M000101251

Palgrave Studies in Agricultural Economics and Food Policy

Series Editor
Christopher Barrett
Cornell University
Ithaca, NY, USA

Agricultural and food policy lies at the heart of many pressing societal issues today and economic analysis occupies a privileged place in contemporary policy debates. The global food price crises of 2008 and 2010 underscored the mounting challenge of meeting rapidly increasing food demand in the face of increasingly scarce land and water resources. The twin scourges of poverty and hunger quickly resurfaced as high-level policy concerns, partly because of food price riots and mounting insurgencies fomented by contestation over rural resources. Meanwhile, agriculture's heavy footprint on natural resources motivates heated environmental debates about climate change, water and land use, biodiversity conservation and chemical pollution. Agricultural technological change, especially associated with the introduction of genetically modified organisms, also introduces unprecedented questions surrounding intellectual property rights and consumer preferences regarding credence (i.e., unobservable by consumers) characteristics. Similar new agricultural commodity consumer behavior issues have emerged around issues such as local foods, organic agriculture and fair trade, even motivating broader social movements. Public health issues related to obesity, food safety, and zoonotic diseases such as avian or swine flu also have roots deep in agricultural and food policy. And agriculture has become inextricably linked to energy policy through biofuels production. Meanwhile, the agricultural and food economy is changing rapidly throughout the world, marked by continued consolidation at both farm production and retail distribution levels, elongating value chains, expanding international trade, and growing reliance on immigrant labor and information and communications technologies. In summary, a vast range of topics of widespread popular and scholarly interest revolve around agricultural and food policy and economics. The extensive list of prospective authors, titles and topics offers a partial, illustrative listing. Thus a series of topical volumes, featuring cutting-edge economic analysis by leading scholars has considerable prospect for both attracting attention and garnering sales. This series will feature leading global experts writing accessible summaries of the best current economics and related research on topics of widespread interest to both scholarly and lay audiences.

More information about this series at
http://www.palgrave.com/gp/series/14651

Prabhu Pingali • Anaka Aiyar
Mathew Abraham • Andaleeb Rahman

Transforming Food Systems for a Rising India

palgrave
macmillan

Prabhu Pingali
Tata-Cornell Institute for Agriculture
and Nutrition
Cornell University
Ithaca, NY, USA

Anaka Aiyar
Tata-Cornell Institute for Agriculture
and Nutrition
Cornell University
Ithaca, NY, USA

Mathew Abraham
Tata-Cornell Institute for Agriculture
and Nutrition
Cornell University
Ithaca, NY, USA

Andaleeb Rahman
Tata-Cornell Institute for Agriculture
and Nutrition
Cornell University
Ithaca, NY, USA

Palgrave Studies in Agricultural Economics and Food Policy
ISBN 978-3-030-14408-1   ISBN 978-3-030-14409-8   (eBook)
https://doi.org/10.1007/978-3-030-14409-8

Cover illustration: Dinodia Photos / Alamy Stock Photo

This Palgrave Macmillan imprint is published by the registered company Springer Nature Switzerland AG.
The registered company address is: Gewerbestrasse 11, 6330 Cham, Switzerland

FOREWORD

India poses some of the greatest puzzles in the world for agricultural economists and food policy analysts. How does a country with some of the most selective universities in the world, and home to some of the planet's most technologically advanced companies, nonetheless have an agriculture sector still surprisingly dependent on smallholders practicing rain-fed cultivation using decades- or centuries-old methods? How is it that some of the world's wealthiest families live among the largest number of undernourished people in the world? How can some of the most logistically sophisticated supply chains in the world coexist alongside agricultural input and output value chains that routinely fail poorer farmers? These and similar juxtapositions make the food systems of India especially fascinating and complex.

The study of India's food systems is valuable not just for educational purposes, however. The prospective human well-being impacts of solutions to the various obstacles that impede India's various food sub-systems hold enormous promise. For the past several years, the Tata-Cornell Institute for Agriculture and Nutrition (TCI), led by Professor Prabhu Pingali, has been at the forefront of field-based, multi-disciplinary, rigorous scientific research to unpack the complexity of India's food systems and to identify and evaluate prospective solutions. This volume shares with readers the fruit of findings by TCI and its collaborators, along with what seem the blueprints for many years' efforts by them and dedicated others.

Professor Pingali and his co-authors, Drs. Anaka Aiyar, Mathew Abraham and Andaleeb Rahman, use a Food Systems Approach (FSA) to frame a fascinating exploration of the multiple mechanisms that leave a tragically large number of Indians malnourished. The integrative FSA lens helps Pingali et al. weave together compelling evidence as to how a highly successful agricultural research and extension system's intense focus on staple cereals—especially rice and wheat—has led over time to nutrient imbalances in the food system that contribute to both obesity/overweight and micronutrient (i.e., mineral and vitamin) deficiencies without fully resolving the undernourishment challenge. They likewise explain how lagging smallholder productivity growth interacts with poor sanitation and lack of access to clean drinking water to compound the nutrient composition of India's food systems and lead to widespread malnutrition amidst plenty. They clearly explain how dramatic urbanization compels changing institutions, structures and technologies in farming and in post-harvest value chains, and how climate change is increasingly exerting similar pressures. And social institutions and cultural customs, not least of which the evolving roles women play in rural India, feature prominently throughout the volume. At a time when the term "intersectionality" has grown popular in political discussions, Pingali et al. illustrate the concept's power when applied to the study of food systems in which biophysical, commercial, cultural, demographic, economic and sociopolitical forces all intersect.

The diversity of experiences among India's states—many the size of independent nations elsewhere in the world in terms of both land mass and population—mirrors what one observes within global regions such as Latin America, Africa or Southeast Asia. Indeed, that immense diversity poses a significant challenge to studying India; one always risks misleading homogenization. The authors skillfully navigate between general descriptions of national-level policies and phenomena and much more local, state-level assessments of specific experiences. Pingali et al.'s diagnostic assessment of appropriate goals and agendas for specific sub-national-scale food systems avoids the sorts of vacuous statements that so often characterize one-size-fits-all descriptions. Their analyses emphasize nuanced differences among the vast nation's sub-populations.

The careful analyses in this volume merit attention because the Indian case is of global importance. Furthermore, the dramatic structural transformation India has been undergoing for the past half century offers instructive lessons for the rest of the low- and middle-income world. Pingali et al.'s systematic, FSA-based diagnostic method as well as their conclusions deserve careful consideration by those working on similar challenges elsewhere in the globe. The context of this book may be distinctively Indian, but many of the challenges the authors describe and the prospective solutions they advance are remarkably general.

It is a great pleasure to include Prabhu Pingali, Anaka Aiyar, Mathew Abraham and Andaleeb Rahman's outstanding book in the Palgrave Studies in Agricultural Economics and Food Policy series. I recommend it enthusiastically to all students of India, of the process of international development, of food systems and human health and nutrition outcomes, and of thoughtful, multidisciplinary research.

Cornell University, Ithaca, NY, USA   Christopher B. Barrett

PREFACE

Over the past several decades, India has witnessed consistently high economic growth rates, often among the fastest in the developing world. The country has made significant gains in reducing poverty levels, and its urban middle class is projected to rise rapidly, both in terms of size and income levels. Despite positive economic growth trends, the country continues to struggle with malnutrition manifested in terms of high rates of child stunting and wasting that are substantially higher than other countries with similar economic growth experience and at similar stages of structural transformation. Even while India struggles to address the undernutrition problem, emerging trends in overweight and obesity portend to a future public health crisis in non-communicable diseases.

India's food and agriculture policy have historically focused on enhancing supplies and access to staple grains, especially rice and wheat, and thereby have had considerable success in reducing the incidence of hunger in the country. While it is true that millions still suffer from hunger, imagine what the situation would have been if the country did not invest in productivity improvement for the major staples through the Green Revolution. However, the laser focus on enhancing rice and wheat supplies may have inadvertently resulted in the crowding out of the more nutritious grains, such as millets and other coarse cereals, and pulses. Staple-grain-focused policies may have also created disincentives for farmers to diversify their production systems in response to rising market demand for non-staple food, such as fruit, vegetables and livestock products. The imbalance in protein, vitamin and micronutrient supply in the food system is a major cause of the high incidence of malnutrition in India.

Poor sanitation, lack of access to clean drinking water and low levels of women's empowerment are other proximate reasons for the persistence of malnutrition in India.

This book provides a detailed assessment of the major paradoxes of the Indian growth story, one in which we see the simultaneous existence of regional inequality, rural and urban food insecurity, intractable malnutrition problems and the growing incidence of overweight and obesity. We examine the nexus of economic development, agricultural production and nutrition through the lens of a "Food Systems Approach (FSA)". Central to our vision for a robust food system is a future where nutrition-secure individuals have the capability and the opportunity to improve their health through greater access to a balanced and healthy diet. In order to implement a holistic approach towards economic welfare and nutrition security, we link the goals for agricultural development, health and nutrition and economic development with each other. We bring together the latest data and scientific evidence from the country to map out the current state of food systems and nutrition outcomes. We place India within the context of other developing country experiences and highlight India's status as an outlier in terms of the persistence of high level of stunting while following the global trends in overweight and obesity. We discuss the policy and institutional interventions needed for promoting a nutrition-sensitive food system and the multi-sectoral strategies needed for simultaneously addressing the chronic undernutrition and emerging over-nutrition problems in India.

This book is a major output of the Tata-Cornell Institute for Agriculture and Nutrition (TCI) at Cornell University. It draws on and builds upon the policy analysis and learnings at TCI during its first five years. TCI was established with a generous gift given to Cornell University by the Tata Trusts, a philanthropic branch of the Tata Group. The endowment was made possible by the vision of Mr. Ratan Tata, the former chairman of India's Tata Group and a Cornell alumnus from the class of 1962. TCI is a long-term research initiative focused on solving problems of poverty, malnutrition and rural development in India. It is specifically focused on understanding and addressing the malnutrition conundrum using a multi-sectoral and multi-disciplinary approach. TCI's research and projects in India consider the factors that influence both a household's ability to access food—such as income, employment and the ability to afford safe, high-quality and diverse foods in sufficient quantities—and the individual's ability to absorb and utilize his or her share of the household's total food/nutrient basket, which could differ depending on the individual's age, gender, level of empowerment, household dynamics, cultural practices or even physiological life stage (e.g., pregnancy and infancy require different diets and care practices).

We are grateful to the TCI team for their support in bringing this book together. We are particularly thankful to the TCI scholars for the stimulating discussions during the weekly research group meetings and to Bhaskar Mittra, Jessica Ames, Kiera Crowley and Mary Catherine French for their support, advice and assistance during various stages of writing the book.

We hope the research and policy prescriptions presented in this book will be useful to food and agricultural policy analysts and nutrition and development practitioners and policy makers. While the book is focused on India, we believe the book's takeaways are applicable to other developing countries facing similar persistence of malnutrition and the emerging concerns of rising NCDs. We hope you enjoy reading the book.

Ithaca, NY, USA
Prabhu Pingali
Anaka Aiyar
Mathew Abraham
Andaleeb Rahman

AUTHOR BIOGRAPHIES

Prabhu Pingali is Professor of Applied Economics and Founding Director of the Tata-Cornell Institute for Agriculture and Nutrition (TCI) at Cornell University.

Mathew Abraham is Assistant Director of the Tata-Cornell Institute for Agriculture and Nutrition (TCI), Cornell University.

Anaka Aiyaris Post-Doctoral Associate with the Tata-Cornell Institute for Agriculture and Nutrition (TCI), Cornell University.

Andaleeb Rahman is Post-Doctoral Associate at the Tata-Cornell Institute for Agriculture and Nutrition (TCI), Cornell University.

CONTENTS

ABBREVIATIONS

AEZ	Agro-ecological Zones
APMC	Agriculture Produce Marketing Committee
BNI	Biological Nitrification Inhibition
CA	Conservation Agriculture
CAGR	Compounded Annual Growth Rate
CCT	Conditional Cash Transfer
CF	Contract Farming
CIMMYT	International Maize and Wheat Improvement Center
CMERI	Central Mechanical Engineering Research Institute
CPB	Conventional Plant-Breeding
CSA	Climate Smart Agriculture
DALYS	Disability Adjusted Life Years
DBT	Direct Benefit Transfer
FAO	Food and Agriculture Organization of the United Nations
FCI	Food Corporation of India
FCP	Food Chain Partnership
FDI	Foreign Direct Investment
FFV	Fresh Fruits and Vegetables
FPOs	Farmer Producer Organizations
FPS	Fair Price Shops
FSA	Food Systems Approach
GDP	Gross Domestic Product
GEAC	Genetic Engineering Approval Committee
GHG	Greenhouse Gases
GM	Genetically Modified
GMO	Genetically Modified Organism
GOI	Government of India

GR	Green Revolution
HIV	Human Immunodeficiency Virus
HYV	High-Yielding Varieties
IBSC	Institutional Biosafety Committees
ICAR	Indian Council of Agricultural Research
ICDS	Integrated Child Development Scheme
ICEX	Indian Commodity Exchange Limited
ICT	Information and Communication Technologies
IDA	Iron Deficiency Anemia
IRRI	International Rice Research Institute
ISFM	Integrated Soil Fertility Management
ITC	Indian Tobacco Company
JLG	Joint Liability Groups
KCC	Kisan Credit Card
LGP	Length of Growing Periods
LMIC	Low- and Medium-Income Countries
MCX	Multi Commodity Exchange
MDMS	Mid-Day Meal Scheme
MGNREGA	Mahatma Gandhi National Rural Employment Guarantee Act
MNC	Multi-National Companies
MSP	Minimum Support Price
NABARD	National Bank for Agriculture and Rural Development
NAFED	National Agricultural Cooperative Marketing Federation
NBSS&LUP	National Bureau of Soil Survey and Land Use Planning
NCD	Non-communicable Disease
NCDEX	National Commodity & Derivatives Exchange
NFHS	National Family Health Survey
NFSA	National Food Security Act
NHPS	National Health Protection Scheme
NMCE	National Multi-Commodity Exchange of India Ltd.
NSEL	National Spot Exchange Limited
NSS	National Sample Survey
PC	Producer Companies
PDIL	Projects and Development India Ltd.
PDS	Public Distribution System
PMGSY	Pradhan Mantri Gram Sadak Yojana
R&D	Research and Development
R2R	Rural to Rural
R2U	Rural to Urban
ReMS	Rashtriya eMarket Services Pvt. Ltd.
RSBY	Rashtriya Swasthya Bima Yojana
SAU	State Agricultural Universities

SDG	Sustainable Development Goals
SEWA	Self-Employed Women's Association
SFAC	Small Farmers' Agribusiness Consortium
SPMRM	Shyama Prasad Mukherji Rurban Mission
SSA	Sub-Saharan Africa
ST	Structural Transformation
U2R	Urban to Rural
U2U	Urban to Urban
UBI	Universal Basic Income
UCX	Universal Commodity Exchange
UIDAI	Unique Identification Authority of India
UP	Uttar Pradesh
USDA	United States Department of Agriculture
VC	Vertical Coordination
WTO	World Trade Organization

LIST OF FIGURES

LIST OF TABLES

CHAPTER 1

Indian Food Systems towards 2050: Challenges and Opportunities

1.1 Motivation

The Green Revolution in the 1970s followed by the liberalization of the Indian economy in the 1990s has been credited with shepherding India onto a path of high growth. Over the last decade, increases in per capita incomes, greater urbanization rates, increase in literacy rates, population growth and poverty reduction have characterized this high growth process. While agricultural development has brought about income generating opportunities to some in the farming sector, in a small farm dominant country like India, poor infrastructure and a lack of institutional support have excluded many small-holders from benefiting from the growth process. At the macro level, the growth process has been highly inequitable, benefiting some states more than others. At the consumer end, increases in income and income generating opportunities continue to coexist with poverty and poor health outcomes. The latter is reflected in the simultaneous prevalence of undernourishment, over-nutrition and micronutrient deficiencies in the country. These conundrums reflect the major paradoxes of the Indian growth story, where we see the simultaneous existence of regional inequality, rural and urban food insecurity and the growing incidence of a triple burden of malnutrition.

Aside from tackling these challenges, looking ahead to 2050 and beyond, we see important trends of unequal growth and climate change challenges threatening India's ability to sustainably and equitably manage an economic and nutrition transformation. Current regional inequality in

© The Author(s) 2019
P. Pingali et al., *Transforming Food Systems for a Rising India*,
Palgrave Studies in Agricultural Economics and Food Policy,
https://doi.org/10.1007/978-3-030-14409-8_1

economic development is a major challenge due to differences in initial resource endowments and nationalized policies that has placed states on different structural transformation pathways. Some states today resemble poor countries in sub-Saharan Africa, while rapidly developing states resemble counterparts in Latin America. Continuing down this policy pathway will have negative implications, for both national political stability and economic development as we look ahead. Boosting agricultural productivity is critical for economic growth and development in India. Agricultural production, however, affects and is affected by climate change. Productivity growth influenced by increasing demand for higher value agricultural produce will lead to increased greenhouse gas emissions and water and soil degradation, accentuating production risks in agriculture. Through its negative impact on food availability, access, nutrition and affordability, climate change will reduce the effectiveness of policies aimed at increasing food and nutrition security for the future. Feeding a growing population that is both richer and more urban has significant implications for future food systems. Linking urban food demand with rural prosperity, while ensuring environmental sustainability will be essential to ensure both urban and rural food security.

1.2   Approach

Much of the prior literature has reflected on the importance of either the development of the agricultural sector, the role of economic growth or the importance of food security for ensuring greater and more equitable economic development. Even works that look at the intersection of these groups focus only on increasing production as a means to increase economic growth or focus on managing consumption as a means for improving health and productivity. They do not evaluate the intersectionality of these domains and their spillovers on the economic, ecological or health systems within the country. Thus, we see the existence of policies that increase productivity in agriculture at the expense of the environment, policies that increase economic growth while also increasing regional inequality and hurting small farmers, and top-down policies that aim to reduce undernutrition without any discussion on how to tackle growing obesity. These policy recommendations remain palliative at best, often treating the symptoms but not the core problems in the economy. Most of these approaches have also not considered the implications of the changing economic, demographic and climatic landscape of the future.

With a view to address the current challenges in the Indian development paradox and in light of the future challenges faced by the country, this book looks at the nexus of economic development, agricultural production and nutrition through the lens of a "food systems approach (FSA)". A traditional FSA looks for opportunities to strengthen the linkages between agricultural production and consumption with the aim to strengthen nutrition access for individuals and households. The motivation of our FSA model is to expand both opportunities to strengthen nutrition access and to enhance capabilities of individuals so that they can access new opportunities in ways to increase their welfare. Creation of new opportunities and capabilities for increasing farm production and productivity, reducing malnutrition and improving labor productivity and facilitating greater structural transformation that is also inequality reducing are the main goals of the approach.

In order to implement a holistic approach towards welfare development and nutrition security, we link the goals for agricultural development, health and nutrition and economic development with each other (Fig. 1.1). We bring together the latest data and scientific evidence from the country to map out the current state of food systems. In this book we (1) highlight the nature of food system challenges in India, (2) provide goals and set a food systems

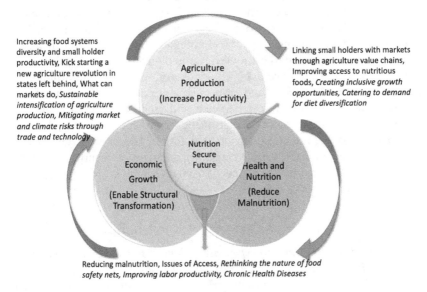

Fig. 1.1   The multi-sectoral approach for food system transformation

agenda for the future for different subnational units in India based on their current structural transformation experience and (3) emphasize policy and institutional interventions that are needed to address these challenges.

The book will be organized along the lines of the food systems framework provided in Fig. 1.1. We first dive into the question about who the new rural and urban consumer of the future would be. We identify their dietary needs and preferences, health challenges and how consumer markets would evolve to meet these changing requirements. We then take a deep dive into challenges for farming in India. We study the farmer, their input usage patterns, institutional challenges in adopting new farming practices and challenges in accessing markets to sell non-staple agricultural products. We highlight issues of access that fall out of intra-household inequalities or social institutions that affect nutrition access. We then travel along the agricultural supply chain and identify the transaction costs and bottlenecks that have prevented a free flow of foods from the farm to the plate. We also identify institutional failures that have prevented market signals from transforming the agricultural landscape away from staple grain production in the country. We identify the challenges for implementing acceptable food quality and food safety standards. Side by side with these insights, we also provide data and evidence on the current food systems challenges from external forces such as the overuse of the environment and the projections from climate change. We study the role of research and development, new technologies, subnational unit-focused policy and the growth of the knowledge and digital economy in mitigating these production and price risks. The book not only aims to inform policy makers on proper actions and respective consequences for future food systems, it also provides researchers new and exciting avenues to conduct research on nutrition security. Additionally, by providing a fresh and holistic perspective on the challenges for the future, and an overview of the policies that are available towards ensuring greater food security, this work aims to increase citizen awareness and engagement in developing food systems of the future.

1.3   Key Takeaways from the Book

1. *The differential growth experience of Indian states can be explained by their initial investments in agricultural productivity growth and their subsequent focus on robust non-agricultural employment growth.* (Chap. 2)

While India's overall GDP growth rate has been consistently high for the past few decades, there are significant inter-state disparities in growth performance. In Chap. 2, we compare Indian states with countries, in terms of the per capita GDP, and we find that some of the poorest states in India have per capita GDP levels that are comparable to some of the poorest countries in sub-Saharan Africa. On the other hand, the most progressive states in India have per capita GDP levels that are comparable to the emerging economies of Southeast Asia and Latin America. These stark differences in the regional growth experience are also reflected in other indicators such as nutrition or poverty. For example, undernutrition in Madhya Pradesh continues to remain a key nutrition challenge, but in Kerala, rising obesity has brought the problem of over-nutrition into focus. Similarly, while rural poverty in Punjab has reduced due to agricultural development, in Orissa, low agricultural productivity and the lack of alternate employment opportunities has resulted in high rural poverty levels. Indian states have also experienced different levels of structural transformation; less than 20% of the population remains in agriculture in the high-income states, while that figure is over 40% in the *lagging states.*

Based on their overall economic performance, in Chap. 2, we group Indian states into three categories—*agriculture-led states, urbanizing states* and *lagging states*—and attempt to explain their growth performance over the past 60 years. The categories are based on three outcomes of economic development; these are state GDP per capita, the share of agriculture in GDP and urbanization rate. Both in the *agriculture-led states* and *urbanizing states,* agricultural growth, kickstarted by the Green Revolution, played a crucial role in catalyzing economic growth. However, states such as Punjab and Andhra Pradesh continue to focus on agriculture with a concentration on staple grain production and consequently have seen a slowdown in their prospects for further income growth. On the other hand, *urbanizing states* such as Gujarat and Maharashtra started with investments in agriculture as an engine of growth but then reinvested their agricultural incomes in developing vibrant industrial and commercial sectors. *Lagging states* such as Bihar and Odisha were bypassed by the Green Revolution due to poor agro-climatic and infrastructural constraints and continue to be on a low growth trajectory. Prospects for future growth in the *lagging states* are still linked to agriculture, but perhaps in looking beyond staple grains, and towards meeting the rising demand for food diversity elsewhere in the country by enhancing the productivity of coarse cereals, pulses and high-value crops and livestock.

2. *Meeting the growing urban demand for food and other agricultural products and non-farm employment provides new growth opportunities for rural economies; the challenge is to ensure that it is inclusive of the poor.* (Chap. 3)

As India grows through a rapid process of urbanization, both with the expansion of the mega-cities as well as the smaller cities and district towns, the food policy challenge will increasingly become one of sustainably feeding the cities. Provisioning the cities is the new growth opportunity for rural areas and could lead to accelerated rural transformation. Through organized upstream and downstream network of activities, the urban facing agribusiness, value chains could absorb surplus agricultural labor and provide them with jobs, especially for the youth and women. Employment in logistics, like aggregation, storage, processing and so on, at the agribusiness upstream and food-related services such as restaurants at the downstream could potentially be leveraged as the channel of employment generation.

Such inclusive transformation of rural spaces—by including those who are left out regarding access to non-farm employment—is essential to remove rural poverty. One of the channels for propelling stagnant agricultural growth is to strengthen the rural-urban continuum which provides ample opportunities to the small farmers and other rural population with greater opportunities to share in the fruits of urban economic growth. Indian policies have not focused on the small towns and the middle spaces to create job opportunities. Recognizing these newer urban settlements and then providing them with urban amenities could be a springboard for non-farm diversification. The benefits of local economies can be realized through the creation of urban-rural clusters that supply goods and services both for consumption and for agricultural production in households. While urbanization and changing employment patterns offer opportunities for a more diversified food system, the challenge lies in ensuring these transformations are smooth and contribute to sustainable poverty reduction.

3. *Diet transition and the rising demand for food diversity is not matched with a commensurate rise in the supply of non-staple foods leading to poor access to more nutritious food.* (Chap. 4)

Diet transition is an important outcome of the structural transformation process. Chapter 4 discusses the two stages of dietary transition with structural transformation. In the first stage, economic growth and rise in per capita income induce diet diversification. Consumer preferences move away from *quantity* to *quality*, substituting traditional staples with non-staples, such as fruit, vegetables and livestock products. In the second stage, the effects of globalization of the economy are reflected in an increase in the consumption of processed food which are rich in proteins, sugars and fats. This diet transition in India is increasingly evident. Chapter 4 provides data on the diet transition in India, specifically the declining share of staple grains—rice and wheat—in household diets across all income groups in urban as well as rural populations, though the degree of transition varies considerably. At the same time, we observe the rise in the diversity of food groups consumed, such as fruit, vegetables and livestock products. However, it is clear that access to food diversity is not equitable and that the poor are significantly disadvantaged in this regard.

With a clear shift away from cereals, it is important to ensure other nutritive food items are available at affordable prices. It is clear, however, that the supply of non-staple foods has not matched the rising demand as manifested in the rising and volatile relative prices of these foods. Without access to nutritive substitutes, dietary diversity would suffer. Protein-rich items such as pulses and animal-based protein items have seen an increase in the prices as well as its volatility, primarily driven by greater demand for these products. Similarly, the highly seasonal supply of fruits and vegetables and lack of storage infrastructure to smoothen prices makes access to nutritious food at affordable prices a challenge for consumers, especially the poor. At the same time, access to processed foods has increased significantly, even in rural areas, and often at prices that are substantially below those of more nutritious fresh food and pulses. Chapter 5 provides data that shows that India may be tripping into a rising over-nutrition and obesity problem, even as it tries to solve the undernutrition problem, due to poor access and affordability of nutrition-rich diets.

4. *While progress is being made on undernutrition, the emerging nutrition transition towards over-nutrition and the rising incidence of non-communicable diseases requires a move away from policies that promote calorie sufficiency to ones that promote food system diversity.* (Chap. 5)

Similar to the experience of other countries that have undergone greater structural transformation, India has made progress towards reducing hunger and reducing undernutrition while witnessing significant economic growth. Over the last three decades, the country has managed to reduce undernutrition by at least ten percentage points across all individual groups. On the other hand, obesity and NCD rates are rising among urban and rural populations, albeit at a slower rate in the latter. Chapter 5 argues that increased dietary diversity is associated with lower prevalence of hidden hunger and higher nutrient adequacy ratios for individuals. It also presents the case that the lack of diet diversity and excessive carbohydrates and sugar consumption is associated with higher risk of obesity and NCDs.

Given this close relationship between dietary diversity of households and nutrition outcomes, ensuring that households can access diverse foods requires interventions at two levels. First is to ensure that there is greater availability of food diversity within the local system. The second set of interventions would need to improve the affordability of these diets. Effective food policy, hence, becomes tantamount to a nutrition sensitive food system which enables transition towards a healthier diet. Policy debates around food security in India have mainly focused upon ensuring adequate access to calories through a continued focus on staple grain production. However, trends around dietary changes and nutrition transition provide a compelling case for questioning the existing paradigm and open up conversations around access to a good quality and balanced diet. Focus on staples has affected incentives to develop markets for non-staples, thus affecting their supply and increasing price uncertainty. Creating new opportunities for the food system diversification, to cater to changing consumer demand, should thus become a focus for policy makers. Chapter 5 also presents the multi-sectoral pathways towards improved nutrition outcomes, such as access to clean drinking water and sanitation, gender empowerment and behavior change and so on.

5. *The objectives and design of India's safety net programs, whether food or cash based, need to evolve with economic growth and the changing nutritional needs of the marginalized populations.* (Chap. 6)

Safety nets have been an essential part of the poverty reduction policies in India by contributing to risk management and reducing vulnerability for a large section of the population. Chapter 6 argues for the future role of safety nets to be more *transformational* rather than vulnerability reducing. Overall effectiveness of safety nets would depend to a large extent on how they are combined with structural reforms and long-term interventions to increase human capabilities and address structural poverty through that. Synergies between agriculture and safety nets, therefore, become essential. Public work, life-cycle based food assistance programs need to be dovetailed into the local agrarian economy.

Regarding the future of safety nets, it is essential to take into account the changing nature of the economic structure, demographic changing, and future livelihood patterns. Urbanization, especially, poses a challenge as well as opportunity in restructuring the safety net architecture. Current policies have not taken into account the fact that India would be more urban than rural by 2050. Most of the existing food-based policies have a greater rural presence. Public works program Mahatma Gandhi National Rural Employment Guarantee Act (MGNREGA) has only been designed for the rural areas, assuming rural employment is the only concern. With rising urbanization, urban informality and unemployment in urban areas, especially among the educated, raise important challenges for the food systems going ahead.

In the case of food-based safety nets, innovations are limited by the modalities of grain procurement. To supply rice and wheat through Public Distribution System (PDS), a massive food grain procurement structure has come about which incentivizes only staples and other more nutritive food products are crowded out. Not only consumers are at a disadvantage due to restricted choice, but the idea of a nutrition-sensitive food system is undermined. It is therefore essential to break the staple grain procurement-storage-distribution interlocked channel. But these interlocked incentives are deeply mired into India's rural political economy. It is one of the major hurdles to India's food system.

6. *Promoting small farm commercialization and diversification serves the dual objectives of enhancing farm incomes while improving the supply and access to food system diversity.* (Chap. 7)

The rising demand for diversified agricultural products has brought about opportunities and challenges for the Indian agricultural sector. The opportunities come from increasing demand for diversified and higher value crops that can improve agricultural incomes and improved access to a varied food basket at the household level. Commercialization of smallholders' farms is an essential pathway to improved rural incomes and better access to diversified and nutritious food. The major challenges, however, are problems associated with the supply side conditions such as poor access to markets, credit, purchased inputs, technology and extension services that have hindered commercialization and made income opportunities inaccessible to many small farm producers. Rising rural wages due to growth in non-farm employment opportunities add to the challenges of commercializing small farms.

Chapter 7 assesses the major institutional innovations associated with mitigating some of the transaction costs associated with market entry and resolving problems associated with achieving economies of scale. Aggregation models such as producer organizations and cooperatives, where smallholders organize themselves in groups to jointly access resources and market their produce, have shown to reduce transaction costs and benefit from the resulting economies of scale. Lagging regions of Eastern and Northeastern India are a particular challenge regarding small farm commercialization. With investments in markets and agricultural infrastructure, such as irrigation, warehouses and cold storage facilities, and a supportive policy environment, such as promoting contract farming, it is possible for these regions to leap frog from the current subsistence systems to commercial operations that are focused on supplying urban demand for food diversity.

7. *Effective aggregation models, such as producer groups, can help reduce the high transaction costs of small farms accessing urban food value chains, especially for fresh food.* (Chap. 8)

With increasing demand for quality and high-value agricultural produce, alternative value chains and newer marketing platforms have emerged. Vertical coordination (VC) by which retailers form direct linkages with farms, bypassing traditional markets, has been growing in India's more progressive states. Newer marketing platforms where farmers can participate in online auctions and trading such as eNAM and Rashtriya eMarket Services Pvt. Ltd (ReMS) in Karnataka and warehousing platforms such as the National Commodity & Derivatives Exchange (NCDEX) eMarkets Limited to hedging price risks can be viable alternatives to existing traditional markets. VC can be more relevant for perishable crops and farmers in regions with good linkages to market (*agriculture-led growth states*), while futures and warehousing platforms can be useful for non-perishable commodities and can emerge in low potential areas such as those in *lagging states*.

Institutional interventions, such as Farmer Producer Organizations (FPOs) and cooperatives, can offset scale disadvantages faced by small farms in supplying to the modern value chains as well as access to electronic markets and futures trading platforms. By reducing the risk associated with the adoption of new crop technologies and reducing transaction costs in market access, these interventions could help in farm diversification as well as better price realizations in the output market.

In Chap. 8, we highlight some recommendations that differ by the stage of development a particular state is in. In the *lagging states* with low agricultural productivity, FPOs have the potential to enable greater commercialization, enabling greater yields. Linkages to output markets will help incentivize the production of pulses and coarse grains, given their comparative advantage. In *agriculture-led states* and *urbanizing states*, alternative models such as contract farming are more likely to succeed since farms in these areas are already highly commercialized. Enabling conditions for contract farming through mechanisms to enforce contracts and allowing retailers and processors to transact directly with farmers, especially in the cash crops, could be the way forward. Here, aggregation models can help reduce organization costs of engaging with a more significant number of small farms and reduce contracting costs that often exclude small farm contracts. Policy measures to financially support FPO emergence and extend financial and insurance-based services, linking them to information and extension services and enabling market linkages by improving connectivity, will further incentivize group formation and establish linkages across the value chain.

8. *Technology will continue to play a vital role in enhancing smallholder productivity and competitiveness, but it's time to look beyond staple grains, and take a holistic view of the technological options for promoting a diverse food system.* (Chap. 9)

Technology in the past has played a critical role in enabling food security in the developing world. The Green Revolution helped in increasing yields of wheat and rice, making many countries like India self-sufficient in these grains. One main reason the Green Revolution was successfully implemented was that it was a public sector intervention that was scale-neutral, allowing small and marginal producers to adopt them. The limitation of these technologies was that they were focused on the main staple grains— rice and wheat—and to regions where irrigation resources were available, leading to interregional and intercrop disparities. The impact these technologies had on the environment because of poor management was also high, leading to depletion of water tables and land degradation.

Chapter 9 makes the case that technology remains critical in the face on the new food security challenges India will face, as it seeks to meet the demand for quantity as well as quality and food system diversity. First- and second-generation GM technologies hold promise in improving returns to farming through reduced cost of production and increasing resilience and the nutritive value of crops. Crop improvement technologies are a priority for the more nutritious crops, especially coarse cereals, such as millets, and pulses. Yield improvements coupled with the effective management of resources (nutrient, water, natural resources) are essential to improve efficiency and achieve sustainable intensification.

Unlike Green Revolution technologies which were public sector generated, technological innovations today are generated in the private sector and hence pose challenges of access for small farms. This is true for crop production and post-harvest technologies. Institutional interventions that enable public sector access to private sector innovations and to adapt them to small farm conditions are crucial. Farm aggregation models could also help small farms access modern technologies for enhancing the productivity of non-staple crops and livestock.

9. *Climate change can have significant adverse impacts on agricultural productivity, rural incomes and welfare; in addition, it can pose serious risks to the nutritive value of the food system since it can have a disproportionately higher effect on non-staple foods.* (Chap. 10)

The impact of rising temperatures on the major staples, such as rice and wheat, is well studied. Declining productivity of these crops can be expected with rising temperatures. However, less well understood is the impact of climate change on crops that are important to the poor, such as millets and sorghum. Also, less studied are the impacts of climate change on a more nutritious food system, such as its impacts on the productivity of fruit, vegetables, pulses and livestock products. Given the lack of technologies currently available to safeguard productivity and the lack of information about climate impacts on these foods, vulnerability of non-staple crop production becomes a major food security concern for the future. Safeguarding the production of these crops and livestock will be important to the goal of achieving nutrition security. Climate change can also have adverse impacts on production systems in the rain-fed areas, particularly those in the semi-arid and the arid fringe areas. Higher temperatures could drive some of these areas out of crop and livestock production activities, especially where irrigation infrastructure is not well established.

Chapter 10 argues that continuing down the current path of development without integrating adaptation and mitigation strategies will have serious negative repercussions on food security within the country. Side by side with adaptation strategies, integrating mitigation strategies that reduce overall carbon foot print will contribute to the global goals of GHG mitigation and help reduce global food systems risks. Policies to encourage investments in clean energy sources, climate-smart infrastructure, preservation and conservation of biodiversity and groundwater management processes have been important steps taken in this direction by the government of India as well as individual state governments. It is also important that these policies not only operate at the level of strategy but that progress and goals can be measured and tracked.

As we look ahead, climate policies for the future should allow diversification of the food system in ways that enhance the environment while improving the nutrition content of foods produced and ensuring equity in access. In order to truly create a food system that ensures nutrition security of all individuals, climate change risks must not be understated, and appropriate actions towards its mitigation need to be adopted.

10. *Food and agricultural policy need to transition from a focus on quantity to emphasize quality, diversity and safety; it should also leverage multi-sectoral synergies with economic growth, improved access to clean drinking water and sanitation and behavior change for promoting improved diets.* (Chap. 11)

This book brings agricultural sector-led developmental approach to the center of policy formulation to ensure nutrition security and rural prosperity for greater welfare. India's recent history has shown that smallholder agricultural productivity growth kickstarted overall economic growth, rural poverty reduction and structural transformation of the economy. However, the predominant focus of agricultural policy on the productivity growth of the major staples—rice and wheat—resulted in significant interregional growth disparities and poor nutrition outcomes. While these policies played an important role in ensuring calorie sufficiency across the country and thereby led to substantial reduction in the incidence of hunger, they tended to inhibit diversification of the food systems and hence the overall supply of micronutrient-rich food. In order to make substantial progress in tackling the problem of malnutrition, both micronutrient malnutrition and the emerging problem of obesity, India's food and agricultural policy needs to move towards promoting food system diversity. This would require clear strategies for diversification of production systems in order to improve the access and affordability of nutritious food, such as fresh fruit, vegetables, pulses and livestock products, and it would also require strategies for promoting individual diet diversity.

In addition, the quality of health and hygiene environment also plays a major role in reducing malnutrition. Poor hygiene environments increase disease burden and sickness and affect nutrient absorption. Improving water and sanitation infrastructures is essential to reduce the spread of disease, especially waterborne diseases. Behavior change programs that promote healthy diets and seek to improve household health environment by encouraging water storage practices, encouraging hand washing before water use and after toilet use and encouraging cleanliness in the surrounding environment have been effective in reducing malnutrition around the world. Finally, interventions that increase education of girl children and women, delay child marriages, provide households information on economic opportunities for women and increase safety at workplaces have been known to impact both nutrition outcomes for women and their children. Research has shown that women's empowerment leads to positive nutrition and health outcomes, especially for young children.

CHAPTER 2

Economic Growth, Agriculture and Food Systems: Explaining Regional Diversity

2.1 Introduction

The Green Revolution of the 1960s transformed India from a net importer of food to a self-sufficient agricultural giant. This *agriculture-led growth* of the 1970s, along with liberalization policies of the 1990s, has been credited with catalyzing the country's remarkable growth in the last two decades. In 2017, India became the sixth largest economy in the world, beating France and closely tied with the UK. Agricultural growth in the country has come to be associated with green paddy fields and overflowing storehouses of surplus grains. Economic development has created globally competitive companies and metropolises. The global face of the Indian labor force is both cosmopolitan and high skilled. Increasing incomes per capita of individuals, as represented by the growing size of the Indian middle class, has brought with it both reduction in overall poverty and a decrease in hunger and undernutrition across the country. On the global platform, India has emerged as a thought leader in discussions related to climate change, poverty and development and international trade. This economic progress of the country has come about due to its structural transformation[1] (ST) from a subsistence agriculture-based economy to

---

[1] Structural transformation is a process of economic development during which an economy reallocates economic activities across its agriculture, industry and service sectors (Herrendorf, Rogerson, & Valentinyi, 2013). ST is characterized by the declining share of the agricultural sector and a declining share of agricultural employment (P. Pingali, 2007a)

© The Author(s) 2019   15
P. Pingali et al., *Transforming Food Systems for a Rising India*,
Palgrave Studies in Agricultural Economics and Food Policy,
https://doi.org/10.1007/978-3-030-14409-8_2

one that has a modernizing agricultural system over the last five decades. In line with the predictions of ST theory, India has also seen a decline in agricultural share in GDP, an increase in labor productivity, growth in urbanization and a reduction in poverty during this time.

Discussing India's growth success as if it is a pan-India phenomenon overshadows the disparate experiences in its subnational growth process (U. Kumar & Subramanian, 2012; Kurian, 2000; Panagariya, Chakraborty, & Rao, 2014; P. Pingali & Aiyar, 2018). After growing by 1–2% between the 1960s and 1980s, India began to grow by 3–4% year on year in the post-liberalization era and around 6–7% over the last one and a half decades. A back of the envelop calculation suggests that there have been at least half of the Indian states that doubled incomes in the first 35 years after independence and then in approximately half the time doubled their incomes again. In other states, state GDP increased by less than double over the entire period (1960–2017). Even though doubling incomes within 60 years is impressive in and of itself, these divergent development experiences across states have created disparities in their development outcomes. The outcome of this regional disparity is reflected in Fig. 2.1. While India leads the South Asia experience for growth, some states such as Bihar and Uttar Pradesh have worse economic outcomes compared to some countries in sub-Saharan Africa. Other states such as Delhi and Goa are comparable to countries in Latin America. These stark differences in the regional growth experience are also reflected in other indicators such as nutrition or poverty. For example, undernutrition in Madhya Pradesh continues to remain a key nutrition challenge, but in Kerala, rising obesity has brought the problem of over-nutrition into focus. Similarly, while rural poverty in Punjab has reduced due to agricultural development, in Orissa,

---

even as the value added of agriculture and agricultural productivity increases. This phenomenon is driven by either (1) faster growth of value added in other sectors, industry or services, which drives changes in employment patterns (Chenery, 1960), or (2) through agriculture-led productivity growth which itself can stimulate demand for non-agricultural products and non-agricultural employment (B. B. F. Johnston & Mellor, 1961). Both of these growth strategies increase rental incomes from factors of production whose productivity has increased through this process. This creates a virtuous cycle of economic growth. Over time, ST processes have come to be associated with greater economic growth, increase in productivity of factors of production, a reduction in the share of the agricultural sector in GDP, increase in the rates of urban-led growth, increase in incomes, poverty reduction, better nutritional security and greater diet diversity (Chenery, 1960; Pingali, Ricketts, & Sahn, 2015; P. C. Timmer, 1988; P. C. Timmer & Akkus, 2008; P. Webb & Block, 2013).

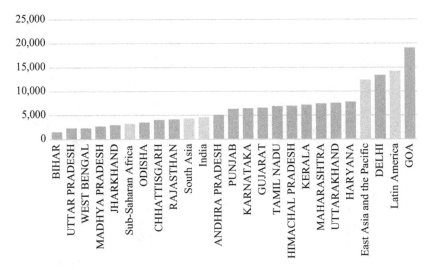

Fig. 2.1 International comparisons in GDP per capita (PPP in constant 2011 international $). Source: National Accounts Statistics & World Bank DataBank (2015–16); based on authors calculations

it remains high and spatially determined. Similarly, measures such as night light intensity—which capture economic activity and levels of urbanization—suggest higher development in the south and northwest areas of the country compared to others (Fig. 2.2).

In this chapter, we propose two major arguments to explain the regional divergence in growth. The first argument builds on the idea that states in India have structurally transformed differentially based on their comparative advantages. In Fig. 2.3, we see that each state in India has started its process of ST at different levels in the 1960s as well as transformed over time at a different pace. Absolute advantages in returns to land, labor and capital played a major role in determining the level at which states started in the development process. However, comparative advantages led to states benefiting differentially from national growth policies. Between the 1950s and 2000s, national growth policies supported either heavy industry development, the development of the agricultural sector, the development of small-scale industries or the service sector (Fig. 2.4). As a consequence, investments made by states in developing "within state" comparative advantages created new avenues for growth. Along with serendipitous changes in aggregate demand, driven by either changes in the local or global economy, these state

Night Light Intensity (lumens), 1992 and 2013

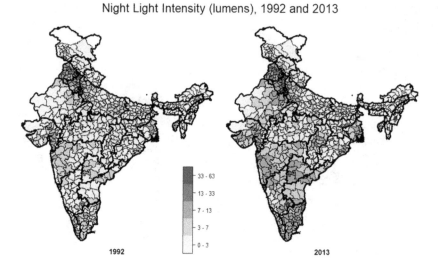

Fig. 2.2 Growth of urban areas. Source: AidGeo Data; based on authors calculations

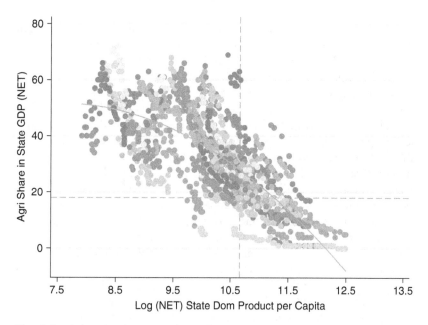

Fig. 2.3 Subnational structural transformation in India (1960–2017). Source: National Accounts Statistics; based on authors calculations

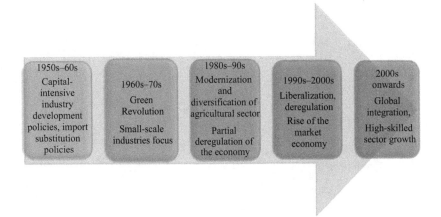

Fig. 2.4 Indian policy priorities over time

policies in concert with the national policies led to a divergence in the regional growth experience (Bhalla & Singh, 1997; Kurian, 2000; Ghosh, 2006; Bhattacharya & Sakthivel, 2004).

The second argument is embedded in the concept of labor market frictions. In this chapter, we argue that high search and entry costs into urban and non-agricultural labor markets have prevented a smooth outmigration of underemployed labor from the agricultural sector to the non-agricultural sector. During the ST process, economic growth is theorized to be accompanied by a reduction in the share of people employed in agriculture. As unemployed individuals migrate towards new opportunities in the non-agricultural sector, labor productivity in agriculture and hence returns to agriculture are expected to increase. However, in India, the decline in the share of agriculture in GDP has not been associated with a commensurate decline in agricultural employment share in total employment. Compared to countries with similar experiences in ST such as the Philippines and Nigeria, agricultural employment share continues to remain high (Fig. 2.5). This fact is further reiterated in Table 2.1. Here we see that agricultural share in total employment has nearly halved from 1991 to 2011, decreasing from 57% to 28%. However, states have been transitioning at different paces. Less than 20% of the population remains engaged in agriculture in Goa and Kerala, but in states like Mizoram and Andhra Pradesh, slightly more than 40% of employment still comes from the agricultural sector. In spite of urban wages growing faster than rural

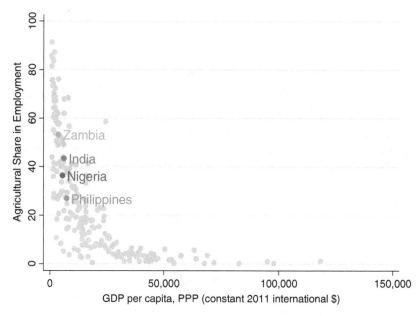

Fig. 2.5 Global comparison of agricultural employment share. Source: National Accounts Statistics & World Bank DataBank (2015–16); based on authors calculations

wages (Bhagat, 2017; Kone, Liu, Mattoo, Ozden, & Sharma, 2016; Munshi, 2011; P. Pingali, 2007b, 2015), census records indicate that rural to rural migration patterns dominate migration streams and many individuals continue to work as agricultural laborers (Fig. 2.6). This implies that labor markets have not been able to employ surplus underemployed labor from the agricultural sector and agricultural labor productivity continues to remain low with vast differences by region.

In order to illuminate the above mechanisms that have impacted regional diversity in growth, in this chapter, we forward evidence from the literature from India. We show that regional comparative advantages (or the lack of it) in resource availability may have benefited some regions over others. In combination with the growth of local and global demand for goods and services, these comparative advantages in inputs have exacerbated subnational divergence in the growth experience. Second, we discuss various labor market frictions that have inhibited a smooth transition of labor from agricultural to the non-agricultural sectors. We show that rural to rural migration in the agricultural sector can be explained by the difference in

Table 2.1 Employment transition during structural transformation

Year	The share of agricultural employment in total employment					
	<20%	20–30%	30–40%	40–50%	>50%	Country average (%)
1991		Goa	Kerala	Gujarat, Haryana, West Bengal	Himachal Pradesh, Punjab, Assam, Maharashtra, Mizoram, Rajasthan, Tamil Nadu, Karnataka, Manipur, Orissa, Sikkim, Arunachal, Meghalaya, Andhra Pradesh, Madhya Pradesh, Uttar Pradesh, Nagaland, Bihar	57
2001	Goa, Kerala	Assam, Gujarat, Haryana, Himachal Pradesh, J&K, Jharkhand, Manipur, Orissa, Punjab, Tripura, West Bengal	Karnataka, Madhya Pradesh, Maharashtra, Mizoram, Rajasthan, Tamil Nadu, Uttarakhand, UP	Andhra Pradesh, Arunachal Pradesh, Bihar, Chhattisgarh, Meghalaya, Nagaland		32
2011	Goa, Kerala	Assam, Haryana, Himachal Pradesh, J&K, Jharkhand, Orissa, Punjab, Sikkim, Uttarakhand, UP, TN, Tripura, West Bengal	Arunachal Pradesh, Bihar, Chhattisgarh, Gujarat, Karnataka, Manipur, Meghalaya, Nagaland, Madhya Pradesh, Maharashtra, Rajasthan	Andhra Pradesh, Mizoram		28

Source: Author's calculations based on census data

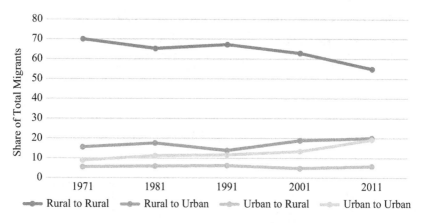

Fig. 2.6   Migration patterns over time. Source: V. K. Singh, Kumar, Singh, and Yadava (2011) and census 2011 migration tables; based on authors calculations

agricultural productivity across states. Low rural to urban migration, more characteristic of the agricultural to non-agricultural migration, has been slower due to poor access to appropriate skills, in addition to geographical challenges that migration poses.

2.2   EXPLAINING INTER-STATE DIVERGENCE IN STRUCTURAL TRANSFORMATION

It is a widely recognized fact that the main driver for the ST process in India was the Green Revolution that began soon after India's independence.[2] To address concerns of food insecurity, rural poverty and low agricultural surplus, policy makers pushed for a nationally oriented agricultural productivity growth policy.[3] Modern high-yielding varieties (HYV) of seeds and

[2] While some may argue that Nehruvian policies on industrial substitution enabled capital accumulation in the country, it is a well-recognized fact that it was the Green Revolution that spread technology into the rural heartland of India. This change played a greater role in poverty reduction, thus stimulating the Indian economy.

[3] It is important to mention that India had already set in place national-level policies for import substitution industrialization policies in the 1950s. However in the 1960s, a burgeoning food deficit, high rural poverty and low rates of urbanization and lack of savings and capital resource accumulation turned policy focus towards development through agriculture. After the Green Revolution created agricultural surplus and put the economy on the process for ST, there was a renewed focus on industrial development. This allowed states where agriculture productivity was still low to invest more in other sectors.

fertilizer technology were first introduced in the late 1960s and early 1970s, in states with high agro-climatic potential and irrigation infrastructure that were considered highly suitable for agricultural intensification and yield enhancing technical change (G. S. Bhalla & Singh, 1997; C. H. H. Rao, 1975, 1994; G. S. Bhalla & Tyagi, 1989). Due to their comparative advantages in farming, northwestern states such as Punjab and Haryana and the southern delta regions in Andhra Pradesh and Tamil Nadu quickly adopted HYV of wheat and rice and, within a short period, became the leaders of the Green Revolution, both regarding food production and productivity. States in the east, such as Bihar and Orissa, that were rich in agricultural lands lost out due to the poor technology suitability, poor infrastructure and lack of institutional support (Bajpai & Sachs, 1996; Prahladachar, 1983).

Between the 1980s to the 2000s, greater development and growth from the agricultural sector was driven by diversification of cropping systems away from staple food grains to cash crop production and by greater use of fertilizers as inputs in production (G. S. Bhalla & Singh, 1997). Some states such as Kerala which did not have a comparative advantage in staple grain production capitalized on the growing demand for fruit, spices and rubber from local and global markets, and invested in tropical plantations (M. G. Rao, Shand, & Kalirajan, 1999). Semi-arid zones of Central India adopted the new crops and varieties of cotton and oil and reoriented their agricultural systems towards the production of these cash crops. Agriculture in these states was able to benefit from the growth in demand for cotton and oil seed that occurred post the staple grain revolution. As a result, these states witnessed a transformation in their agricultural sectors, while states such as Bihar, UP, MP[4] and Odisha that continued to remain focused on staple grain production lost out.

Side by side with the agricultural transformation,[5] the industrial (non-agricultural) policies that were instituted in the 1950s began to

[4] In Pingali, Mittra, and Rahman (2017), authors discuss the MP transformation. Over the last two decades, MP has made tremendous progress towards reforming the agricultural system by utilizing low labor costs and high cropping area availability. MP is now a major supplier to the PDS system and has overtaken Punjab and other states in staple grain production. However, agricultural productivity, though increasing, continues to remain low.

[5] In this chapter we interchangeably use the concept of the Green Revolution and the agriculture revolution. Here with the former we mean the introduction of new high-yielding varieties of wheat and rice, along with innovations in irrigation, water use and fertilizer and pesticide use that revolutionized agriculture in India. The agriculture revolution refers to the Green Revolution along with the diversification of cropping systems across the country that came up in response to changing local and global demand for high-value products such as tea, coffee, rubber and so on.

bear fruit in the 1980s (Aghion, Burgess, Redding, & Zilibotti, 2008; Bhattacharya & Sakthivel, 2004; S. E. Ghani, Grover, Kerr, & others, 2016; M. Ghosh, 2006; U. Kumar & Subramanian, 2012; Rodrik & Subramanian, 2004). The direct impact of the Green Revolution had been twofold. One, it decreased rural poverty, thus stimulating aggregate demand from rural areas (Pingali, 2012). Two, as more agricultural capital and labor surplus was released through rapid increases in productivity into the industrial sector, returns to industrial investments began to pay off. For example, during the initial stages of the Green Revolution, growing needs for construction and power in agriculture drove demand for manufacturing products. Thus some states which had not benefited from the Green Revolution refocused their development strategies, on their comparative advantage, in developing their non-agricultural sectors. In Panagariya et al. (2014), authors discuss that state policies, with regard to urban land ceiling ownership, labor policies, capital markets, small industry policies and bankruptcy laws, varied across states. This created distortions to the returns in capital and labor endowments both across industries and across states. Thus different types of industries (capital or labor intensive) developed in some states vis-a-vis others. Given that India was a closed economy during this time, locally determined demand for goods and services eventually drove profitability across industries. This contributed to cross-sector differences in growth and thus subnational differential growth rates as well.

However, by the 1990s, the liberalization of the Indian economy created another force of divergence in the structural transformation experience. Integrating the economy into the global playing field led to different trends in non-agricultural growth that varied by sectors and states (Chakravorty, 2003; S. E. Ghani et al., 2016). In the literature, there were many reasons attributed to how comparative advantages were created and altered across states during this time. Existence of poor performing state monoliths that could not compete in the international markets, divergence in input factor productivity due to different speeds of tariff deregulation and a political economy that had supported incumbent firms over others pre-liberalization were hypothesized to have affected comparative advantages across states (Kurian, 2000; Rodrik & Subramanian, 2004; Aghion et al., 2008; Kumar & Subramanian, 2012). States that produced goods with high global demand, using the factor of production in which they had a comparative advantage, thus saw an increase in their GDPs relative to states that did not. For example, the fertilizer industry grew faster in response to liberalization, but the iron and steel industry slowed down since local industries were not competitive with global suppliers (Aghion et al., 2008; U. Kumar & Subramanian, 2012). This led to states like Gujarat, whose industries were focused on fertilizer production, growing faster than states like Bihar, which relied on iron and steel production. Among those who had stimulated their economic growth through agricultural development, states that focused only on the production of crops for domestic demand were not able to keep pace with those who diversified their agriculture into export-oriented crops.

The liberalization of the economy and its integration into the world of internet technology created another wedge in the inter-state development processes. In some states, globalization of the economy in combination with comparative advantages created through human capital investments in the past and reforms in the telecom sector facilitated a service sector transformation (Amirapu & Subramanian, 2015; Arnold, Javorcik, Lipscomb, & Mattoo, 2012; Nagaraj, 2009). States like Maharashtra, Karnataka and Tamil Nadu, which had invested heavily in high-skilled human capital development as well as in technology infrastructure, greatly benefited from the technology boom that was driving the growth of the high-skilled global service sector. This growth process then led to a further divergence between growth experiences across states. However, this also leads to further divergence in the intra-state development experience. Since several Indian states focused on high skill employment as opposed to labor-intensive job creation, this stalled movement of labor out of rural areas. The rising disparity incomes between rural and urban areas and the rise in the informal, low-skilled service sector employment relative to more formal employment was one of the negative consequences.

2.2.1   Characterizing ST by Development Process Adopted

To capture the disparate structural transformation processes that caused subnational divergence and hence discuss its implications for food systems looking ahead, we classify states into three categories—*agriculture-led growth states, urbanizing states* and *lagging states*. To identify which states belong in these categories, we use three major outcomes in the structural transformation process. The first outcome that is used in the state classification is GDP per capita. In our model GDP per capita represents both income levels and the productivity of individuals. We classify states into

Table 2.2   Classification of states

Typology	Agriculture-led growth states	Urbanizing states	Lagging states
Criteria	Low urbanization rates and high GDP per capita share of agriculture are relatively high	High urbanization rates and high GDP per capita share of agriculture are reducing	Low urbanization rates and low GDP per capita and low productive agricultural sector drive growth
States	Punjab, Haryana, Andhra Pradesh, Himachal Pradesh	Kerala, Goa, Maharashtra, Tamil Nadu, Gujarat, Karnataka, Telangana, Uttarakhand	Bihar, MP, UP, Odisha, Jharkhand, Chhattisgarh, West Bengal, Rajasthan, J&K, northeast states

high GDP per capita or low GDP per capita depending on whether they are above or below the average state GDP per capita across the country. The second outcome we use is the share of agriculture in GDP. A high (or low) agricultural share in GDP (compared to the mean) represents the relative importance of the agricultural sector in contributing to economic development within the state. The third outcome measure is urbanization rates. A high (or low) rate of urbanization represents the relative importance of the non-agricultural sector in contributing to GDP growth. Combing these three outcome measures, we classify states into the three categories (as shown in Table 2.2). We classify states with high GDP per capita, where agriculture continues to remain an important contributor to GDP growth and low urbanization rates as *agriculture-led growth states*. We classify states with high GDP per capita and high urbanizing rates as *urbanizing states*. Finally, in places with low GDP per capita and low rates of urbanization, we classify states as *lagging states*.

In line with our description in the previous section on the subnational growth experience, in *agriculture-led growth states*, a high productive agricultural sector, stimulated by the introduction of the Green Revolution, is the engine of economic growth. These economies were among the first to adopt new technologies for staple crop production. This led to an increase in their agricultural productivity and production and played a key role in transforming their economic landscape. While the Green Revolution played an important role in creating a sizeable agriculture surplus, some of these states have not reinvested the same in the non-agricultural sectors. This explains the relatively low urbanization rates. States such as Punjab, Haryana, Himachal Pradesh and Andhra Pradesh represent this development paradigm.

The second group of states in our model are the *urbanizing states*. In these states, economic development started with the Green Revolution. Many of these states were either able to reinvest surpluses created during their Green Revolution or were able to attract investments of surpluses from neighboring states into the development of their non-agricultural sectors. For example, Delhi attracted much of the agricultural surplus investments from Punjab, while Telangana was able to redirect agricultural surpluses from Andhra Pradesh's Green Revolution for its development. Alongside these changes, investments in human capital development, aggressive infrastructure development policies, rapid urban agglomeration and other non-agricultural development policies also paid off. In some of these states, growth has been driven by the manufacturing sectors, while in others a high-skilled service industry has been the major driver of growth. Examples of such states would include Maharashtra, Tamil Nadu, Gujarat, Uttarakhand, Karnataka, Telangana.[6]

The last category are the *lagging states*. Due to the technology unsuitability in these regions, many of these states did not see the widespread adoption of Green Revolution HYV seeds when it was first rolled out in the 1970s. In the next phase of the Green Revolution, dominated by cash crop production, price policies for staple production distorted incentives to diversify into non-staple agricultural production. Thus many of these states were not able to take advantage of the comparative advantages they had in the production of non-staple crops. As a result, they continued to rely on a low productive agricultural sector to drive their structural transformation while other states forged ahead. In the absence of strong non-agricultural development policy, urbanization rates remained low relative to other groups as well. States such as Bihar, Rajasthan, Madhya Pradesh, Orissa, Uttar Pradesh, Jharkhand, Chhattisgarh and Jammu and Kashmir belong to this category.[7]

[6] A caveat for this classification is that there exists a lot of inter-group variation in the ST experience of states. For example, the factors that led to Tamil Nadu's growth are different from the factors that led Kerala to become urbanized. Similarly, agriculture-led transformation in Punjab is dominated by staple crops, but cash crops can better explain Himachal's progress towards ST. However for the sake of parsimony, we bundle states together. This allows us to capture the broad historical experiences of states as well as identify some major trends by group as we look ahead. As we move forward, researchers would have to develop state-specific policies that reflect on the various trends within states. We leave this exercise to the future academic researchers and policy makers.

[7] In this chapter, states from the North east are included into the 'special category states' classification since this region received concessions on central taxes and financial redistributions in order to develop their institutions and economies. While we acknowledge that there is a lot of variation between these states in terms of the ST experience, their

2.2.2   An Empirical Exercise on Characterizing ST in India

In Table 2.3, we see the outcomes of the different development process mentioned in the previous section. In the table, we regress state GDP per capita on a number of fixed effects controlling for lags (up to five years). In this model, the province fixed effects control for differences in institutions and other time invariant factors that were common within the province. The time fixed effects account for changes in access to technology or politics and so on that may have impacted states differently over time. In column 1 (and 3), the constant term represents the annual year-on-year increase in GDP per capita (and percentage change) over time that is exogenous to these changes. It shows how much faster growing states increased their GDP per capita over time. This inequality increasing feature of states economic growth patterns is reflected in Fig. 2.3, which compares differences in the way that state transformed between the 1960s to recent times. From column 2 onward, we introduce two more fixed effects. First, we divide up the year variable into decadal dummies. These dummies represent the different timelines of the planning committee of India within which they introduced different technologies and policies to facilitate ST in India. In the 1960s and 1970s (D1 & D2), for example, the main policy focus was on building agricultural systems. In the 1980s (D3), small industry development became a national focus. In the 1990s (D4), trade liberalization and deregulation became the main focus of development strategies. In the 2000s (D5), the high-skilled service sector, facilitated by the internet technology boom across the world became a key driving force. Since the main focus of policy kept changing between these decades, the additional variation from the changing institutional context we feel is captured by adding these dummies. Second, to capture the differential effects of policy on state-wise development, we then interact the decadal dummies with the type of ST that has come to characterize state-wise development. In columns 2 and 4, our preferred specifications, we include a full set of interactions that account for both the development experience of the state and the decade fixed effects. As one would expect, states with ST led by agriculture greatly benefited from the early changes made during the Green Revolution. These states

economies remain weak compared to the rest of the country. This makes them comparable in outcomes to the *lagging states*. Thus, in other chapters, figures or tables, where there is no data on these states, the experience of *lagging states* will be assumed to represent their experience as well.

Table 2.3 Per capita growth over time

Variables	(1)	(2)	(3)	(4)
	NSDP PC	NSDP PC	Log NSDPPC	Log NSDPPC
Lagging × D1	5,064**	−731.2*	0.379*	0.301
	(2,147)	(375.9)	(0.190)	(0.212)
Lagging × D2	−925.0	−1,515**	−0.0772	−0.0317
	(3,159)	(594.0)	(0.134)	(0.120)
Lagging × D3	−2,523	−440.6	−0.0888	−0.0818
	(2,212)	(323.7)	(0.115)	(0.0992)
Lagging × D4	−4,051**	−228.1	−0.0136	−0.0196
	(1,917)	(326.4)	(0.0986)	(0.0774)
Lagging × D5	−4,242	−365.6	0.208	0.277
	(3,429)	(447.2)	(0.233)	(0.196)
Lagging × D6	−6,598	−251.3	0.260	0.357
	(5,449)	(757.6)	(0.251)	(0.216)
High Ag × D1	8,276*	−1,156**	1.174***	1.467***
	(4,405)	(427.2)	(0.271)	(0.171)
High Ag × D2	7,324**	−1,527**	0.949***	0.798***
	(3,072)	(570.1)	(0.127)	(0.128)
High Ag × D3	9,178***	−593.2	1.035***	0.855***
	(1,994)	(368.3)	(0.0949)	(0.0957)
High Ag × D4	13,859***	78.72	1.129***	0.936***
	(2,606)	(741.6)	(0.0811)	(0.0872)
High Ag × D5	28,789***	1,489**	1.255***	0.917***
	(4,262)	(685.1)	(0.237)	(0.195)
High Ag × D6	42,487***	1,674	1.308***	0.875***
	(6,915)	(1,183)	(0.247)	(0.255)
Urbanizing × D1	−12,164	2,463***	0.623***	0.911***
	(9,068)	(839.5)	(0.147)	(0.214)
Urbanizing × D2	−13,782	2,897***	0.480***	0.788***
	(11,472)	(838.4)	(0.144)	(0.169)
Urbanizing × D3	−9,961	3,056***	0.534***	0.807***
	(9,142)	(651.7)	(0.126)	(0.165)
Urbanizing × D4	1,314	5,274***	0.581***	0.855***
	(4,528)	(1,394)	(0.148)	(0.145)
Urbanizing × D5	23,021***	5,781***	0.804***	0.773***
	(2,421)	(910.8)	(0.164)	(0.174)
Urbanizing × D6	58,910***	8,817***	1.016***	0.638**
	(7,312)	(2,176)	(0.211)	(0.277)
Constant	52,464***	4,005**	10.21***	9.834***
	(4,379)	(1,523)	(0.191)	(0.276)
Observations	1,340	1,188	1,340	1,188

(continued)

Table 2.3 (continued)

Variables	(1)	(2)	(3)	(4)
	NSDP PC	NSDP PC	Log NSDPPC	Log NSDPPC
R-squared	0.909	0.989	0.917	0.936
State FE	YES	YES	YES	YES
Year FE	YES	YES	YES	YES
Decade FE	YES	YES	YES	YES
Lags	NO	YES	NO	YES
Robust SE	YES	YES	YES	YES

Robust standard errors in parentheses—clustered by state, ***$p < 0.01$, **$p < 0.05$, *$p < 0.1$
NSDP PC—National State Domestic Product per capita, Log NSDP PC—log values of NSDP PC—represents year-on-year growth
High Ag—high agricultural productive states, Spl Cat—special category states; *lagging states* are the baseline comparison groups
FE—refers to fixed effects, lags—include five lags for NSDP PC values

grew around 14% each year in the first decade and then around 8% on average every year. *Urbanizing states*, which diversified out of staple grains and agriculture, grew steadily around 9% year on year over the entire time. *Lagging states*, which focused their agriculture on staples on the other hand, grew very slowly in the first three decades. Much of their 2–3% growth has come from the post-liberalization times.

2.3   TRANSITION FROM THE AGRICULTURE TO THE NON-AGRICULTURAL SECTOR: FRICTIONS AND SEARCH COSTS IN LABOR MARKETS

During the process of ST, economic growth brings new employment opportunities in the fast growing non-farm economy (Johnston & Mellor, 1961). As the number of opportunities to engage in the non-farm rural sector increases, many opportunities for employment and growth also come to situate themselves in urban agglomerations such as peri-urban areas, towns and cities. Agglomeration of skills and capital in these urban units are known to speed up the process of growth, thus pushing up urban wages faster than rural wages. Hence, historically, it has been common to see large numbers of people migrating from rural to urban areas to avail the benefits of this growth (Barrett, Christian, & Shiferaw, 2017; Johnston, 1970; Johnston & Mellor, 1961; P. Pingali, 2010).

In India, while cities have grown in size and economic opportunities have increased, an important criticism of the ST process is that there has been a very low rural to urban migration rates in response to these changes. The employment share of agriculture in total employment has not fallen as fast as the decrease in the value added of agriculture in GDP. In line with this observation, migration data from the census 2011 reveals that rural to rural migration has dominated patterns for working age males. The major occupational choice for these types of migrants are agricultural laborer-related jobs, which explains why agricultural share in labor remains high even though India has undergone structural transformation. Rural to urban migration, often characterized by the transition of jobs from the agricultural to the non-agricultural sector, has been increasing, albeit too slowly (Fig. 2.4). This is in spite of the fact that urban unemployment continues to remain high and increasing demand for urban services continues to drive up wages (Binswanger-Mkhize, 2013; Munshi & Rosenzweig, 2016).[8] To explain this conundrum, in this section, we propose explanations on the market dynamics and illuminate the different search or entry costs that have impacted labor markets and hence migration patterns in India. In a future chapter, we highlight the micro-level constraints involved for income diversification of households.

2.3.1   The Push and Pull of Migration in Response to Disequilibria in Labor Markets

We classify labor markets in India into those for low skills and those for high skills. The low-skilled labor markets in India are characterized by lower human capital investments in education. Sectors such as agriculture, construction, mining and low value added industries and (non-agricultural) services determine the labor demand. In the absence of signals for worker quality, which generally come from education, social networks play an important role in reducing search costs. Social networks also help reduce monitoring costs and costs of contract enforcement

---

[8] Many peri-urban areas continue to remain classified as rural based on a hard and fast census classification for urban areas. Experts who tend to use these census definitions tend to underestimate the amount of urbanization in the country, and hence migration rates at best underestimate the true migration rates between rural and urban areas.

for employers in these low-skilled labor markets. In high-skilled labor markets, firms from sectors such as finance, medical care, education and research and technology development determine labor demand. Entry costs, reflected by costs of accessing good quality education, restrict labor supply and the total skills available for firms to access. In these markets, social networks play a smaller role in determining employment opportunities. Firms instead rely on observable worker quality, experience working in other firms and educational levels of individuals as credible signals in the hiring process.

All states in India have some combination of these markets depending on their level of ST. In Tamil Nadu and Gujarat, firms demanding high-skilled labor can be found in both urban and semi-urban areas. Higher levels of ST in these states create demand for both high-skilled and low-skilled workers in urban areas. This creates the pull factor for labor out of agricultural jobs and out of rural areas. In order to replace these outmigrants, wages in rural areas increase to attract new labor. This creates a pull for able-bodied and productive migrants from other states where rural labor markets may be depressed due to economic conditions. In states such as Madhya Pradesh and Orissa, the low-skilled labor supply is large, but employment opportunities outside the local labor market may not exist due to low worker productivity. In these states, migrants from rural areas will often participate in low-skilled labor markets closer to their homes. Thus, these various factors contribute to four internal migration patterns documented in the Indian census (Table 2.4).

The first type of migration is the rural to rural (R2R) transition, which records the percentage of individuals who transition between rural areas of residence from one census survey to the next. The second type of migration is rural to urban (R2U) migration. This migration reflects the movement of individuals from rural residences to urban residences. According to the labor market theories, during ST, greater urban growth, driven by growth in the non-agricultural sector, is expected to stimulate demand for this type of transition. The third and fourth types of migration pattern are the urban to urban (U2U) and the urban to rural (U2R) migration. For the former, high levels of urbanization both between and within states determine migration patterns. For those migrating from urban to rural areas, age and gender

Table 2.4 Migration patterns over time

Year	Group	Rural to rural	Rural to urban	Urban to rural	Urban to urban
1971	Male	53.2	26.6	6.4	13.8
	Female	77.6	10.7	5	6.7
	Total	70	15.6	5.5	8.9
1981	Male	45.6	30	7	17.4
	Female	73.3	12.5	5.6	8.6
	Total	65.2	17.6	5.9	11.3
1991	Male	43.43	31.6	7.2	17.8
	Female	76.5	8.4	5.8	9.3
	Total	67.2	13.9	6.2	11.7
2001	Male	36.4	34.2	6.3	23.1
	Female	72.3	13.5	4.2	10
	Total	62.9	18.9	4.8	13.4
2011	Male	33.9	30.2	7.1	28.8
	Female	64.0	15.7	5.2	15.1
	Total	54.9	20.1	5.8	19.3

Source: Singh et al. (2011), census 2011

play a major role. This type of migration is dominated by older aged individuals migrating for retirement and by women migrating for marriage. Within states, the level of ST and proximity to urban centers can influence migration patterns. For example, locational advantages such as proximity to Delhi explain greater R2U migration for work related employment from Haryana. High urbanization, low migration costs and the promise of high incomes per capita encourage the inmigration of low-skilled workers from neighboring states. R2R migration patterns would be larger in *lagging states* like Bihar. Low urbanization rates and low incomes per capita reduce incentive for rural to urban migration in favor of rural to rural migration. Individuals are more likely to move between rural areas within the state. U2U migration patterns would be larger for *urbanizing states* like Maharashtra. High rates of urbanization, greater access to the global economy and more opportunities for urban-oriented economic growth create the impetus for driving the migration of both high-skilled and low-skilled individuals towards its urban areas (Census Report, 2001, pp. 23–24).

2.3.2   Explaining High R2R Migration Rates: Moving Low-skilled Agricultural Labor Between Low and High ST States

In 2011, nearly 55% of total migration involved individuals moving between rural areas of India. These transition patterns tend to dominate the migration story of India and are often used to drive home the point that ST processes have not been sufficient in India. In this section, we argue instead, embedded in the macro statistics are the pull factors created by low-skilled agricultural labor markets in high ST areas vis-a-vis low ST areas. In high ST states, for example, increase in productivity of agriculture has driven up the labor costs of low-skilled agricultural laborers (S. Bhalla, 1979). In response to these pull factors, labor from low ST areas migrate towards job opportunities in these agricultural labor markets.

There are two reasons for a migrant from a low productive agricultural labor market to move to a high productive but low-skilled agricultural labor market. One, as long as the expected wages at the destination are higher than their current wages, migrants will prefer to move between labor markets that maximize their wages given their skills, knowledge and preferences for work (Fields, 2011; Harrison & Leamer, 1997; Lipton, 1980). Other factors that influence the cost of migration such as proximity to home town or linguistic and ethnic proximity to members at the destination can influence both where the individual may choose to migrate as well as how long they choose to stay (Harris & Todaro, 1970; Todaro, 1969). These costs also differ based on educational qualifications, the strength of social networks and opportunity costs of migration (Fields, 1975; Lipton, 1980). High intra-district figures and high rural to rural migration may thus reflect rational responses of migrant households to local labor market frictions rather than failed outcomes of urbanization or ST. In low-skilled agricultural labor markets, wages are higher in high ST states than low ST states as evidenced from the literature (Fig. 2.7). As a result, workers from low ST areas migrate into agricultural markets in high ST states. In 2001 migration census report, migration from Bihar (0.14 million) and Uttar Pradesh (0.24 million) dominated inmigration figures to Punjab. Work employment was cited as the main reason for migration by male migrants from UP (72.1%) and Bihar (82.2%).[9]

---

[9] While one would ideally like to have migration transition probabilities between states by sector, this data is not available. However, it is reasonable to assume that rural to rural migration rates from Bihar to Punjab are higher than rural to urban migration rates between these states.

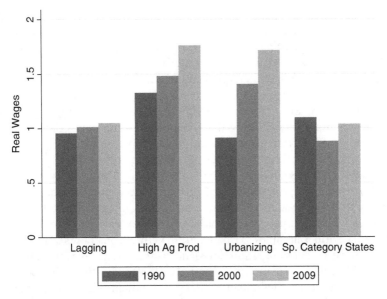

Fig. 2.7 Agriculture wage differentials by state classifications. Source: ICRISAT VDSA meso-level data; based on authors calculations

2.3.3 Explaining Low R2U Migration Rates: Illuminating Frictions That Affect the Speed of Transition

Urban markets are thought to house non-agricultural production centers that grow during ST. The ST theory predicts that non-agricultural sector growth, represented by greater urbanization and industrial growth, creates the major pull factors for migration out of rural areas. Thus ST is expected to bring with it high rural to urban migration rates (B. Bhattacharyya, 1985; Fields, 1975, 2011; Lipton, 1980; Todaro, 1969; Zhang & Song, 2003). In India, both urbanization, as well as wage differentials between urban and rural markets, have been increasing with ST. In response to these changes, one would expect that there would an increase in the R2U migration rates. However, based on census migration data, we see that R2U migration statistics has been increasing rather slowly. Experts have argued that even though 30% of India reports migrating over ten years, most of the migration is by women moving for marriage and males moving for employment within their districts.[10] Temporary migration, a situation where individuals may enter urban labor markets for six or fewer months, has been the defining feature of this type of migration (Bhagat, 2017; Kone et al., 2016; Mitra & Marayama, 2009; Pandey, 2014; Tumbe, 2014). Low R2U migration in the presence of high wage differentials and unemployment represent a contradiction to the expected growth process as determined by ST.

At the micro level, experts have highlighted the role of language, caste, religion and age in explaining the phenomena of high rates of temporary migration of low-skilled workers and low occupational mobility in urban areas (Munshi, 2011; Munshi & Rosenzweig, 2006, 2016). In China (Rozelle, Taylor, & DeBrauw, 1999) and Mexico (Taylor & Wyatt, 1996), authors find that poorly defined land rights often prevent laborers from selling their unproductive lands and moving out of agriculture. The literature also finds that proximity to urban areas also plays a role in determining migration outcomes. Urban infrastructure constraints also impose costs on permanent migration since land costs in urban areas are extremely high (Bhagat, 2017; Imbert & Papp, 2014; Pandey, 2014). These entry costs along with poor human capital development add to labor market frictions and reduce incentives for workers from rural areas to respond to urban labor market demand. If the probability of finding a job is low due to lack of information, this will discourage rural to urban migration in the presence of urban unemployment and rising wages (B. Bhattacharyya, 1985; Fields, 2011; Lipton, 1980).

At the macro level, low levels of ST in states or low growth of the non-agricultural sectors reduces pull factors that are essential for migration to take place. Looking at the data on the migration probabilities between states, one sees that geographical proximity of *urbanizing states* determines migration patterns. In 2001, Maharashtra saw the greatest increase in migrants with over 3.2 million people entering the state. Of those migrating, 81% moved into urban areas. Delhi welcomed an additional 2.2 million people. Much of the migration to these *urbanizing states* came from *lagging states*. More than 70% of male migrants to these states reported that they migrated for work and employment.

[10] Urban population growth doubled between 1901 and 2001, then increased 8% between 2001 and 2011. This growth has come from (1) high urban fertility rates (around 2.0), and urban fertility has reached this level only recently. Till 2001 it was above 2, which meant that urban population growth was driven by those living in urban areas. (2) Migration to cities—this has been a smaller portion of the total urban growth for now. However, it will change soon as migration has urban fertility rates that have fallen below replacement rates in 2011.

2.3.4 Changing Demographic Structure and Its Impact on Rural Productivity

In India, outmigration is characterized by welfare reducing factors at the point of origin. Overall, highly educated, young, productive and rich male individuals migrate first followed by their nuclear families (Census, 2001; Kone et al., 2016; Pandey, 2014; Tumbe, 2014; Zhang & Song, 2003). Reverse migration or the process of moving from urban to rural areas also contributes to changing the socio-demographic profile of villages for those left behind (Census, 2001). Among those participating in U2R migration, marriage is the largest driver of female migration and old age is the largest driven of male migrants. Thus outmigration of young workers and inmigration of women and older individuals create a village economy characterized by older age individuals and women and children. These groups are then expected to manage the farm and hence drive the rural economy. In Munshi and Rosenzweig (2016), authors show that outmigration greatly impacts the strength and wealth of the social network, increasing vulnerability of those who are left behind. Migrant remittances are often used to pay back the debt incurred for helping a family member migrate or in replacing farm labor with automated tools of production. Desai and Banerji (2008) show that women who are left behind exhibit independence and better empowerment indicators only if they do not already live with an extended family. Living with extended family decreases their agency in supporting the household.

In such situations, there are three important things to note. One, over time, women and older individuals often become an important part of the labor force in agriculture in rural areas. In the last census, the female to male ratio of women working in the agricultural sector had increased both over time and with greater amounts of GDP per capita. Figure 2.8 reiterates the importance of focusing on increasing agricultural productivity of women to stimulate rural growth in the future. Two, without access to financial markets to invest gains from migration or non-agricultural markets to spend their cash on, rural economies may not benefit from net migration. Thus investments in increasing access to banks or other savings instruments will be important for stimulating investments and hence growth in the non-farm rural sector. Three, as rural fertility remains high and child mortality continues to reduce, there is bound to be an increase in the number of young individuals who will become eligible to participate

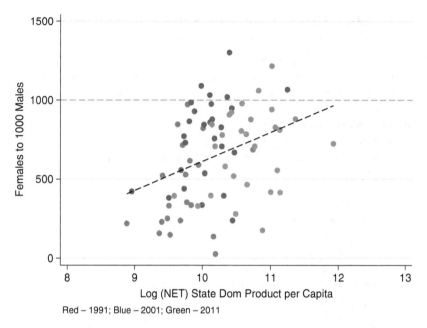

Fig. 2.8 Growing participation of women in agriculture. Source: Census 1991, 2001 & 2011; based on authors calculations

in the labor markets over time. Lack of access to proper education or health facilities due to poor rural infrastructure and poor access to nutrition will reduce the productivity of the future labor force. This will reinforce the existence of a low productive rural economy, thus impacting future efforts towards stimulating greater structural transformation.

2.4   Conclusion

As of 2018, India has become the sixth largest economy in the world displacing France from this position. The emergence of the country on the global stage is evident in its growing per capita incomes and its emergence as a global economic and thought leader. However, India's growth experience has been marred by subnational divergence. This has led to the emergence of states like Goa and Delhi whose development experiences compare to high growth countries in Latin America, while states like Bihar and Uttar Pradesh are now more comparable to some of the low-income countries in sub-Saharan Africa. In the former, development is driven by a high growth urban economy, while the latter's development is weighed down by a low productive agricultural sector.

In this chapter, we deliberate upon the reasons behind the divergent subnational growth experience. Overall there are four major takeaways. First we find that the Green Revolution, which played an important role in catalyzing economic growth in many states across the country, did not benefit all states. States (currently *lagging states*) which did not have any comparative advantages in the production of rice and wheat have been left behind in the development process. Instead, those states that have built their agricultural sectors on comparative advantages such as ease of access to global markets, agro-climatic advantages, high-skilled farm capacity for production have been the ones to benefit from technology advances of the Green Revolution. In many of the fast growing states, agricultural value added and agricultural productivity remains high and continues to grow, reiterating the role of a productive agricultural sector in supporting the growth process. In *lagging states*, staple-grain-focused agricultural policies and rigid procurement policies lock small farmers into staple grain production even when they have no comparative advantages in its production. The lack of documentation of landownership and the increase in fragmentation of land have also been linked to poor investments in productivity-enhancing inputs, thus leading to low yields. This creates a vicious cycle of low yields and low returns to farming and keeps small farmers in their subsistence mode of production especially in *lagging states*.

Second, our analysis of the development process reveals that serendipitous changes in national (aggregate) demand (pre-1990s) or global demand (post-1990s) and the readiness of states to direct their economic sectors to respond to this demand have been the key ingredients in propelling them forward. States that have been more flexible in their development approach, focusing on developing industries in which they have comparative advantages in resource availability, have been more successful in enabling greater ST. In *urbanizing states*, even though the Green Revolution provided the impetus for growth, development strategies that have focused on comparative advantages, in skill and infrastructure availability, rather than absolute advantages, say in availability of land, have proved successful for ST. Thus national policies that keep states locked into a single type of development strategy have now become high-risk strategies. Even states focused on *agriculture-led growth* need to actively redirect their economies to benefit from global opportunities for growth based on their comparative advantages in high-value crop production, for example. In this regard, investment strategies that increase the productivity of resources are important towards ensuring long-term development.

Third, embedded in our discussion on the macro factors that impact growth is the assumption that if economies are to structurally transform, a robust non-agricultural sector will be needed. The non-agricultural sector creates the pull factor that helps redirect underemployed agricultural labor from low productivity to higher productivity jobs. This non-agricultural sector growth can come from the non-farm rural sector as well as urban areas. While we discuss this in more detail in Chap. 3, in this chapter, we argue that reducing labor market frictions will increase participation in the non-farm (or non-agricultural sector) and is key to facilitate faster ST. This involves reducing search costs and entry costs into rural and urban non-farm labor markets. For example, we identify that human capital investments reduce both search and entry costs and are needed for greater occupational mobility. Additionally, information about labor market returns, increasing safety in the workplace and access to role models who come from the same caste and community can also be important inputs into reducing barriers to entry. Four, a major trend that we see emerging for the future is the growing importance of women in the agricultural sector. On-farm labor-saving technology which enhances productivity and reduces drudgery is essential for kickstarting a Green Revolution 2.0, especially in low productive regions. However, technology adoption can enhance on-farm productivity only if it accounts for issues of access that are impacted often by gender, poor education, lack of land tenure rights or lack of access to financial markets. These labor market frictions need to be addressed through appropriate rural development and human capital enhancing policies.

Looking ahead, we see three important drivers for economic growth that will impact the speed of ST within the country. First, recent research has shown that climate change has created a non-trivial threat to future production. Studies have already documented the negative effects of temperature and rainfall shocks on agricultural productivity, labor productivity and health of individuals within the country (Majra & Gur, 2009; E. Somanathan & Somanathan, 2009). This poses a major challenge for development policies as there is expected to be regional disparities in the intensity of impacts due to climate change. Thus economic policy needs to simultaneously invest in creating comparative advantages for growth while reducing greenhouse gas emissions through appropriate climate change mitigation policies. Second, extrapolating on the current demographic and migration trends from the country, we see that over the next 30 years, a greater number of young Indians are expected to enter the workforce. However only healthy individuals will have the ability to participate in growth processes to their full capacity. Also, current trends in industry growth indicate the growing preference of mechanization and labor-saving technologies in production processes. Creating a clear pathway for young people to benefit from economic growth opportunities that a mechanized ST process brings with it, which, simultaneously addressing the human capital challenge of better nutrition and health, will be an important policy commitment. Three, rapid urbanization of population poses a major challenge if it is not inclusive of the rural growth. Looking ahead, tying rural development to urban food growth requires policy innovations in agricultural development, food supply chains, food safety nets and non-farm economic opportunities. These commitments will be important towards ensuring the long-term sustainability of economic development processes.

REFERENCES

Aghion, P., Burgess, R., Redding, S., & Zilibotti, F. (2008). The unequal effects of liberalization: Theory and evidence from India. *American Economic Review, 98*(4), 1397–1412. https://doi.org/10.1257/aer.98.4.1397

Amirapu, A., & Subramanian, A. (2015). *Manufacturing or services? An Indian illustration of a development dilemma.* CGD Working Paper Series No. 409.

Arnold, J., Javorcik, B., Lipscomb, M., & Mattoo, A. (2012). *Services reform and manufacturing performance: Evidence from India.* Retrieved from http://www.cepr.org/pubs/new-dps/dplist.asp?dpno=8011

Bajpai, N., & Sachs, J. D. (1996). *Trends in inter-state inequalities of income in India.* Development Discussion Papers (No. 528), p. 25.

Barrett, C. B., Christian, P., & Shiferaw, B. A. (2017). The structural transformation of African agriculture and rural spaces: Introduction to a special section. *Agricultural Economics, 48*(5), 1–9. https://doi.org/10.1111/agec.12382

Bhagat, R. B. (2017). *Migration and urban transition in India: Implications for development migration and urban transition in India: Implications for development.* United Nations expert group meeting on Sustainable Cities, Human Mobility and International Migration. Retrieved from http://www.un.org/en/development/desa/population/events/pdf/expert/27/papers/V/paper-Bhagat-final.pdf

Bhalla, G. S., & Singh, G. (1997). Recent developments in Indian agriculture: A state level analysis. *Economic and Political Weekly, 32*(13), A2–A18.

Bhalla, G. S., & Tyagi, D. S. (1989). Spatial pattern of agricultural development in India. *Economic and Political Weekly, 24*(25), 46–56.

Bhalla, S. (1979). Real wage rates of agricultural labourers in Punjab, 1961–77: A preliminary analysis. *Economic and Political Weekly, 14*(26), A57–A68. Retrieved from http://www.jstor.org/stable/4367735

Bhattacharya, B. B., & Sakthivel, S. (2004). Regional growth disparity in India: Comparison of pre- and post-reform decades. *Economic and Political Weekly, 39*(10), 1071–1077.

Bhattacharyya, B. (1985). The role of family decision in internal migration: The case of India. *Journal of Development Economics, 18*, 51–66.

Binswanger-Mkhize, H. P. (2013). The stunted structural transformation of the Indian economy: Agriculture, manufacturing and the rural non-farm sector. *Economic and Political Weekly, 48*, 5–13. Retrieved from https://www.epw.in/journal/2013/26-27/review-rural-affairs-review-issues/stuntedstructural-transformation-indian

Census. (2001). *Migration Tables. Census of India* (Vol. 1).

Chakravorty, S. (2003). Industrial location in post-reform India: Patterns of inter-regional divergence and intra-regional convergence. *Journal of Development Studies, 40*(2), 120–152. https://doi.org/10.1080/00220380412331293797

Chenery, H. B. (1960). Patterns of industrial growth. *American Economic Review, 50*(4), 624–654.

Desai, S., & Banerji, M. (2008). Negotiated identities: Male migration and left-behind wives in India. *Journal of Population Research, 25*(3), 337–355. https://doi.org/10.1007/BF03033894

Fields, G. S. (1975). Rural-urban migration, urban unemployment and underemployment, and job-search activity in LDCs. *Journal of Development Economics, 2*(2), 165–187. https://doi.org/10.1016/0304-3878(75)90014-0

Fields, G. S. (2011). Labor market analysis for developing countries. *Labour Economics, 18*(Suppl. 1), S16–S22. https://doi.org/10.1016/j.labeco.2011.09.005

Ghani, S. E., Grover, A., Kerr, W. R., & Others. (2016). Spatial development and agglomeration economies in services—Lessons from India (June).

Ghosh, M. (2006). Economic growth and human development in Indian states. *Economic and Political Weekly, 41*(30), 3321–3329. Retrieved from http://www.jstor.org/stable/4418499

Harris, J. R., & Todaro, M. P. (1970). Migration, unemployment and development: A two-sector analysis. *American Economic Review, 60*(1), 126–142.

Harrison, A., & Leamer, E. (1997). Labor markets in developing countries: An agenda for research. *Journal of Labor Economics, 15*(3), S1–S19. https://doi.org/10.2307/2535423

Herrendorf, B., Rogerson, R., & Valentinyi, A. (2013). Two perspectives on preferences and structural transformation. *American Economic Review, 103*(7), 2752–2789.

Imbert, C., & Papp, J. (2014). Short-term migration, rural workfare programs and urban labor markets: Evidence from India. *Center for Economic Policy Research* [Google Scholar].

Johnston, B. B. F. (1970). Agriculture and structural transformation in developing countries: A survey of research. *Journal of Economic Literature, 8*(2), 369–404.

Johnston, B. B. F., & Mellor, J. W. (1961). The role of agriculture in economic development. *American Economic Review, 51*(4), 566–593.

Kone, Z. L., Liu, M. Y., Mattoo, A., Ozden, C., & Sharma, S. (2016). *Internal borders and migration in India*. Policy Research Working Paper No. 8244.

Kumar, U., & Subramanian, A. (2012). Growth in India's states in the first decade of the 21st century: Four facts. *Economic and Political Weekly, XLVIII*(3), 48–57.

Kurian, N. J. (2000). Widening regional disparities in India: Some indicators. *Economic and Political Weekly, 35*(7), 538–550. Retrieved from http://www.jstor.org/stable/4408933

Lipton, M. (1980). Migration from rural areas of poor countries: The impact on rural productivity and income distribution. *World Development, 8*(1), 1–24. https://doi.org/10.1016/0305-750X(80)90047-9

Majra, J. P., & Gur, A. (2009). Climate change and health: Why should India be concerned? *Indian Journal of Occupational and Environmental Medicine, 13*(1), 11.

Mitra, A., & Marayama, M. (2009). Rural to urban migration: A district-level analysis for India. *International Journal of Migration, Health and Social Care, 5*(2), 35–53.

Munshi, K. (2011). Strength in numbers: Networks as a solution to occupational traps. *Review of Economic Studies, 78*(3), 1069–1101. https://doi.org/10.1093/restud/rdq029

Munshi, K., & Rosenzweig, M. (2006). Traditional institutions meet the modern world: Caste, gender, and schooling choice in a globalizing economy. *American Economic Review, 96*(4), 1225–1252. https://doi.org/10.1257/aer.96.4.1225

Munshi, K., & Rosenzweig, M. (2016). Networks and misallocation: Insurance, migration, and the rural-urban wage gap. *American Economic Review, 106*(1), 46–98. https://doi.org/10.1257/aer.20131365

Nagaraj, R. (2009). Is services sector output overestimated? An inquiry. *Economic and Political Weekly, 44*(5), 40–45. Retrieved from http://www.jstor.org/stable/40278458

Panagariya, A., Chakraborty, P., & Rao, M. G. (2014). *State level reforms, growth, and development in Indian states* (Vol. 3). Studies in Indian Economic Policies.

Pandey, A. K. (2014). Spatio-temporal changes in internal migration in India during post reform period. *Journal of Economic & Social Development, X*(1), 107–116.

Pingali, P. (2007a). Agricultural growth and economic development: A view through the globalization lens. *Agricultural Economics, 37*(Suppl. S1), 1–12. https://doi.org/10.1111/j.1574-0862.2007.00231.x

Pingali, P. (2007b). Westernization of Asian diets and the transformation of food systems: Implications for research and policy. *Food Policy, 32*(3), 281–298. https://doi.org/10.1016/j.foodpol.2006.08.001

Pingali, P. (2010). Chapter 74 Agriculture renaissance: Making 'agriculture for development' work in the 21st century. In P. Pingali & R. Evenson (Eds.), *Handbook of agricultural economics* (pp. 3867–3894). Elsevier. Retrieved from http://www.sciencedirect.com/science/article/pii/S1574007209040742

Pingali, P. (2012). Green revolution: Impacts, limits, and the path ahead. *Proceedings of the National Academy of Science, 109*(31), 12302–12308. https://doi.org/10.1073/pnas.0912953109

Pingali, P. (2015). Agricultural policy and nutrition outcomes—Getting beyond the preoccupation with staple grains. *Food Security, 7*(3), 583–591. https://doi.org/10.1007/s12571-015-0461-x

Pingali, P., & Aiyar, A. (2018). *Diversity in development: An inter-state differences in the India growth story.*

Pingali, P., Mittra, B., & Rahman, A. (2017). The bumpy road from food to nutrition security—Slow evolution of India's food policy. *Global Food Security, 15*, 77–84. https://doi.org/10.1016/j.gfs.2017.05.002

Pingali, P., Ricketts, K., & Sahn, D. E. (2015). The fight against hunger and malnutrition: The role of food, agriculture, and targeted policies. In D. E. Sahn (Ed.), *Agriculture for nutrition.* Oxford, UK: Oxford University Press.

Prahladachar, M. (1983). Income distribution effects of the green revolution in India: A review of empirical evidence. *World Development, 11*(11), 927–944.

Rao, C. H. H. (1975). *Technological change and the distribution of gains in Indian agriculture.* Macmillan Company of India.

Rao, C. H. H. (1994). *Agricultural growth, rural poverty and environmental degradation in India.* Oxford University Press.

Rao, M. G., Shand, R. T., & Kalirajan, K. P. (1999). Convergence of incomes across Indian states—A divergent view. *Economic and Political Weekly, 34*(13), 769–778.

Rodrik, D., & Subramanian, A. (2004). *From Hindu growth to productivity surge: The mystery of the Indian growth transition.* NBER Working Paper Series No. w10376.

Rozelle, S., Taylor, J. E., & DeBrauw, A. (1999). Migration, remittances, and agricultural productivity in China. *American Economic Review, 89*(2), 287–291. https://doi.org/10.1257/aer.89.2.287

Singh, V. K., Kumar, A., Singh, R. D., & Yadava, K. N. S. (2011). Changing pattern of internal migration in India: Some evidences from census data. *International Journal of Current Research, 3*, 289–295.

Somanathan, E., & Somanathan, R. (2009). Climate change: challenges facing India's poor. *Economic and Political Weekly, 44*(31), 51–58.

Taylor, J. E., & Wyatt, T. J. (1996). The shadow value of migrant remittances, income and inequality in a household—Farm economy. *Journal of Development Studies, 32*(6), 899–911.

Timmer, P. C. (1988). Chapter 8 The agricultural transformation. *Handbook of Development Economics, 1,* 275–331. https://doi.org/10.1016/S1573-4471(88)01011-3

Timmer, P. C., & Akkus, S. (2008). *The structural transformation as a pathway out of poverty: Analytics, empirics and politics.* Working Paper No. 150, Washington, DC.

Todaro, M. P. (1969). A model of labor migration and urban unemployment in less developed countries. *The American Economic Review, 59*(1), 138–148. https://doi.org/10.2307/1811100

Tumbe, C. (2014). The Great Indian Migration Wave, 1870–2010, Persistence & Consequences. Mimeo, The Economic Growth Center, Yale University.

Webb, P., & Block, S. (2013). Nutrition information and formal schooling as inputs to child nutrition. *Economic Development and Cultural Change, 52*(4), 801–820.

Zhang, K. H., & Song, S. (2003). Rural-urban migration and urbanization in China: Evidence from time-series and cross-section analyses. *China Economic Review, 14*(4), 386–400. https://doi.org/10.1016/j.chieco.2003.09.018

CHAPTER 3

Rural Livelihood Challenges: Moving out of Agriculture

3.1 INTRODUCTION

Narratives around poverty, hunger, food security and nutrition—largely subsumed in the food system—are intrinsically linked to the development of the rural economy. Rural economic structure is constantly reshaped by forces of urbanization, expanding markets, returns to livelihood opportunities, changes in land use patterns and the inherent socio-demographic structure of villages. Also, the reliance on cultivation as the main source of livelihood in rural areas is declining with the growth of smaller towns and non-farm livelihood opportunities. Thus, the future of agricultural work will look very different from what we have seen.

The theory of structural transformation suggests a decline in agriculture's share in total output and employment over time. As people move out of agriculture, household income and access to non-farm economic opportunities—rather than just farm-level production diversity or farm incomes—become equally important predictors of household food and nutrition security. This is driven by the fact that, as agricultural systems modernize and markets develop, there is an increasing separation between the production and consumption decisions of households (Pingali & Sunder, 2017). As a result, home consumption declines and food security concerns progressively become an issue of *access* rather than *availability*. To enhance access to nutrition and food, when most households progressively become net consumers of food, household income becomes the

© The Author(s) 2019

P. Pingali et al., *Transforming Food Systems for a Rising India*,
Palgrave Studies in Agricultural Economics and Food Policy,
https://doi.org/10.1007/978-3-030-14409-8_3

most important instrument for improving welfare.[1] The logical question therefore ensues: how can one increase income earning opportunities in rural areas such that it increases food security and welfare? The development world has taken note of the fact that income diversification is key to rural development, poverty reduction and food security and the same applies to India as well. Along the path of structural transformation, the non-farm sector in India has gains in prominence becoming an important pathway for increasing food security.

In the last four decades, Indian rural output has increased by almost seven times—Rs. 3,199 billion to Rs. 21,107 billion at 2004–05 prices—but the share of agriculture in rural income has reduced from 72.4% to 39.2% (Chand, Srivastava, & Singh, 2017). Pathways from agriculture to nutrition mostly assume farming—as a source of income and food—to be the most important means to access food in rural economies. However, a greater share of households in rural India now rely on markets to access food.[2] Nationally representative data suggests that 88% of farming households rely on some form of non-farm income sources to sustain their livelihoods (Chandrasekhar & Mehrotra, 2016). Non-farm income is therefore becoming an important source of food security and dietary diversity (Mishra & Rahman, 2018). Livelihood and income diversification out of farming have been considered as desirable for enabling greater structural transformation. By moving underemployed agricultural labor towards non-farm economic opportunities, it is expected to enhance capabilities and raise household living standards (Ellis, 1998). During times of distress such as weather shocks, non-agricultural labor supply is generally found to increase enabling income diversification and consumption smoothening (Ito & Kurosaki, 2009).

Against this background, this chapter discusses the evolving role of non-farm income in determining household food security and nutrition in rural India through diversification of incomes and livelihoods. We build upon the idea that promotion of the rural non-farm economy should be an important component of India's rural transformation strategy. We paint a comprehensive portrait of the changing nature of the rural economic structure, blurring of rural-urban distinctions, and how this poses a challenge as well as opportunity to create employment for labor leaving the agricultural sector. The analytical lens of a food system approach here is

---

[1] See chapter on health for discussion on the pathways to reduce malnutrition.

[2] In 2011–12, 84% of India's population was classified as net consumers of rice, much of which was purchased in the market (CITE).

particularly helpful in imagining *rural* as farm production and beyond—encompassing various food-related non-farm activities such as storage, processing, distribution and transportation of food in addition to many other services which do not necessarily fall within the realm of food production but provide livelihood opportunities to the rural population.[3]

3.2   Non-farm Sector as Part of the Development Strategy

Livelihood diversification and non-farm employment are important levers for rural economic growth. Across developing countries, the success of the Green Revolution led to the idea of a "unimodal" agrarian structure (Tomich et al., 1995). It was believed that agricultural growth through productivity-enhancing strategies could generate economy-wide growth multipliers, leading to across-the-board income growth and employment generation. While agricultural growth did propel growth and structural transformation in many countries, demographic pressure, preponderance of small farms, declining share of household income from agriculture and commercialization have changed the role of agriculture in future economic growth. Hazell (2018) recognizes a growing differentiation within the agricultural sectors of developing countries. Imagining the future of agriculture, based upon experience in the last 100 years, Hazell argues that the development strategies for rural areas should now prioritize poverty reduction as part of long-term agricultural growth strategy and foster an environment of gainful job creation. Agricultural issues should be focused towards smallholders, specifically increasing their commercially viability through connecting them to markets. Economic changes have reconfigured the roles of culture, institutions, gender and access to human capital in rural areas. At the same time, quality education and health infrastructure, in addition to the issue of access to land, irrigation and other natural resources are increasingly becoming important. Policy focus, therefore, should be on quality jobs, better labor market participation, higher wages and reductions in rural poverty. These arguments further those of Mellor and Johnston (1984) who had argued that reducing poverty and its various manifestations including malnutrition require a concerted attempt of "…interacting forces, characterized as a ring, that link nutritional need, generation of effective demand for food on the part of

---

[3] Many of these points will be discussed in the following chapters.

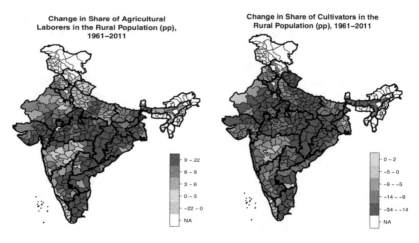

Change in Share of Agricultural
Laborers in the Rural Population (pp),
1961–2011

Change in Share of Cultivators in the
Rural Population (pp), 1961–2011

Fig. 3.1 Change in the agricultural workforce. Source: Data from Indian Census 1961–2011, based on author's calculations (Note: We have used data for the major Indian states, and district boundaries represent the 1971 divisions for the sake of comparability over time.)

the poor, increased employment, a strategy of development that structures demand towards goods and services which have a high employment content, production of wage goods, and an emphasis on growth in agriculture". The development strategy path followed by a nation, therefore, is central to how the food equation balances.[4]

The transformation of the workforce in India away from low-productivity agricultural sector into manufacturing and other tertiary activities has been slow. More than 60% of the rural workforce continues to be employed in agriculture-based livelihoods, despite the share of agriculture output being around 17%. There has been a decline in the share of cultivators, but the share of agricultural labor increased; the desired transition from rural to urban occupation did not take place (Fig. 3.1). Poorer regions specially continue to have a greater share of the rural workforce primarily engaged in agriculture, either as cultivators or wage laborers. In the *urbanizing states*, and those where agriculture is the driving force, the share of the workforce employed in cultivation is lower (Fig. 3.2). The share of those employed in agriculture—in cultivation and agricultural labor—is highest

[4] The food equation is the term used by Malthus in his 1978 "Essay on Population" as a race between food and population. A balanced food equation implies food sufficiency where domestic food demand is met by overall supplies.

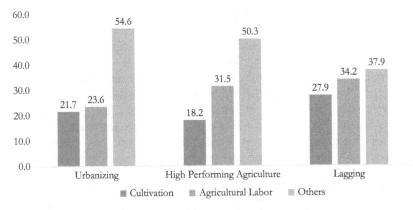

Fig. 3.2 Labor share by state classification. Source: Data from Census of India 2011; based on author's calculations

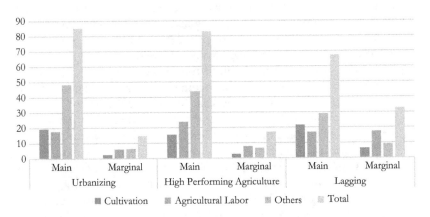

Fig. 3.3 Nature of work: main and marginal workers (in %). Source: Data from Census of India 2011; based on author's calculations

among the *lagging states*. Further distinguishing between main and marginal occupation further elucidates the above point. In the *lagging states*, a greater share of the workforce is also a marginal worker (Fig. 3.3). More advanced states have a lower share of marginal cultivators while the *lagging states* have marginal workers who are spread across agricultural and non-agricultural occupations. These differentiations help us underscore the point that while India's structural transformation largely has often been dubbed as "stunted" (Binswanger-Mkhize, 2013), more nuance lies in subnational variations. Regional variation in land fragmentation and poor access to capital with smallholders has further stifled the desired pace of structural transformation in the lagging regions.

Dynamic changes in the rural economy were historically brought about by Green Revolution productivity increase. These gains, however, were limited to regions which could specialize in the production of staple crops and had better agro-climatic endowments, irrigation and road infrastructure and institutional structures that allowed for better governance of natural resources, such as land and water rights.[5] In the case of high-productive agriculture states which benefited from the Green Revolution, rise in farm incomes and demand for labor induced higher wage rates which stimulated rural non-farm activities. Rural transformation and greater non-farm employment were brought about by the "pull" forces implying relatively higher returns in the non-farm sector. Income from the non-farm sector is potentially a major poverty-reducing strategy and often picks up the slack when agriculture is not doing well (Haggblade, Hazell, & Reardon, 2010). It is a widely accepted fact that agricultural households engage in a wide range of economic activities apart from cultivation. A recent nationally representative survey of farmers reflects this phenomenon: only 12% of the households whose primary source of income is cultivation are not engaged in any secondary activity (Chandrasekhar & Mehrotra, 2016).

For the first time, in 2012, a greater share of Indian population worked in the non-farm sector. Between 2005 and 2012, about 50 million jobs were created in the non-farm sector, while 34 million jobs were lost in agriculture (Chand, Saxena, & Rana, 2015).[6] As the non-farm sector is increasingly becoming more important for Indian rural economy, the official line of thinking on India's agrarian society too has begun to acknowledge rural employment as more than cultivation and agricultural labor. In an interview, Dr. Ramesh Chand, member, agriculture, a government think-tank, NITI Aayog, said, "…it is not proper to view rural India as only an agricultural economy. Now two-third of the economy of rural India is non agriculture and only one-third is agriculture."[7] He adds,

---

[5] Structural transformation by regions has been dealt with in detail in Chap. 2.

[6] A report by McKinsey Global Institute titled "India's Labour Market: A new emphasis on gainful employment" presents a similar figure. It says that during 2011–15, 33 million non-farm jobs were created, while the number of agricultural jobs declined by 26 million.

[7] https://www.firstpost.com/business/research-on-agrarian-distress-is-inadequate-we-need-some-proper-indicator-says-ramesh-chand-of-niti-aayog-4795141.html. Accessed on July 24, 2018.

"Ultimately, like China, Japan or any small farm economy, we need to move in the direction of part-time farmers. We recognise that one or two acres will not give them income, they have to earn from other sources. In many cases it is already happening, but we have to move as a development strategy."

3.2.1   *Distributional Implications of Non-farm Income*

Investing in the growth of the non-farm sector is hailed as an important development strategy because of its potential for the redistribution of incomes. Non-farm income acts as a redistribution mechanism in a number of ways (Lanjouw & Lanjouw, 2001). First, by producing more afford-able and lower quality goods consumed mostly by the poor, rural industrial production leads to lower local prices. Second, non-farm economic opportunities provide a source of employment to those for whom agriculture may not provide sustenance and therefore helps to absorb the growing rural labor force, especially in the states which are lagging. Third, through increasing rural livelihood avenues, these types of economic activities help slow down temporary migration (*ibid*).

India's growth experience suggests a steep rise in inter-personal inequality (Jayaraj & Subramanian, 2013; Motiram & Naraparaju, 2015). As the central agrarian question in India remains the availability of productive land, non-farm sector helps maintain income for the landless and the smallholder. It is fairly well established that Indian agriculture is dominated by smallholders, and fragmentation of land is the root cause of poverty and inequality in rural areas (Chakravorty, Chandrasekhar, & Naraparaju, 2016). Land fragmentation leads to a reduction in the mean plot size below the threshold beyond which mechanization becomes a challenge. This further lowers the economic viability of farms (Deininger, Monchuk, Nagarajan, & Singh, 2017). While redistribution of land is not a politically attractive option and the consolidation of holdings is operationally challenging, promotion of non-farm opportunities seems to be a more pragmatic way of increasing the income of smallholders and other rural poor. Given the greater pro-poor incidence of non-farm income, historically marginalized sections of the rural society—which have lower access to land and capital—have benefited substantially from the non-farm sector employment despite its casual nature. Similarly, women also benefit from the non-farm sector as their access to resources such as land and jobs remains limited (Lei, Desai, & Vanneman, 2017). Reduction in inequality requires greater access to non-farm jobs which are formal. While non-farm jobs reduce inequality through alleviating unequal access to land (Joshi & Lanjouw, 2016), formal sector employment would ensure it is more sustainable.

3.3   COMPOSITION OF THE RURAL NON-FARM SECTOR IN INDIA

The important question, however, is to understand the nature of non-farm sector to understand its welfare implications. Traditionally, the rural non-farm sector comprises of a highly heterogeneous portfolio of activities including services and small-scale manufacturing industries which cater to agricultural input needs and meet the demands of rural consumers (Haggblade et al., 2010). Rural non-farm employment includes food processing or clothing manufacture in the manufacturing sector, in addition to services such as motor repair, or other skilled or unskilled work. Non-farm workers could also be self-employed through small-scale enterprises and petty trade (Reardon, Stamoulis, & Pingali, 2007). The nature of the non-farm sector changes as one travels towards villages located closer to towns and other urban centers.

With overall economic growth, better rural infrastructure and declining rural-urban travel time distances, the composition of the rural non-farm sector in India has changed; construction and manufacturing sectors have become major employment sources. According to the estimates based on the National Sample Survey (NSS), construction sector employs 30.1% of the total non-agricultural employment (Chand et al., 2017). Manufacturing employment, on the other hand, stands at 22.1%, while services employ 45.1% of the labor force. Unprecedented growth in the construction and the service sector over the last decade has led to a greater number of jobs but also led to greater casualization of the labor force. Lack of formal written contracts between the construction workers and their employers raises the issue of job quality. Even among the formal sector employees in the non-farm economy, such as manufacturing or services, only 60% have a formal contract, depriving a majority with no social security benefits (Saha & Verick, 2017). Introduction of the public employment programs, such as MGNREGA, have also facilitated a faster move towards the rural non-farm sector, yet these livelihood avenues are a last resort means for those in the lower income quintile, casting doubts on the long-run welfare of this transition.

It has been argued that the rise in agricultural productivity abets non-farm activity (T. Reardon, 1997). In the long run, the expansion of the non-farm sector leads to higher agricultural wages which act as the indirect channel of rural poverty reduction (Lanjouw, 2007). In the Indian context, where education levels are low and vocational skills limited, the non-farm sector is a lucrative alternative for the poor. Over the long run, with a reduction in poverty and investment in future human capital, the non-farm sector could be the springboard for greater economic mobility. The promise of the non-farm sector for abetting human capital investment returns in long-term economic mobility, however, rests on its ability to provide equitable access to quality education, access to well-functioning credit markets as well as the strengthening of the rural-urban linkages.

With agriculture becoming commercialized and a large share of the country expected to be urban by 2050, most households would be buying food from the market, and hence access to food and nutritional security, therefore, would mostly be determined through the income pathway. Indian policy makers thus face a precarious challenge where they not only need to ensure cultivation is remunerative for greater rural income but also create an enabling environment where quality non-farm economic activities are accessible to a wider rural population which are at a disadvantage because of lack of education, skills, social networks and financial capital.

3.4   Urbanization and Growth of the Rural Economy

Urbanization is an outcome of the development process and is intrinsically linked to the evolving food systems. We discuss how urbanization is reshaping diets in Chap. 5. Here, we examine the role of urbanization in contributing to the rural economy through greater employment opportunities. We will specifically address the challenge of meeting the growing urban need for food and other rural resources while at the same time ensuring sustainable rural growth.

Urban areas benefit from agglomeration effects and economies of scale because they can attract a skilled workforce and production inputs are more easily available (Glaeser & Maré, 2001). The concentration of economic activities leads to technological spillovers and reduced costs of infrastructure provisions. Theoretically, urban economic growth can contribute to reducing rural poverty through two main channels: absorption of surplus labor and productivity spillovers. As per the classic Lewisian model, surplus rural labor is absorbed in the urban sector, leading to higher rural wages (Lewis, 1954). Rural poverty reduction is also influenced through greater urbanization and the rise in the demand for rural products. Urban economic growth also affects rural incomes through remittances. The lack of labor-intensive manufacturing sector and adequate urban employment has been one of the reasons why the share of labor in agriculture has not declined commensurate with its declining share in overall output. Similarly, low levels of permanent migration suggest hindrance to rural-urban mobility. At the same time, India's growth story across the globe is of its sprawling metropolises with an abundance of technically skilled manpower and seats of global innovation. The question of our time is therefore how to leverage India's urbanization for greater rural prosperity.

As India is expected to be 60% urban by 2050, better infrastructure and communication networks are expected to reduce physical distance and cultural barriers between rural and urban residents. Agriculture, therefore, may no longer continue to be the defining feature of the economic and cultural life in rural areas. This rural transformation—an essential part of structural transformation—entails greater interaction along the rural-urban spaces, thereby promoting agricultural productivity and greater marketable surpluses. This could then facilitate overall production diversification, new forms of livelihood and better infrastructure provision in rural areas. Spatial boundaries across the rural-urban dichotomies are increasingly getting blurred as with larger rural areas becoming indistinguishable from the small urban areas, especially regarding the occupational patterns and built-up area characterizations (Chatterjee, Murgai, & Rama, 2015). The right set of public policies, however, are essential to ensure smooth, inclusive and sustainable urbanization for structural transformation to take place.

It is now fairly well-established that urbanization has been a significant contributor to rural poverty reduction since 1991 by providing rural households with a greater number of livelihood opportunities during the period when agriculture has largely remained largely stagnant (Chatterjee, Murgai, Narayan, & Rama, 2016). However, understanding the variegated nature of urbanization is crucial to understand its impact on rural poverty. Urbanization is generally imagined to be the growth of larger metropolises which misses the point that most of the urban population resides in smaller towns. Breaking the monolith of "urban" into its various kinds is therefore very important. Against the common notion which equates urbanization with big cities and planning, Indian urbanization has been noted to have a *subaltern* character, which implies a rapid rise in settlement agglomerations, which are often not classified as urban by the Indian census operations (Denis, Zerah, & Mukhopadhyay, 2012). The other way to represent these transitions is to call it *R Urbanism* or *Rurality* where urban is rapidly integrating with the rural (Chandrasekhar & Mukhopadhyay, 2017; Revi et al., 2006). Subaltern urbanization, with a growth of small towns in the last decade, has been more prominent in the poorer states (B. Chaudhuri, Chatterjee, Mazumdar, & Karim, 2017). The urban transition has already matured in the more developed states.

3.4.1   Emergence of Smaller Towns

Rural non-farm economy along with the secondary towns contributes significantly to inclusive growth patterns and poverty reduction during the process of rural transformation (Christiaensen & Todo, 2014). Compared to major urban agglomerations, rural poverty reduction is much stronger if the urban economic growth is driven by smaller towns. These towns provide easier connectivity to the rural hinterland, encouraging labor mobility as well as better access to markets and amenities, including access to human capital. In India, despite all the focus on metropolitan cities as engines of growth, it is actually the smaller towns which have had the biggest impact on poverty reduction during the last two decades (Chatterjee et al., 2016; Gibson, Datt, Murgai, & Ravallion, 2017). Along the spatial gradient—where the strict rural and urban definitions become blurry—agglomeration effects around smaller cities have been the highest as they have led to many high-performing rural places (Li & Rama, 2015).

In regions where agriculture is the dominant sector and farmers are prosperous, clusters of small towns have emerged. Many of these small towns are market towns often referred to as *mandi* towns which are centers for agriculture inputs and marketing (Kapur & Krishnamurthy, 2014). Without expanding enough to become cities, these regions lie along the rural-urban continuum where the principal economic activities are essentially linked to agriculture and consumer demand emanating out of farm income. They comprise facilities for cultivation, input distribution and agricultural marketing yards as well as provide essential consumer goods and services to the villages nearby. Economic activities in smaller towns typically include manufacturing, trades and services.

Middle spaces between the village and small towns are settlements which Indian census operations call as *census towns*. India's census operations define *census towns* (CTs) as urban areas if it has a population of at least 5,000 people, population density is greater than 400 persons per square kilometer and at least 75% of the main male workforce is employed in the non-farming sector. While this is the standard classification of what is considered as "urban" in India, CTs are peculiar in the way that despite being urban, these settlements continue to be administered as rural areas. The number of census towns between 2001 and 2011 saw a threefold increase from 1,362 to 3,894 contributing to 30% of the urban population growth, reflecting *in situ* urbanization (Pradhan, 2013). Unlike CTs, *statutory towns* (with a population of less than 100,000), which either have a municipal corporation, cantonment board or notified town area committee have grown at a relatively slower pace, while census towns have almost doubled from 7.4% to over 14% (Mukhopadhyay, Zérah, Samanta, & Maria, 2016). The rise of census towns together with a greater increase in the built-up area therefore suggests a gross underestimation of urbanization in India.

So, what happens in these census towns and why are they relevant for agricultural growth? These newer towns have become the hub of economic activity and commerce for the rural markets (*ibid*). Proximity to rural areas has also allowed these market towns to become centers for growth, where much of the rural demand for new services and goods are met. This has also allowed them to be distant from the uncertainties of larger metropolises. These smaller towns have not only generated non-farm employment avenues and contributed to greater rural poverty alleviation but are also the largest growing market for the FMCG sector (Nielsen & CII, 2012). Many of the small towns or even census towns are zones of transition from an agrarian economy to a more diversified one where manufacturing and services have a greater role. The pace of change, however, varies by the stage of regional rural transformation. There is a different pattern in the regions where agriculture has not been a part of the structural transformation process. In those regions, smaller towns have a greater share of those employed in agriculture. Smaller towns provide employment avenues to those who wish to or are forced to transition out of farming. This is reflected in the greater share of marginal workers in the small towns and rapid emergence of smaller towns and large villages along the poorer regions of Indo-Gangetic plains—like in UP and Bihar (Mukhopadhyay, 2017). Stagnant agriculture, chronic underemployment and insufficient job creation in the region have led to the non-farm economy along the rural-urban spaces emerging as the main providers of economic sustenance.

3.4.2   Peri-urban Areas and Agricultural Growth

The urban-rural distinction is blurring fast. It is also becoming increasingly hard to distinguish between census towns and towns with urban administrative status. Villages proximate to census towns are not very different from those proximate to statutory towns (Mukhopadhyay, 2017). Instead of a rural-urban binary, we now have a *rural-urban continuum* which is expanding along with structural transformation of the economy. As villages have begun to exhibit urban characteristics, this phenomenon is often referred to as *peri-urbanization*. Peri-urban regions are considered as mixed or transitory spaces, undergoing rapid and multiple transformations (Dupont, 2005). While there are issues of disentangling the rural-urban dichotomy, peri-urban agriculture could be a significant contributor to poverty alleviation and food security. Assuming that commuters live in peri-urban areas, Chandrasekhar (2011) estimates them as around 32 million (4.3% of the rural population) in India. These commuting workers are primarily engaged in manufacturing, construction and other retail or wholesale sector. Peri-urban regions have become important hubs helping the diversification of economic activity through creating agglomeration effects, and access to amenities and generation of non-farm employment. In villages located closer to towns, the share of non-farm activities could be as large as 70% (Sharma, 2016). Villages near towns also participate more in intensive agriculture and have higher wages, and households tend to have greater income and consumption expenditure (*ibid*). Against the common understanding that manufacturing is only restricted to urban areas, formal manufacturing activities in India too have moved from urban to rural environments in the last decade, while urban areas comprise the informal service sector jobs (Ghani, Goswami, & Kerr, 2012). A substantial share of government and other public sector formal jobs like banking are also located in the rural areas, where people commute daily to work. This form of mobility is reflected in a large share of urban to rural commuter shares.

3.5   POLICY STRATEGIES TO ENCOURAGE THE GROWTH OF THE NON-FARM SECTOR IN INDIA

Dividing non-farm employment into three categories—regular employment (generally salaried), casual employment (daily wage) and self-employment—Lanjouw and Murgai (2009) note that regular non-farm employment is the most sought after. Compared to the other two, regular employment in the non-farm sector is associated with higher income and greater stability, but also requires greater skill and better human capital. The challenge for a more vibrant food system is to ensure that movement towards non-farm employment is not a step-down. In this section, we will highlight some of the policy strategies which could be prioritized to encourage the non-farm sector in India.

3.5.1   Focus on Agriculture and Rural Infrastructure

A vibrant agricultural sector is essential to the growth of non-farm sector because of the large dependence on it for food security and employment. Most of the rural households do earn a certain part of their income from agriculture while diversifying their income portfolio in India (Chandrasekhar & Mehrotra, 2016). Agricultural income therefore not only increases the agency of households to command food but also provides resources to take control over other aspects of lives such as investing in children's education, setting up a new enterprise leading to greater accumulation of assets. There could be four major categorizations of the agricultural growth and non-farm linkages (Lanjouw & Lanjouw, 2001; Reardon, 1997; Haggblade & Hazell, 1989). Through *production linkages*, agriculture connects to non-farm suppliers of raw materials and farm inputs. There are *consumption linkages* when the gains from agricultural income are spent on locally produced non-farm goods. Through the supply of labor to non-agricultural activities during the lean season, and investment in non-agricultural activities, agriculture is connected to the economy through *factor market*. There are *productivity* linkages through reduced food prices. These linkages, however, assign primacy to the agriculture as a driver of these connections. The reverse takes place too when newer industries could ignite the demand for agricultural products. Similarly, productivity linkages could be induced by the non-farm sector through better input supply, product marketing or investment from non-farm earnings into agriculture for better seeds and fertilizer variety leading to enhanced agricultural productivity.

An important aspect of restructuring the rural economy is to remove structural constraints to credit and markets. More remunerative non-farm employment avenues are heavily determined by the density of social networks and family ties, if not by the required degree of skills and training. Often it is the poorest who lack these and are locked out of this market because of marginalized social groups or small land holding. Investment in rural infrastructure goes a long way in reducing the economic distance between rural and urban areas. Reduction in this distance abets rural transformation, integrates markets and thereby facilitates greater access to non-farm employment opportunities, especially for women. Evaluating the impact of a national road expansion program in India, Aggarwal (2018) shows how road infrastructure contributes significantly—through greater dietary diversity and higher agricultural input usage—to the food system. Lei et al. (2017) highlight the importance of rural roads for female employment. Studying the impact of rural road scheme in India, Asher and Novosad (2018), however, caution against assuming road construction, that is, reduction in geographic distance, as the only form of required rural investment. They show that road construction in India led to a 10 percentage point decrease in the share of agricultural workers at the expense of a similar increase in wage labor. Much of this movement took place outside of the village, but it is not permanent migration. These impacts are most pronounced among the groups with the lowest costs and highest potential gains from participation in labor markets: households with small landholdings and working age men. Interestingly, they find that the movers are not the primary income earners of the household. They find that new paved roads under the *Pradhan Mantri Gram Sadak Yojana* (PMGSY) improve available transportation services facilitating the reallocation of labor out of agriculture. Rural infrastructure is important, but it is only one of the many possible solutions in abetting non-farm occupational transitions. Non-farm opportunities did not increase in the rural areas; rather roads become a conduit for accessing employment in nearby towns. This finding highlights the fact that road infrastructure is only one way, not the most effective maybe, to increase rural productivity. Better results can be had by facilitating easier movement of labor to areas of better opportunity which point to the importance of urban infrastructure to facilitate rural-urban migration.

3.5.2   Governing Census Towns as Urban Areas

The understanding of rural transformation in India is seriously limited by lack of due recognition to the fact that a large share of rural settlements exhibit urban characteristics, be it through census definitions or as reflected in their built-up areas. Former Union Minister for Rural Development Jairam Ramesh had famously pointed out to this by referring to these spaces as *trishanku* (middle world). The lack of acknowledgement of changing rural forms also undermines the economic potential of these areas for structural transformation. Future growth of the rural-urban continuum and the creation of greater non-farm opportunities are restricted by the administrative framework which continues to regard census towns as rural areas despite their urban demographic and economic characteristics. It must to be noted that most of the census towns are not near the mega-cities; rather they are dispersed throughout the country, which underscores the greater importance of connecting these spaces to rural areas through moving to urban governance of these spaces. By recognizing these multiple patterns of urbanization, especially its *subaltern* nature, rural areas could attract investments, job creation and ultimately the benefits from urban growth in the vicinity.

The current government has launched a new program known as the *Shyama Prasad Mukherji Rurban Mission (SPMRM)*, with the objective of developing a "… *cluster of villages that preserve and nurture the essence of rural community life with focus on equity and inclusiveness without compromising with the facilities perceived to be essentially urban in nature, thus creating a cluster of "Rurban villages"*. Under the scheme, 300 rural growth clusters would be created around the country to facilitate local and regional development through higher investments, better infrastructure and service provision in rural areas. The problem with the scheme again lies in not recognizing these changing spaces as urban. The scheme envisages cluster of villages (geographically contiguous with a population of around 25,000–50,000 in plain/coastal areas and of about 5,000–15,000 in desert/hilly/tribal areas) would fall under Gram Panchayats in the same administrative block. The government has designed an agenda for the program on how it wants to facilitate urbanization of the rural (Singh & Rahman, 2018). Looking at some of the census towns which resemble these potential clusters, Mukhopadhyay et al. (2016) have shown that public service provisioning such as solid waste management and street lighting in census towns is fairly similar to that of villages. Without an appropriate change in the governance frameworks, rural transformations would continue to be constrained.

3.5.3   Linking Food Systems to the Jobs Agenda

Food systems extend far beyond agricultural land and production and provide food, energy and nutrition to the population. At the same time, they also serve an economic and social role through enhancing household access to food. Access comes through income and better jobs. As the food system cut across agriculture, health and nutrition, poverty and the environment, it can also be leveraged to create jobs. Most new jobs in the rural areas would be created in the non-farm sector. As the agricultural value chains develop, there would be greater demand for those who can work in related logistics, from aggregation to storage and processing. With the right set of skills to youth, these sectors could become a major source of job creation. Similarly, rural employment which links to agricultural inputs and mechanization are expected to develop fast with the spread of technology and cellphones.[8] *Hello Tractor* in Nigeria is a stellar example of leveraging technology to generate employment avenues in rural areas. Small farmers who cannot afford tractors use this *Uber*-like facility for on-demand temporary access to tractors. An aggregator in the village arranges for these demands. In India, newer organizations like Gold Farm are using Farming as a Service (FaaS) model where farm equipment can be hired through cellphones or call centers.

Emerging modern food value chains, which include storage, processing, distribution, transportation and retail at the mid-stream and food preparation, and restaurants at the end-stream offer multiple avenues to create gainful employment. These are also the sectors where youth and women can be employed in larger numbers. In a recent report, *Future of Food: Shaping the Food System to Deliver Jobs,* by the World Bank, some of these aspects are highlighted in the developing world context (Townsend, Benfica, Prasann, & Lee, 2017). This is especially true for villages in the vicinity of cities or towns. Planners should think of creating agriculture hubs (e.g., processors, agro-industries, storage, packers) for structured food value chains. This would enable an easier transportation of food to the urban population while generating downstream employment concerning moving agricultural produce off the farm and into or through the supply chain. With rural transformation, the size of agribusiness and agricultural value chains increase relative to the farm economy. For example, the agribusiness sector is about half the

---

[8] https://www.thebetterindia.com/137361/gold-farm-equipment-aggregator-startup-raises-capital/

economic size of farming in sub-Saharan Africa. In relatively more developed countries of Asia and Latin America, it is about two to three times the size of agriculture; across the developed world, it could be more than ten times as large. In the post-harvest season, when the labor demand in agriculture is low, agribusiness and food value chains offer significant avenues for employment growth. It has been shown that 10% growth in organized food processing leads to 5% employment growth in this sector (World Bank, 2015). As per capita incomes increase and eating patterns shift, the demand for jobs in these off-farm segments of the food system will increase. Capitalizing on the same could employ the skilled as well as semi-skilled youth in the hinterlands.

3.5.4   Skill Enhancement and Investment in Human Capital

A challenge for policy makers in India, however, has been to provide skills and increase the workforce participation of rural women. A stylized fact is that most rural women in India work on their household farm as unpaid labor. According to the latest census figures, workforce participation rate of rural women is only 30% compared to 53% for rural males. Another fundamental feature of women in rural India is their low human capital. On 58% of the rural women are literate compared to 77% of rural men. This implies that almost one-fourth of rural non-farm workers in India are illiterate. Lack of education and the required skills inhibit a smooth transition into the non-farm sector. Since construction sector does not require much skills, this sector provides the greatest share of non-farm work. The formal service sector which provides a better quality of employment and written contracts, however, requires more skilled and educated workers. Skilled and educated workers, however, are short in supply. This is a major problem with generating non-farm employment which stems from poor schooling quality in early childhood to lack of vocational training post formal schooling years. While India prides itself in achieving a near-universal school enrolment ratio, it has an abysmal record of actual learning outcome of children (Kingdon, 2007). For the firms, the shortage of skilled labor stems in two ways: lack of a sufficient number of trained personnel and trained people lacking in the required job skills (Mehrotra, 2014). This has been attributed to the outdated syllabus at these vocational institutes which create a mismatch between the quality of training and requirements of the job.

A major challenge for policy makers in India, therefore, is providing quality skills to the workers. Lack of skills has been a major impediment for female employment too. Through the National Policy for Skills

Development and Entrepreneurship in India, the government is trying to increase women labor participation through skilling and gender main-streaming of skills. Policy should take a cue from the work of NGOs like the Self-Employed Women's Association (SEWA) where they impart train-ing and skills to women so that they can start their own business. This needs to be prioritized through focusing on the potential of emerging job opportunities through food system transformations in food retail as upstream-downstream opportunities along the agricultural value chains.

3.5.5   *Quality of Non-farm Sector*

The quality of jobs being created in the non-farm sector can be dubbed as ordinary—informal and casual—regarding their potential for rural trans-formation and lowering structural poverty. The poor quality of rural non-farm sector jobs especially for women leads to greater withdrawal from the labor market (Chatterjee et al., 2015). Poverty, vulnerability to poverty, and informal employment status are highly associated. Around 79% of workers who work in the informal sector can be classified as poor without any job or social security (NCEUS, 2008). These workers not only work at low wages, but their working conditions are also miserable. Informality is not particularly specific to rural areas. Even for urban dwellers and migrant, employment and jobs opportunities for the low-skilled workers is nothing but precarious (Breman, 2016).

3.6   Conclusion

There are clear complementarities between the development of agricul-tural and non-agricultural sectors (Foster & Rosenzweig, 2007). As the agricultural share in the GDP declines, rural non-farm economy becomes a conduit for the resource flows from agriculture to other sectors. Non-farm economic activities are therefore central to the overall processes of economic growth and changes in the food systems.

Changing economic structure, livelihood opportunities, urban growth opportunities and the commercialization of agriculture—in the course of the structural transformation process—lead to the greater role of markets in accessing food. As a result, means to household food access in the future would be influenced by earning capacities. Farming households would rely on the market value of their produce to access food, whereas the earning capacity of the households dependent upon the non-agricultural sector for livelihood would depend upon wages. The blurring of the rural-urban distinction and greater ease of commute are expected to diversify the portfolio of economic opportunities available to the rural households. Greater fragmentation of landholdings would further increase the role of non-farm sector in facilitating labor movement out of agriculture. This process would lead to a change in the profile of agricultural workers, and economic activities would increasingly become wage-oriented similar to the experience of the developed world. Rising urbanization and urban consumption demand would create fertile opportunities for the non-agricultural workforce to migrate, commute and get employment in food value chains.

Attainment of SDGs—zero hunger and a poverty-free world—therefore depends crucially on how rural areas transform and the nature of their inclusiveness. Given the slow pace of rural transformation in India, the potential for leveraging food systems to propel the growth of the non-farm sector is immense. Through organized upstream and downstream networks of activities with the emergence of greater agribusiness opportunities, surplus agricultural labor—especially youth and women—are expected to be employed in value chain processes. Such inclusive transformation of rural spaces—by including those who are left out of non-farm employment—is essential to reduce rural poverty.

The other important channel for propelling agricultural growth is to strengthen the rural-urban continuum which provides ample opportunities to the small farmers and other rural population to share in the fruits of urban economic growth. Till now, policy makers in India have not recognized the potential of small towns and the peri-urban spaces to create job opportunities. Recognizing these newer urban settlements and providing them with urban amenities could be a catalyst for non-farm diversification. Local agglomeration economy benefits could be realized through creating clusters of urban-rural spaces which feed the consumer services demand for agricultural households as well as the market for new inputs, technologies and information. The rural-urban continuum would create alternatives to less remunerative migration often resorted as a strategy to escape poverty and hunger and benefit from agglomeration effects from the poorer regions.

While urbanization and changing employment patterns offer opportunities for a more diversified food system, the challenge lies in ensuring these transformations are smooth and contribute to sustainable poverty reduction. Most importantly, the quality of human capital is key to chartering a swifter pace of structural transformation. It has been well documented that India's economic growth has not been able to generate sufficient employment in the manufacturing sector. Similarly, quality service sector jobs require specific skills depending on emerging job requirements; labor transition into the non-farm sector is difficult for most of the farm-based labor. Despite achieving universal enrolment in primary schools, learning outcomes remain low. Similarly, the lack of vocational educational facilities further limits the opportunities to transition into more gainful and formal employment avenues. These are some of the structural issues which have held back the transformation of India's economy in general.

References

Aggarwal, S. (2018). Do rural roads create pathways out of poverty? Evidence from India. *Journal of Development Economics, 133*, 375–395. https://doi.org/10.1016/j.jdeveco.2018.01.004

Asher, S. E., & Novosad, P. M. (2018). *Rural roads and local economic development*. Policy Research Working Paper 8466, World Bank Group, Washington, DC.

Binswanger-Mkhize, H. P. (2013). The stunted structural transformation of the Indian economy: Agriculture, manufacturing and the rural non-farm sector. *Economic and Political Weekly, 48*, 5–13. Retrieved from https://www.epw.in/journal/2013/26-27/review-rural-affairs-review-issues/stuntedstructural-transformation-indian

Breman, J. (2016). At work in the informal economy of India: A perspective from the bottom up (OIP). *OUP Catalogue.*

Chakravorty, S., Chandrasekhar, S., & Naraparaju, K. (2016). *Income generation and inequality in India's agricultural sector: The consequences of land fragmentation.* Indira Gandhi Institute of Development Research, Mumbai Working Papers. Indira Gandhi Institute of Development Research, Mumbai, India. Retrieved from https://econpapers.repec.org/RePEc:ind:igiwpp:2016-028

Chand, R., Saxena, R., & Rana, S. (2015). Estimates and analysis of farm income in India, 1983–84 to 2011–12. *Economic and Political Weekly, 50*(22), 139–145.

Chand, R., Srivastava, S. K., & Singh, J. (2017). *Changing structure of rural economy of India implications for employment and growth.* New Delhi: NITI Aayog.

Chandrasekhar, S. (2011). Workers commuting between the rural and urban: Estimates from NSSO data. *Economic and Political Weekly, 46*(46), 22–25. Retrieved from http://www.jstor.org/stable/41319397

Chandrasekhar, S., & Mehrotra, N. (2016). Doubling farmers' incomes by 2022. *Economic & Political Weekly, 51*(18), 10–13.

Chandrasekhar, S., & Mukhopadhyay, A. (2017). The changing nature of rurality: Reframing the discourse on migration and commuting. In *Rural labour mobility in times of structural transformation* (pp. 183–207). Singapore: Springer Singapore. https://doi.org/10.1007/978-981-10-5628-4_9

Chatterjee, U., Murgai, R., Narayan, A., & Rama, M. (2016). *Pathways to reducing poverty and sharing prosperity in India: Lessons from the last two decades.* World Bank.

Chatterjee, U., Murgai, R., & Rama, M. (2015). Employment outcomes along the rural-urban gradation. *Economic & Political Weekly, 50*(26 & 27), 5–10. Retrieved from http://www.epw.in/system/files/pdf/2015_50/26-27/Employment_Outcomes_along_the_RuralUrban_Gradation.pdf

Chaudhuri, B., Chatterjee, B., Mazumdar, M., & Karim, S. (2017). Income ranking of Indian states and their pattern of urbanisation. In E. Denis & M.-H. Zérah (Eds.), *Subaltern urbanisation in India. Exploring urban change in South Asia* (pp. 91–118). https://doi.org/10.1007/978-81-322-3616-0_4

Christiaensen, L., & Todo, Y. (2014). Poverty reduction during the rural–urban transformation—The role of the missing middle. *World Development, 63*, 43–58. https://doi.org/10.1016/j.worlddev.2013.10.002

Deininger, K., Monchuk, D., Nagarajan, H. K., & Singh, S. K. (2017). Does land fragmentation increase the cost of cultivation? Evidence from India. *The Journal of Development Studies, 53*(1), 82–98. https://doi.org/10.1080/00220388.2016.1166210

Denis, E., Zerah, M.-H., & Mukhopadhyay, P. (2012). Subaltern urbanisation in India. *Economic and Political Weekly.* Retrieved from https://www.epw.in/journal/2012/30/review-urban-affairs-review-issues/subaltern-urbanisation-india.html

Dupont, V. (2005). *Peri-urban dynamics: Population, habitat and environment on the peripheries of large Indian metropolises: An introduction.* CSH Occasional Paper 14, Centre de Sciences Humaines, New Delhi.

Ellis, F. (1998). Household strategies and rural livelihood diversification. *Journal of Development Studies, 35*(1), 1–38. https://doi.org/10.1080/00220389808422553

Foster, A. D., & Rosenzweig, M. R. (2007). Chapter 47, Economic development and the decline of agricultural employment (pp. 3051–3083). https://doi.org/10.1016/S1573-4471(07)04047-8

Ghani, E., Goswami, A. G., & Kerr, W. R. (2012). *Is India's manufacturing sector moving away from cities?* Policy Research Working Papers, The World Bank. https://doi.org/10.1596/1813-9450-6271

Gibson, J., Datt, G., Murgai, R., & Ravallion, M. (2017). For India's rural poor, growing towns matter more than growing cities. *World Development, 98*, 413–429. https://doi.org/10.1016/j.worlddev.2017.05.014

Glaeser, E. L., & Maré, D. C. (2001). Cities and skills. *Journal of Labor Economics, 19*(2), 316–342. https://doi.org/10.1086/319563

Haggblade, S., & Hazell, P. (1989). Agricultural technology and farm-nonfarm growth linkages. *Agricultural Economics, 3*(4), 345–364.

Haggblade, S., Hazell, P., & Reardon, T. (2010). The rural non-farm economy: Prospects for growth and poverty reduction. *World Development, 38*(10), 1429–1441. https://doi.org/10.1016/j.worlddev.2009.06.008

Hazell, P. (2018). Urbanization, agriculture and smallholder farming. In R. Serraj & P. Pingali (Eds.), *Agriculture and food systems to 2050: Global trend, challenges and opportunities* (pp. 137–160). Singapore: World Scientific.

Ito, T., & Kuroki, T. (2009). Weather risk, wages in kind, and the off-farm labor supply of agricultural households in a developing country. *American Journal of Agricultural Economics, 91*(3), 697–710. https://doi.org/10.1111/j.1467-8276.2009.01270.x

Jayaraj, D., & Subramanian, S. (2013). On the inter-group inclusiveness of India's consumption expenditure growth. *Economic and Political Weekly, XLVIII*(10), 65–70.

Joshi, B., & Lanjouw, P. (2016). Non-farm diversification, inequality and mobility in Palanpur. *Economic and Political Weekly, 51*(26–27), 43–51.

Kapur, D., & Krishnamurthy, M. (2014). *Market towns and the dynamics of India's rural and urban transformations.* Working Paper, International Growth Center.

Kingdon, G. G. (2007). The progress of school education in India. *Oxford Review of Economic Policy, 23*(2), 168–195. https://doi.org/10.1093/oxrep/grm015

Lanjouw, J. O., & Lanjouw, P. (2001). The rural non-farm sector: Issues and evidence from developing countries. *Agricultural Economics, 26*(1), 1–23. https://doi.org/10.1111/j.1574-0862.2001.tb00051.x

Lanjouw, P. (2007). Does the rural nonfarm economy contribute to poverty reduction. In S. Haggblade, P. B. R. Hazell, & T. Reardon (Eds.), *Transforming the rural nonfarm economy: Opportunities and threats in the developing world* (pp. 55–82). Johns Hopkins University Press.

Lanjouw, P., & Murgai, R. (2009). Poverty decline, agricultural wages, and non-farm employment in rural India: 1983–2004. *Agricultural Economics, 40*(2), 243–263. https://doi.org/10.1111/j.1574-0862.2009.00373.x

Lei, L., Desai, S., & Vanneman, R. (2017). *Village transportation infrastructure and women's non-agricultural employment in India: The conditioning role of community gender context.* IHDS Working Paper No. 2017-2.

Lewis, W. A. (1954). Economic development with unlimited supplies of labour. *The Manchester School, 22*(2), 139–191. https://doi.org/10.1111/j.1467-9957.1954.tb00021.x

Li, Y., & Rama, M. (2015). *Households or locations? Cities, catchment areas and prosperity in India.* World Bank Policy Research Working Paper No. 7473.

Mehrotra, S. (2014). *India's skills challenge: Reforming vocational education and training to harness the demographic dividend.* Oxford University Press.

Mellor, J. W., & Johnston, B. F. (1984). The world food equation: Interrelations among development, employment, and food consumption. *Journal of Economic Literature, 22*(2), 531–574.

Mishra, S., & Rahman, A. (2018). Does non-farm income affect food security? Evidence from India. Mimeo.

Motiram, S., & Naraparaju, K. (2015). Growth and deprivation in India: What does recent evidence suggest on "Inclusiveness"? *Oxford Development Studies, 43*(2), 145–164. https://doi.org/10.1080/13600818.2014.988693

Mukhopadhyay, P. (2017). Does administrative status matter for small towns in India? In E. Denis & M.-H. Zérah (Eds.), *Subaltern urbanisation in India: An introduction to the dynamics of ordinary towns* (pp. 443–469). New Delhi: Springer India. https://doi.org/10.1007/978-81-322-3616-0_17

Mukhopadhyay, P., Zérah, M.-H., Samanta, G., & Maria, A. (2016). *Understanding India's urban frontier: What is behind the emergence of census towns in India?* The World Bank. https://doi.org/10.1596/1813-9450-7923

National Commission for Enterprises in the Unorganised Sector (NCEUS). (2008). *Report on definitional and statistical issues relating to informal economy.*

Nielsen, & CII. (2012). *Emerging consumer demand: Rise of the small town Indian.*

Pingali, P., & Sunder, N. (2017). Transitioning toward nutrition-sensitive food systems in developing countries. *Annual Review of Resource Economics, 9*(1), 439–459. https://doi.org/10.1146/annurev-resource-100516-053552

Pradhan, K. C. (2013). Unacknowledged urbanisation. *Economic and Political Weekly.* Retrieved from https://www.epw.in/journal/2013/36/special-articles/unacknowledged-urbanisation.html

Reardon, T. (1997). Using evidence of household income diversification to inform study of the rural nonfarm labor market in Africa. *World Development, 25*(5), 735–747. https://doi.org/10.1016/S0305-750X(96)00137-4

Reardon, T., Stamoulis, K., & Pingali, P. (2007). Rural nonfarm employment in developing countries in an era of globalization. *Agricultural Economics, 37,* 173–183. https://doi.org/10.1111/j.1574-0862.2007.00243.x

Revi, A., Prakash, S., Mehrotra, R., Bhat, G. K., Gupta, K., & Gore, R. (2006). Goa 2100: The transition to a sustainable RUrban design. *Environment and Urbanization, 18*(1), 51–65. https://doi.org/10.1177/0956247806063941

Saha, P., & Verick, S. (2017). Casualization and shift of rural workers to non-farm activities. In *Rural labour mobility in times of structural transformation* (pp. 127–150). Singapore: Springer Singapore. https://doi.org/10.1007/978-981-10-5628-4_7

Sharma, A. (2016). Urban proximity and spatial pattern of land use and development in rural India. *The Journal of Development Studies, 52*(11), 1593–1611. https://doi.org/10.1080/00220388.2016.1166207

Singh, C., & Rahman, A. (2018). Urbanising the rural: Reflections on India's National RUrban Mission. *Asia & the Pacific Policy Studies, 5*(2), 370–377. https://doi.org/10.1002/app5.234

Tomich, T. P., Kilby, P., & Johnston, B. F. (1995). *Transforming agrarian economies: Opportunities seized, opportunities missed.* Cornell University Press.

Townsend, R., Benfica, R. M., Prasann, A., & Lee, M. (2017). *Future of food: Shaping the food system to deliver jobs.* Washington, DC: World Bank.

World Bank. (2015). *Ending poverty and hunger by 2030: An agenda for the global food system.* Retrieved from http://documents.worldbank.org/curated/en/700061468334490682/pdf/95768-REVISED-WP-PUBLIC-Box391467B-Ending-Poverty-and-Hunger-by-2030-FINAL.pdf

CHAPTER 4

Diet Diversity and the Declining Importance of Staple Grains

4.1 INTRODUCTION

Nutrition transition is an important outcome of the structural transformation process (Timmer, 2017). It is understood as the phenomenon that captures changes in households' dietary intake, eating practices and physical activity patterns amidst economy-wide changes (Popkin, 1997). Dietary patterns are influenced by the process of structural transformation in two stages (Pingali & Khwaja, 2004). During the first stage, economic growth and rise in per capita income induce diet diversification. Consumer preferences move away from *quantity* to *quality*, substituting traditional staples with non-staples. In the second stage, the effects of economic globalization are reflected in an increase in the consumption of processed foods which are rich in proteins, sugars and fats. Such structural changes lead to certain improvements in the quality of life, and improved health and hygiene requirements which lead to a decline in the food quantity requirements (Pingali & Sunder, 2017). At the same time, consumer preference for taste attributes of the food increases and diets begin to diversify. These changing dietary preference demands are met through an expansion of agribusiness value chains and the transformation of food systems.

© The Author(s) 2019
P. Pingali et al., *Transforming Food Systems for a Rising India*,
Palgrave Studies in Agricultural Economics and Food Policy,
https://doi.org/10.1007/978-3-030-14409-8_4

Nutrition transition in India is increasingly evident. The share of staple grains—rice and wheat—is declining, and households are moving towards a diversified diet (Pingali, 2006). According to the NSSO consumption expenditure surveys, the share of monthly expenditure on cereals and cereal products came down from 41.1% to 10.8% in rural India between 1971–72 and 2011–12. For urban areas, cereal expenditure shares declined from 23.4% to 6.6%. There has been an increase in the share of expenditure of non-staples. Over the next few decades, a rising Indian population, greater urbanization, increases in per capita incomes and demographic changes in the population would create new challenges for food systems.

Agricultural systems would need to respond to the changing demand of the population through more diversified production patterns. Greater income and globalization of diets have led to greater demand for diverse food, produced globally as well as imported from abroad. For a healthy nutrition transition to take place, food systems should have a sufficient supply of nutrient-rich food items and the policy push to promote healthy diets.[1] While every country goes through this transition along the process of economic development, the nutrition-related health outcomes along the process may vary. In the next chapter, we discuss the changing burden of nutrition and health that takes place during the structural transformation process. Understanding the nature of nutrition transition, and how it shapes and is shaped by the food systems, is essential for public health and nutrition policy.

Building on this thread, this chapter asks the following questions: What is the nature of changing food demand in India as we look towards 2050? What does it imply for the food systems? Do these dietary changes imply better nutritional outcomes? Are these changes contributing to the rising concern of the "triple burden" of malnutrition? These questions are important from the perspective of rising incidence of obesity and non-communicable diseases. Implicit in this chapter is the assumption that a lack of a healthy workforce and a high incidence of undernourished children will put a limit on a country's future growth trajectory. Given that the future demographic predictions—growing numbers of working-age people entering India's labor force—poor diets and poor health would lead to the loss of the potential returns from this "demographic dividend".

---

[1] In the chapters on agricultural supply, we discuss options for catering to diversified production systems and commercialization of farms so that they can benefit from the growing urban demand for food.

4.2   THE NATURE OF CHANGING FOOD DEMAND

By 2021, India is expected to overtake China as the most populous country in the world. With around 1.38 billion people (almost 17% of the world), changing food habits—dietary quality as well as quantity—have ramifications for future consumption demand and food systems. *Westernization* of diets and the agri-food system transformation are central to understanding the nature of future demand in India (Pingali, 2007; Reardon & Timmer, 2014). Traditional food systems and food policy were conceptualized around the emergency response to drought and hunger mitigation, a common feature of the Indian agrarian economy prior to the 1970s. Breakthroughs in grain production technology because of the Green Revolution led to self-sufficiency in food production. Food security concerns therefore evolved from food availability to access. Similarly, rising income because of agricultural productivity growth and its economy-wide effects facilitated greater demand for the consumption of non-cereals relative to staples. The first stage of India's nutrition transition was completed with the achievement of food self-sufficiency. The challenge of food availability therefore has been addressed. The new challenge lies in the access and affordability of a nutritious diet. With an increase in the demand for high-value agricultural products such as fruits and vegetables, dairy and meat and processed foods, India has now entered the second stage of this nutrition transition. Indian diets are now becoming more *westernized*, influenced by a multitude of factors such as rising income, demographic transition, urbanization and the spread of retail chains or supermarkets. Urbanization, demographic changes, globalization and exposure to new types of food have not only brought about lifestyle changes but have considerably changed Indian food consumption patterns too.

Consumption data from subsequent rounds of the National Sample Survey (NSS) appropriately reflects these dietary changes (Fig. 4.1). There has been a secular decline in the household share of food expenditure, across both rural and urban areas. In 1972–73, 72.9% of monthly expenditure was allocated to food items in rural India which has come down to 52.9% in 2011–12. The share of food expenditure in urban areas is lower than rural shares and has come down significantly from 64.5% to 42.6% during the same time. This is consistent with Engel's Law which states that the proportional share of food expenditure declines in the household budget with growth in income: over time and across income classes. The declining share of food expenditure, however, also reflects the

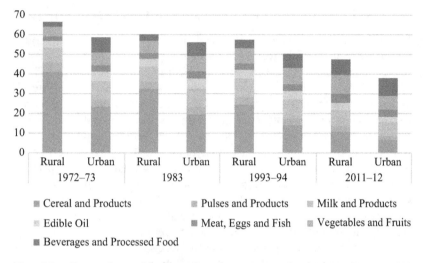

- Cereal and Products   Pulses and Products   Milk and Products
- Edible Oil   Meat, Eggs and Fish   Vegetables and Fruits
- Beverages and Processed Food

Fig. 4.1 Share of monthly expenditures on various food items. Source: NSS
Surveys; based on authors calculations

move towards a more diversified diet with an increase in income. This
confirms the Bennett's Law which states that lifestyle changes accompanied by the opportunity cost of women's time and urbanization lead to a
reduction in the demand of staple food items and hence a proportional
share of food expenditures. One can see that the decline in the share of
food consumption has been accompanied by a proportionately higher
decline in the share of expenditure on cereals, while expenditure on non-
cereals like vegetables, fruit, dairy products, edible oils, meat products,
beverages and other processed food has increased. A compelling case for
the changing dietary preferences can be discerned through food expenditure elasticities. These elasticity estimates reflect how an additional increase
in household expenditure would be spent on the food. Commodities with
higher expenditure elasticities would imply that the consumers would
spend an extra unit of income gain on the particular item. Joshi and
Kumar (2016) calculate these elasticities which show that consumers prefer an additional income on food and beverages, followed by animal protein items (meats, fish and eggs) (Fig. 4.2). Consumer food preference is
the lowest for cereals followed by coarse cereals.

These statistics strongly reflect the notion that India is undergoing a
nutrition transition where higher incomes facilitate greater consumption
of non-cereal food products, processed food and eating out. The changing

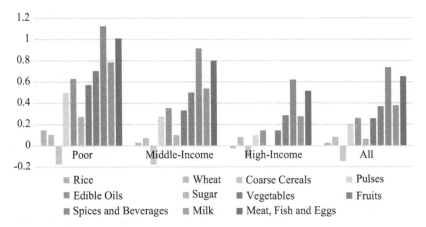

Fig. 4.2 Expenditure elasticity for food items by household class. Source: Joshi and Kumar (2016)

nature of food demand reflects Indian consumers' desire to move away from staple dominated diets. With time, Indian consumers—urban and rural—are moving towards the calorie threshold at which greater income leads to substitution away from cereals. Staples are the cheapest source of calories. They are essential for the diet, especially for the poor, to address hunger. Once households surpass a subsistence level of energy intake, their marginal utility from extra calories declines and they substitute towards food products with non-nutritional attributes such as taste (Jensen & Miller, 2010). The diversification of diets also comes at a cost. Evidence suggests a preference for variety and quality to increase over time across the entire population distribution, even the poorest households (Rahman, 2017). Greater income and rising monetary value of time use allow households to afford that. Poverty estimates for rural India for the years 2001–12 suggest that districts with a lower incidence of poverty have a greater share of food expenditure on non-cereals compared to cereals (Fig. 4.3). There is also a decline in the dietary practices with a change in poverty levels which leads to a decline in average calorie consumption while overall nutritional and other health outcomes continue to improve. Occupational changes which require less strenuous labor, improvements in health, hygiene and sanitary conditions across India have reduced the need for greater energy intake (Deaton & Drèze, 2009; Duh & Spears, 2016). Looking ahead, therefore, one can convincingly argue that consumption demand for these non-staples is expected to drive the future food system.

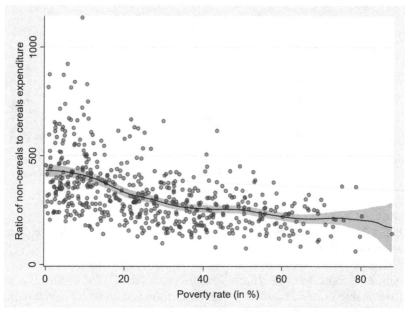

Fig. 4.3 District-level association between share of expenditure on non-cereals to cereals and poverty levels in rural India. Source: NSSO 2011–12; based on authors calculations

4.3   TRANSFORMATION IN THE AGRI-FOOD SYSTEMS

Rising demand for high-value products, eating out and processed food has coincided with the growth of restaurants and fast-food chains and the emergence of modern food value chain. Newer forms of food value chains have affected how food travels from farm to fork. The expansion of modern value chains through large modern supermarkets or mega-markets have gradually started replacing small convenience stores, at least in the urban centers. The proliferation of retail chains—of varying quality, tastes and affordability catering to all sections of the society—and changing time use of women, too, have affected how India eats.

Reardon and Timmer (2014) identify five interlinked transformations of the agri-food system occurring across Asia: (1) urbanization, (2) diet change, (3) agri-food system transformation, (4) rural factor market transformation and (5) intensification of farm technology (the agricultural transformation).

Broader developments in the food system have made the staple grain self-sufficiency paradigm of food security redundant. During the early years of the Green Revolution, "grow more" policy objectives for the rising population disregarded the food supply chain and urban food demand (Reardon & Timmer, 2014). Almost five decades later, urban food economy has increasingly become important with a greater share of the population living in urban areas and changing dietary patterns of the consumers and greater movement of people and products along the rural-urban continuum. Food growers are now more sensitive to urban food demands. Further, labor mobility from rural to urban areas and the rise in rural incomes have further facilitated the changes in rural dietary patterns. Changing food demand is also characterized by a growing consumer preference for internationally acceptable grades and standards that signal quality and nutritional diversity in food and food products and align with their health, food safety and environmental concerns (Eaton, Meijerink, & Bijman, 2008; Narayanan, 2014; Poulton, Dorward, & Kydd, 2010; Roy & Thorat, 2008; Swinnen & Maertens, 2007).

One of the key drivers of agri-food systems and future food demand in India is the expansion of the modern food retail industry during the last decade. Market research reports suggest that the number of supermarkets have increased from 500 in 2006 to 8,500 in 2016.[2] With an annual growth of around 15%, India's food retail industry is ranked as the sixth largest in the world. Currently, it is valued at 380 billion USD (USDA, 2018). It contributes to a substantial part of the overall economic output and has grown because of favorable changes in demographics along with increasing disposable incomes. Much of the retail sector continues to be unorganized, but there has been a significant growth when organized brands were almost non-existent. The emergence of modern retail in India has taken place in three stages (Reardon, Lansing, Minten, & Ababa, 2011). It began with the expansion of government retail chains during the 1960s/1970s. In the second stage, there was a proliferation of chain of cooperative retail stores starting in the 1970s and 1980s, followed by the rapid increase in the presence of private retail chains beginning slowly in the 1990s which picked up pace during the 2000s. In the last decade, private retail stores have become even more prominent with the advent of Foreign Direct Investment (FDI)

[2] https://www.statista.com/statistics/791302/india-number-of-supermarkets. Accessed on November 13, 2018.

in retail. Supermarkets are now spreading across the country. Studies have shown that organized modern retail is growing quite faster than the unorganized retail sector in India. The number of modern retail stores in Delhi, for example, has more than doubled during 2003–09 with the private sector modern retail comprising 6.5% of the processed food markets and about 3–4% of the fresh produce (Minten, Reardon, & Sutradhar, 2010). Comparing these estimates to the value of food and agricultural exports from India, Minten et al. (2010) find the contribution of modern retail to be close to 41% of this number, which is remarkable given that the Indian food retail market is still in its infancy. Greater penetration of the food retail market in India is also a result of changes in economic and demographic structure: rise in incomes and the emergence of a middle class; urbanization driven by rapid growth small and medium towns, apart from the larger urban metropolis. Greater public infrastructure (roads and communication channels) enabling better rural-urban connectivity; and remittance-based economies and global integration of the economy and people. With FDI in retail being approved, the availability of processed foods would vastly increase, especially catering to the well-off urban population more connected to the global consumption trends and with sufficient disposable income.

Together with the expansion of food retail, there has also been a significant change in how India eats. Entry of foreign brands like McDonald's, Pizza Hut, Domino's and others during the 1990s and greater participation of women in the workforce, at least in the urban areas, eating out is increasingly becoming a common feature. More than 25% of the households report to eating out every month (Gaiha, Jha, & Kulkarni, 2013). Quite understandably, people in the major metropolitan cities eat out the most, followed by the urban population in nonmetro urban areas and then by the rural population. With greater urbanization in the future, the eating out feature of the Indian population is further expected to increase. While consumption from local vendors and small eateries has always been a feature of Indian diets, the emergence and consolidation of indigenous brands like *Haldiram's* and *Barbeque Nation*, among others, have also affected Indian diets. Greater integration with the global economy, and the rise of an aspirational "middle class" with it, has played its role in bringing this change in consumption patterns, providing an opportunity for the modern agri-food systems to evolve.

4.4   URBANIZATION, CULTURAL AND DEMOGRAPHIC CHANGE

Urbanization and demographic changes have been the key drivers of nutrition transition. The processes of urbanization, changing environments (physical and economic) as well as dietary preferences interact to influence urban diets and nutritional outcomes. According to the Census 2011 figures, 33% of the Indian population is classified as urban. However, using other methods of urban concentration, the proportion of India's population living in areas with urban-like features stands much higher at 55.3%. According to UN World Urbanization Prospects, India's urban population share would equal that of the middle-income countries by 2050 (Fig. 4.4). Rising population along the peripheries of major metropolitan cities— beyond the official administrative boundaries of major cities like Delhi, Mumbai, Hyderabad and Kolkata—has led to greater urban agglomeration effects leading to a rising demand for restaurants and other related business opportunities. Overall urbanization rates of India, however, mask the degree of urban food demand. A study by Ablett et al. (2007) finds that by 2006, 29% of India's population lived in cities, yet urban consumers contributed to 43% of all expenditures on food consumption. As India urbanizes more, future consumer food demand would begin to resemble that of east and southeast Asian countries where urban consumers account for more than two-thirds of overall food expenditures (Reardon, 2015).

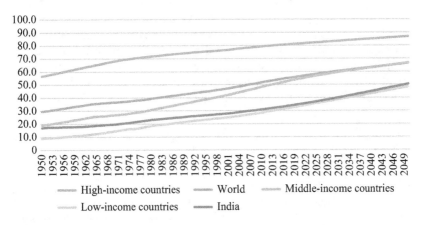

Fig. 4.4 Projected share of urban population. Source: UN World Urbanization Prospects

A notable feature of India's demographic change is the emergence of a middle class which consists of around 600 million, or half of India's population (Krishnan & Hatekar, 2017). Multinational corporations have been betting on this rising middle class and emerging consumer economy in India (Ablett et al., 2007). Reduction in poverty and greater consumer demand for food quality is expected to create significant potential growth for the food industry. India's new urban middle class comprising of many single working youths, nuclear families and working couples, travelling internationally and living metropolitan lifestyles, has led to the westernization of food preferences (Pingali & Khwaja, 2004). Greater frequency of dining out, tasting alternative cuisines and the reliance on ready-to-eat foods reflect the same. This has resulted in a significant increase in the number of restaurants, food courts and internationally branded eateries across India's large cities. The market value of food restaurants in the food service industry has more than trebled in the last decade, from 70.5 to 230.1 billion USD between 2010 and 2019.[3]

Greater migration (domestic and international), cable television and the penetration of the Internet have also played their role in the rising demand for processed food products and the food service industry. Changing dietary practices aren't only restricted to urban areas as greater rates of spatial diffusion of cultural habits have influenced dietary patterns even in rural areas. While the urban elites may emulate western diets, rural population imitates the consumption practices of those in urban areas.[4] There is also an ongoing process of *convergence* as well as *adaptation* of dietary practices across regions (Kennedy, Nantel, & Shetty, 2004). While convergence refers to greater similarity in diets—decline in staple consumption and increase in the demand for pulses, animal-based proteins and fruits and vegetables—dietary adaptation implies the adjustment of diets to the changing pace of urban lifestyles. In households where both parents often commute long distances and work long hours,

[3] https://www.statista.com/statistics/676084/value-of-restaurants-in-food-service-industry-india/. Accessed on November 13, 2018.

[4] Government statistics on food consumed away from home (FAFH) is often under-reported (Smith, 2015). Consumption expenditure surveys conducted by the National Sample Survey Organization (NSSO) of India collect information on the quantity consumed and expenditure incurred on a set of food items. Earlier they collected information on the consumption of "cooked meals" as a single item in their food consumption module which aimed to capture FAFH at the household level. It is only recently that they have moved to more detailed FAFH sub-categories to capture the prevalence of eating out.

consumers eat more meals outside the home and purchase more brand-name processed foods. Time constraints arising from the greater participation of women—primarily responsible for cooking at home—in the household reliance on purchased or packaged processed food have further seen an increase.

4.5   Concerns for the Food Systems

While the changing food demand is suggestive of the nutrition transition and offers the potential for growth of the agribusiness industry and ushering in the modern food value chains, it also poses a challenge for the food systems regarding what is produced and consumed and ultimately its effect on human health. Greater diversification of the food consumption basket—because of increase in the consumption of processed and packaged food, away-from-home meals, edible oils and sugar-sweetened beverages—has led to concerns of a high incidence of obesity and other non-communicable diseases. While over-nutrition has increased, average calorie consumption has declined. With the changing nature of occupations, better means of transportation and mechanization of agriculture, there has been a reduction in physical activity and the advent of a more sedentary lifestyle among the working-class population. Changes in lifestyle along with an improvement in disease environment have led to a lowering of the total energy intake (Deaton & Drèze, 2009). Reduction in calorie requirements, however, has coincided with a rise in the quality of diets as measured through dietary diversity (Shankar et al., 2017). On average, the number of food groups consumed by the households increased from 8.8 (out of 12 food groups) to 9.7 between 1990 and 2012 in rural India. In urban areas, it increased from 9.3 to 9.5 groups. Per capita calorie intake declined by 8.6% and 2.4% during 1983–2005 in rural and urban areas, respectively.

4.5.1   Rise in the Consumption of Convenience Food

Since the 1990s, there has been a greater shift towards the consumption of "convenience food" as eating out has increased along with the greater consumption of processed food, beverages and other packaged items which have higher salt, fat or sugar content, often associated with the incidence of chronic non-communicable diseases (NCDs). The consumption of these unhealthy commodities is rapidly rising across most low- and medium-income countries

(LMICs) because of greater availability and access. Understanding these transformations along with economic and social changes is important to understand future food demand. With the increase in the money value of time as wages rise, more and more women participate in the workforce, and convenience food not only becomes affordable but also frees up time. The issue of energy-dense snack items high in fat content is now increasingly becoming a feature of household consumption in low-income populations across rural and urban areas. Consider the following passage from a news article about slums in New Delhi:

> …"Most children have tea and phan [rusk] for breakfast," said Najma, a feisty worker who went door to door to conduct the study. "Mothers have to leave early on work so they give the babies what they eat." Food is cooked twice at home: rice, roti, dal [mostly masoor since it's the cheapest], sabzi [mostly potatoes], but never green leafy vegetables or fruit or milk. Meals are interspersed with Maggi, popcorn and a variety of chips, which kill the appetite for a full meal. It isn't just that children like their taste, there is an economic rationale to rely on junk food. A packet of Maggi noodles costs Rs 10 while a meal of rice, dal and vegetables would cost approximately three times that amount. (Mohan, 2015)

The cost of food from the local carts and other cheap processed food is often less than the cost of cooking food at home, especially when both parents work. Consumption of these unhealthy food items, in an increasingly dynamic economy, is often an economic choice for the poor. Even in rural India, the consumption of convenience foods like chips, chocolate, bakery products, soft drinks and other sugar-sweetened beverages is extremely common among school-going children (Gupta, Downs, Ghosh-Jerath, Lock, & Singh, 2016). With 60% of India's population under 30 years of age and many of them on the move, various formal and informal retail food sellers provide eating convenience food options. There has been a steady expansion of restaurants and fast-food eating joints in India. Many global brands have opened up their retail chains in India, specifically focusing on the younger section of India's population. Based upon a household survey of slums in Delhi, Singh, Gupta, Ghosh, Lock, and Ghosh-Jerath (2015) find that on average households spend around 11% of their monthly food expenditure on snacks, while 15% of the working member reported eating lunch outside. While higher-income households may rely on more packaged convenience foods, for the households with poor socioeconomic, often the local vendors are the purchase point. Food hygiene and dietary safety, therefore, become very pertinent concerning diets of the poor. From the policy perspective, these changes are often ignored as food consumption from hawkers, and wet market stall operators are not appropriately captured in the NSSO surveys used to estimate dietary patterns (Smith, 2015).

4.5.2   Food Prices and Inflation

A major concern, which affects food security and dietary diversification, especially for the poor, is the rise in food prices. Food inflation is among one of the most pressing challenges for India's food policy as higher levels of inflation have been a feature of the economy in the last decade. Rise in food prices directly affect the diets and nutritional status of households (Brinkman, de Pee, Sanogo, Subran, & Bloem, 2010). In India, the food price inflation episode between 2006 and 2009 led to an increase in the risk of child malnutrition (Vellakkal et al., 2015). This connection stems from a decline in the quantity of food consumed and dietary quality through an increase in the cost of the food basket. With a clear shift, away from cereals, it is important to ensure other nutritive food items are available at affordable prices. Without access to nutritive substitutes, dietary diversity would suffer. Protein-rich items such as pulses and animal-based protein items have seen an increase in the prices as well as its volatility (Fig. 4.5). This was famously referred to as "protein inflation" by the former deputy

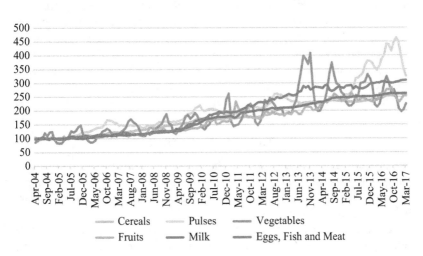

Fig. 4.5 Wholesale Price Index (WPI) for food items. Source: Office of the Economic Adviser, Govt. of India, Ministry of Commerce and Industry

governor of India's central bank (Gokarn, 2011). Increase in the price of protein-rich items like eggs, meat, fish, milk is primarily driven by greater demand for these products (Sekhar, Roy, & Bhatt, 2017). Similarly, the highly seasonal supply of fruits and vegetables and the lack of a storage infrastructure to smoothen prices make effective food price policy and, hence, become tantamount to a nutrition-sensitive food system which enables transition towards a healthier diet.

4.5.3   Implications for Health, Nutrition and Environment

While greater dietary diversity has been welfare enhancing, the consumption of more protein and fats together with a decline in the levels of physical activity as a result of urbanization and changes in occupational patterns have led to the greater prevalence of obesity, coronary heart disease, diabetes and other non-communicable diseases among the Indian population. According to an estimate by Misra et al. (2011), nutrition transition has led to an "epidemic of diet-related non-communicable diseases (DR-NCDs)" which begins with maternal nutritional deprivation causing low birth weight among infants, "…which, coupled with early childhood 'catch-up growth', leads to obesity in early childhood, thus predisposing to NCDs later in life". This raises an important challenge from the public health perspective. There are distinct regional patterns in diets which have implications for the various aspects of NCDs. As one moves from rural to urban areas, there is an increase in energy and salt consumption, but the share of calories from rice declines, while the share of oils, fruit, pulses and legumes increases (Joy et al., 2017). This suggests that while urban consumers had a greater likelihood of being obese, they are less likely to be underweight. Their study suggests beneficial as well as detrimental impact of diets on health because of dietary changes in India.

4.6   Conclusion

Indian diets are changing. While this nutrition transition may be slower compared to other developing countries like China or those in Latin America, the influence of the forces of globalization on Indian dietary habits cannot be denied. Urbanization and globalization have enabled easier access to fat and sugar-rich food items which appeal to the innate sensory preferences. Changing consumer preferences—driven by income growth, demographic changes and globalization effects—for more diversified foods have increased the demand for foods other than staples.

Accelerated nutrition transition for the low-income countries, however, may not be beneficial if the supply of healthy food items is absent from the food value chain (Drewnowski & Popkin, 2009). The traditional notion of more developed countries as the only ones with fat-rich diets is no longer true. Across the developing world, there has been a decline in the importance of cereals, while consumption of animal-based protein, and processed, and purchased food is on the increase. These trends are consistent across rural as well as urban areas, though the degree of transition may vary. Demand-side challenges for food security in India need to factor in these changes. Policy debates around food security in India till now have mainly focused upon ensuring adequate access to calories through a continued focus on staple-grain production. However, emerging trends around dietary changes and nutrition transition provide a compelling case for questioning the existing paradigm and opening up conversations around access to good quality, and balanced diet. In order to bring a more nutritious and diverse food system, accessibility and affordability aspects of food security needs to be stressed. Creating new opportunities for the food systems to augment supply of more nutritious food for this changing demand should thus become a policy focus.

While modern food retail in India is still in its infancy, it is already expanding rapidly, at least in urban areas. With greater rural infrastructure and purchasing power, it is expected to penetrate rural areas soon. An emerging policy challenge is the rising consumption of packaged/ processed food and the growing phenomena of eating out. Increases in the rates of obesity and overweight are widely documented, from urban and rural areas in the poorest countries of sub-Saharan Africa and South Asia to populations in countries with higher income levels. While these are some of the manifestations of nutrition transition, its ill-effects regarding the rising incidence of NCDs need to be actively managed. Modernizing supply chains, better food safety standards and incentives for encouraging a more health-oriented food industry would be a crucial step towards that. While saying this, we are fully aware of the issue of the acute levels of undernutrition in India. We do not intend to gloss over this aspect of mal-nutrition and the consumer demand from the lower end of the income strata. What we argue is for a more nutrition-sensitive food system which addresses the issue of undernutrition as well as obesity. The long-term policy challenge lies in enabling a diversified food system where a better and more diversified diet becomes affordable to all sections of the society.

In addition to the nutritional challenges for food demand, greater com-petition for land, water, and energy, its related environmental costs pose critical challenges for the food systems to supply affordable and nutritious food (Godfray et al., 2010). Similarly, urbanization which is considered as a harbinger of nutrition transition also poses challenges regarding diet quality and over-nutrition. The "messy" nature of urbanization is reflected in the fact that 65.5 million Indians live in urban slums according to Census 2011, and 13.7% of the urban population lives below the official poverty line. Greater concentration of poor in the urban areas, often with poor access to infrastructure and services, is further expected to impose challenges on the food system. Policy should therefore factor in the dynamic nature of growth and the changing nature of consumer demand for nutritious food systems.

REFERENCES

Ablett, J., Baijal, A., Beinhocker, E., Bose, A., Farrell, D., Gersch, U., ... Gupta, S. (2007). The 'Bird of Gold': The rise of India's consumer market. San Francisco: McKinsey Global Institute.

Brinkman, H.-J., de Pee, S., Sanogo, I., Subran, L., & Bloem, M. W. (2010). High food prices and the global financial crisis have reduced access to nutritious food and worsened nutritional status and health. The Journal of Nutrition, 140(1), 153S–161S. https://doi.org/10.3945/jn.109.110767

Deaton, A., & Drèze, J. (2009). Food and nutrition in India: Facts and interpretations. Economic and Political Weekly, 47(7), 42–65. https://doi.org/10.2307/40278509

Drewnowski, A., & Popkin, B. M. (2009). The nutrition transition: New trends in the global diet. Nutrition Reviews, 55(2), 31–43. https://doi.org/10.1111/j.1753-4887.1997.tb01593.x

Duh, J., & Spears, D. (2016). Health and hunger: Disease, energy needs, and the Indian calorie consumption puzzle. The Economic Journal, 1–32. https://doi.org/10.1111/ecoj.12417

Eaton, D., Meijerink, G., & Bijman, J. (2008). Understanding institutional arrangements—Fresh fruit and vegetable value chains in East Africa. Markets, Chains and Sustainable Development Strategy and Policy Paper No. XX.

Gaiha, R., Jha, R., & Kulkarni, V. S. (2013). How pervasive is eating out in India? Journal of Asian and African Studies, 48(3), 370–386. https://doi.org/10.1177/0021909612472040

Godfray, H. C. J., Beddington, J. R., Crute, I. R., Haddad, L., Lawrence, D., Muir, J. F., ... Toulmin, C. (2010). Food security: The challenge of feeding 9 billion people. Science, 327(5967), 812–818. https://doi.org/10.1126/science.1185383

Gokarn, S. (2011). The price of protein. *Macroeconomics and Finance in Emerging Market Economies*, 4(2), 327–335. https://doi.org/10.1080/17520843.2011.593908

Gupta, V., Downs, S. M., Ghosh-Jerath, S., Lock, K., & Singh, A. (2016). Unhealthy fat in street and snack foods in low-socioeconomic settings in India: A case study of the food environments of rural villages and an urban slum. *Journal of Nutrition Education and Behavior*, 48(4), 269–279.e1. https://doi.org/10.1016/j.jneb.2015.11.006

Jensen, R. T., & Miller, N. H. (2010). A revealed preference approach to measuring hunger and undernutrition (No. 16555). In Intergovernmental Panel on Climate Change (Ed.), *NBER Working Paper Series*. Cambridge, UK: Cambridge University Press.

Joshi, P., & Kumar, P. (2016). Food demand and supply projections to 2030: India. In F. Brouwer & P. K. Joshi (Eds.), *International trade and food security: The future of Indian agriculture, Part 2* (pp. 29–63). CABI Publishing.

Joy, E. J., Green, R., Agrawal, S., Aleksandrowicz, L., Bowen, L., Kinra, S., … Dangour, A. D. (2017). Dietary patterns and non-communicable disease risk in Indian adults: Secondary analysis of Indian Migration Study data. *Public Health Nutrition*, 20, 1–10. https://doi.org/10.1017/S1368980017000416

Kennedy, G., Nantel, G., & Shetty, P. (2004). *Globalization of food systems in developing countries: Impact on food security and nutrition*. FAO.

Krishnan, S., & Hatekar, N. (2017). Rise of the new middle class in India and its changing structure. *Economic and Political Weekly*, 52(22), 40–48. Retrieved from https://www.epw.in/journal/2017/22/special-articles/rise-new-middle-class-india-and-its-changing-structure.html

Minten, B., Reardon, T., & Sutradhar, R. (2010). Food prices and modern retail: The case of Delhi. *World Development*, 38(12), 1775–1787. https://doi.org/10.1016/j.worlddev.2010.04.002

Misra, A., Singhal, N., Sivakumar, B., Bhagat, N., Jaiswal, A., & Khurana, L. (2011). Nutrition transition in India: Secular trends in dietary intake and their relationship to diet-related non-communicable diseases. *Journal of Diabetes*, 3(4), 278–292. https://doi.org/10.1111/j.1753-0407.2011.00139.x

Mohan, S. (2015, June 1). Junk food is feeding a malnutrition epidemic in Delhi's slums. *Scroll*. Retrieved from https://scroll.in/article/728525/junk-food-is-feeding-a-malnutrition-epidemic-in-delhis-slums

Narayanan, S. (2014a). Profits from participation in high value agriculture: Evidence of heterogeneous benefits in contract farming schemes in Southern India. *Food Policy*, 44, 142–157. https://doi.org/10.1016/j.foodpol.2013.10.010

Pingali, P. (2006). Westernization of Asian diets and the transformation of food systems: Implications for research and policy. *Food Policy*, 32(3), 281–298. https://doi.org/10.1016/j.foodpol.2006.08.001

Pingali, P. (2007). Westernization of Asian diets and the transformation of food systems: Implications for research and policy. *Food Policy, 32*(3), 281–298. https://doi.org/10.1016/j.foodpol.2006.08.001

Pingali, P., & Khwaja, Y. (2004). *Globalisation of Indian diets and the transformation of food supply systems.* Citeseer.

Pingali, P., & Sunder, N. (2017). Transitioning toward nutrition-sensitive food systems in developing countries. *Annual Review of Resource Economics, 9*(1), 439–459. https://doi.org/10.1146/annurev-resource-100516-053552

Popkin, B. M. (1997). The nutrition transition and its health implications in lower-income countries. *Public Health Nutrition, 1*(1), 5–21.

Poulton, C., Dorward, A., & Kydd, J. (2010). The future of small farms: New directions for services, institutions, and intermediation. *World Development, 38*(10), 1413–1428. https://doi.org/10.1016/j.worlddev.2009.06.009

Rahman, A. (2017). *Food elasticity estimates for rural India: Preference for food variety and between group substitutions.*

Reardon, T. (2015). The hidden middle: The quiet revolution in the midstream of agrifood value chains in developing countries. *Oxford Review of Economic Policy, 31*(1), 45–63. https://doi.org/10.1093/oxrep/grv011

Reardon, T., Lansing, E., Minten, B., & Ababa, A. (2011). Surprised by supermarkets: Diffusion of modern food retail in India. *Journal of Agribusiness in Developing and Emerging Economies, 1*(2), 134–161. https://doi.org/10.1108/JADEE-10-2013-0040

Reardon, T., & Timmer, C. P. (2014). Five inter-linked transformations in the Asian agrifood economy: Food security implications. *Global Food Security, 3*(2), 108–117. https://doi.org/10.1016/j.gfs.2014.02.001

Roy, D., & Thorat, A. (2008). Success in high value horticultural export markets for the small farmers: The case of Mahagrapes in India. *World Development, 36,* 1874–1890.

Sekhar, C. S. C., Roy, D., & Bhatt, Y. (2017). *Food inflation and food price volatility in India: Trends and determinants.* IFPRI Discussion Papers, International Food Policy Research Institute (IFPRI). Retrieved from https://econpapers. repec.org/RePEc:fpr:ifprid:1640

Shankar, B., Agrawal, S., Beaudreault, A. R., Avula, L., Martorell, R., Osendarp, S., … Mclean, M. S. (2017). Dietary and nutritional change in India: Implications for strategies, policies, and interventions. *Annals of the New York Academy of Sciences, 1395*(1), 49–59. https://doi.org/10.1111/nyas.13324

Singh, A., Gupta, V., Ghosh, A., Lock, K., & Ghosh-Jerath, S. (2015). Quantitative estimates of dietary intake with special emphasis on snacking pattern and nutritional status of free living adults in urban slums of Delhi: Impact of nutrition transition. *BMC Nutrition, 1*(1), 22. https://doi.org/10.1186/s40795-015-0018-6

Smith, L. C. (2015). The great Indian calorie debate: Explaining rising under-nourishment during India's rapid economic growth. *Food Policy, 50,* 53–67. https://doi.org/10.1016/j.foodpol.2014.10.011

Swinnen, J. F. M., & Maertens, M. (2007). Globalization, privatization, and vertical coordination in food value chains in developing and transition countries. *Agricultural Economics, 37,* 89–102. https://doi.org/10.1111/j.1574-0862.2007.00237.x

Timmer, C. P. (2017). Food security, structural transformation, markets and government policy. *Asia and the Pacific Policy Studies, 4*(1), 4–19. https://doi.org/10.1002/app5.161

USDA. (2018). GAIN Report No. IN8081. Retrieved from https://gain.fas.usda.gov/Recent%20GAIN%20Publications/Retail%20Foods_New%20Delhi_India_6-28-2018.pdf

Vellakkal, S., Fledderjohann, J., Basu, S., Agrawal, S., Ebrahim, S., Campbell, O., … Stuckler, D. (2015). Food price spikes are associated with increased malnutrition among children in Andhra Pradesh, India. *The Journal of Nutrition, 145*(8), 1942–1949. https://doi.org/10.3945/jn.115.211250

CHAPTER 5

The Nutrition Transformation: From Undernutrition to Obesity

5.1 Introduction

As structural transformation changes countries from subsistence agriculture economies to modernized economies, countries undergo a nutrition-related transition[1] (Griffiths & Bentley, 2001). High rates of undernutrition[2] come down and population health improves. However, even as undernutrition decreases, experiences of some countries in the recent past have shown that obesity rates may increase due to over-nutrition[3] and this can decrease overall gains made to health during the

---

[1] In the previous chapter, we use the definition of the nutrition transition as described in Popkin (1997), which refers to the dietary transformation that are related to ST. In this chapter the nutrition transformation refers to the changing burden of nutrition-related health problems that constitute the triple burden of malnutrition—we build on the Griffiths and Bentley (2001) conceptualization here.

[2] At its broadest level, undernourished individuals are those who do not have access to one or more essential nutrients in their diets. Being undernourished, represented by individuals who are either underweight (too thin for their age), wasted (too thin for their height and age) or stunted (too short for their age) compared to a well-nourished reference population, is one type of undernourishment. Another type of undernourishment is called hidden hunger. This manifests itself as deficiencies of essential micronutrients such as vitamins or minerals in the human body.

[3] Over-nourished individuals, on the other hand, are those who consume an excess of a particular macronutrient—calories in particular. This condition is represented by overweight and obesity outcomes which are determined by the age, gender, height and weight of the individual in relation to a similar well-nourished group.

© The Author(s) 2019   93
P. Pingali et al., *Transforming Food Systems for a Rising India*,
Palgrave Studies in Agricultural Economics and Food Policy,
https://doi.org/10.1007/978-3-030-14409-8_5

nutrition transition. When food systems focus narrowly on ensuring food security but do not think more broadly about ensuring nutrition security, this problem of obesity and hence malnutrition can become synonymous with the problem of poverty and low incomes. Thus, poor nourishment and poor health may increase during structural transformation. In India too, economic growth, agricultural development and a keen policy focus on nutrition-related health improvements have brought with it a reduction in hunger and undernutrition rates across the country. Between the NFHS I (1992–93) and NFHS IV (2015–16) surveys, undernutrition rates for children under the ages of five have fallen. The incidence of stunting has decreased by 13 percentage points, and underweight rates have decreased by 24 percentage points. Between NFHS III (2005–06) and NFHS IV (2015–16), the percentage of adult women and men who are underweight has decreased by 13 pp and 15 pp (respectively). However, within the last decade, the over-nutrition prevalence rate has doubled within the country (see Fig. 5.1). Given its close association with the incidence of non-communicable diseases, this phenomenon has created new and serious challenges for the health of individuals. In the long term, increasing risks for malnutrition may have repercussions for economic development, agriculture and health.

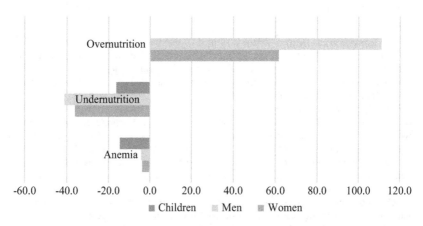

Fig. 5.1 Percentage point changes in the triple burden of malnutrition in India. Source: NFHS 2005–06 and NFHS 2015–16; based on authors calculations

In the previous chapter, we have seen that the demand for food per capita, demand for diverse foods and demand for eating out has kept pace with rising per capita incomes. If food systems cannot respond appropriately to the growing demand for nutrients with an adequate supply response, this may reduce the effectiveness of current policy interventions in meeting their goals of lowering undernutrition and hidden hunger. Additionally, in Chaps. 2 and 3, we have seen that forces of ST have led to a divergence in the growth experience across regions and the agricultural and non-agricultural sectors. If food systems cannot address the problem of income inequality, this may impact a household's ability to access and purchase diverse and quality nutrients from markets. These factors have important (negative) implications for the Indian experience.

In this chapter, we explore the food system's role in reducing the triple burden of malnutrition[4] and moving towards a healthier population. We bring forward evidence from the literature that illuminates the pathways through which malnutrition is impacted as well as discuss interventions from India that have been successful in reducing poor nutrition outcomes thus far. We also bring forward evidence from international contexts on other potential interventions available for reducing malnutrition and lay out different options that can help regulate the nutrition transition that we see unfolding in the country today.

---

[4] The triple burden of malnutrition encapsulates the coexistence of a large number of undernourished individuals side by side with over-nourished people in the presence of high levels of micronutrient deficiencies within a given population. At its broadest level, undernourished individuals are those who do not have access to one or more essential nutrients in their diets. Being undernourished manifests itself as individuals who are either underweight (too thin for their age), wasted (too thin for their height and age) or stunted (too short for their age) compared to a well-nourished reference population. Calorie deprivation and protein energy deficiency are some of the major causes of this type of undernourishment. Another type of undernourishment is called hidden hunger. This manifests itself as deficiencies of essential nutrients such as vitamins or minerals called micronutrients. Diseases such as anemia, night blindness, rickets, scurvy and so on are outcomes of these deficiencies. Over-nourished individuals on the other hand are those who consume an excess of a particular macronutrient, calories in particular. This condition is represented by overweight and obesity outcomes.

5.2   CURRENT STATE OF THE TRIPLE BURDEN
OF MALNUTRITION IN INDIA

The triple burden of malnutrition is particularly an acute problem for India. For one, the latest NFHS estimates show that around 30% were too thin for their age and gender (underweight)[5] and 38% of all children under the ages of five were too short for their age and gender (stunted). With regard to the former, India did far worse regarding prevalence both across ST and when compared to other countries (Fig. 5.2). However, with regard to stunting indicators, it can be seen that poor states in India have comparable outcomes to countries from the SSA regions, while more developed states are closer to world averages (Fig. 5.3). Poor nutrition outcomes are known to lower cognitive skills, lower educational outcomes, lower productivity and lower wages in adults who were malnourished as children compared to adults who were not (Alderman, Hoddinott, & Kinsey, 2006; Black et al., 2013; Chen & Zhou, 2007; Hoddinott,

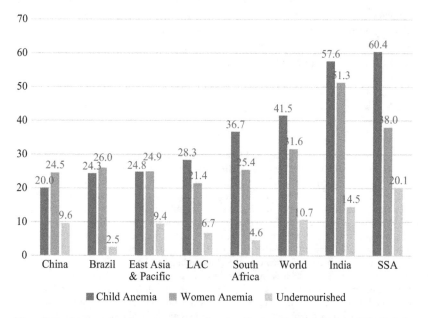

Fig. 5.2 International comparisons in the share of malnutrition (2015–16). Source: World Bank DataBank; based on authors calculations

[5] Most of the improvements came from moving people out of the severely malnourished cases into the moderately malnourished.

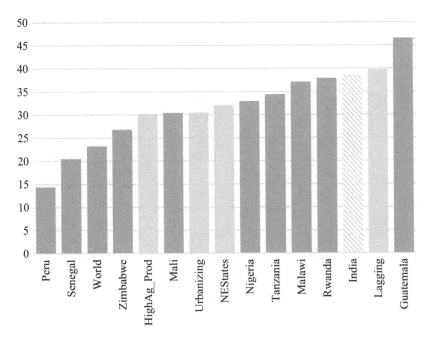

Fig. 5.3 Share of stunted children under 5 years (2015–16). Source: NFHS 2015–16 and World Bank DataBank; based on authors calculations

Maluccio, Behrman, Flores, & Martorell, 2008; Roseboom, de Rooij, & Painter, 2006; T. J. Roseboom et al., 2001; Victora et al., 2008; Akresh, Verwimp, & Bundervoet, 2013; Gørgens, Meng, & Vaithianathan, 2012; Lumey et al., 2007; Stein et al., 2008). In addition to greater mortality risks for children, studies have also shown that adults who were undernourished in childhood have greater incidence of non-communicable diseases than those who were properly fed (Chen & Zhou, 2007; Gørgens, 2002; T. Roseboom et al., 2006). While one can still argue that there has been progress towards reducing stunting, underweight between the 2005 and 2015 National Family Health Surveys (NFHS) across all levels of state-wise development, the incidence of wasting has increased during this time (Fig. 5.4). Wasting occurs when children are too thin for their respective heights, ages and gender. This indicator has been correlated with lower access to food in the short term as well as increased mortality risks for children under the ages of five. An increase in this indicator reflects the speed of, or lack thereof, progress in comprehensively reducing food insecurity and undernutrition within the country.

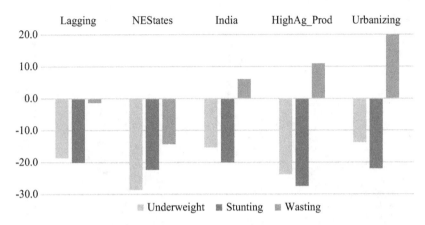

Fig. 5.4   Percentage change in the undernutrition in children under five by state classification. Source: NFHS 2005–06 and NFHS 2015–16; based on authors calculations

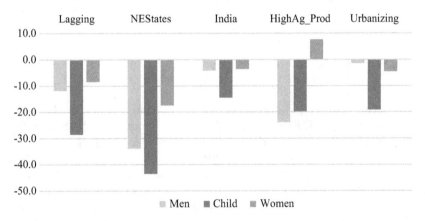

Fig. 5.5   Percentage change in anemia prevalence by state classifications. Source: NFHS 2005–06 and NFHS 2015–16; based on authors calculations

Two, the problem of hidden hunger, or micronutrient deficiency, in India continues to remain acute. For example, the current incidence rates of anemia for men (23%), women (53%) and children (58%) are higher than incidence rates of the same group of individuals in poor countries such as those in sub-Saharan Africa (Fig. 5.5). Of those who are anemic, iron deficiency anemia (IDA) is believed to affect around 60% of all individuals (Murray et al., 2012).

This disease has been correlated with greater fatigue and lower productivity. Other essential nutrients such as iodine and vitamin A too, that are important inputs into biological processes, have not yet been able to find a way into the Indian diet (Jha, Gaiha, & Sharma, 2009). For women in India, reducing anemia continues to remain extremely difficult to tackle compared to other groups. Between the NFHS III & IV, anemia incidence decreased by 3.6 percentage points for non-pregnant women in comparison to men whose anemia decreased by 4.2 percentage points. Both these groups were not targeted for any interventions. In states which have had a history of high productive agricultural systems, anemia rates of women have increased during this time. This is a cause of concern given that this micronutrient deficiency has been linked with higher maternal mortality in adults as well as lower cognitive development and higher infant mortality rates (Akhtar et al., 2013; Allen, Peerson, & Olney, 2009; Bobonis, Miguel, & Sharma, 2004; Brabin, Hakimi, & Pelletier, 2001; Jones et al., 2016; Rasmussen, 2001).

Three, while the country continues to grapple with the problem of undernutrition, experts have called to attention the unprecedented increase in obesity rates, both in rural and urban areas in the country (R. Jha et al., 2009; Meenakshi, 2016; P. Pingali, 2007; Popkin, 1997, 1999; Sengupta, Angeli, Syamala, Dagnelie, & Schayck, 2015; Sturm, Ringel, & Andreyeva, 2004; Swinburn et al., 2011). Traditionally, obesity has been viewed as a luxury good associated with higher per capita incomes and a greater level of structural transformation (Popkin, 1997, 1999). However, obesity rates have increased at an alarming rate in the last ten years—doubled for men and increased by 62% for women (Fig. 5.6). Even across states, it would seem that poorer states are worse affected by the changes in obesity rates compared to richer states. Obesity is a known risk factor for non-communicable diseases (NCDs) such as diabetes, heart disease, cancer and other chronic diseases. Even in the country, higher incidence of high sugar is correlated with high obesity in states (Fig. 5.7). In the United states, in addition to health risks, obesity has also been found to explain lower incomes, productivity and wages in addition to lower long-term health (Alaimo, Olson, & Frongillo, 2001; Cawley, 2015; Wang, McPherson, Marsh, Gortmaker, & Brown, 2011).

The fourth but important characteristic of the malnutrition problem in India is that it remains a problem for women and children regardless of the level of economic development in the country. Even though multiple interventions have targeted changes to move the indicators on these groups, the stickiness of the problem is reflected both in economic outcomes and in the inequities remaining more or less constant over time. Regarding anemia prevalence, over-nutrition or even undernutrition, the

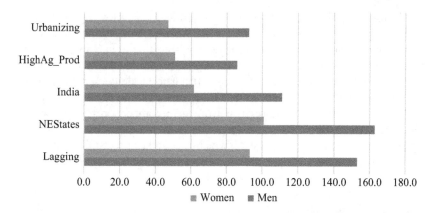

Fig. 5.6 Percentage change in obesity incidence by state classifications. Source: NFHS 2005–06 and NFHS 2015–16; based on authors calculations

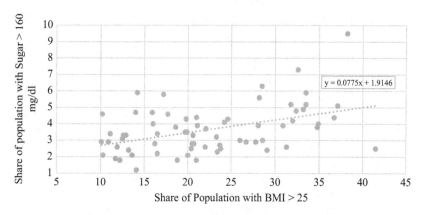

Fig. 5.7 Relationship between the risk of diabetes and over-nutrition in adults. Source: NFHS 2015–16; based on authors calculations

prevalence rates continue to remain the highest for these groups. When women are undernourished, research has found that this leads to low labor productivity, health and economic development of the household. This has negative intergenerational spillovers on the health of children for whom the woman is the major care giver. When children are undernourished in their childhood, this has been linked to poor adult education, health and productivity outcomes (Alderman et al., 2006; Almond & Currie, 2011; Gutierrez, 2013; J. Hoddinott et al., 2008; J. A. Maluccio et al., 2009; Plessow et al., 2015).

5.3   Pathways Towards Better Nutrition Outcomes

Policy makers and scientists around the world have learned that reducing malnutrition is not just about making more food or even more healthy food available for individuals to consume. There are many other channels through which individuals are prevented from accessing adequate food or nutrients. To capture the complexity of the problem of access, we build on the nutrition framework proposed by Pingali and Ricketts (2014) that encompasses the main pathways relevant in our food systems approach. At its broadest level, there are two main units of analysis in this framework—the household and the individual. Malnutrition arises from the lack of access to diverse diets for households. This arises due to the lack of availability of diverse foods in a local ecosystem (Fig. 5.10, quadrant 1) as well as due to income insecurity that impacts the affordability of a balanced diet (Fig. 5.10, quadrant 2). This translates into low food security and poor diet diversity across households and thus enhances risks involved in being malnourished. With regard to ensuring greater availability of diverse foods within a local ecosystem, corresponding nutrition and agriculture-related interventions play an important role in access. Income uncertainty that arises from socio-economic disadvantages is known to limit households' ability to access foods. Thus interventions that create safety nets to protect households against income shocks can play a key role in improving access. Within households, intra-household dynamics (Fig. 5.10, quadrant 3) and the health environment (Fig. 5.10, quadrant 4) determine nutrition access and hence explain differences in nutrition outcomes between members. With regard to risk factors that arise from intra-household dynamics, age, gender, relationship to the head of household and so on play an important role in determining access to food. This dynamic is reflected in Figs. 5.8 and 5.9, where one sees that women and children have the highest rates of malnutrition compared to male members. Finally is the effect of the health environment which is impacted by disease burden as well as water and sanitation quality within households. By affecting human biological processes that help in the absorption of nutrition, a poor health environment becomes an important risk factor in determining malnutrition levels (Fig. 5.10).

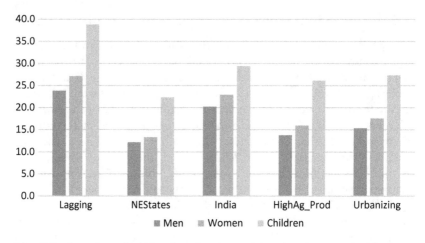

Fig. 5.8   Intra-household burden of undernutrition share by state classifications. Source: NFHS 2015–16; based on authors calculations

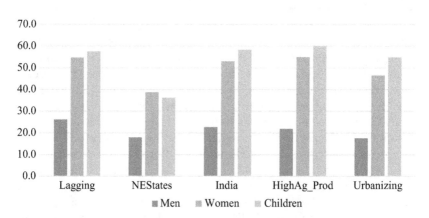

Fig. 5.9   Intra-household burden of anemia by state classification. Source: NFHS 2015–16; based on authors calculations

In this chapter, we add the effects of the growing incidence of NCDs, rising economic inequality and threats from climate change to the framework. NCDs can directly reduce individuals' ability to absorb food by impacting their health. If women are more susceptible to health shocks from NCDs, this can worsen the problem of access to nutrition and can also negatively impact children's health outcomes (Shetty et al., 2012).

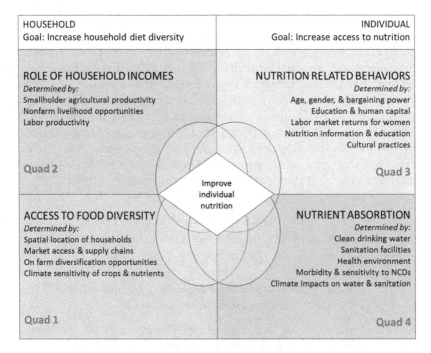

Fig. 5.10   Pathways to better nutrition

Increase in NCDs can also lower the productivity of household members, thus impacting how much food there would be available to consume. Exposure to secondary health risks increases the probability of catastrophic health episodes and thus reduces income security of households. An unanticipated health episode is known to be a major risk factor in the impoverishment of households (Krishna, 2011). Rising economic inequality reduces the number of economic opportunities available for households to participate in the process of development. This creates a self-reinforcing vicious cycle of low income and low ST. States with low ST do not have the institutional capacity to implement successful poverty alleviation programs. Given that labor is a major input into agricultural production in these regions, poor health of individuals in these states translates into low agricultural productivity. Poor health also prevents individuals from participating in economic development activities that may be available in high growth states, thus locking individuals and their respective states into a suboptimal equilibrium of poor health and poor economic development. This reduces the ability of states to participate in catch-up growth. Finally, threats from climate change have brought new, unanticipated negative spillovers to economic development, health and agriculture. By increasing uncertainty in agricultural production, climate change threatens to increase food price volatility, decrease access to food for poor households, decrease the nutrient content of crops as well as decrease the health environment.[6] These shocks will threaten efforts made towards improving nutrition outcomes. In the next section, we summarize the evidence from the literature with regard to the pathways as well as the experience of these interventions along these pathways in enabling greater nutrition.

5.4   EVIDENCE ON PATHWAYS AND THEIR CORRESPONDING FOOD, AGRICULTURE AND NUTRITION INTERVENTIONS

5.4.1   Pathways to Reduce Household Malnutrition Through Diet Diversification

According to the Food and Agriculture Organization of the United Nations (FAO), "Dietary diversity is a qualitative measure of food consumption that reflects household access to a variety of foods, and is also a proxy for nutrient adequacy of the diet of individuals" (Kennedy, Ballard, & Dop, 2011). Diet diversity of households is known to be correlated with better nutrition (Arimond & Ruel, 2004; Busert et al., 2016; J. Hoddinott & Yohannes, 2002; Pingali & Sunder, 2017; Popkin, Horton, Kim, Mahal, & Shuigao, 2001; J. H. Rah et al., 2010). For example, increased dietary diversity has been associated with lower prevalence of hidden hunger and higher nutrient adequacy ratios for individuals (Arimond & Ruel, 2004; Ruel, 2003; Steyn, Nel, Nantel, Kennedy, & Labadarios, 2006). In households with greater consumption of animal-based products such as milk, eggs or meat, children who are not breastfed have lower stunting and wasting as well (Ruel, 2003). Lack of diet diversity has more recently been linked to a higher risk of obesity (Azadbakht & Esmaillzadeh, 2011; Nicklas, Baranowski, Cullen, & Berenson, 2001). Given this close relationship between dietary diversity of households and nutrition outcomes, ensuring that households can access diverse foods requires interventions at

---

[6] More evidence on these factors can be found in the chapter on climate change.

two levels. First is to ensure that there is greater availability of food diversity within the local system. The second set of interventions would need to improve the affordability of these diets. In this section, we discuss the various interventions that have been currently implemented in India with regard to improving nutrition by targeting household diet diversity.

5.4.1.1   Improving Access to Food Diversity

In India, staple grain policy has subsidized the production of calorie dense foods (P. Pingali, 2015). While these policies have successfully increased staple grain productivity and hence economic outcomes and nutrition in some parts of the country, it has also led to a regional divergence in outcomes. Agricultural households from low ST areas have low cropping diversity, low ability to participate in markets as well as some of the worse nutrition outcomes in the country. *Staple grain fundamentalism* in agricultural policy has preoccupied policy makers in investing in productivity enhancing staple-grain-focused technologies at the cost of developing similar biotechnologies for non-staple crops (Pingali, 2012). This strategy has increased vulnerability in the production of non-staples, especially in areas which are not properly irrigated. As climate change threatens the production of crops, lack of technology for drought-resistant, heat-resistant and flood-resistant non-staples increases vulnerability of the same.[7] On the demand side, as discussed in Chap. 4, the growth of the retail sector and organized sector and increased expenditures on non-staples reflects the increase in demand and hence willingness to spend on these goods. Urban dietary demand, for example, has been rising quite rapidly across all states, especially in those regions that are more developed (Fig. 5.11). Agricultural (rural) households too are spending a larger fraction of their incomes on non-staples (such as meat, pulses, fruits and vegetables) purchased from the markets (S. Subramanian & Deaton, 1996; Deaton, 1987). These demand factors create non-trivial production challenges and challenges for their distribution. These supply and demand factors have important implications for the availability of nutrients and diverse foods at the household level. If climate shocks increase uncertainty in food production and hence increase volatility of food prices, poor households will be more vulnerable to shocks food security and hence malnutrition (Jensen, 2000).

Currently, research on the safety net programs such as the Mid-Day Meal Scheme (MDMS) and the Public Distribution System (PDS) have shown mixed results regarding their impact on improving household diet

---

[7] These factors are discussed in more detail in Chap. 7.

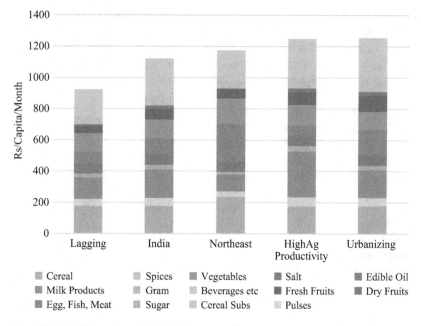

Fig. 5.11 Urban household dietary-spending patterns in India (2011–12). Source: Food Consumption Expenditure report NSSO 2011–12; based on authors calculations

diversity. Research on the Integrated Child Development Scheme (ICDS) program has shown it to be mildly effective in reducing undernutrition in children and mothers who are beneficiaries of the program. In areas where Anganwadi health workers have been compensated for performance, there has been greater short-term progress in addressing malnutrition (Dubowitz et al., 2007; P. Singh, 2015). Thus having a strong locally oriented health task force has been an important complementary investment required for improving undernutrition outcomes. Evaluations of the MDMS has shown its effectiveness in reducing undernutrition of school-aged children, especially from families who suffered from shocks such as droughts (Singh, Park, & Dercon, 2013). Rahman (2016) and Kishore and Chakrabarti (2015) have linked universal access to the PDS with greater household diet diversity. However, in a study by Kaushal and Muchomba (2015), the author found that PDS access may not have a clear impact on nutrition outcomes. The challenges in implementation that have led to this mixed evidence on their impact will be discussed in more detail in the next chapter.

On the other end of the malnutrition burden, research has shown that rising obesity and NCD prevalence has been linked to consumption of excessive carbohydrates and sugar in diets. Staple grain crops and sugar crops have been long favored by agricultural and PDS procurement policies in the country. By artificially keeping consumption prices low, experts have speculated that this has led to overconsumption of these foods in diets. According to Arora, Pillai, Dasgupta, and Garg (2014) increased consumption of sugar and fat products in diets is a major risk factor in explaining the rise in obesity in India. Anjana et al. (2015) found that increased intake of refined cereals was highly correlated with increased diabetes incidence especially when time spent on sedentary activities (such as watching television and sitting) was high and abdominal obesity was high. Shrivastava, Misra, Mohan, Unnikrishnan, and Bachani (2017) have found evidence that South Asians consumed more calories from carbohydrates and their foods had a greater glycemic index compared to their European counterparts. These dietary patterns have been linked to greater NCD risks. However, research in this area is new and needs to be further developed. In addition, given that it is a new phenomenon, interventions have not yet been incorporated into policy making.

Micronutrient deficiency (hidden hunger) is the third component of the triple burden that has been linked to lower diet diversity of households. At various points in the country's history, the nutrition department has run information campaigns on better diets and nutrition. A cross-sectional study on the effectiveness of advertisement campaigns on purchasing iodized salt found that it reduced undernutrition of children, but the authors found the effects to be very small (S. Kumar & Berkman, 2015). In the 1990s, famous national advertising campaigns that encouraged the consumption of milk and eggs became a part of nutritional messaging in the country. Even though knowledge about the benefits of these products grew, there have been no experimental evaluations of the impact of these information and communication programs on household diet diversity or nutritional outcomes thus far. In the chapter on policy (11), we discuss the possibility of introducing laws for increasing food safety, fortification of foods and biofortification of crops as methods to improve access to micronutrients in food at the economy level and hence at the household level.

5.4.1.2 *Increasing Household Incomes*

When the level of income or the number of employment-generating opportunities that households have access to is low and the probability that households are impacted by productivity shocks is high, households faced greater income insecurity. By reducing the ability of households to plan ahead and thus purchase diverse foods from markets, income insecurity reduces the affordability of nutritious diets and thus increases malnutrition. In households from more developed states in India, greater income security (incomes per capita) and more market access (greater employment opportunities) have been found to be correlated with higher dietary diversity and lower levels of undernutrition (Koppmair, Kassie, & Qaim, 2017; Sibhatu, Krishna, & Qaim, 2015). Agricultural households from these areas too have greater income-generating capability and hence better access to nutritious foods and hence better nutrition outcomes. In *lagging states* in India, agricultural households are more likely to consume food from their own farms (P. Pingali, Mittra, & Rahman, 2017). Research from other similar subsistence agriculture contexts has shown that access to home gardens or livestock related livelihood opportunities can improve diet diversity and nutrition in such contexts (Ali, Ahmed, & Islam, 2008; Berti, Krasevec, & FitzGerald, 2004; Jones, Shrinivas, & Bezner-Kerr, 2014; Masset, Leroy, & Frongillo, 2007).

Looking at effective interventions across the country, commercialization of the agricultural production system is an important pathway to increase ST, reduce rural poverty and reduce rural malnutrition. In order to enable greater commercialization, reducing transaction costs in participating supply chains (Abraham & Pingali, 2017) as well as strengthening the participation of the retail sector in procurement and distribution of foods from small farms is an important way forward (Boselie, Henson, & Weatherspoon, 2003; Reardon, Timmer, & Minten, 2012; Thomas Reardon & Minten, 2011).[8] As seen in Chap. 3, non-farm incomes and remittances from migrants have also been found to play an important role in increasing income security and diet diversity as well as reducing malnutrition in rural households (Babatunde & Qaim, 2010; Binswanger-Mkhize, 2012; Imai, Gaiha, & Thapa, 2015; Owusu, Abdulai, & Abdul-Rahman, 2011; Benjamin, Reardon, Stamoulis, & Winters, 2002; Binswanger-Mkhize, 2013). Also, interventions that reduce costs of migrating, rural infrastructure projects that increase access to urban markets and rural development programs that stimulate local markets can thus alleviate malnutrition by increasing household incomes. In urban areas as well, income per capita, permanent employment opportunities and better-quality urban infrastructure are known to be correlated with greater diet diversity as well as lower undernutrition. However, there is very little research on the pathways that impact urban food (in)security (Maxwell, 1999). Moving forward, urbanization trends in

---

[8] This will be discussed in Chap. 8.

India will reconfigure the importance of urban food security in the nutrition debates. Developing interventions that focus on improving urban food security will become important as we look ahead.

The second pathway that reduces the affordability of nutritious diets and thus increases household-level malnutrition is unanticipated shocks to household productivity. In this regard, poor households are more likely to be impacted by unanticipated catastrophic events such as health, weather or food price shocks. This increases their vulnerability and thus impacts malnutrition. Research has shown that in the absence of appropriate financial tools to hedge against short-term production risks, crop price shocks tend to translate into worse malnutrition outcomes of households (Bellemare, 2015; De Brauw, 2011; Ivanic & Martin, 2008; R. T. Jensen & Miller, 2008). For example, in Nicaragua, undernutrition in children worsened when incomes of small farmer households growing coffee were hurt by price shocks from the international coffee markets (Maluccio, 2005). In other instances, weather-related shocks such as lower rainfall or longer droughts have been found to worsen nutrition outcomes of both children and adults. For example, famines caused by extended periods of drought have been linked to a reduction in the long-term productivity of adults who experienced these shocks when they were in utero. Providing adequate protection through crop or weather insurance is thus important towards ensuring that households are protected against lower nutrition outcomes. Health shocks can be devastating for household food security and nutritional outcomes (Strauss & Thomas, 1998; R. M. Townsend, 1994, 1995; Asfaw & Braun, 2004). Krishna (2011) has documented an unanticipated health shock to the breadwinner of the family can impoverish households. In the short term, health spending can increase household debt, thus reducing household access to nutritious foods. In the long run, the productivity of households can reduce if children are taken out of school to work or women have to participate in labor markets that pay them lower wages.

At the economy level, structural transformation and economic growth has led to changing preferences in diets and has increased opportunity costs of home food preparation (due to rising wages). These phenomena have been correlated with greater demand for eating diverse foods and eating more processed foods available at supermarkets and restaurants (Pingali, 2006; Popkin, 1999, 2003).[9] These changes are reflected both in

---

[9] See Chap. 4 for discussion on patterns and factors of this phenomenon.

the growth in expenditure shares in household spending on non-staples, such as milk, eggs and meat relative to staples, and in the greater demand for *eating out* (Gaiha, Jha, & Kulkarni, 2013). While many of these dietary changes have been linked to lower undernutrition and hidden hunger outcomes, Anjana et al. (2015) found that increased intake of refined cereals, fruits and vegetables, dairy products, and monounsaturated fatty acid was correlated with increased diabetes when sedentary activities and abdominal obesity of individuals was also high. There is some evidence to show that greater income per capita has increased the consumption sugary and fat-based products (Gaiha et al., 2013; V. Gupta, Downs, Ghosh-Jerath, Lock, & Singh, 2016; P. Pingali, 2006). Consumption of these types of foods has been associated with greater obesity incidence. Also, Arora et al. (2014) argue that doubling in the per capita consumption of these products over the last 15 years can be correlated with increases in obesity in the country. However obesity is still a new phenomenon in India. Hence there has been very little research done so far to understand the income effects of food demand on obesity in the country. Also thus far the obesity phenomenon is largely urban and is linked to higher incomes per capita, but research from developed country contexts finds that as the difference in incomes per capita increases, obesity incidence becomes a burden for poorer populations. In the absence of a food system that accounts for this issue of access, obesity becomes a major threat to future health systems.

5.4.2   Pathways to Reduce Individual Malnutrition by Improving Access

Across India and in all types of malnutrition indicators, women and children do far worse than the adult males. Within the same household as well, it is common to see that women, children or older-age adults are more malnourished than the adult male or breadwinner. Even between children, boys are known to have better nutrition outcomes than girls. There are two major explanations for the intra-household variation in malnutrition outcomes. First, observable traits such as gender, age, education and labor force participation often determine who has access to nutrition within households. Households tend to invest their scarce resources towards individuals who have the highest potential to improve household welfare. Even if not directly observed, intra-household dynamics such as bargaining power, time use patterns and cultural beliefs and practices can also create unanticipated trade-offs between household members and thus moderate their access to food and nutrition. Even in completely egalitarian and altruistic households, the health environment often plays a role in increasing morbidity and sickness. Combined with age, health stock of individuals and their access to food, a poor health environment creates barriers to nutrient absorption. Lack of water or sanitation facilities and high incidence of communicable diseases increase morbidity of children and hence reduce their ability to access nutrition. For older adults, age and susceptibility to NCDs also increases morbidity and hence affects their nutrition outcomes. These factors contribute to intra-household dynamics that result in nutrition outcomes that differ across individuals who live within the same household.

5.4.2.1 *Inducing Positive Nutrition Behaviors Within Households*
Within households, nutrition disparities are the outcome of six important channels. One, in many poor agricultural households, the low opportunity cost of time, reflected by low (agricultural) wages of women and girls relative to men and boys, creates a nutrition-productivity spiral in favor of the men and at the expense of women. This problem is particularly harsh in income-constrained households where members may allocate more market work to the higher-paid members, thus reinforcing a productivity nutrition trade-off in their favor (J. R. Behrman & Deolalikar, 1993, 1990; Deolalikar, 1988). These trade-offs become salient when households experience income shocks. For example, nutritional outcomes of women and girl children worsen when there are agriculture-related shocks such as droughts or floods, during price shocks and during labor market shocks such as health shocks, migration-related shocks and economic downturns (Agüero & Marks, 2011; Akresh, Verwimp, & Bundervoet, 2011; Alderman et al., 2006; Baez & Santos, 2007; D'Souza & Jolliffe, 2013; del Ninno & Lundberg, 2005; Ferreira & Schady, 2009; J. Hoddinott, 2006; R. Jensen, 2000). Two, women are often relegated to household tasks such as water and firewood collection or threshing and harvesting on the fields. These tasks are energy intensive, but they are undervalued in the market (H. R. Barrett et al., 2005; Kadiyala, Harris, Headey, Yosef, & Gillespie, 2014). Even though there is no strong evidence that malnutrition outcomes of children worsen when mothers go back to work, women maybe expected to stay home and involve themselves in child care (Bennett, 1988; Glick & Sahn, 1998; Kes & Swaminathan, 2006; Leslie, 1988). These services too are undervalued and thus women's (girls) household contributions tend to be undervalued in favor of men (boys) thus reducing access.

Studies from Mexico have found that changing returns to household work through cash transfers for girl children can be one way to help reduce their time spent on household work and to keep them in schools (Parker & Skoufias, 2000). Three, Jayachandran and Pande (2017) found the oldest male child within a household had better nutrition-related outcomes compared to similar children in Africa. However, any other child (with a higher birth order) fared worse than a comparable group of children from the same context. Hoddinott and Kinsey (2001) and Maccini and Yang (2009) also found that when there were rainfall shocks, within the same household, girls' malnutrition and schooling outcomes worsened in relation to boys' malnutrition outcomes. Thus discriminatory practices based on birth order of gender often lead to different nutrition outcomes between groups of children within the same households. Four, intra-household bargaining literature shows that when women have more bargaining power within households nutritional outcomes of all members improve. For example, when households are headed by women rather than men, the nutrition outcomes of children are better in the former even if their incomes were lower on average (Headey, 2013; C. Johnson & Rogers, 1993). Multiple authors have found that women's education is a powerful channel through which household malnutrition, as well as intergenerational health outcomes of children, can improve (Case & Ardington, 2006; Currie & Moretti, 2003; Oreopoulos, Page, & Stevens, 2006; Thomas, Strauss, & Henriques, 1991). Intra-household bargaining power of women is also reflected in the amount of freedom they have to control resources when they belong to male-dominated households. Multiple researchers have found that increase in empowerment of women within households, represented by greater financial control and more physical mobility outside the home, played an important role in improving child nutrition indicators (Imai, Annim, Kulkarni, & Gaiha, 2014; Shroff, Griffiths, Adair, Suchindran, & Bentley, 2009; M. R. Shroff et al., 2011). Thus increasing women's education, bargaining power and empowering women to take decisions within households will be important towards decreasing intra-household disparities. Five, within households, it can also be the case that households may not have proper information on nutritional behaviors that can impact malnutrition. In sub-Saharan Africa, evaluations of behavior change communication programs on breastfeeding have been found to be effective in increasing knowledge, duration of breastfeeding and health outcomes especially for babies whose mothers are HIV positive (Coovadia et al., 2007; Thior et al., 2006). Interventions such as the distribution of vitamin A and iron tablets in India have been unsuccessful in reducing micronutrient deficiency since households lack information on the benefits of following treatment protocols properly. Six, cultural practices often prevent women and children from accessing the necessary care from interventions that are focused on improving their health. In some cases, cultural beliefs about the micronutrients' effects on health play a role in reducing whether women and children continue treatment. For example, in India, Nichter (2008) found that women were discouraged to take iron supplements since midwives from the villages believed it would increase the size of the baby in utero and thus increase complications for child mortality in women who were giving birth. However, the flip side to the argument was that women who were anemic were highly susceptible to maternal mortality risks. Changing these behaviors require education interventions for all household members, informational campaigns about the importance of nutrition and economic growth policies that are inclusive.

Programs such as the ICDS focus on addressing malnutrition by providing pregnant women and new mothers with reproductive healthcare such as ante-natal checkups, nutrition supplements such as iron tablets, nutritious meals and information on managing nutrition intake during their pregnancies. For newborn children, the ICDS provides post-natal care, monitors anthropometric health of newborn children and educate mothers on the importance of breastfeeding and eating healthy. Information on nutrition supplements and nutrition intake for children are also provided to new mothers with the view to change behavior. Evaluations of these programs have found that iron-related nutrition outcomes of children improved after women were educated on the same (Kapur, Sharma, & Agarwal, 2003). With regard to undernutrition, additional interventions such as encouraging early initiation of breastfeeding practices were found to be more effective than just providing individuals with more information on nutrition practices (Kumar, Goel, Mittal, & Misra, 2006). Introduction of complementary feeding practices along with breastfeeding was found to be associated with better nutrition outcomes for children in some areas as well (Menon, Bamezai, Subandoro, Ayoya, & Aguayo, 2015). In states such as Maharashtra, regular monitoring of babies and mothers and strict protocols to identify and treat groups that are at high risk of malnutrition have played an important role in reducing its severity. Greater citizen involvement has also been thought to be the key motivation for creating efficient systems in Maharashtra. The MDMS program, on the other hand, has been found to be an extremely cost-effective program in improving nutrition outcomes of students. Afridi (2010) found that for less than Rs. 20 a day, a child attending a school with access to MDMS reduced their daily dietary calorie deficiency by 30%, iron deficiency by 10% and reduced protein deficiency by 100%.

India has some of the world's worst rates of anemia for men, women and children, and this burden exists across states and economic development outcomes in the country. Anemia has been linked to the lack of micronutrient availability in diets and is known to have many long-term negative health effects on individuals as well. Many interventions implemented by the health department in India have focused on improving the last mile access with regard to micronutrients. For example, distribution of vitamin A and iron capsules for pregnant women and babies have long been part of the strategy to improve reproductive and child health in the country. However, there have not been many rigorous evaluations of these programs. For example, Semba et al. (2010) found some evidence that vitamin A interventions in India did reduce child undernutrition, especially wasting in children. However, the effects were modest at best. In cases where it has worked, experts have shown that there are significant improvements to child health. Adhvaryu and Nyshadham (2016) found that when children were exposed to iodine supplementations in utero, they were more like to have better health and cognitive outcomes compared to a sibling who was not exposed.

The other important and growing phenomenon in the malnutrition burden is obesity incidence. A systematic review of the nature of obesity within households reveals that in less developed countries, obesity is an outcome of income and is equally prevalent between men and women in rich households. However, greater economic development becomes associated with obesity of women in the lower income strata, but male obesity tended to more malleable to economic growth (Dinsa, Goryakin, Fumagalli, & Suhrcke, 2012). In these contexts, obesity of women is also associated with a higher premium in labor markets regarding reduced wages as well as greater health spending (Cawley, 2004, 2010). These effects are known to spill over on poor health outcomes that have negative effects for both women and their children. In India, S. Gulati et al. (2013) find that socio-economic indicators and the lack of knowledge on obesity explain the high overweight rates of girls and boys in urban schools. However, other than the income and information pathways, there is very little known about why women and children may be susceptible to obesity in the country. Given its challenges for health, this becomes an extremely crucial investment area as we think ahead to improve nutrition outcomes.

5.4.2.2   *Improving Nutrient Absorption by Investing in the Health Environment*

Poor nutrition and a poor health environment have an endogenous relationship. Among the factors that increase this vulnerability are the age of the individual and their health stock. Children who are undernourished or anemic, for example, are more susceptible to diseases in the health environment (Horton & Ross, 2003; Thakur, Chandra, Pemde, & Singh, 2014). Similarly, children who have higher morbidity have worse malnutrition outcomes (Clasen et al., 2014; Miguel & Kremer, 2015). This endogeneity reinforces the problem of poor nutrient absorption for children. A poor health environment can be an outcome of low quality of drinking water, inadequate sewerage facilities, proximity to fecal contamination by livestock and humans and poor hygiene in water and sanitation practices. As disease burden increases in the surrounding areas, constant exposure to disease reduces individuals' ability to absorb nutrition from foods that they eat.

In India, much of the disease burden still comes from diarrhea incidence. Diarrhea is an outcome of bacterial and viral infections that can be transmitted through an unclean environment. In Fig. 5.12, we see the strong correlation between low sanitation infrastructure and diarrhea incidence in children. Hammer and Spears (2016) and Spears, Ghosh,

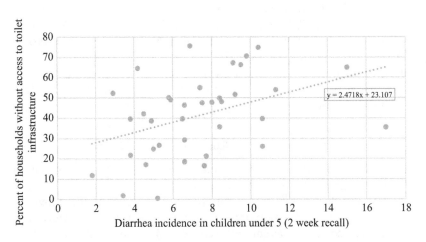

Fig. 5.12 Relationship between diarrhea prevalence and lack of sanitation. Source: NFHS 2015–16; based on authors calculations

and Cumming (2013) showed that in India, reduction in stunting was correlated with a reduction in open defecation in villages through the construction of toilet infrastructure. In the *lagging states* of Madhya Pradesh and Orissa, Clasen et al. (2014) and Patil et al. (2014) showed that constructing toilets could not help reduce diarrheal infections since households did not engage in clean sanitation behaviors even after the infrastructure became available. Supplementing investments made in constructing infrastructure for water and sanitation services, along with BCC interventions, has been found to be most effective in improving nutrition in many other developing countries. Having access to clean water and engaging in hygienic practices for sanitation-related cleanliness was found to be effective in lowering disease burden and hence improving nutrition outcomes in India (Lee, Rosenzweig, & Pitt, 1997; Mangyo, 2008). Rah et al. (2015) found that in areas where the primary care givers encouraged clean drinking water practices such as washing hands before eating and after using the toilet, stunting-related malnutrition decreased. In places where households consume water stored in containers, sanitizing water storage facilities through the addition of chlorine tablets has been found to decrease the spread of disease (Mengistie, Berhane, & Worku, 2013). Other practices such as boiling water before consuming it and encouraging people to wash hands with soap before they eat has been found to be effective in the fight against diarrhea (Biran et al., 2008). Other health-related interventions such as vaccinations against communicable diseases, distribution of deworming tablets, provision of bed nets to reduce the spread of mosquitoes and malaria have also been found to be effective in improving child health (Lim et al., 2011; Miguel & Kremer, 2015). By reducing morbidity, these interventions improve the nutrition absorption capacity of children and thus can contribute to the fight against malnutrition.

5.5   Challenges for the Future

Moving the country from high undernutrition to low undernutrition while simultaneously preventing an increase in obesity needs to be a key goal for enabling a smooth transition towards better health. However tackling high undernutrition, micronutrient deficiency or high prevalence of obesity requires different interventions that address key challenges based on the malnutrition type. In Fig. 5.13, we see that obesity has become a problem of high incomes, while undernutrition is correlated

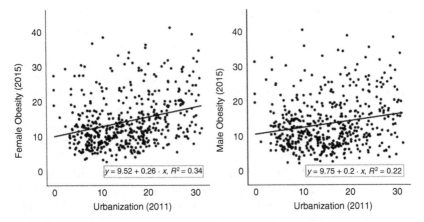

Fig. 5.13 District-level association between urbanization and obesity. Source: Census 2011 and NFHS 2015–16; based on authors calculations

with low ST. Hence interventions need to address the specific nutrition-economic growth context of ST that aligns with each state. For example, tackling obesity in *urbanizing states* like Kerala would need to become the key focus of state development policies while tackling undernutrition in *lagging states* like UP needs to remain a priority. Within each of these categories, identifying the main channel through which malnutrition is impacted should be identified both by state and by district. For example, in more hilly areas of Chhattisgarh, solving the problem of access to food maybe more important for reducing undernutrition while improving sanitation access might be more effective in the plains of Madhya Pradesh. Similarly, improving nutrition education and positive nutrition behaviors might be key in Tamil Nadu where white collar jobs dominate economic growth while improving food grades and safety in Maharashtra would improve access to nutrition in urban areas, where much of food is accessed by eating out. Thus, looking ahead there is a need for more state specific research for identifying the most important pathway through which the threat for malnutrition can be reduced.

There are three additional challenges for the triple burden of malnutrition as we look ahead to 2050. The first challenge is tackling the rising incidence of NCDs. As per the report (MoHFW, 2017), nearly 62% of all deaths in the country are due to NCDs. This number has nearly doubled in the last two decades. Urbanized states have the highest DALYs[10] from premature deaths while *lagging states* have the lowest this far. NCDs account for 35% of premature deaths of individuals between the ages of 15 and 39 and 74% of all deaths for individuals between the ages of 40 and 69 in the country. Among the NCDs, cardiovascular diseases, chronic respiratory diseases, cancers and diabetes explain more than 80% of all deaths. DALYs from diabetes incidence has increased by 80% and unhealthy diets, higher blood pressure, high cholesterol and overweight now account for 25% of risk associated with NCDs.[11] Urbanized states have seen the greatest increase in NCDs and also have the highest increases in obesity incidence (MoHFW, 2017). Given demographic projections for the future, increasing trends for urbanization and increasing incidence of obesity, there is a credible threat that NCDs will become a liability for health systems as well look ahead. This will not only impact malnutrition outcomes; it will lead to a reduction in the productivity of individuals as well as lower economic growth outcomes in the long run.

The second major threat comes from climate change. Changing rainfall patterns, an increase in the number of heat days and increased air and water pollution will worsen the health environment. By reducing access to essential resources such as water and increasing disease burden, climate change will increase the risks for malnutrition. Current research has shown that air and water pollution too can directly impact the health environment and thus health and mortality. Climatic risk factors will also directly impact the rate of incidence of NCDs and hence pose a further threat to progress made towards improving health (Kjellstrom, Holmer, & Lemke, 2009; Majra & Gur, 2009; Myers et al., 2017; Patz, Campbell-Lendrum, Holloway, & Foley, 2005; Watts et al., 2015). Through the agricultural system, climate change also threatens to impact nutrition by reducing food availability and nutrient content in crops. Literature has suggested that women and children will be more vulnerable as climate change threatens access to water and other natural resources which occupy Cooperative Marketing Federation (much of the time use patterns for these groups. All these factors will further reduce the effectiveness of interventions currently designed to address malnutrition.

---

[10] DALYS—Disability Adjusted Life Years—years of healthy life lost due to premature death and suffering. DALYS = years of life lost + years lived with disability.

[11] The latter has increased from 10% in the 1990s.

The third challenge is the problem of growing income inequality across geographical space and incomes. The malnutrition transformation predicts that as incomes increase, undernutrition first decreases and is followed by an increase in over-nutrition. However, with higher levels of development, greater income inequality leads to over-nutrition incidence transitioning away from the rich towards a problem of the poor and less privileged. This transition is driven by increased access to unhealthy processed foods from supermarkets, higher opportunity costs related to home meal preparation as well as greater demand for diet diversity. In India, we are in the process of moving towards high over-nutrition even before we have successfully tackled the problem of undernutrition. This transition can be explained by both the growing income inequality within the country as well as the limited success of current interventions to tackle the undernutrition problem. Given that some states will progress more quickly towards completing their ST, guiding their economies away from a malnutrition transition through appropriate policy interventions that are best suited to the development experiences of the states will be important as we look ahead.

5.6   CONCLUSION

Similar to the experience of other countries that have undergone a greater structural transformation, India has made progress towards reducing hunger and reducing undernutrition as it emerges into the global stage. Over the last three decades, the country has managed to reduce undernutrition by at least ten percentage points across all individuals. However, tackling micronutrient deficiency continues to remain a challenge for policy makers. Anemia rates of children and women have remained stubbornly high and are still comparable to those in sub-Saharan African countries, which themselves have been on a lower transformation pathway. Much of the progress made towards tackling this problem has now been marred by the fast increasing rates of overweight individuals. This new phenomenon has blindsided policy efforts. While one may be tempted to argue that increasing obesity may itself represent the role of fast rising incomes (as experienced by many other countries), its rate of increase and its indirect effects on non-communicable diseases are extremely concerning. NCDs currently explain around 62% of all deaths in India, a doubling of the rate since the early 2000s. Much of the increase in NCDs has come from diseases such as heart conditions and diabetes which are closely related to issues of food access and malnutrition. This abrupt shift in the distribution of the triple burden of malnutrition is unprecedented, and experts and policy makers have become concerned about its impacts for the health of individuals both in the short term and the long term. In the short term, malnutrition has been found to lower labor productivity and reduce household food security. In the long term, growing numbers of unhealthy populations place a large public health burden on the Indian health system to deliver health services. This may affect the potential for long-term economic development.

Through this chapter, we provide an account of the pathways through which malnutrition can be reduced. We identify four such pathways using a food systems approach. At the household level, access to diverse diets and income security play a major role with regard to increasing food security and reducing malnutrition. Research has shown that helping households diversify their diets by increasing access to diverse foods through markets as well as increasing income and livelihood opportunities is important for tackling malnutrition. For obesity reduction as well, having access to nutritious diets, reducing overconsumption of calories from sugar as well as increasing income security, will play an important role. Within the household, intra-household dynamics with regards to food access and the quality of the surrounding health environment determine an individual's ability to absorb nutrition from food. Women and children in households are thus especially vulnerable to malnutrition compared to men. Research from developed country contexts suggests that these dynamics play out obesity risks as well. Higher obesity has been found to be associated with poor economic outcomes and lower intergenerational health for women. Spillovers from increasing obesity rates often impact incidence and mortality related to NCDs as well. Thus, improving welfare in the future involves a continued commitment towards the reduction of undernutrition and micronutrient deficiencies, as well as increasing commitment towards reducing risk factors for obesity and thus NCDs.

In this chapter, we present evidence on the success of various interventions that have been implemented in India to tackle the issue of malnutrition. Our chapter also highlights areas where more research or evidence is required to understand how malnutrition can be reduced. For example, we show that there is very little known on the pathways through which obesity can be reduced. Similarly, though there have been many interventions to reduce hidden hunger or micronutrient deficiencies, there is little known on what has worked or not. Also, we discuss the importance of investing in other channels for reducing undernutrition such as reducing communicable disease incidence through vaccinations and increasing access to clean and safe drinking water. We also highlight the differences in the national and regional policy responses to the nutrition issue and argue that a decentralized approach is now more relevant in tackling malnutrition. For example, we propose that discussions on reducing obesity need to become more important in the food policy debates in *urbanizing states*, while their agricultural policies need to focus on increasing rural income security. In *lagging states* on the other hand, food and agricultural policy needs to remain focused on reducing undernutrition and hidden hunger. In addition, we highlight the risks that climate change, rising NCDs and regional inequality pose to tackling malnutrition. These phenomena, we argue, increase health systems risks associated with malnutrition and will derail progress made towards achieving better health if not addressed. Thus achieving the goal for nutrition security for the future will require interventions that simultaneously tackle the multiple challenges that impact the triple burden of malnutrition.

References

Abraham, M., & Pingali, P. (2017). Transforming smallholder agriculture to achieve the SDGs. In L. Riesgo, S. Gomez-Y-Paloma, & K. Louhichi (Eds.), *The role of small farms in food and nutrition security*. Springer.

Adhvaryu, A., & Nyshadham, A. (2016). Endowments at birth and parents' investments in children. *The Economic Journal, 126*(593), 781–820.

Afridi, F. (2010). Child welfare programs and child nutrition: Evidence from a mandated school meal program in India. *Journal of Development Economics, 92*(2), 152–165. https://doi.org/10.1016/j.jdeveco.2009.02.002

Agüero, J. M., & Marks, M. S. (2011). Motherhood and female labor supply in the developing world: Evidence from infertility shocks. *Journal of Human Resources, 46*(4), 800–826. https://doi.org/10.1353/jhr.2011.0002

Akhtar, S., Ahmed, A., Randhawa, M. A., Atukorala, S., Arlappa, N., Ismail, T., & Ali, Z. (2013). Prevalence of vitamin A deficiency in South Asia: Causes, outcomes, and possible remedies. *Journal of Health, Population, and Nutrition, 31*(4), 413–423. Retrieved from http://www.ncbi.nlm.nih.gov/pmc/articles/PMC3905635/

Akresh, R., Verwimp, P., & Bundervoet, T. (2011). Civil war, crop failure, and child stunting in Rwanda. *Economic Development and Cultural Change, 59*(4), 777–810. https://doi.org/10.1086/660003

Akresh, R., Verwimp, P., & Bundervoet, T. (2013). Civil war, crop failure, and child stunting in Rwanda. *Economic Development and Cultural Change, 59*(4), 777–810.

Alaimo, K., Olson, C. M., & Frongillo, E. A., Jr. (2001). Low family income and food insufficiency in relation to overweight in US children: Is there a paradox? *Archives of Pediatrics and Adolescent Medicine, 155*(10), 1161–1167. https://doi.org/10.1001/archpedi.155.10.1161

Alderman, H., Hoddinott, J., & Kinsey, B. (2006). Long term consequences of early childhood malnutrition. *Oxford Economic Papers, 58*(3), 450–474. https://doi.org/10.1093/oep/gpl008

Ali, M. Y., Ahmed, M. M., & Islam, M. B. (2008, April). *Homestead vegetable gardening: Meeting the need of year round vegetable requirement of farm family.* In National Workshop on Multiple Cropping held at Bangladesh Agricultural Research Council, Farmgate, Dhaka, Bangladesh, pp. 23–24.

Allen, L. H., Peerson, J. M., & Olney, D. K. (2009). Provision of multiple rather than two or fewer micronutrients more effectively improves growth and other outcomes in micronutrient-deficient children and adults. *The Journal of Nutrition, 139*(5), 1022–1030. https://doi.org/10.3945/jn.107.086199

Almond, D., & Currie, J. (2011). Killing me softly: The fetal origins hypothesis. *Journal of Economic Perspectives, 25*(3), 153–172. https://doi.org/10.1016/j.surg.2006.10.010.Use

Anjana, R. M., Sudha, V., Nair, D. H., Lakshmipriya, N., Deepa, M., Pradeepa, R., … Mohan, V. (2015). Diabetes in Asian Indians—How much is preventable? Ten-year follow-up of the Chennai Urban Rural Epidemiology Study (CURES-142). *Diabetes Research and Clinical Practice, 109*(2), 253–261. https://doi.org/10.1016/j.diabres.2015.05.039

Arimond, M., & Ruel, M. T. (2004). Dietary diversity is associated with child nutritional status: Evidence from 11 demographic and health surveys. *The Journal of Nutrition, 134*(July), 2579–2585.

Arora, N. K., Pillai, R., Dasgupta, R., & Garg, P. R. (2014). Whole-of-society monitoring framework for sugar, salt, and fat consumption and noncommunicable diseases in India. *Annals of the New York Academy of Sciences, 1331*(1), 157–173. https://doi.org/10.1111/nyas.12555

Asfaw, A., & Braun, J. v. (2004). Is consumption insured against illness? Evidence on vulnerability of households to health shocks in rural Ethiopia. *Economic Development and Cultural Change, 53*(1), 115–129.

Azadbakht, L., & Esmaillzadeh, A. (2011). Dietary diversity score is related to obesity and abdominal adiposity among Iranian female youth. *Public Health Nutrition, 14*(1), 62–69.

Babatunde, R. O., & Qaim, M. (2010). Impact of off-farm income on food security and nutrition in Nigeria. *Food Policy, 35*(4), 303–311. https://doi.org/10.1016/j.foodpol.2010.01.006

Baez, J. E., & Santos, I. V. (2007). Children's vulnerability to weather shocks: A natural disaster as a natural experiment. Syracuse University, Mimeo.

Barrett, H. R., Browne, A. W., Hyder, A. A., Maman, S., Nyoni, J. E., Khasiani, S. A., ... Sohani, S. (2005). The pervasive triad of food security, gender inequity and women's health: Exploratory research from sub-Saharan Africa. *Community Development Journal, 29*(3), 203–214.

Behrman, J. R., & Deolalikar, A. B. (1990). The intrahousehold demand for nutrients in rural South India individual estimates, fixed effects, and permanent income. *The Journal of Human Resources, 25*(4), 665–696.

Behrman, J. R., & Deolalikar, A. B. (1993). The intrahousehold distribution of market labour supply in rural South India. *Oxford Bulletin of Economics and Statistics, 55*(4), 409–421.

Bellemare, M. F. (2015). Rising food prices, food price volatility, and social unrest. *American Journal of Agricultural Economics, 97*(1), 1–21. https://doi. org/10.1093/ajae/aau038

Benjamin, D., Reardon, T., Stamoulis, K. G., & Winters, P. (2002). *Promoting farm/non-farm linkages for rural development—Case studies from Africa & Latin America*. Rome: FAO.

Bennett, L. (1988). The role of women in income production and intra-household allocation of resources as a determinant of child nutrition and health. *Food and Nutrition Bulletin, 10*(3), 16–26.

Berti, P. R., Krasevec, J., & FitzGerald, S. (2004). A review of the effectiveness of agriculture interventions in improving nutrition outcomes. *Public Health Nutrition, 7*(5), 599–609. https://doi.org/10.1079/PHN2003595

Binswanger-Mkhize, H. P. (2012). India 1960–2010: Structural change, the rural non-farm sector, and the prospects for agriculture. In *Center on Food Security and the Environment Stanford Symposium Series on Global Food Policy and Food Security in the 21st Century, Stanford University*. Citeseer.

Binswanger-Mkhize, H. P. (2013). The stunted structural transformation of the Indian economy: Agriculture, manufacturing and the rural non-farm sector. *Economic and Political Weekly, 48*, 5–13. Retrieved from https://www.epw. in/journal/2013/26-27/review-rural-affairs-review-issues/stuntedstructural-transformation-indian

Biran, A., Rabie, T., Schmidt, W., Juvekar, S., Hirve, S., & Curtis, V. (2008). Comparing the performance of indicators of hand-washing practices in rural Indian households. *Tropical Medicine & International Health, 13*(2), 278–285.

Black, R. E., Victora, C. G., Walker, S. P., Bhutta, Z. A., Christian, P., de Onis, M., ... Uauy, R. (2013). Maternal and child undernutrition and overweight in low-income and middle-income countries. *The Lancet, 382*(9890), 427–451. https://doi.org/10.1016/S0140-6736(13)60937-X

Bobonis, G. J., Miguel, E., & Sharma, C. P. (2004). *Iron deficiency anemia and school participation*. Poverty Action Lab Paper (No. 7), pp. 1118–1120.

Boselie, D., Henson, S., & Weatherspoon, D. (2003). Supermarket procurement practices in developing countries: Redefining the roles of the public and private sectors. *American Journal of Agricultural Economics, 85*(5), 1155–1161.

Brabin, B. J., Hakimi, M., & Pelletier, D. (2001). An analysis of anemia and pregnancy-related maternal mortality. *The Journal of Nutrition, 131*(2), 604S–615S.

Busert, L. K., Neuman, M., Rehfuess, E. A., Dulal, S., Harthan, J., Chaube, S. S., … Manandhar, D. S. (2016). Dietary diversity is positively associated with deviation from expected height in rural Nepal—3. *The Journal of Nutrition, 146*(7), 1387–1393.

Case, A., & Ardington, C. (2006). The impact of parental death on school outcomes: Longitudinal evidence from South Africa. *Demography, 43*(3), 401–420.

Cawley, J. (2004). The impact of obesity on wages. *The Journal of Human Resources, 39*(2), 451. https://doi.org/10.2307/3559022

Cawley, J. (2010). The economics of childhood obesity. *Health Affairs, 29*(3), 364–371. https://doi.org/10.1377/hlthaff.2009.0721

Cawley, J. (2015). An economy of scales: A selective review of obesity's economic causes, consequences, and solutions. *Journal of Health Economics, 43*, 244–268. https://doi.org/10.1016/j.jhealeco.2015.03.001

Chen, Y., & Zhou, L.-A. (2007). The long-term health and economic consequences of the 1959–1961 famine in China. *Journal of Health Economics, 26*(4), 659–681.

Clasen, T., Boisson, S., Routray, P., Torondel, B., Bell, M., Cumming, O., … Schmidt, W. P. (2014). Effectiveness of a rural sanitation programme on diarrhoea, soil-transmitted helminth infection, and child malnutrition in Odisha, India: A cluster-randomised trial. *The Lancet Global Health, 2*(11), e645–e653. https://doi.org/10.1016/S2214-109X(14)70307-9

Coovadia, H. M., Rollins, N. C., Bland, R. M., Little, K., Coutsoudis, A., Bennish, M. L., & Newell, M.-L. (2007). Mother-to-child transmission of HIV-1 infection during exclusive breastfeeding in the first 6 months of life: An intervention cohort study. *The Lancet, 369*(9567), 1107–1116.

Currie, J., & Moretti, E. (2003). Mother's education and the intergenerational transmission of human capital: Evidence from college openings. *The Quarterly Journal of Economics, 118*(4), 1495–1532.

D'Souza, A., & Jolliffe, D. (2013). Conflict, food price shocks, and food insecurity: The experience of Afghan households. *Food Policy, 42*, 32–47. https://doi.org/10.1016/j.foodpol.2013.06.007

De Brauw, A. (2011). Migration and child development during the food price crisis in El Salvador. *Food Policy, 36*(1), 28–40. https://doi.org/10.1016/j.foodpol.2010.11.002

Deaton, A. (1987). Estimation of own- and cross-price elasticities from household survey data. *Journal of Econometrics, 36*(1–2), 7–30.

del Ninno, C., & Lundberg, M. (2005). Treading water. The long-term impact of the 1998 flood on nutrition in Bangladesh. *Economics and Human Biology, 3*(1), 67–96. https://doi.org/10.1016/j.ehb.2004.12.002

Deolalikar, A. B. (1988). Nutrition and labor productivity in agriculture: Estimates for rural South India. *The Review of Economics and Statistics, 70*(3), 406–413.

Dinsa, G. D., Goryakin, Y., Fumagalli, E., & Suhrcke, M. (2012). Obesity and socioeconomic status in developing countries: A systematic review. *Obesity Reviews, 13*(11), 1067–1079. https://doi.org/10.1111/j.1467-789X.2012. 01017.x

Dubowitz, T., Levinson, D., Peterman, J. N., Verma, G., Jacob, S., & Schultink, W. (2007). Intensifying efforts to reduce child malnutrition in India: An evaluation of the Dular program in Jharkhand, India. *Food and Nutrition Bulletin, 28*(3), 266–273.

Ferreira, F. H. G., & Schady, N. (2009). Aggregate economic shocks, child schooling, and child health. *The World Bank Research Observer, 24*(2), 147–181. https://doi.org/10.1093/wbro/lkp006

Gaiha, R., Jha, R., & Kulkarni, V. S. (2013). How pervasive is eating out in India? *Journal of Asian and African Studies, 48*(3), 370–386. https://doi. org/10.1177/0021909612472040

Glick, P., & Sahn, D. E. (1998). Maternal labour supply and child nutrition in West Africa. *Oxford Bulletin of Economics and Statistics, 60*(3), 325–355.

Gørgens, T. (2002). Selection and stunting effects of famine: A case study of the Great Chinese Famine.

Gørgens, T., Meng, X., & Vaithianathan, R. (2012). Stunting and selection effects of famine: A case study of the Great Chinese Famine. *Journal of Development Economics, 97*(1), 99–111. https://doi.org/10.1016/j.jdeveco.2010.12.005

Griffiths, P. L., & Bentley, M. E. (2001). The nutrition transition is underway in India. *The Journal of Nutrition, 131*(10), 2692–2700. http://doi. org/0022-3166/01

Gulati, S., Misra, A., Colles, S. L., Kondal, D., Gupta, N., Goel, K., ... Bhardwaj, S. (2013). Dietary intakes and familial correlates of overweight/obesity: A four-cities study in India. *Annals of Nutrition and Metabolism, 62*(4), 279–290. https://doi.org/10.1159/000346554

Gupta, V., Downs, S. M., Ghosh-Jerath, S., Lock, K., & Singh, A. (2016). Unhealthy fat in street and snack foods in low-socioeconomic settings in India: A case study of the food environments of rural villages and an urban slum. *Journal of Nutrition Education and Behavior, 48*(4), 269–279.e1. https://doi. org/10.1016/j.jneb.2015.11.006

Gutierrez, F. H. (2013). *Long-term consequences of early life health shocks: Evidence from the 1980s Peruvian crisis.*

Hammer, J., & Spears, D. (2016). Village sanitation and child health: Effects and external validity in a randomized field experiment in rural India. *Journal of Health Economics, 48*, 135–148. https://doi.org/10.1016/j.jhealeco.2016. 03.003

Headey, D. D. (2013). Developmental drivers of nutritional change: A cross-country analysis. *World Development, 42*(1), 76–88. https://doi.org/10.1016/j.worlddev.2012.07.002

Hoddinott, J. (2006). Shocks and their consequences across and within households in Rural Zimbabwe. *Journal of Development Studies, 42*(2), 201–321.

Hoddinott, J., & Kinsey, B. (2001). Child growth in the time of drought. *Oxford Bulletin of Economics and Statistics, 63*(4), 409–436. https://doi.org/10.1111/1468-0084.t01-1-00227

Hoddinott, J., Maluccio, J. A., Behrman, J. R., Flores, R., & Martorell, R. (2008). Effect of a nutrition intervention during early childhood on economic productivity in Guatemalan adults. *The Lancet, 371*(9610), 411–416. https://doi.org/10.1016/S0140-6736(08)60205-6

Hoddinott, J., & Yohannes, Y. (2002). *Dietary diversity as a food security indicator*. Discussion Paper (No. 136), International Food Policy Research Institute (IFPRI), Food Consumption and Nutrition Division, Washington, DC.

Horton, S., & Ross, J. (2003). The economics of iron deficiency. *Food Policy, 28*(1), 51–75.

Imai, K. S., Annim, S. K., Kulkarni, V. S., & Gaiha, R. (2014). Women's empowerment and prevalence of stunted and underweight children in rural India. *World Development, 62*, 88–105.

Imai, K. S., Gaiha, R., & Thapa, G. (2015). Does non-farm sector employment reduce rural poverty and vulnerability? Evidence from Vietnam and India. *Journal of Asian Economics, 36*, 47–61. https://doi.org/10.1016/j.asieco.2015.01.001

Ivanic, M., & Martin, W. (2008). Implications of higher global food prices for poverty in low-income countries. *Agricultural Economics, 39*, 405–416. https://doi.org/10.1111/j.1574-0862.2008.00347.x

Jayachandran, S., & Pande, R. (2017). Why are Indian children so short? The role of birth order and son preference. *American Economic Review, 107*(9), 2600–2629.

Jensen, R. (2000). Agricultural volatility and investments in children. *American Economic Review, 90*(2), 399–404. https://doi.org/10.1257/aer.90.2.399

Jensen, R. T., & Miller, N. H. (2008). The impact of food price increases on caloric intake in China. *Agricultural Economics, 39*(1), 465–476. https://doi.org/10.1111/j.1574-0862.2008.00352.x

Jha, R., Gaiha, R., & Sharma, A. (2009). Calorie and micronutrient deprivation and poverty nutrition traps in rural India. *World Development, 37*(5), 982–991. https://doi.org/10.1016/j.worlddev.2008.09.008

Johnson, C., & Rogers, B. L. (1993). Children's nutritional female-headed households in the Dominican Republic. *Social Science & Medicine, 37*(11), 1293–1301.

Jones, A. D., Hayter, A. K. M., Baker, C. P., Prabhakaran, P., Gupta, V., Kulkarni, B., … Kumar, P. U. (2016). The co-occurrence of anemia and cardiometabolic disease risk demonstrates sex-specific sociodemographic patterning in an urbanizing rural region of southern India. *European Journal of Clinical Nutrition,* *70*(3), 364–372.

Jones, A. D., Shrinivas, A., & Bezner-Kerr, R. (2014). Farm production diversity is associated with greater household dietary diversity in Malawi: Findings from nationally representative data. *Food Policy, 46,* 1–12.

Kadiyala, S., Harris, J., Headey, D., Yosef, S., & Gillespie, S. (2014). Agriculture and nutrition in India: Mapping evidence to pathways. *Annals of the New York Academy of Sciences, 1331*(1), 43–56. https://doi.org/10.1111/nyas.12477

Kapur, D., Sharma, S., & Agarwal, K. N. (2003). Effectiveness of nutrition education, iron supplementation or both on iron status in children. *Indian Pediatrics, 40*(12), 1131–1144.

Kaushal, N., & Muchomba, F. M. (2015). How consumer price subsidies affect nutrition. *World Development, 74,* 25–42. https://doi.org/10.1016/j.worlddev.2015.04.006

Kennedy, G., Ballard, T., & Dop, M. C. (2011). *Guidelines for measuring household and individual dietary diversity.* FAO.

Kes, A., & Swaminathan, H. (2006). Gender and time poverty in sub-Saharan Africa. In *Gender, time use, and poverty in Sub-Saharan Africa* (pp. 13–38). World Bank.

Kishore, A., & Chakrabarti, S. (2015). Is more inclusive more effective? The 'New Style' public distribution system in India. *Food Policy, 55,* 117–130. https://doi.org/10.1016/j.foodpol.2015.06.006

Kjellstrom, T., Holmer, I., & Lemke, B. (2009). Workplace heat stress, health and productivity—An increasing challenge for low and middle-income countries during climate change. *Global Health Action, 2*(1), 2047.

Koppmair, S., Kassie, M., & Qaim, M. (2017). Farm production, market access and dietary diversity in Malawi. *Public Health Nutrition, 20*(2), 325–335.

Krishna, A. (2011). *One illness away: Why people become poor and how they escape poverty.* Oxford University Press.

Kumar, D., Goel, N. K., Mittal, P. C., & Misra, P. (2006). Influence of infant-feeding practices on nutritional status of under-five children. *The Indian Journal of Pediatrics, 73*(5), 417–421. https://doi.org/10.1007/BF02758565

Kumar, S., & Berkman, L. F. (2015). Association of inadequately iodized salt use with underweight among young children in India. *Asia Pacific Journal of Public Health, 27*(2), 185–194.

Lee, L., Rosenzweig, M. R., & Pitt, M. M. (1997). The effects of improved nutrition, sanitation, and water quality on child health in high-mortality populations. *Journal of Econometrics, 77*(1), 209–235. https://doi.org/10.1016/S0304-4076(96)01813-1

Leslie, J. (1988). Women's work and child nutrition in the Third World. *World Development, 16*(11), 1341–1362.

Lim, S. S., Fullman, N., Stokes, A., Ravishankar, N., Masiye, F., Murray, C. J. L., & Gakidou, E. (2011). Net benefits: A multicountry analysis of observational data examining associations between insecticide-treated mosquito nets and health outcomes. *PLoS Medicine, 8*(9), e1001091. https://doi.org/10.1371/journal.pmed.1001091

Lumey, L. H., Stein, A. D., Kahn, H. S., van der Pal-de Bruin, K. M., Blauw, G. J., Zybert, P. A., & Susser, E. S. (2007). Cohort profile: The Dutch Hunger Winter families study. *International Journal of Epidemiology, 36*(6), 1196–1204. https://doi.org/10.1093/ije/dym126

Maccini, S., & Yang, D. (2009). Under the weather: Health, schooling, and economic consequences of early-life rainfall. *American Economic Review, 99*(3), 1006–1026. https://doi.org/10.1257/aer.99.3.1006

Majra, J. P., & Gur, A. (2009). Climate change and health: Why should India be concerned? *Indian Journal of Occupational and Environmental Medicine, 13*(1), 11.

Maluccio, J. A. (2005). Coping with the coffee crisis in Central America: The role of the Nicaraguan Red de Protección Social. *FCND Discussion Papers, 188*(Feb.), 44.

Maluccio, J. A., Hoddinott, J., Behrman, J. R., Martorell, R., Quisumbing, A. R., & Stein, A. D. (2009). The impact of improving nutrition during early childhood on education among Guatemalan adults. *The Economic Journal, 119*(537), 734–763. https://doi.org/10.1111/j.1468-0297.2009.02220.x

Mangyo, E. (2008). The effect of water accessibility on child health in China. *Journal of Health Economics, 27*(5), 1343–1356.

Masset, E., Leroy, J. L., & Frongillo, E. A. (2007). Can interventions to promote animal production ameliorate undernutrition? *The Journal of Nutrition, 137*(10), 2311–2316.

Maxwell, D. (1999). The political economy of urban food security in Sub-Saharan Africa. *World Development, 27*(11), 1939–1953. https://doi.org/10.1016/S0305-750X(99)00101-1

Meenakshi, J. V. (2016). Trends and patterns in the triple burden of malnutrition in India. *Agricultural Economics, 47*(S1), 115–134. https://doi.org/10.1111/agec.12304

Mengistie, B., Berhane, Y., & Worku, A. (2013). Household water chlorination reduces incidence of diarrhea among under-five children in rural Ethiopia: A cluster randomized controlled trial. *PLoS One, 8*(10), e77887.

Menon, P., Bamezai, A., Subandoro, A., Ayoya, M. A., & Aguayo, V. (2015). Age-appropriate infant and young child feeding practices are associated with child nutrition in India: Insights from nationally representative data. *Maternal & Child Nutrition, 11*(1), 73–87.

Miguel, E., & Kremer, M. (2015). Worms: Identifying impacts on education and health in the presence of treatment externalities. *Econometrica, 72*(1), 159–217.

MoHFW. (2017). *India: Health of the nation's states.* MoHFW Report.

Murray, C. J. L., Vos, T., Lozano, R., Naghavi, M., Flaxman, A. D., Michaud, C., ... Lopez, A. D. (2012). Disability-adjusted life years (DALYs) for 291 diseases and injuries in 21 regions, 1990–2010: A systematic analysis for the Global Burden of Disease Study 2010. *The Lancet, 380*(9859), 2197–2223. https://doi.org/10.1016/S0140-6736(12)61689-4

Myers, S. S., Smith, M. R., Guth, S., Golden, C. D., Vaitla, B., Mueller, N. D., ... Huybers, P. (2017). Climate change and global food systems: Potential impacts on food security and undernutrition. *Annual Review of Public Health, 38*(1), 259–277. https://doi.org/10.1146/annurev-publhealth-031816-044356

Nichter, M. (2008). *Global health: Why cultural perceptions, social representations, and biopolitics matter.* University of Arizona Press.

Nicklas, T. A., Baranowski, T., Cullen, K. W., & Berenson, G. (2001). Eating patterns, dietary quality and obesity. *Journal of the American College of Nutrition, 20*(6), 599–608.

Oreopoulos, P., Page, M. E., & Stevens, A. H. (2006). The intergenerational effects of compulsory schooling. *Journal of Labor Economics, 24*(4), 729–760.

Owusu, V., Abdulai, A., & Abdul-Rahman, S. (2011). Non-farm work and food security among farm households in Northern Ghana. *Food Policy, 36*(2), 108–118. https://doi.org/10.1016/j.foodpol.2010.09.002

Parker, S., & Skoufias, E. (2000). *The impact of PROGRESA on work, leisure and time allocation.* Washington, DC: International Food Policy Research Institute.

Patil, S. R., Arnold, B. F., Salvatore, A. L., Briceno, B., Ganguly, S., Colford, J. M., Jr., & Gertler, P. J. (2014). The effect of India's total sanitation campaign on defecation behaviors and child health in rural Madhya Pradesh: A cluster randomized controlled trial. *PLoS Medicine, 11*(8), e1001709.

Patz, J. A., Campbell-Lendrum, D., Holloway, T., & Foley, J. A. (2005). Impact of regional climate change on human health. *Nature, 438*(7066), 310.

Pingali, P. (2006). Westernization of Asian diets and the transformation of food systems: Implications for research and policy. *Food Policy, 32*(3), 281–298. https://doi.org/10.1016/j.foodpol.2006.08.001

Pingali, P. (2007). Westernization of Asian diets and the transformation of food systems: Implications for research and policy. *Food Policy, 32*(3), 281–298. https://doi.org/10.1016/j.foodpol.2006.08.001

Pingali, P. (2012). Green revolution: Impacts, limits, and the path ahead. *Proceedings of the National Academy of Science, 109*(31), 12302–12308. https://doi.org/10.1073/pnas.0912953109

Pingali, P. (2015). Agricultural policy and nutrition outcomes—Getting beyond the preoccupation with staple grains. *Food Security, 7*(3), 583–591. https://doi.org/10.1007/s12571-015-0461-x

Pingali, P., & Sunder, N. (2017). Transitioning toward nutrition-sensitive food systems in developing countries. *Annual Review of Resource Economics, 9*(1), 439–459. https://doi.org/10.1146/annurev-resource-100516-053552

Pingali, P. L., & Ricketts, K. D. (2014). Mainstreaming nutrition metrics in household surveys—Toward a multidisciplinary convergence of data systems. *Annals of the New York Academy of Sciences, 1331*(1), 249–257. https://doi.org/10.1111/nyas.12597

Plessow, R., Arora, N. K., Brunner, B., Tzogiou, C., Eichler, K., Brügger, U., & Wieser, S. (2015). Social costs of iron deficiency anemia in 6–59-month-old children in India. *PLoS One, 10*(8). https://doi.org/10.1371/journal.pone.0136581

Popkin, B. M. (1997). The nutrition transition and its health implications in lower-income countries. *Public Health Nutrition, 1*(1), 5–21.

Popkin, B. M. (1999). Urbanization, lifestyle changes and the nutrition transition. *World Development, 27*(11), 1905–1916. https://doi.org/10.1016/S0305-750X(99)00094-7

Popkin, B. M. (2003). The nutrition transition in the developing world. *Development Policy Review, 21*(5–6), 581–597. https://doi.org/10.1111/j.1467-8659.2003.00225.x

Popkin, B. M., Horton, S., Kim, S., Mahal, A., & Shuigao, J. (2001). Trends in diet, nutritional status, and diet-related noncommunicable diseases in China and India: The economic costs of the nutrition transition. *Nutrition Reviews, 59*(12), 379–390.

Rah, J. H., Akhter, N., Semba, R. D., De Pee, S., Bloem, M. W., Campbell, A. A., … Kraemer, K. (2010). Low dietary diversity is a predictor of child stunting in rural Bangladesh. *European Journal of Clinical Nutrition, 64*(12), 1393.

Rah, J. H., Cronin, A. A., Badgaiyan, B., Aguayo, V. M., Coates, S., & Ahmed, S. (2015). Household sanitation and personal hygiene practices are associated with child stunting in rural India: A cross-sectional analysis of surveys. *BMJ Open, 5*(2), e005180.

Rahman, A. (2016). Universal food security program and nutritional intake: Evidence from the hunger prone KBK districts in Odisha. *Food Policy, 63*, 73–86. https://doi.org/10.1016/j.foodpol.2016.07.003

Rahman, A. (2017). *Food elasticity estimates for rural India: Preference for food variety and between group substitutions.*

Rasmussen, K. M. (2001). Is there a causal relationship between iron deficiency or iron-deficiency anemia and weight at birth, length of gestation and perinatal mortality? *The Journal of Nutrition, 131*(2), 590S–603S.

Reardon, T., & Minten, B. (2011). Surprised by supermarkets: Diffusion of modern food retail in India. *Journal of Agribusiness in Developing and Emerging Economies, 1*(2), 134–161. https://doi.org/10.1108/20440831111167155

Reardon, T., Timmer, C. P., & Minten, B. (2012). Supermarket revolution in Asia and emerging development strategies to include small farmers. *Proceedings of the National Academy of Sciences, 109*(31), 12332–12337. https://doi.org/10.1073/pnas.1003160108

Roseboom, T., de Rooij, S., & Painter, R. (2006). The Dutch famine and its long-term consequences for adult health. *Early Human Development, 82*(8), 485–491.

Roseboom, T. J., Van Der Meulen, J. H. P., Ravelli, A. C. J., Osmond, C., Barker, D. J. P., & Bleker, O. P. (2001). Effects of prenatal exposure to the Dutch famine on adult disease in later life: An overview. *Molecular and Cellular Endocrinology, 185*(1–2), 93–98.

Ruel, M. T. (2003). Operationalizing dietary diversity: A review of measurement issues and research priorities. *The Journal of Nutrition, 133*(11), 3911S–3926S.

Semba, R. D., de Pee, S., Sun, K., Campbell, A. A., Bloem, M. W., & Raju, V. K. (2010). Low intake of vitamin A-rich foods among children, aged 12–35 months, in India: Association with malnutrition, anemia, and missed child survival interventions. *Nutrition, 26*(10), 958–962.

Sengupta, A., Angeli, F., Syamala, T. S., Dagnelie, P. C., & Schayck, C. P. v. (2015). Overweight and obesity prevalence among Indian women by place of residence and socio-economic status: Contrasting patterns from "underweight states" and "overweight states" of India. *Social Science and Medicine, 138*, 161–169. https://doi.org/10.1016/j.socscimed.2015.06.004

Shetty, P., Victora, C. G., Adair, L., Fall, C., Hallal, P. C., Martorell, R., ... Group, M. and C. U. S. (2012). India's diabetes time bomb. *Nature, 485*(7398), S14.

Shrivastava, U., Misra, A., Mohan, V., Unnikrishnan, R., & Bachani, D. (2017). Obesity, diabetes and cardiovascular diseases in India: Public health challenges. *Current Diabetes Reviews, 13*(1), 65–80.

Shroff, M., Griffiths, P., Adair, L., Suchindran, C., & Bentley, M. (2009). Maternal autonomy is inversely related to child stunting in Andhra Pradesh, India. *Maternal & Child Nutrition, 5*(1), 64–74.

Shroff, M. R., Griffiths, P. L., Suchindran, C., Nagalla, B., Vazir, S., & Bentley, M. E. (2011). Does maternal autonomy influence feeding practices and infant growth in rural India? *Social Science & Medicine, 73*(3), 447–455.

Sibhatu, K. T., Krishna, V. V., & Qaim, M. (2015). Production diversity and dietary diversity in smallholder farm households. *Proceedings of the National Academy of Sciences, 112*(34), 10657–10662.

Singh, A., Park, A., & Dercon, S. (2013). School meals as a safety net: An evaluation of the midday meal scheme in India. *Economic Development and Cultural Change, 62*(2), 275–306.

Singh, P. (2015). Performance pay and information: Reducing child undernutrition in India. *Journal of Economic Behavior & Organization, 112*, 141–163.

Spears, D., Ghosh, A., & Cumming, O. (2013). Open defecation and childhood stunting in India: An ecological analysis of new data from 112 districts. *PLoS One, 8*(9), e73784. https://doi.org/10.1371/journal.pone.0073784

Stein, A. D., Wang, M., Digirolamo, A., Grajeda, R., Ramakrishnan, U., Ramirez-zea, M., ... Inter-, S. (2008). Nutritional supplementation in early childhood, schooling, and intellectual functioning in adulthood. *Archives of Pediatrics & Adolescent Medicine, 162*(7), 612–618.

Steyn, N. P., Nel, J. H., Nantel, G., Kennedy, G., & Labadarios, D. (2006). Food variety and dietary diversity scores in children: Are they good indicators of dietary adequacy? *Public Health Nutrition, 9*(5), 644–650.

Strauss, J., & Thomas, D. (1998). Health, nutrition, and economic development. *Journal of Economic Literature, 36*(2), 766–817.

Sturm, R., Ringel, J. S., & Andreyeva, T. (2004). Increasing obesity rates and disability trends. *Health Affairs, 23*(2), 199–205.

Subramanian, S., & Deaton, A. (1996). The demand of food and calories. *Journal of Political Economy, 104*(1), 133–162.

Swinburn, B. A., Sacks, G., Hall, K. D., McPherson, K., Finegood, D. T., Moodie, M. L., & Gortmaker, S. L. (2011). The global obesity pandemic: Shaped by global drivers and local environments. *The Lancet, 378*(9793), 804–814. https://doi.org/10.1016/S0140-6736(11)60813-1

Thakur, N., Chandra, J., Pemde, H., & Singh, V. (2014). Anemia in severe acute malnutrition. *Nutrition, 30*(4), 440–442.

Thior, I., Lockman, S., Smeaton, L. M., Shapiro, R. L., Wester, C., Heymann, S. J., … Kim, S. (2006). Breastfeeding plus infant zidovudine prophylaxis for 6 months vs formula feeding plus infant zidovudine for 1 month to reduce mother-to-child HIV transmission in Botswana: A randomized trial: The Mashi Study. *JAMA, 296*(7), 794–805.

Thomas, D., Strauss, J., & Henriques, M. (1991). How does mother's education affect child height? *The Journal of Human Resources, 26*(2), 183–211.

Townsend, R. M. (1994). Risk and insurance in village India. *Econometrica, 62*(3), 539–591.

Townsend, R. M. (1995). Consumption insurance: An evaluation of risk-bearing systems in low-income economies. *Journal of Economic Perspectives, 9*(3), 83–102. https://doi.org/10.1257/jep.9.3.83

Victora, C. G., Adair, L., Fall, C., Hallal, P. C., Martorell, R., Richter, L., … Group, M. and C. U. S. (2008). Maternal and child undernutrition: Consequences for adult health and human capital. *The Lancet, 371*(9609), 340–357.

Wang, Y. C., McPherson, K., Marsh, T., Gortmaker, S. L., & Brown, M. (2011). Health and economic burden of the projected obesity trends in the USA and the UK. *The Lancet, 378*(9793), 815–825. https://doi.org/10.1016/S0140-6736(11)60814-3

Watts, N., Adger, W. N., Agnolucci, P., Blackstock, J., Byass, P., Cai, W., … Cooper, A. (2015). Health and climate change: Policy responses to protect public health. *The Lancet, 386*(10006), 1861–1914.

CHAPTER 6

Reimagining Safety Net Programs

6.1 INTRODUCTION

Safety nets—food and non-food based—have been the cornerstone of India's emerging social security regime. While these safety programs have existed for a while, the last 15 years have seen the emergence of a welfare policy structure in India. Driven by the rights-based initiative, which recognized basic entitlements to work, food and education as a fundamental right of the citizen, safety net programs have been enshrined in the constitution. The five main programs which provide a semblance to the social security architecture in India—Public Distribution System (PDS), Integrated Child Development Scheme (ICDS), Mid-Day Meal Scheme (MDMS), Mahatma Gandhi National Rural Employment Guarantee Scheme (MGNREGS) and pensions for widows and elderly—have played a crucial role in the reduction of poverty, increasing incomes, and reducing malnutrition.[1] However, these schemes have also been heavily criticized for their design, targeting errors and corruption which leads to very high costs of operations. Other alternatives have been proposed which incorporate the benefits of technological advancements in monitoring and better targeting. Yet, the design of these safety net programs have been a continuing debate in policy circles.

---

[1] In the previous chapter, we have discussed the potential role of safety nets in reducing the triple burden of malnutrition.

© The Author(s) 2019   135
P. Pingali et al., *Transforming Food Systems for a Rising India*,
Palgrave Studies in Agricultural Economics and Food Policy,
https://doi.org/10.1007/978-3-030-14409-8_6

The policy debate in India on the safety nets is grappling with the following questions. First, should the schemes be targeted towards poor or be universally applicable? Second, should the social security benefits be in the forms of in-kind transfers or the beneficiaries be handed cash of an equivalent amount to choose their consumption bundle? Third, should these social security schemes be replaced with an unconditional Universal Basic Income (UBI)? While payments for pensions or public works program are intrinsically cash based, the cash versus kind argument is most relevant for the food assistance programs like PDS and ICDS. Reading the debate closely, one gleans that much of this debate is more ideological than evidence-based. The idea of improving nutritional outcomes is only implied in these deliberations without explicit consideration to the role of safety net programs in tackling the multiple emerging nutritional challenges as seen in the previous chapter. Part of this confusion stems from the fact that the benefits and costs of safety net programs are difficult to evaluate and compare since they do not make a clear distinction between its role as income support and nutritional assistance.

Given India's regional divergent experience of structural transformation, in this chapter, we explore the ability of safety nets to create a sufficient floor for those who are disadvantaged. The challenge of a nutrition-sensitive food system lies in its ability to respond to the current nature of economic transformation and food demand. Given the pressures of urbanization, dietary transition, demographic changes, higher rural-urban mobility, establishment of newer food value chains, changing consumer preferences, ecological degradation and the processes of globalization, these changes create new challenges for food safety nets regarding delivering food safely to individuals who are disadvantaged. The rise in urban population implies greater share of net food consumers in the future who would rely on traditional as well as commercial food value chains for accessing food. This would increase competition for food safety nets which have played a role in the procurement and distribution of food. Less physically demanding jobs and better sanitation environment further reduces the number of calories needed and increases demand for diverse nutrients. Competition for land and dwindling natural resources like water influences the choice of the crop among farmers. Development of markets and connection to modern value chains provide farmers with greater avenues for growing commercial crops which further influences the food system diversity. Given these expected changes in the future, we ask the following question: how should safety nets be designed to ensure better nutrition outcomes? What kind of safety net programs would help to improve diets and nutritional outcomes?

To answer this question, we first examine the range of existing safety nets in India and their implications for the food system. We describe the *why*, *how* and *what* of the safety nets regarding their conception, their subsequent achievements and failures, and their potential future. We deliberate upon the usefulness of these programs with a keen eye on the changing nature of food demand and discuss ways to improve these programs. We argue that the policy makers should think hard on whether the same objectives which these programs intend to achieve today would stay relevant in the future too. Here, we also align the debates around poverty, consumption demand, supply considerations and how all these factors square up with the relevance of these safety nets.

6.2   The Role of Safety Nets in the Food Systems

The idea of social safety nets became popular in the global policy dialogues during the 1980s and 1990s as a part of the humanitarian and developmental debates (Croppenstedt, Knowles, & Lowder, 2017). The World Development Report 1990 discussed the inclusion of safety nets as income support during periods of stress and calamities, as one of the planks of the "New Poverty Agenda". Gradually, ideas around safety nets began to use it as a lever for addressing economic shock and reduction in chronic poverty. Without a clear definition around the kind of safety nets to be pursued, it was broadly understood to be a set of interventions aimed at reducing risks and vulnerability—social and economic—to alleviate extreme poverty and deprivation. Safety nets became an essential part of the poverty eradication agenda in developing countries given the imperfections of credit and insurance market which ensures the citizens against any unanticipated income shocks. Gradually, it expanded to address specific concerns of hunger and nutrition. Greater scholarship on the disadvantages faced by women, children and the elderly further led to calls for specifically designed safety nets which ensures the well-being and agency of the most marginalized.

There are multiple other pathways through which safety nets contribute to the food system. First, through the income pathway, transfers—in-kind or direct—add to household income which enables food diversification, investment in human capital and overall productivity. Greater income support potentially leads to higher investment in education and health of children enabling a better quality of human capital which has implications for future productivity and earning capacity. For the cultivating households, greater resources help overcome liquidity and credit constraints which influences greater investment in agriculture and livestock. It also frees up resources and creates avenues to move out of agriculture. Second, food assistance or income transfer programs ensure inter-temporal consumption smoothing and food access as livelihood options in developing countries often follow a cyclic process. Third, safety nets targeted at women or children have implications for intra-household food access. Supplementary food and nutritional assistance programs at various stages of the life cycle lead to greater reduction in enhancing human capital. In the long run, such interventions lower the probability of intergenerational poverty. Similarly, income transfers focused at women in the household enhances their economic status and bargaining power in the economy. Fourth, safety nets promote local economic growth especially when it involves agriculture. Greater productivity improves production capacity and stimulates demand for locally grown agricultural products.

As food systems evolve along the stages of economic development, so does the need, design and role of safety nets. Fiscal ability to spend on safety nets by the government also changes with economic development. Given the structural transformation of the Indian economy, this chapter deliberates upon how safety nets should be envisaged in the future anticipating economic growth, demographic transitions and technological advancement.

6.3   Safety Net Programs in India

India has a long history of safety net programs. These programs, however, were largely driven by policy concern such as weather shocks, price risk, social control and so on. There has not been a concerted effort at creating a social security architecture aimed at addressing the issues of poverty and vulnerability. For example, PDS was introduced during the 1940s to shield urban consumers against food shortages. A public works program was introduced in the state of Maharashtra during the early 1970s after prolonged droughts and in 1977. The Maharashtra government introduced the Employment Guarantee Act employing nearly half a million workers. ICDS, too, was initiated during the 1970s, though on a pilot basis. It was only in the last two decades that a holistic safety net design began to emerge.

Table 6.1   Description of major safety net programs in India

	Targeted population	Nature of the program	Objectives
PDS	Poor	In-kind food transfers	Hunger reduction
ICDS	Children and mothers	Supplemental food assistance	Nutritional assistance
MDMS	School going children	Hot cooked meals	Classroom hunger mitigation
MGNREGS	Universal rural population	Public works program	Rural livelihoods
Pensions	Widows and elderly	Income transfer	Poverty among elderly
RSBY	Poor	Health insurance	Safeguard against health shocks induced poverty

Recent reforms in the safety net programs coincided with the spectacular pace of economic growth and the consequent distributional concerns of growth such as lack of its "inclusiveness". Safety net expansions have provided economic security to a large section of the poorer population. The bulk of the social security expenditures comprise five major programs: PDS, ICDS, MDMS, MGNREGS and pension schemes (Drèze & Khera, 2017). A brief description of these programs is provided in Table 6.1 in terms of its objectives, targeted population and the nature of transfer. According to a ballpark estimate by Narayanan and Gerber (2017), the central government of India spent around 1.7% of the gross domestic product (GDP) on the combined operations on PDS, ICDS, MDMS and MGNREGA in 2013–14.[2] In the last ten years, the budget outlay on these programs has increased substantially. Expenditure on ICDS has almost quadrupled from Rs. 40 billion in 2006–07 to almost Rs. 160 billion in 2016–17 (Fig. 6.1). Food subsidy and MGNREGS comprise the largest share of expenditure and have seen the greatest increase too.[3] Despite huge outlays, these programs have been heavily criticized for being prone to corruption, ineffective in reaching

[2] Arriving at an exact estimate for these schemes is non-trivial because the outlays and expenditures on food assistance programs in government statistics also include the expenses on food procurement and stocking operations. Further, state governments may spend over and above the central government's expenditures, making the calculations imprecise.

[3] It must be noted that food subsidy also includes the food procurement operations. It is very difficult to get data which differentiates PDS from overall food subsidy.

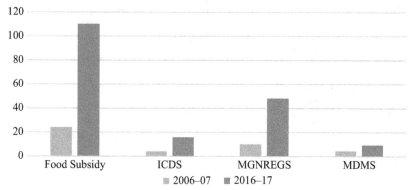

Source: Government Budget Documents

Fig. 6.1 Budget expenditures on major safety nets (in Rs. '00 billion)

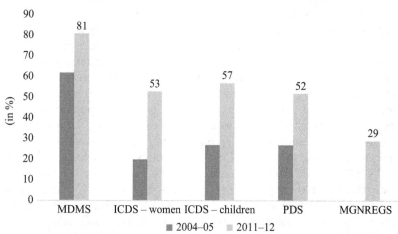

Source: All figures from MGNREGS from Drèze and Khera (2017) based upon the Indian Human Development Surveys (IHDS I and II).
MGNREGS figures are only for rural households.

Fig. 6.2 Coverage and expansion of major social safety net programs

the poor and therefore a huge fiscal drain. The last decade, however, has seen a substantial improvement in the coverage and utilization of these programs. Using longitudinal data between 2004–05 and 2011–12, Drèze and Khera (2017) highlight the extent of this expansion (Fig. 6.2). MDMS is the most popular scheme and its access among school going children improved from 62% in 2004–05 to 81% in 2011–12. Substantial improvement in the usage of ICDS and PDS are also evident.

Safety nets always wrestle with the problem of identifying the best design where the benefits are disproportionately higher to the non-poor households. At the same time, there have to be sufficient incentives for the beneficiaries to work. These challenges are further compounded among the poor and developing countries where the proportion of people requiring support remains very high compared to the fiscal resources at their disposal. Usefulness or efficacy of the social safety net has therefore been a very active policy debate in India. While it has been unanimously acknowledged that a large share of the Indian population is poor and needs some sort of support against anticipated and unanticipated economic shocks, the debate has mostly veered around what is the most efficient and economical way to build a safety net architecture. Arguments have put across, therefore, to promote growth as a poverty reduction and channel resources into more productive investments. Some have argued that social assistance should rely more on narrow targeting. There have been calls for moving towards a cash-based transfer replacing the in-kind food assistance through PDS. Of late, there has been a debate around the usefulness of a UBI to all households.

6.4   FOOD-BASED SAFETY NET PROGRAMS

With a life-cycle approach to food security, food assistance at various stages of life is provided through PDS, MDMS and ICDS. Under the umbrella of the National Food Security Act (NFSA), these programs aim at providing nutrition to nutritional assistance for pregnant and lactating mothers, infants, school going children and senior citizens. NFSA, as it was passed in the Indian parliament in 2013 states that its objective is to "… provide for food and nutritional security in human life cycle approach, by ensuring access to adequate quantity of quality food at affordable prices to people to live a life with dignity and for matters connected therewith or incidental thereto". NFSA further aims to expand the coverage of PDS to about two-thirds of India's population—75% and 50% of the rural and urban population respectively—under PDS. Eligible monthly entitlements include 5 kg of grains per person at a highly subsidized prices of Rs. 3/2/1 per kg for rice/wheat/coarse grains. The identified poorest of the poor households, however, will continue to receive 35 kg of food grains per month. Other nutritional assistance include cooked meals to mothers during pregnancy and six months after childbirth in addition to maternity benefit of not less than Rs. 6,000 (100 USD). For children up to 14 years of age, NFSA entitles nutritious meals. In cases where entitled food grains or meals are unable to be provided, the beneficiaries are entitled to a food security allowance. We will discuss PDS, ICDS and MDMS here in detail and their relevance for food and nutritional security.

PDS was introduced as a food security mechanism during the World War period under colonial rule. The original idea being that the rural areas have greater access to food while urban residents need food provisions during times of scarcity. The PDS expanded its rural presence only in the 1970s as the Green Revolution led to food surpluses. In a bid to incentivize farmers to produce more, the government announced a minimum support price (MSP). Farmers were free to sell to the government at the MSP which remained lower than the market prices and provided a floor price. To ensure an outlet for this huge procurement operation, the government opened more rural Fair Price Shops (FPS) which led to the expansion of PDS. At the same time, inefficiencies like leakages and corruption were rampant in this procurement-stocking-distribution system, given its huge size. Initially designed as a universal scheme, PDS was curtailed to a targeted program in 1997 as India adopted a structural adjustment program to bring down the subsidies. Various state governments, in the meanwhile, continued to have a non-targeted PDS in pursuance of a more populist political regime. PDS has been criticized as being poorly designed, leaky, beset with targeting errors, corruption-prone and a drain on the fiscal capacity of the government. The most essential challenge in a targeted program is how to identify beneficiaries. India has failed abysmally when it comes to the targeting of its welfare programs for the poor (Jha & Ramaswami, 2010; Kotwal & Ramaswami, 2014). For various schemes, the government of India classifies households as poor and non-poor. Recent estimates provided in the Economic Survey of India 2017–18 indicate that targeting errors continue to persist (Government of India, 2018). Only 28% in the bottom 40% of the household access PDS, while 36% of the benefits accrue to the non-poor (Table 6.2).

Identification of poor is beset with conceptual and administrative challenges. The criteria for identifying poor household are often vague, and the information on those indicators are hard to collect (Hirway, 2003). At the lowest level of administration, such as villages and urban local bodies, political favoritism often leads to poor being left out of the schemes meant for them (Panda, 2015). In a targeted program like PDS, identification of

Table 6.2 Targeting of PDS and MGNREGS (in %)	PDS	MGNREGA
Non-beneficiaries	40	65
Among the beneficiaries		
Leakages	36	20
Benefits to non-poor	36	43
Benefits to the bottom 40%	28	37

Source: Economic Survey 2017–18, p. 200, Fig. A5

beneficiaries has been the major issue. Many states—for example, Tamil Nadu, Himachal Pradesh, Chhattisgarh and parts of Odisha—have therefore made PDS entitlements universal, thereby obviating the need for targeting. These states have performed better in take-up rates and had lower leakages after universalization (Drèze, Himanshu, Khera, & Sen, 2015). The recent expansion of the PDS has come about through an expansion of the number of beneficiaries through a more "inclusive approach" as the exclusion of the non-poor often gets less political support and suffers the risk of being sabotaged by the politically powerful non-poor groups. Despite the success of universal PDS in many states, most of the states continue having a targeted PDS. The share of targeted beneficiaries, however, is expected to expand across most of the poorer regions under the NFSA.

ICDS began as an experiment aimed at nutritional assistance to pregnant and lactating mothers and children under six years of age in 1975. In those days, child mortality in India was very high, while health and community-based systems were hardly present. Mid-term appraisal of the 11th 5-year plan (2007–12) pointed to serious underperformance of the ICDS and its ineffectiveness in reducing undernutrition among children. ICDS was criticized for its poor design and implementation. During the last decade, however, ICDS has remarkably improved its performance driven by advocacy efforts by civil society coalitions calling for "nutrition to be a priority on the national agenda" (Balarajan & Reich, 2016). Advocacy by civil society groups along with active interventions by the Supreme Court of India brought about significant changes in the ICDS design and implementation. Coverage of ICDS was expanded, provisions were made universal from a targeted one, and the provision of hot cooked meals was introduced. Concerns about ICDS however still exist which include inadequate infrastructure, issues of unskilled and underpaid staff and political will for its implementation (N. Rao & Kaul, 2018).

Political will and therefore ICDS performance again vary by states. Relatively limited focus only on children between 0 and 3 years of age has also been questioned (Drèze & Khera, 2017).

While ICDS was designed to address the issue of early childhood development and maternal nutrition supplementation, the MDMS is a school feeding program which aimed at increasing enrolment and reducing "classroom hunger" among primary school students. MDMS is the biggest school lunch program in the world (Khera, 2006). It was introduced in 1995 as the "National Programme for Nutritional Support for Primary Education". MDMS wasn't much of a success until 2001 when its coverage was expanded to all the states of India. In the initial phase, not all schools had the right infrastructure in place to provide "cooked meals", and "dry ration" was mostly distributed. Since 2001, active intervention by the Supreme Court of India and local civil society organizations have led to mandatory provisions of cooked meals to all primary school children. MDMS now provides meals consisting of 300 calories and 8–12 grams of protein daily to all the children attending primary schools.

MDMS, as it was conceived, did manage to increase school enrolment rates; however its impact on child nutrition has been a concern as food supplementation and its quality was low. Initially, MDMS suffered from the availability of infrastructure and financial resources. With improvements in those aspects, concerns now exist around the quality of nutrition supplementations. Nutrient content of the school meals is low in comparison to the daily requirements for protein, fat, iron and other micronutrients. Often these schemes become a tool for promoting a sectarian agenda, such as the prohibition of eggs from the meals. Some states have banned eggs under MDMS, promoting vegetarianism.[4] By depriving essential nutrients at early stages of life, politicians take to propagating cultural and religious dogmatism. The other issues which require immediate attention to make MDMS more effective is adequate infrastructure at schools, sufficient and trained staff, better nutrient composition of the food and adequate accountability mechanisms in place (Khera, 2013). There are also glaring food safety concerns as MDMS has often been in the news related to issues of hygiene with some cases leading to deaths.[5]

[4] http://www.huffingtonpost.in/2015/06/02/how-politics-and-religious-dogma-deny-eggs-to-indias-severely-m/

[5] http://www.bbc.com/news/world-asia-india-23342003

6.4.1   Impact of Food-based Safety Net Programs on Nutrition

Evidence of the effects of these food-based safety nets on nutrition in India remains unclear (Pingali & Rao, 2016). It is limited by lack of availability of longitudinal data, choice of metrics for evaluating their impact, the appropriate period for analysis and the different geographical contexts. As a measure of nutrition, studies have mostly focused on the intermediated indicators of nutrition such as food intake and dietary diversity. The impact of food safety nets could be divided into two periods—before and after 2005 when these programs were revived by the government. Studies which used data before 2005 find no effect of PDS on nutrition (Kaushal & Muchomba, 2015; Kochar, 2005; Tarozzi, 2005). Recent empirical studies, however, do provide evidence of a positive effect of PDS, on nutrient intake as well as dietary diversity (Kishore & Chakrabarti, 2015; Krishnamurthy, Pathania, & Tandon, 2017; Rahman, 2016). Similarly, reforms in the functioning of ICDS have led to a significant impact in reducing malnutrition. Jain (2015) finds that children receiving supplementary meals are taller compared to others—the effect being significantly higher for the girl child. Even in eastern states of India, where governance and performance of safety nets are reportedly poor (*ibid*), Mittal and Meenakshi (2015) find a decline in the prevalence of undernutrition among children who benefited from ICDS. MDMS, too, has had a positive impact on nutrition, especially during times of economic distress. Access to MDMS increases daily intake of essential macronutrients—calories and protein—among school children (Afridi, 2010). In another study, Singh, Park, and Dercon (2013) underscore the role of MDMS as a safety net for children who faced droughts in early years of life. They find that despite economic shocks, there was an improvement in child anthropometric measures for children with access to MDMS.

6.4.2   Calorie-based Food Assistance

One of the reasons for the failings of food-based safety net programs in India has been its excessive focus on calorie-based supplementation. By focusing solely on the availability and access to calories, extant food policy has been proven to be a detriment to the nutritional challenge. The rising prevalence of obesity and the persistence of micronutrient deficiencies now comprise a significant share of the "triple burden of malnutrition" (Meenakshi, 2016). Calorie assistance programs, unfortunately, are not designed to deal with these emerging public health challenges. With surplus production and food assistance programs, we have adequate mechanisms in place to ensure that households have sufficient food to eat; however, ensuring food security may not translate into better nutrition. India's food policy has missed this nuanced aspect of nutrition. From the perspective of human rights and ethics, the recognition of the right to food and enactment of NFSA has its heart at the right place, but it fails to consider the imperatives of a dynamic food system, which reflects changing consumption preferences and nutritional needs (de Brauw & Suryanarayana, 2015). By explicitly focusing on a minimum calorie adequacy idea, NFSA neglects crucial aspects of nutritional security such as dietary diversity and hidden hunger due to micronutrient deficiency. This leads to a pressing question—how should we design our food assistance programs to address malnutrition in its multiple dimensions?

6.5   Non-food-based Safety Nets

Along with the food-based safety nets and employment guarantee schemes in rural areas, MGNREGS provides the basic existing architecture to India's social welfare regime. MGNREGS is a national-level public works program, on the lines of the Maharashtra Employment Guarantee Act of 1977. Under the MGNREGS, all adults in a rural household are guaranteed 100 days of unskilled manual work. MGNREGS is the largest social security scheme in the world which entitles the citizens to "right to work", and hence it is obligatory upon the government to provide work when demanded. The benefits of public works program as a safety net lies in the aspects of self-selection and creation of durable assets. Those who demand work are engaged in building durable assets like roads, canals, ponds and wells across rural India. This would address the issues of rural livelihood as well as infrastructure at the same time. Under the scheme, a minimum wage-material ratio of 60:40 is to be maintained.[6] MGNREGS was envisaged as a program to generate employment as well as create "durable assets" which would help agriculture through creating rural infrastructure. Its performance in creating assets despite incurring high costs has led critics to refer to it as "doles for creating holes". On the operational side of it, MGNREGS, like other safety net programs also suffers from inefficiencies

---

[6]Wage here represents the amount in total paid as wages to the workers. The rest is the amount spent on materials for the public works program.

such as corruption, delayed payment or lower wages to workers as a result of local political coalitions, for example, between post office officials and panchayat members, which often goes unnoticed.[7]

However, income earned from MGNREGS has proved to be nutrition enhancing. Using a panel data on households, Ravi and Engler (2015) find that participation in MGNREGS had a significant impact in increasing food expenditures and a significant reduction in the number of meals foregone by households. Similarly, Liu and Deininger (2010) find a positive impact of MGNREGS on consumption expenditure, asset accumulation as well as nutrient intake: calorie and protein. Wages play an important role in the income pathway to nutrition. A study by Azam (2012) shows how MGNREGS had a positive effect on agricultural wages. Contributing to the human capital, participation in the MGNREGS by women had a positive effect on the educational outcomes of children (Afridi, Mukhopadhyay, & Sahoo, 2016).

6.6   POLITICAL ECONOMY OF THE SAFETY NET

Safety nets, which Indian policymakers have designed and we discuss here can be classified as benefits which help in "consumption smoothing" rather than "mean shifting", thereby addressing vulnerability to poverty rather than its chronic manifestation (Devereux, 2002). Chronic poverty is addressed if there is an increase in factor productivity (of labor, land and capital). How much India's current and emerging safety net architecture would be able to address factor productivity is the policy question. Programs like PDS, ICDS, MDMS or pension schemes are relevant for reducing vulnerability especially to kids and elderly who cannot generate independent livelihoods of their own. Programs focused on kids have larger implications for human capital and future productivity. Public works and food assistance programs, therefore, have been more hotly contested regarding their design to achieve the desired outcome.

Part of the problem lies in the fact that safety nets are enmeshed in political incentives which inhibit reforms in the program design. PDS reforms are essentially linked to the government's farm support policies. Rice and wheat provided through PDS are procured through a system of pre-announced minimum support prices (MSP) which ensures a remunerative price to

---

[7] MGNREGS payments are made through post offices, and the panchayat leader is the sanctioning authority as the scheme is decentralized to the lowest tier of government administration.

farmers. Initial expansion of PDS during the 1970s largely leveraged on the productivity growth that resulted from Green Revolution technologies. To promote agricultural production, the government incentivized food production through minimum support price (MSP) and amassed massive amounts of grain. These food grains found an outlet through PDS into the hands of poor consumers. Agricultural growth in the Indo-Gangetic plains—which benefited from the Green Revolution—led to a powerful political lobby of agriculturists whose interests are aligned with greater farm procurement of staple grains, which were distributed through the PDS. The interlocked farmer-consumer incentive system has made it politically challenging to introduce reforms in the PDS. While supporting agriculture makes for sound economics and politics, the procurement-stocking-distribution model in the food system has led to perverse incentives for the farmers. Procurement through MSP mainly takes place for rice and wheat, which disincentivizes the production of other crops. Evidence suggest that rice-wheat dominance has led to the displacement of traditionally grown nutritious crops like coarse cereals and pulses. Such lopsided agricultural production patterns not only affect variety and essential nutrients in the food system but also undermine biodiversity.

It has been widely established that the increase in expenditure on safety nets of late has been attributed to the greater role of state governments primarily driven by three factors: history of political legacy, social coalitions and resultant political party competition, and political leaders' influence in strengthening state capacity for program delivery (Deshpande, Kailash, & Tillin, 2017). Since the 1990s, there has been a greater role of the regional parties in central politics enabling the state governments to have a greater say in the policy space (Kennedy, 2017). The role of politics in enabling a more egalitarian and better designed safety nets in the southern states of India has been there for long, but sub-national politics has gained greater traction of late. For example, while policy legacies could explain improved safety nets in southern states of India like Kerala and Tamil Nadu, reforms in Odisha and Chhattisgarh are a result of political populism espousing egalitarian concerns of the state party leaders. Greater influence of regional political settlements and their influence over safety nets could be a function of the demands of democracy and electoral accountability. The influence of electoral politics on the design of the safety nets cannot be denied. Negotiating the needs of an evolving food system in the political space is something food policy has always grappled with. Policy interventions which focus on nutrition may be considered less attractive to gain electoral patronage, while direct food assistance, which is more tangible and more immediate, benefits the voters. Moving the focus to nutritional improvements—the distal outcome of food assistance—hence gets ignored. The consumer interests, therefore, get more enmeshed with the producer incentives. Innovations in food delivery mechanisms are becoming a more distant proposition.

6.7   The Possible Future of Safety Nets in India

Regardless of these challenges, it is an accepted fact that safety nets have been instrumental in alleviating poverty and improving the lives of millions across the world, and they will be a critical tool to fight poverty and better developmental outcomes in India too.

6.7.1   Citizenship Rights or Hand-Outs?

Envisaging the future of safety nets in India needs a reflection on the genesis of these programs and the recent reforms. There are two paradigms of social protection—citizenship and charity (Kidd, 2017). Under the citizenship paradigm, redistribution is considered as a public good and governments invest heavily in safety nets. The charity paradigm, however, looks to support the poor with *hand-outs* and has relatively lower spending on the social assistance programs. The developed world follows the citizenship paradigm, while lower developed countries follow the charity paradigm. With the strengthening of democracy and economic growth, even the low and middle-income countries like India are moving towards a citizenship paradigm based safety net, which gives the citizen a sense of entitlement (Daigneault, 2014).

India's safety net paradigm—based upon rights-based approach—exhibits a similar pattern. The language of social citizenship rights through safety nets also reduces the likelihood of class-based conflict (Jayal, 2013). There could be multiple other hypotheses for India to move towards a citizenship-based paradigm of safety nets (Kapur & Nangia, 2015). Theories of "social citizenship" in democracies initially entail civil rights (such as freedom of speech, faith and others), gradually moving to political rights, and finally the social rights which is the driver of welfare state expansion. The "compensation hypothesis" of Karl Polanyi states that expansion of welfare state takes place as economic insecurities increase with the spread of the free market and economic integration across countries as a result of globalization. The third hypothesis emerges from the power resources theory, according to which emergence of welfare regimes reflect class-related distribution and strengthening of partisan politics as reflected in organized demand by labor and other disadvantaged groups for protection. These hypotheses, however, are merely suggestive of the possible factors behind the emerging social welfare narrative in India with no conclusive evidence (*ibid*). Regardless of the exact motivation, it cannot be denied that the current safety net architecture in India is a combination of democratic needs, competitive politics, rising economic insecurity and genuine concerns for the poor. More importantly, safety nets in the country is going to stay, and expand further. The direction and design of the same is the issue of debate.

6.7.2   Newer Forms of Safety Nets: Health Insurance

With the right to food and work formally enshrined in the country's constitution, health insurance under the larger ambit of the *Ayushman Bharat* program is now emerging as the newer form of safety net, albeit partly private sector based, as a departure from the current solely publicly financed programs. In the 2018 budget, the government of India launched a new National Health Protection Scheme (NHPS) aiming to cover almost half of the population with a yearly family insurance cover of Rs. 5 lakhs. The antecedent of NHPS was the Rashtriya Swasthya Bima Yojana (RSBY), a health insurance program targeted specifically at the families falling below the poverty line, introduced in 2008. Under RSBY, beneficiaries (five members of the family which includes the head of household, spouse and up to three dependents) are entitled to hospitalization coverage up to Rs. 30,000 (roughly equivalent to 500 USD) for illnesses which require hospitalization. RSBY is implemented through insurance companies and provides the beneficiaries an option of choosing between public and private hospitals. Insurance premium subsidies (Rs. 750 equivalent to 12 USD annually) are shared by the Union and State governments on a 3:1 basis. The beneficiary pays a sum of Rs. 30 (0.5 USD) every year as a registration/renewal fee. State governments have introduced their versions of health insurance programs like *Yeshasvini* in Karnataka and *Aarogyasri* in Andhra Pradesh. NHPS fundamentally differs from RSBY in the sense that the former is an entitlement; all eligible households are covered once the scheme is operationalized. NHPS is a part of the *Ayushman Bharat*—healthy and prosperous India—a program which also includes setting up of 1.5 lakh healthcare centers. These centers would provide for comprehensive healthcare facilities for maternal and child health services in addition to non-communicable diseases, free essential drugs and diagnostic services. The overarching objective of this enhances productivity and well-being and enables a supporting platform for unanticipated wage loss and impoverishment.

Health insurance is a necessary inclusion to the set of safety nets in India since health shocks are one of the major causes of households falling into poverty in India (Krishna, 2011). In contrast to other safety nets which attempt to bring households out of poverty, subsidized health insurance schemes are useful protection against catastrophic health expenditures and hence lower the probability of falling into poverty.

6.7.3   Stage of Structural Transformation and Urbanization of Safety Nets

Urban population is expected to increase. While urban poverty in India is relatively lower than rural poverty, greater urban population increase in the future would lead to "urbanization of poverty" (Ravallion, 2002). Urban poverty has its peculiar features which include income volatility, informality in jobs and living conditions, poor social services and less cohesive community and social networks (Gentilini, 2015). The urban poor often live in locations with the poor quality of hygiene and exposure to infectious disease environment. Given a robust link between access to clean water and sanitation facilities with nutrition, the urban poor are at high levels of risk of malnutrition. Lack of adequate social protection schemes in urban areas further compound these problems. Urban residents, being net consumers of food, are also more exposed to fluctuations in prices. Informality and a high degree of inequality have been a feature of India's urbanization which makes urban poor highly vulnerable in the absence of appropriate social support programs (Roy, 2009).

In the future, the role of urban safety nets would further increase in importance. Currently, safety nets have a greater rural presence. Increase in the rate of urban poverty and the associated nutritional impacts have often been overlooked in the policy space. While poverty may not be directly related to food or nutritional security, there is a definite link between the two (Maitra & Rao, 2015). Safety nets also need to be attuned to the greater rates of future migration to urban areas. Currently, the entitlement of migrants to the various social security benefits which are not easily transferable which inhibits inter-state labor mobility and hence structural transformation (Kone, Liu, Mattoo, Ozden, & Sharma, 2016).

6.7.4   The Question of Cash Transfers

Should safety nets should be replaced with cash transfers or Direct Benefit Transfer (DBT), as referred to in India, in place of in-kind subsidies? This question has generated a lot of academic as well policy debates in the recent past. DBT in the form of pensions—for elderly, widows and disabled—and MGNREGA payment has attained reasonable success in some states of India. The debate has largely been around PDS. Cash transfers with a lower transaction cost have been proposed as an alternative to the costly and inefficient PDS. Cash, in the hands of beneficiaries, also enables them the choice of their consumption basket. One can argue that PDS is essentially a cash transfer because the marginal propensity of cereal consumption from the PDS subsidy is close to zero (Balasubramanian, 2015). The case for cash transfers is further strengthened by a randomized controlled experiment by Gangopadhyay, Lensink, and Yadav (2015) in Delhi where they find that replacing in-kind food subsidy with cash transfers of equivalent amount does not affect food security. Khera (2014) questions gross generalization of such findings and argues that "one-size-fits-all" approach may not work, given wide regional variation in governance, infrastructure and poverty levels.

There have been multiple arguments in-kind transfers to continue. In India, where poverty levels are high and there is widespread inequality, underdeveloped credit and factor markets, paternalism being a cultural norm, "leaving people to their own devices" through cash transfers may not be a smart policy if the idea is to ensure sufficient protection against food insecurity. Khera (2014) finds that poorer households prefer cash when the PDS works poorly; however, in-kind transfers are preferred when PDS is effective. Consumer preferences also differ by gender. Women are more averse towards cash transfer programs because of restricted physical mobility and challenges of handling official banking procedures (*ibid*). While these are cultural factors, critics of cash transfers have also argued that cash could be diverted into other non-food expenditures. Intra-household resource allocation depends upon patriarchal norms which could lower food access for women and children, undermining overall nutrition. The other important thing to note is the potential benefit of moving to a cash transfer when in-kind transfers have a similar effect on food consumption. Shrinivas, Baylis, Crost, and Pingali (2018) show that almost 83% of the PDS subsidy is spent on food. They also provide suggestive evidence that PDS could have a higher effect on the consumption of nutritious food than an income increase of equivalent amount.

The success of cash transfers critically relies upon the availability of local markets. Most poor in India live in remote parts and their market accessibility is limited and raises concerns of local food availability in the absence of PDS. Cash transfers require other financial infrastructures such as the presence of banks and post offices. India lacks such rural infrastructure, without which a sudden move towards cash could increase distress, at least in the short term. Open market prices exhibit cyclic fluctuations. If cash transfers are not indexed to inflation, the benefits are likely to be eroded. While price indexation may seem a trivial exercise, its operationalization against local price increase, and the awareness among beneficiaries of their entitlement every month is often much discussed.

A significant concern when moving towards a DBT is *what does the government do with the huge amount of food grains which the government procures from the farmers to incentivize production?* Without an in-kind transfer through PDS, food procurement would only lead to further increase in the enormous quantities of rice and wheat which India already has a huge stock lying in its godowns. This is a major political economy question which is often not raised while discussing the move to cash transfers. Some proponents have mentioned disbanding food procurement completely, but the policy direction seems contrary to that. The last few years have seen greater food procurement than earlier. The political rhetoric of the time has seen multiple more incentives for the farmer to sell rice and wheat to the government as evident through cases in Madhya Pradesh, Chhattisgarh, Bihar, Uttar Pradesh and Odisha. Government has provided mixed signals on this issue. While it has opened up a discussion around moving towards DBT, it has been encouraging food procurement too.

6.7.5   Universal Basic Income

Given the difficult economics of the safety nets, global interest in the idea of a Universal Basic Income (UBI) has reached Indian shores too. Narratives around replacing the existing safety nets with a UBI have emerged as one of the most engaging debates in recent times. While academics have been talking about it for some time, Economic Survey in 2017 introduces its possibility in the policy debate by considering UBI as *"...a powerful idea whose time even if not ripe for implementation is ripe for serious discussion"*. The survey talks about the potentials of UBI centered on the ideals of "universality, unconditionality, and agency" to "wipe[ing] every tear from every eye". Arvind Subramanian, who is credited with the Economic Survey, is reported to have said that UBI could be leveraged for the "liberation of the cognitive bandwidth" through the provision of a basic minimum level of assistance to the neediest.[8] While the idea of UBI is appealing because it provides freedom—of choosing suitable work and consuming items of choice—operationalizing the same could be a mammoth challenge. The government hopes to leverage the advancements in technology to make this a possibility. The central government has set up the Unique Identification Authority of India (UIDAI) which collects and maintains a database on biometric and demographic identifiers of all residents and issues a 12-digit unique identity number called *Aadhaar*.[9] Clubbing *Aadhaar* with the financial inclusion program, known as the *Jan-Dhan Yojana*, under which every citizen would have a bank account, and the expansion of the coverage of mobile phones—popularly called JAM (*Jan Dhan-Aadhaar-Mobile*) trinity—the government aims to build up a technology-based architecture to make this a reality.

6.7.6   Use of Technology for Efficient Safety Nets

Advancements in the information and communication technologies (ICTs) have definitely revolutionized the flow and timeliness of information across multiple nodes and hence offer a brilliant option to curb leakages and local elite capture—often attributed to poor performance—in the implementation of safety nets. ICT could ensure accountability between the policymakers, service providers, and citizens. JAM trinity is expected to be a game changer regarding how social security programs operate in India. By linking *Aadhaar* (biometric identification) of the beneficiaries with their *Jan Dhan* bank accounts and mobile phones, funds could be directly transferred to the beneficiaries into their bank accounts. This cuts out the intermediaries in the citizen-state interactions. According to the Economic Survey, this would save around about Rs. 3.78 lakh crore (6,000 billion USD) or 4.2% of India's GDP, which is currently spent on key subsidies.[10] While the idea is compelling and is something which the government is seriously considering, ground-level realities produce a sobering picture of the usefulness of

---

[8] https://www.cgdev.org/blog/reducing-poverty-india-with-power-digital-payments-UBI
[9] *Aadhaar* is the world's largest national identification number project.
[10] The estimate also includes subsidies on fertilizers, LPG and other items which are not discussed here.

ICT, at least for now. It has often been found that the biometrics of many beneficiaries, especially among the poorest of the population, is not easily registered on the scanning devices. Lack of electricity and banking infrastructure in some of the remote parts of the country make it cumbersome for the people to access benefits. On account of technological glitches, wage payments are often delayed, irregular or even rejected at times.

Robust ICT systems take time and the required infrastructure needs sophistication and appropriate database security systems. While ICT is increasingly being used for program delivery and effectively so in many places, when would be the right time for India to introduce a cash transfer scheme or UBI, leveraging the available technology and identification system, only time would tell.

6.7.7   Linkage and Synergies with Agriculture

Critics of the narrowly targeted programs have argued that often the entitlements are mere "...*token handouts to make harsh neo-liberal reforms politically palatable, or to avoid taking real actions to redress the structural causes of poverty and vulnerability*" (Devereux, 2002). They highlight the fact that market-based reforms in the developing world left many behind increasing inequality. Social security benefits in some way ameliorate those impacts for the poor. These necessary interventions do not address the structural roots of poverty. We would like to argue that greater investment in agriculture—private and public—and the right incentives for producers should be the way ahead.

A major share of India's population lives in rural areas and is primarily engaged in agriculture-based livelihoods. For India's nutritional security, the challenge lies in ensuring that social security interventions are effective at scale, which requires coordinated investments across sectors to address deep-rooted causes of malnutrition (Kadiyala, Joshi, Mahendra Dev, Nandakumar, & Vyas, 2012). Agriculture as the central focus of tackling nutrition has been widely recognized in the academic as well as policy circles (Tirivayi, Knowles, & Davis, 2016). Safety nets, food insecurity and poverty, and agriculture are inextricably linked in the rural economy, and these synergies make for a more resilient food system. Safety nets could be used to increase productive investments in agriculture leading to overall economic growth through multiple pathways (Hoddinott, 2008). First, safety nets help in generating household assets. Second, they also protect against assets when during times of economic shocks. Third, acting as a risk coping mechanism, they allow households to use their existing resources better. Fourth, by supporting the poor, safety nets contribute to a reduction in inequality and promote growth.

The agricultural sector has been found to more effective in reducing extreme poverty, while the non-agricultural sector has been proven more beneficial in reducing less severe poverty (Christiaensen, Demery, & Kuhl, 2011). Hence, pro-poor policies call for greater investments in agricultural development. Examining trends in poverty and nutrition for 29 countries during the period of economic transformation, Webb and Block (2012) find that the structural transformation leads to increase in total income and poverty reduction faster if there is strong support for agriculture. Reduction in poverty, in turn, leads to better nutrition, especially in rural areas. This transformation, however, brings with it the risks associated with the greater prevalence of obesity and non-communicable chronic diseases. Hence, to avoid these negative consequences, the transition needs careful management through a suitable design of support for smallholder agriculture along with the appropriate health interventions. Existing evidence from Latin America and Africa suggests so. In Latin America, conditional cash transfers have proved to be beneficial in increasing land use, farm implements and livestock ownership. Similarly, in Africa, cash transfer programs have led to greater input use and productive investments in agriculture.

There are enough avenues for greater synergies between the safety net programs and agriculture in India. Rural asset creation through MGNREGS could be leveraged to revitalize agriculture. Rain-fed agriculture, where irrigation facilities are fewer, could be suitable to grow coarse grains and pulses, which could be provided through the PDS. It would be a useful step towards the larger goal of nutritional security with more diversified diets as well as production systems. Food can be produced locally for MDMS, ICDS or PDS, which would not only boost the local economy but would also adhere to the local tastes.

6.7.8   Government Investment in Public Goods

According to the FAO (2015), reliance on social protection alone to address hunger and rural poverty would be a flaw. Safety nets need to be combined with sufficient public and private investments in agriculture along with rural developmental programs to ensure inclusive and sustainable economic growth in addressing the cycle of rural poverty. Illustrations from across the globe also throw up a contrasting result. While countries in East Asia, the Pacific and Southeast Asia have been able to reduce the prevalence of hunger and poverty successfully through safety nets, South Asia and sub-Saharan Africa have shown much slower progress. Social safety nets are crucial for smoothening consumption across the year, avoiding the sale of assets or retaining children in school during times of economic distress. However, other important interventions, such as irrigation, markets, rural infrastructure, promoting agricultural extension services, and facilities for crop and weather insurance play a huge role in reducing the vulnerability of farmers. Some of these programs are not very lucrative from the point of politicians as they do not bring in immediate gains and are less populist.

One must understand that emergence of the social safety architecture in the last two decades is associated with some of the major macro-transformations in the Indian economy as well as a polity. First, the greater intensity of electoral competition has led the emergence of newer political settlements across various interest groups with clearer identification of constituencies and the desired push towards gaining their electoral support. Second, economic growth since the 1990s has increased the government's fiscal capacity to finance greater investment on safety nets. Third, the fiscal capacity has increased, the government's administrative capacity, especially at the local level may have weakened which has led to worsening of the quality of public goods such as schools and hospitals. Safety nets become more alluring to the voters, especially when the quality of public services is on the wane. Elected representatives, on the other hand, use these transfers as an incentive to bypass issues around poor provisioning of public infrastructure.

While India has been effectively trying to weave in a safety net for the poor, the provision of essential public amenities or public goods such as access to clean water, sanitation, electricity, roads and so on hasn't got the desired attention. Kapur and Nangia (2015) attribute this to the government's weak administrative capacity. They argue that by prioritizing safety nets over the creation of durable public goods, India has taken the path followed by many of the Latin American countries, which took to social security spending as a way to reduce poverty. Comparative analysis, however, suggests that in the long run welfare outcomes were better among the East Asian countries which spent more on creating better provisioning of public infrastructure while being a minimalist welfare state.

Nutrition as a public good, too, has never been a priority development agenda until very recent times. Recent improvements in the performance of food-based safety can be attributed to strong advocacy groups and judicial activism in the country which necessitated state intervention. The realization that economic growth is no panacea to improved nutrition and the basic human right of food entitlement has been the bedrock of this movement. This led to powerful rights-based movement championed by the "right to food" initiative which has brought about much expediency to the policy (Gillespie, Haddad, Mannar, Menon, & Nisbett, 2013). Judicial interventions by the Supreme Court of India helped advance the right to food of specific food-deprived populations and significantly contributed to reducing hunger. This was also helped by the center-left alliance which supported the cause of social welfare programs with the expansion and universalization of many of these schemes (Balarajan & Reich, 2016).

6.8   Conclusion

The current set of safety nets in India—ICDS, MGNREGA, PDS and MDMS—provide income and nutritional assistance during different stages of the life cycle of an individual. The essential idea behind these interventions is to enhance individual capabilities and welfare through more equitable access to food and income. Individual capabilities are increased through a reduction in malnutrition, improved labor productivity, better human capital and reduction in overall inequality of opportunity. It has taken almost 70 years since independence to create a basic safety net architecture, which is intrinsically linked to the economy's structural transformation. Economic growth has definitely played a role in the creation of a basic safety net platform. Improvements in the coverage of safety nets during the last 25 years have benefited from the quadrupling of public revenue which has eased out the resource barrier and made its implementation more affordable (Drèze & Khera, 2017). On the demand side, there have been multiple reasons for this expansion. Increase in interpersonal inequality along with economic growth has led to rising demand for expansion in safety net provisions. Citizens in India are now much more empowered, and civil society plays an active role in channelizing the concerns leading to a citizenship paradigm for safety nets. Public policy towards safety nets has also been influenced by electoral concerns. Expansion and improvement in many of these safety net programs have also been influenced by the electoral arithmetic of mobilizing voter support leveraging upon the populistic nature of these schemes. Universalization of these schemes, rather than targeted poverty reduction interventions, suggests a rise in the support by the political elites.

Safety nets, however, have been an essential part of the poverty reduction policies contributing to risk management and vulnerability reduction for a large section of the population. While these interventions have largely been laudable, looking into the future one does need to think about their future role. These policies over time should become more *transformational* rather than just vulnerability reducing. Structural roots of poverty need to be addressed through combining safety nets with structural reforms and long-term interventions with the aim of increasing human capabilities and addressing structural poverty through that. Synergies between agriculture and safety nets, therefore, become essential. Public work and life-cycle-based food assistance programs need to be dovetailed into the local agrarian economy.

The future of safety nets has to take into account the changing nature of the economic structure, demographic changing and future livelihood patterns. Urbanization, especially, poses a challenge as well as opportunity in restructuring the safety net architecture. Current policies which mostly address rural poverty do not consider the fact that India would be more urban than rural by 2050. With rising urbanization, urban informality and unemployment in urban areas, especially educated unemployment, raise important challenges for the food systems going ahead. Movement of labor from rural to urban areas is further going to increase the share of net consumers who need to be shielded away from rising food prices. Observing the nature of transition in a developed country like the United States offers useful clues. In the United States, many of the workers make a living doing multiple odd jobs comprising what they call as a part of *gig economies*. The Government Accountability Office classified about 31% of the workforce in America as "contingent" workers. The rise in informality in the Indian urban sector is not very different, and it may not be a stretch to imagine the condition to be far worse in India where labor regulations are hardly effective.

The issue of safety net design also needs serious considerations. The current system does suffer from problems of corruption and leakages. ICTs could be utilized better to curb these inefficiencies. Research has shown its benefits in improving program effectiveness for MGNREGA and PDS. Identification of beneficiaries through *Aadhaar* has bolstered the case for cash transfers, yet it is important however to recognize the use they could serve without compromising identity security. Many of the loopholes exist regarding biometric authentication using *Aadhaar* which often becomes a hindrance rather than benefits the poor. These inefficiencies should be ironed out.

Innovations in the food-based safety nets are seriously limited by the modalities of grain procurement structure which incentivizes only staples, potentially crowding out more nutritive food products. This not only is disadvantageous for the consumers through restricting choice, but also undermines the idea of a nutrition-sensitive food production system. It is therefore essential to break the staple grain procurement-storage-distribution interlocked channel. These interlocked incentives are however deeply mired in India's rural political economy which is a major obstacle to food system diversification.

We would also like to highlight here that Indian public policy has often undermined the provision of essential public goods and services which are complimentary to safety nets. Public good provisioning has been ignored as expenditure on safety nets have got priority. The poor quality of infrastructure—urban as well rural—is a testimony to that. It has been well established that long-term welfare depends upon the quality of durable public infrastructure as reflected in the success of East Asian countries which reduced poverty despite not having a welfare state.

REFERENCES

Afridi, F. (2010). Child welfare programs and child nutrition: Evidence from a mandated school meal program in India. *Journal of Development Economics, 92*(2), 152–165. https://doi.org/10.1016/j.jdeveco.2009.02.002

Afridi, F., Mukhopadhyay, A., & Sahoo, S. (2016). Female labor force participation and child education in India: Evidence from the National Rural Employment Guarantee Scheme. *IZA Journal of Labor & Development, 5*(1), 7. https://doi.org/10.1186/s40175-016-0053-y

Azam, M. (2012). *The impact of Indian job guarantee scheme on labor market outcomes: Evidence from a natural experiment*. IZA Working Paper 6548, World Bank, pp. 1–34. https://doi.org/10.2139/ssrn.1941959

Balarajan, Y., & Reich, M. R. (2016). Political economy of child nutrition policy: A qualitative study of India's Integrated Child Development Services (ICDS) scheme. *Food Policy, 62,* 88–98. https://doi.org/10.1016/j.foodpol.2016.05.001

Balasubramanian, S. (2015). Is the PDS already a cash transfer? Rethinking India's food subsidy policies. *The Journal of Development Studies, 51*(6), 642–659. https://doi.org/10.1080/00220388.2014.997221

Christiaensen, L., Demery, L., & Kuhl, J. (2011). The (evolving) role of agriculture in poverty reduction—An empirical perspective. *Journal of Development Economics, 96*(2), 239–254. https://doi.org/10.1016/j.jdeveco.2010.10.006

Croppenstedt, A., Knowles, M., & Lowder, S. K. (2017). Social protection and agriculture: Introduction to the special issue. *Global Food Security, 16*(2), 0–1. https://doi.org/10.1016/j.gfs.2017.09.006

Daigneault, P.-M. (2014). Three paradigms of social assistance. *SAGE Open, 4*(4), 1–8. https://doi.org/10.1177/2158244014559020

de Brauw, A., & Suryanarayana, M. (2015). Linkages between poverty, food security and undernutrition: Evidence from China and India. *China Agricultural Economic Review, 7*(4), 655–667. https://doi.org/10.1108/CAER-09-2015-0117

Deshpande, R., Kailash, K. K., & Tillin, L. (2017). States as laboratories: The politics of social welfare policies in India. *India Review, 16*(1), 85–105. https://doi.org/10.1080/14736489.2017.1279928

Devereux, S. (2002). Can social safety nets reduce chronic poverty? *Development Policy Review, 20*(5), 657–675. https://doi.org/10.1017/S1464793106007007

Drèze, J., Himanshu, Khera, R., & Sen, A. (2015). Clarification on PDS leakages. *Economic and Political Weekly, 50*(39), 72–73.

Drèze, J., & Khera, R. (2017). Recent social security initiatives in India. *World Development, 98*, 555–572. https://doi.org/10.1016/j.worlddev.2017.05.035

FAO. (2015). Social protection and agriculture: Breaking the cycle of rural poverty. In *The state of food and agriculture*. Rome.

Gangopadhyay, S., Lensink, R., & Yadav, B. (2015). Cash or In-kind transfers? Evidence from a randomised controlled trial in Delhi, India. *The Journal of Development Studies, 51*(6), 660–673. https://doi.org/10.1080/00220388.2014.997219

Gentilini, U. (2015). Entering the city: Emerging evidence and practices with safety nets in urban areas.

Gillespie, S., Haddad, L., Mannar, V., Menon, P., & Nisbett, N. (2013). The politics of reducing malnutrition: Building commitment and accelerating progress. *The Lancet, 382*(9891), 552–569. https://doi.org/10.1016/S0140-6736(13)60842-9

Government of India. (2018). *Economic survey 2017–2018*.

Hirway, I. (2003). Identification of BPL households for poverty alleviation programmes. *Economic and Political Weekly*, 4803–4808.

Hoddinott, J. (2008). *Social safety nets and productivity enhancing investments in agriculture*. Washington, DC: IFPRI.

Jain, M. (2015). India's struggle against malnutrition—Is the ICDS program the answer? *World Development, 67*, 72–89. https://doi.org/10.1016/j.worlddev.2014.10.006

Jayal, N. G. (2013). *Citizenship and its discontents: An Indian history*. Harvard University Press.

Jha, S., & Ramaswami, B. (2010). How can food subsidies work better? Answers from India and the Philippines. *ADB Economics Working Paper Series, 221*(221), 1–35. https://doi.org/10.2139/ssrn.1721907

Kadiyala, S., Joshi, P. K., Mahendra Dev, S., Nandakumar, T., & Vyas, V. (2012). A nutrition secure India. *Economic and Political Weekly, XLVII*(8), 21–25.

Kapur, D., & Nangia, P. (2015). Social protection in India: A welfare state sans public goods? *India Review, 14*(1), 73–90. https://doi.org/10.1080/147364 89.2015.1001275

Kaushal, N., & Muchomba, F. M. (2015). How consumer price subsidies affect nutrition. *World Development, 74*, 25–42. https://doi.org/10.1016/j.worlddev.2015.04.006

Kennedy, L. (2017). State restructuring and emerging patterns of subnational policy-making and governance in China and India. *Environment and Planning C: Politics and Space, 35*(1), 6–24. https://doi.org/10.1177/0263 774X16630551

Khera, R. (2006). Mid-day meals in primary schools: Achievements and challenges. *Economic and Political Weekly, 41*(46), 4742–4750. Retrieved from http://www.jstor.org/stable/4418915

Khera, R. (2013). Mid-day meals: Looking ahead. *Economic & Political Weekly, 48*(32), 12–14. Retrieved from http://www.righttofoodindia.org/data/mdm/MidDay_Meals_Looking_Ahead.pdf

Khera, R. (2014). Cash vs. in-kind transfers: Indian data meets theory. *Food Policy, 46*, 116–128. https://doi.org/10.1016/j.foodpol.2014.03.009

Kidd, S. (2017). *Citizenship or charity: The two paradigms of social protection.*

Kishore, A., & Chakrabarti, S. (2015). Is more inclusive more effective? The 'New Style' public distribution system in India. *Food Policy, 55*, 117–130. https://doi.org/10.1016/j.foodpol.2015.06.006

Kochar, A. (2005). Can targeted food programs improve nutrition? An empirical analysis of India's public distribution system. *Economic Development and Cultural Change, 54*(1), 203–235. https://doi.org/10.1086/431260

Kone, Z. L., Liu, M. Y., Mattoo, A., Ozden, C., & Sharma, S. (2016). *Internal borders and migration in India.* Policy Research Working Paper No. 8244.

Kotwal, A., & Ramaswami, B. (2014, September). Delivering food subsidy: The state and the market. In *The Oxford handbook of food, politics, and society* (pp. 301–326). Oxford University Press.

Krishna, A. (2011). *One illness away: Why people become poor and how they escape poverty.* Oxford University Press.

Krishnamurthy, P., Pathania, V., & Tandon, S. (2017). Food price subsidies and nutrition: Evidence from state reforms to India's public distribution system. *Economic Development and Cultural Change, 66*(1), 55–90. https://doi.org/10.1086/694033

Liu, Y., & Deininger, K. (2010). Poverty impacts of India's national rural employment guarantee scheme: Evidence from Andhra Pradesh.

Maitra, C., & Rao, D. S. P. (2015). Poverty–food security nexus: Evidence from a survey of urban slum dwellers in Kolkata. *World Development, 72*, 308–325. https://doi.org/10.1016/j.worlddev.2015.03.006

Meenakshi, J. V. (2016). Trends and patterns in the triple burden of malnutrition in India. *Agricultural Economics, 47*(S1), 115–134. https://doi.org/10.1111/agec.12304

Mittal, N., & Meenakshi, J. V. (2015). *Utilization of ICDS services and their impact on child health outcomes: Evidence from three East Indian states*. New Delhi.

Narayanan, S., & Gerber, N. (2017). Social safety nets for food and nutrition security in India. *Global Food Security, 15*, 65–76. https://doi.org/10.1016/j.gfs.2017.05.001

Panda, S. (2015). Political connections and elite capture in a poverty alleviation programme in India. *The Journal of Development Studies, 51*(1), 50–65. https://doi.org/10.1080/00220388.2014.947281

Pingali, P., & Rao, T. (2016). Understanding the multidimensional nature of the malnutrition problem in India. In P. Pingali & G. Feder (Eds.), *Agriculture and rural development in a globalizing world*. Routledge.

Rahman, A. (2016). Universal food security program and nutritional intake: Evidence from the hunger prone KBK districts in Odisha. *Food Policy, 63*, 73–86. https://doi.org/10.1016/j.foodpol.2016.07.003

Rao, N., & Kaul, V. (2018). India's integrated child development services scheme: Challenges for scaling up. *Child: Care, Health and Development, 44*(1), 31–40. https://doi.org/10.1111/cch.12531

Ravallion, M. (2002). On the urbanization of poverty. *Journal of Development Economics, 68*(2), 435–442. https://doi.org/10.1016/S0304-3878(02)00021-4

Ravi, S., & Engler, M. (2015). Workfare as an effective way to fight poverty: The case of India's NREGS. *World Development, 67*, 57–71. https://doi.org/10.1016/j.worlddev.2014.09.029

Roy, A. (2009). Why India cannot plan its cities: Informality, insurgence and the idiom of urbanization. *Planning Theory, 8*(1), 76–87. https://doi.org/10.1177/1473095208099299

Shrinivas, A., Baylis, K., Crost, B., & Pingali, P. (2018). Do staple food subsidies improve nutrition? Unpublished manuscript. Retrieved from http://barrett.dyson.cornell.edu/NEUDC/paper_520.pdf

Singh, A., Park, A., & Dercon, S. (2013). School meals as a safety net: An evaluation of the midday meal scheme in India. *Economic Development and Cultural Change, 62*(2), 275–306.

Tarozzi, A. (2005). The Indian public distribution system as provider of food security: Evidence from child nutrition in Andhra Pradesh. *European Economic Review, 49*(5), 1305–1330. https://doi.org/10.1016/j.euroecorev.2003.08.015

Tirivayi, N., Knowles, M., & Davis, B. (2016). The interaction between social protection and agriculture: A review of evidence. *Global Food Security, 10*, 52–62. https://doi.org/10.1016/j.gfs.2016.08.004

Webb, P., & Block, S. (2012). Support for agriculture during economic transformation: Impacts on poverty and undernutrition. *Proceedings of the National Academy of Sciences, 109*(31), 12309–12314. https://doi.org/10.1073/pnas.0913334108

CHAPTER 7

Enabling Smallholder Prosperity through Commercialization and Diversification

7.1   INTRODUCTION

India will be the most populous country in the world with a population of 1.65 billion citizens by the year 2050. Keeping in mind the need to achieve zero hunger, the two central concerns for food security is how to increase productivity and how to diversify food production. Growth in productivity is needed to eradicate all forms of hunger in the existing population and safeguard the future generation from it, and diversification of production is essential to meet the demand for higher value crops resulting from income growth and ensure more availability of micronutrients. However, the way forward in achieving higher productivity and diversity of foods needs to reduce agriculture's effect on the environment. Adapting agricultural production growth with current and ongoing climate change consequences such as temperature and precipitation change and replenishing natural resources required for agriculture that is lost or on the verge of loss, forms the core supply challenge for global and Indian agriculture.

In India, where a majority of agricultural producers are small and marginal in size, commercialization of farms by which smallholders produce for the market is essential to improve incomes and better access to diversified and nutritious food. The rising demand for diversified agricultural products has brought about opportunities and challenges for India's agricultural sector. The opportunities come from increasing demand for diversified and higher value crops that can improve agricultural incomes

P. Pingali et al., *Transforming Food Systems for a Rising India*,
Palgrave Studies in Agricultural Economics and Food Policy,
https://doi.org/10.1007/978-3-030-14409-8_7

(Pingali, Khwaja, & Madelon, 2005) and improved access to a varied food basket at the household level. The major challenge, however, is the set of problems associated with the supply side conditions such as poor access to credit and other input markets that have hindered commercialization and made income opportunities inaccessible to many producers. In this chapter, we assess the major institutional features of smallholder production challenges and potential solutions to rectify them. Specifically, we look at (a) the benefits and limits of the Green Revolution to determine the current supply and nutritional challenges of the Indian food system, (b) the production constraints smallholder agricultural systems currently face in the context of commercialization and meeting food security and economic growth challenges and (c) the general direction interventions need to take in order to meet the goals of sustained productivity growth and diversification.

7.2   Farm Size, Yields and Regional Disparities— Benefits and Limits of the Green Revolution

A majority of the world's agricultural production takes place on small and marginal farms, and despite recurring predictions that small farms will soon disappear, they have persisted and in many cases have increased in number (Hazell, Poulton, Wiggins, & Dorward, 2010; Hazell, 2018). In India, the average size of landholdings decreased from 1.33 hectares in 2000–01 to 1.15 hectares in 2010–11. Considering these trends, assessing small farm viability becomes critical. Understanding the relationship between land size and productivity is essential to identify the potentials and challenges for small farms. The relationship between size of landholdings and productivity has been debated in the field of rural development and economics for a long time. Since the 1960s, economists have argued that crop productivity per unit of land declined with an increase in farm size (Bardhan, 1973; Mazumdar, 1965; A. Sen, 1962). Referred to as the "small farm paradigm", it was argued that there is an inverse relationship between farm size and productivity. These studies conclude that small farms have an advantage over large farms in per capita productivity due to higher labor utilization (e.g., using family labor) and higher input utilization (e.g., using intensive farming practices). This inverse relationship was a result of imperfect land and labor markets (Bardhan, 1973; A. Sen, 1966). Imperfections in the labor market meant that surplus labor at the household level was available, as off-farm opportunity costs (off-farm wages minus search and travel costs) were higher than on-farm wages, and low-cost labor allowed for substituting lumpy inputs such as capital-intensive equipment (Binswanger & Rosenzweig, 1986; Eastwood, Lipton, & Newell, 2010; Poulton, Dorward, & Kydd, 2010). Imperfect land markets meant that land lease options to access more land for farming was limited (Eswaran & Kotwal, 1986; Hazell et al., 2010) and producers had to utilize their existing resource endowment effectively.

In many Asian countries (where land was scarce and labor abundant), the "small farm paradigm" did hold and was considered a socially optimal outcome (Hazell et al., 2010; Poulton et al., 2010). Johnson and Ruttan (1994) clarify that the size and productivity relations hold when considering scale-neutral inputs associated with the actual production processes such as labor input, monitoring and local knowledge. For these inputs, in the pressure of high monitoring costs (to large farms), small farms are not at a disadvantage and in many cases may have an advantage. However, with factors including access to markets, credit and extension services, technical knowledge and technology, along with lumpy inputs such as management and asset-specific machinery that have high fixed costs and are not scale-neutral, small farms are at a disadvantage (Poulton et al., 2010). Some studies have also shown that the inverse relationship between small size and high productivity disappears when soil quality (Benjamin, 1995; S. S. Bhalla & Roy, 1988), capital market imperfections (Feder, 1985) and unobserved heterogeneities such as climatic variations and quality of management are considered (Eastwood et al., 2010). In countries like India, where wages are on the rise, there has also been a lowering of off-farm opportunity costs, eroding the labor advantage of small farms (Binswanger & Singh, 2017). In this section, we look at agricultural development in India in the context of smallholder production to assess the nature of growth and regional disparity trends in the context of the Green Revolution.

7.2.1 Green Revolution Technologies and Regional and Crop Disparities

The Green Revolution (GR) was a landmark achievement in technological and institutional innovation that brought about the exponential growth in yields of cereals in many developing countries and saw improved food availability (mainly wheat and rice), a rise in per capita incomes and poverty reduction. This was extraordinary because productivity growth took place in line with population growth, which more than doubled, and when land scarcity and land values were rising (Pingali, 2012). Central to the GR strategy was the use of high-yielding variety (HYV) technology in staples such as wheat, rice and maize coupled with appropriate institutional mechanisms to enable widespread adoption across many developing countries (ibid). In countries like India, GR was effectively implemented on small farms because these technologies were (a) scale-neutral and they could be divided and distributed at no extra cost unlike other technologies such as tractors and irrigation (Birner & Resnick, 2010; G. Feder, Just, & Zilberman, 1985; Hazell et al., 2010; Mosley, 2002); and (b) it was an international public good that had adequate input support in the form of state-subsidized fertilizers and pesticides and extension services (Pingali, 2012), allowing for the adoption of these technologies by smallholders in many parts of India. The positive impacts of the GR were that it led to significant increases in the yields of wheat and rice that led to lowering of food prices and increased availability, improving food security, and the resulting income growth led to a reduction of poverty in many parts of India (ibid).

Although GR technologies were scale-neutral allowing for adoption on small farms, they were not resource-neutral (Bernstein, 2010) and this meant adoption was influenced by the smallholder's access to resources such as irrigation, markets and credit. Also, as food security was traditionally defined as calorific security, food policy was excessively focused on the promotion of staple grains such as wheat and rice to make available sufficient amount of calories to the population (Pingali, 2015). Relative to staple grains, other crops such as pulses and coarse cereals received limited focus concerning R&D resulting in limited seed technology development and market support such as direct procurement and support price. Therefore, the regional and crop disparity regarding benefits became stark in the years following the GR, resulting in high interregional inequalities in agricultural development. Much of the eastern region (Bihar, Eastern UP, West Bengal, Odisha and Madhya Pradesh) did not see a change in area under production (Figs. 7.1 and 7.2).

As access to irrigation was vital in determining the regions where GR technologies were implemented, Punjab and Haryana and to a less extent the Indo-Gangetic plains saw an increase in area under production of wheat and rice. Also, in Punjab, the wheat yields are 2 to 2.4 times higher than of other states, and rice yields are 1.5 to 2 times that of states such as Odisha, Maharashtra, Madhya Pradesh and Bihar. During this period, we also see a change in cropping patterns. As the economic benefits of

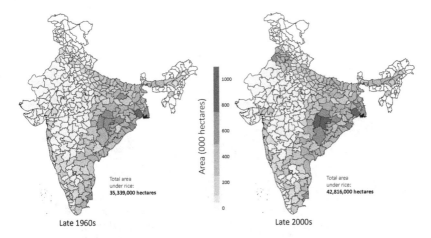

Fig. 7.1 Change in area under production ('000 hectares) of rice between 1960s and 2000s. Source: Ministry of Agriculture and Farmers Welfare, Government of India; based on authors calculation

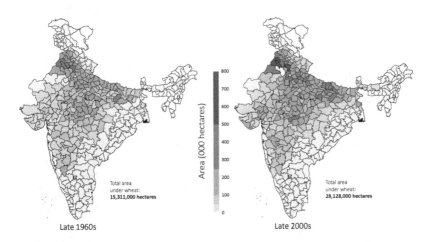

Fig. 7.2 Change in area under production ('000 hectares) of wheat between 1960s and 2000s. Source: Ministry of Agriculture and Farmers Welfare, Government of India; based on authors calculations

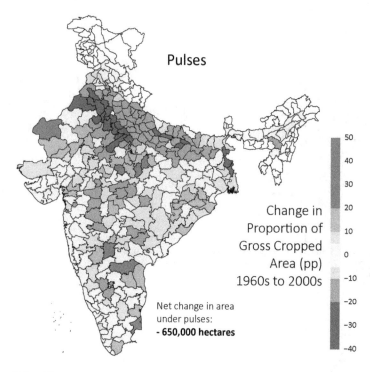

Fig. 7.3 Change in area under production ('000 hectares) of pulses between 1960s and 2000s. Source: Tata-Cornell Institute

increased yields were substantial, it led to the emergence of intensive cropping of wheat and rice in irrigated tracts of India. Figure 7.3 shows the change in the proportion of gross cropped area under pulses in various parts of India. In the irrigated regions that witnessed intense cultivation of wheat and rice, there was a 30–40% drop in area under pulses cultivation, as pulses were substituted for rice cultivation in GR adopted regions and pulses cultivation shifted to the central parts of India (Abraham & Pingali, 2019; Pingali, 2012).

Figure 7.4 shows the per capita availability of various food grains in India from 1951 to 2015. In the case of cereals, we see availability increased from 65.7 to 168 grams per capita per day in wheat and from 158.9 to 186 grams per capita per day in rice to increase production in line with population growth. In the case of pulses where comparable technological

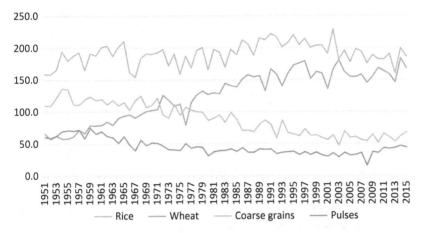

Fig. 7.4 Per capita availability of cereals, coarse grains and pulses in India (1951–2015). Source: Ministry of Agriculture and Farmers Welfare, Government of India

and institutional interventions were missing, production and area under cultivation stagnated, leading to a decline in per capita availability from 60 grams per day per person in 1951 to 43 grams in 2015. Yields witnessed only a marginal increase (251 kg/hectare) in the last 65 years. In the case of coarse grains (such as sorghum, pearl millets, finger millets, barley etc.) per capita availability decreased from 109.6 in 1951 to 67.4 grams per day in 2015. Despite an increase in yields from 579 kg per hectare to 1579 kg per hectare in coarse cereals during the same period, the area under cultivation decreased by about 60%, leading to lower supply.

The advantage of the GR was that it was scale-neutral and could be adopted by small and marginal producers provided they had access to irrigation or were in locations with reduced agro-climatic risk. Institutional support and favorable policy in the form of subsidized inputs and extension services and market support through minimum support prices and direct procurement by the state played a crucial role in enabling and incentivizing adoption. GR was also a watershed in agricultural development that played a critical role in poverty reduction and significantly reducing hunger. The limits of GR were that it was focused on significant staple grains such as wheat and rice and was limited to regions that were not resource constrained. The current challenges for the India food system are to ensure diversification to higher value crops to ensure the availability of nutritious foods and ensure income growths through productivity increases, especially in *lagging states* that did not benefit from the GR. Central to ensuring broad-based growth and development in the agricultural sector is rectifying the institutional and resource constraints of smallholder production. The next section of this chapter discusses the significant production challenges of smallholder agricultural systems in diversification and commercialization.

7.3   Production Challenges—Small Farm Diversification, Commercialization and Risks

Income, urbanization and population growth are the main drivers of demand of agricultural produce, and the supply challenge for the agricultural sector in meeting this demand is two-pronged: one, to increase cereal production to keep up with rising population, and two to ensure the availability of diversified food groups that cater to increasing demand. Commercialization of smallholder agriculture is central to meeting this demand. Commercialization is the process by which farms increase their engagement with input and output markets as they move away from integrated or subsistence farming systems to specialized crop and livestock production (Pingali & Rosegrant, 1995). During the transition, non-traded inputs are substituted for purchased seeds, pesticides and fertilizers that enable production increase and diversification of production and selling in output markets (Carletto, Corral, & Guelfi, 2017; Pingali & Rosegrant, 1995; von Braun, 1995). Commercialization is central to the structural transformation process as greater input market orientation increases the demand for industrial goods and technology essential for production, increases household welfare through employment generation and increased labor productivity and enables the transfer of surplus in the form of food, labor and capital from the agrarian sector to the other sectors.

In India, the regional disparities in rates of commercialization have been varied. Regions that benefited from the GR witnessed growth in yields through the use of high-yielding seed technologies, fertilizers and pesticides, while in unirrigated regions where agro-climatic risks were high, production systems remain semi-commercial due to lower surpluses. The ability to smallholder agriculture to transform from subsistence and semi-commercial farming to commercialized farming requires linkages to factor markets to access credit, land, inputs (seeds, fertilizer and pesticides) and technology. In this section, we look at the significant challenges to diversification, the disadvantages of smallholders to commercialize due to capital market imperfections and changing characteristics of inputs markets.

7.3.1 Small Farms and the Costs of Diversification

Diversification of production at the farm level is critical for food security through increased availability of nutritious food and for improving incomes. However, the ability to diversify is determined by both policy and access to factors of production such as seeds, fertilizer and pesticides, credit and extension services. Food policy in India has traditionally focused on concerns of calorific security, where it aimed to ensure the availability of sufficient calories for its citizens (Varshney, 1998). GR technologies focused mainly on wheat and rice and agricultural policies focused on price support and direct procurement aimed to bring about intensive cereal-based transformations (de Janvry & Subbarao, 1986; Dorward, Kydd, Morrison, & Urey, 2004; Freebairn, 1995; Goldman & Smith, 1995).

In comparison, food grains such as coarse cereals and pulses did not see much technological intervention or market support. The unintended consequence was that it reduced the incentives for the cultivation of micronutrient-rich coarse grains and pulses in favor of wheat and rice affecting the availability of micronutrient-rich foods.

Costs of producing and selling different crops vary depending on their characteristics as commodities or products. Commodities are "Standardized agricultural products that have had little or no processing and often raw materials for further procession" (Schaffner, Schroder & Earle, 1998, p. 6). Products are commodities that are differentiated based on attributes (organic, processed, branded, variety, perishability) or commodities with value addition (Reardon & Timmer, 2007). The notable difference between commodities and products is that commodities are fungible (substitutable) raw materials or produce like corn, wheat, rice, crude oil or iron ore, while products are of higher value, perishable and often require specialized value chains.

The cost dynamics for growing commodities and products are fundamentally different and this influences the ability of farms to diversify. Table 7.1 highlights the various features on which commodities and products differ at the farm level. As products such as fruits and vegetables, milk, and so on are highly differentiated, they may require higher labor inputs, monitoring and higher levels of credit access to procure quality

Table 7.1   Factors influencing costs at the farm level for commodities and products

Characteristics	Products	Commodities
Labor input	Higher labor inputs to manage crops at the farm level. Pesticide and fertilizer application	Relatively low. Labor requirements during sowing and harvesting are high
Monitoring	Higher monitoring is required to control for quality and grade during the growing process	Constant monitoring is not required and this may contribute to lower labor
Credit	Higher labor and monitoring along with the need for quality inputs raises the need to access credit	The level of credit needed will be lower than products
Inputs	Specific inputs such as seeds, medicines, fertilizers and pesticides may be needed, raising the costs of access and negotiation	Subsidized inputs such as seeds, fertilizers and pesticides available, reducing the cost of production and access costs compared to products

inputs as grades and standards requirements for marketing products may be more stringent. This raises the costs of production and management at the farm level for products in comparison to commodities.

The capacity of small farms to diversify from commodities to high-value products has production and management costs and risks associated with them. The willingness of farming households to diversify or stay in semi-commercial production systems will depend on behavioral characteristics such as levels of risk aversion and the ability to withstand and manage those risks. Therefore, access to infrastructure such as irrigation and inputs such as credit and quality inputs in the forms of seeds, fertilizer and pesticides plays an essential role in the ability of smallholders to diversify. Credit availability, changing labor costs and costs of inputs are determining factors not just for diversification but also for agricultural production growth in general.

7.3.2   Challenges in Accessing Factor Markets and Improving Supply—Credit, Labor and Input Costs

The ability of small farms to access credit, labor and inputs such as quality seeds, fertilizers and pesticides determines their capacity to commercialize and improve household level incomes. Access to these factors of production is influenced fundamentally by credit availability. Capital market imperfections limit access to credit for farms with low land endowments because they have limited value as collateral (Besley, 1995a, 1995b; Bhaduri, 1977; J. Ghosh, 2013; P. Ghosh, Mookherjee, & Ray, 2001). As the scope for internally financing agricultural production is limited due to slow turnover of capital for small farms, the need for credit is essential. To assess the potential for smallholder production to commercialize and diversify, we look at the challenges in accessing credit and input markets and the changing dynamics of labor markets.

7.3.2.1 Access to Institutional Credit

The impact increased access to institutional credit has on agricultural productivity in India is well established. Binswanger and Khandker (1992) show that credit access has a positive effect on agricultural output and that it increased the use of fertilizer and investment in livestock and machinery at the farm level. Bhalla and Singh (2010) using a district level analysis show that institutional credit has a positive effect on mechanization and non-labor inputs, and in regions that are technologically backward, the elasticity is much higher. Access to institutional credit (from financial institutions such as banks) is conditioned on the size of landholding and access to irrigation. Financial institutions often do not have enough local knowledge about borrowers regarding their risk profiles, and this makes collateral (irrigated land) an essential criterion for borrowings (Bardhan, 1996). The high cost of acquiring information disqualifies marginal farmers, tenant farmers and households without proper title deeds to the land from accessing credit.

Poor access to banks makes non-institutional sources such as moneylenders and input dealers an important option for credit, affecting profit and growth in the agricultural sector. According to the Situation of Agricultural Households Survey (2014) carried out by the National Sample Survey (NSS), 52% of all agricultural households in India are indebted. The data also revealed the relationship between the size of landholdings and access to formal credit. Figure 7.5 shows the indebtedness in the agricultural sector with the landholding size of agricultural households. The borrowings of households possessing less than two hectares of land (marginal landholders) are higher from informal sources, and the percentage of borrowing from formal sources goes up with an increase in land size.

Since the early 2000s, there has been a significant drive to improve credit access for agricultural producers. Figure 7.6 shows that between

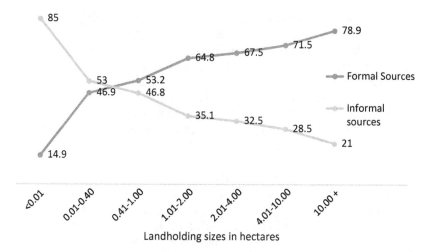

Fig. 7.5 Percentage of indebtedness of different landholding sizes from different sources of credit (2014). Source: Situation of Agricultural Households Survey, NSSO, 2014

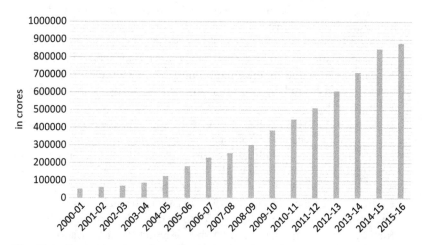

Fig. 7.6 Institutional credit to the agricultural sector (2000–01 to 2015–16). Source: Ministry of Agriculture and Farmers Welfare, Government of India

2000–01 and 2015–16 overall agricultural credit grew 16 times from 52,827 crores to 877,527 at the compounded annual growth rate (CAGR) of 20.6%. However, there are notable regional variations with the southern regions accessing 39% of the total agricultural loans. The *lagging states* in the central and eastern zones receive a lower proportion of 7% and 12%, respectively (Table 7.2). Schemes such as the Kisan Credit Card (KCC)

Table 7.2 Percentage share of agricultural loan (accounts and amounts) and KCC in 2016 in various states/regions

Selected states/regions	Agricultural loans		Kisan Credit Cards	
	Percentage of bank accounts to total	Percentage of loan amount total	Percentage of KCC issued since inception	Percentage of outstanding amount
Andhra Pradesh	6.86	9.80	9.69	5.79
Karnataka	5.32	5.01	6.31	6.67
Kerala	9.06	12.15	3.48	2.01
Tamil Nadu	5.07	3.35	6.61	2.94
Telangana	7.94	8.56	6.63	4.04
South Zone total	*34.24*	*38.87*	*32.73*	*21.45*
Gujarat	3.22	5.15	2.90	5.68
Maharashtra	7.99	7.25	6.93	8.63
Rajasthan	6.58	7.81	5.58	11.14
West Zone total	*17.81*	*20.27*	*15.42*	*25.45*
Haryana	3.21	5.75	2.42	6.45
Himachal Pradesh	0.28	0.59	0.51	0.79
Punjab	2.82	9.78	2.54	10.13
Uttarakhand	0.56	0.73	1.32	1.34
Uttar Pradesh	10.80	4.31	19.50	14.86
Jammu & Kashmir	0.13	0.32	0.47	0.68
North Zone total	*17.80*	*21.48*	*26.77*	*34.25*
Chhattisgarh	7.51	6.02	0.52	1.04
Madhya Pradesh	2.06	0.98	6.12	8.46
Central Zone total	*9.57*	*7.00*	*6.65*	*9.51*
Jharkhand	3.65	4.68	1.27	0.60
Bihar	0.40	0.42	4.54	3.08
Orissa	6.42	2.11	5.25	2.56
West Bengal	9.87	4.51	5.42	2.01
East Zone total	*20.34*	*11.72*	*16.49*	*8.26*
North East states total	*0.24*	*0.67*	*1.95*	*1.09*

Source: Department of Agriculture, Cooperation & Farmers Welfare, Government of India

were introduced in 1998 to improve timely access to short-term loans and simplify the process of screening. Again, regional variation in credit access through this scheme has been varied. Table 7.2 shows that the south and north zones have about twice as many credit cards issued and renewed compared to the central and east zones. Uttar Pradesh accounts for 19.5% of all KCC issued. In a study in the Krishnagiri district of Tamil Nadu, data collected from 120 farmers growing paddy, sugarcane and groundnuts showed that net income and cost of production for farmers with access to KCC were higher (Prakash & Kumar, 2016). The higher cost of production was attributed to the purchase of higher volumes and quality of inputs for production. A study by NABARD (Mani, 2016) with 714 farming households in 6 Indian states showed that farmer with access to KCC saw an average increase in income of 5462 rupees per acre.

In order for these advantages to percolate more widely, there is a need to increase coverage of KCC especially in the east and central regions. The other challenges that have limited access to KCC have been the time taken to sanction them, socioeconomic biases based on caste and landholding size, low credit limit and lack of awareness among farmers that these provisions are available to them (Kumar, Yadav, Jee, Kumar, & Chauhan, 2011; Mani, 2016; Prakash & Kumar, 2016). Addressing these will be essential for smallholder commercialization especially in regions of poor agricultural growth.

7.3.2.2 Changing Labor Costs—Effects of Farm Level and Non-farm Wages

Effective labor utilization of small farms using family labor was the main factor that gave small farms the advantage of higher per capita productivity. As non-farm opportunity costs were higher, labor could substitute capital and lumpy inputs at the farm level leading to efficient labor utilization. In the past two decades, India has seen a growth in real farm wages at the rate of 6.8% per annum and this is expected to rise with further economic growth (Gulati, Jain, & Satija, 2014). Simultaneously there has been a growth of non-farm wages as well resulting from the growth of other sectors and rural social programs, especially the Mahatma Gandhi National Rural Employment Guarantee Scheme (MGNREGS) (Binswanger-Mkhize, 2013; Gulati et al., 2014), leading to an increase in farm level opportunity costs. Binswanger and Singh (2017) observe that rising non-farm wages have pulled family labor out of farms as off-farm opportunity costs decrease. They also note that non-farm wage increase tends to pull family labor out of the agricultural sector and not hired labor, as they may be older with little education. The pull of family labor effectively erodes the advantage of labor utilization and reduces profits, as farm wages of hired labor is high.

Also, because of the migration of productive male labor, an increase in the feminization of agriculture is taking place (Agarwal, 2010; Pattnaik, Lahiri-Dutt, Lockie, & Pritchard, 2018). Mechanization will play an essential role in improving agricultural productivity, adjusting for rising wages and reduction of drudgery in farming. In the process of structural transformation, different countries have addressed wage increases through mechanization replacing wage labor, farmers exiting agriculture for non-farm sectors, diversification to higher value crops to increase income, state expenditure in productivity increasing technologies and raising food prices to support farm incomes (Binswanger & Singh, 2017). However, the major challenge for small farms with credit constraints and lower than optimal size for mechanization, as it is not scale-neutral, remains. Freeing up land lease markets that can enable small farms to lease in the land, capital subsidies to buy equipment in the wake of credit constraints and aggregation of small farms may be a few solutions to enabling this shift.

7.3.2.3 Changing Nature of Input Markets and Access Problems

The change in dependence on input markets by smallholder households as opposed to depending on using inputs sourced at the farm is an integral part of commercialization. Pray and Nagarajan (2014) argue that the transformation of the agricultural input industry went through two stages. Before the Green Revolution, a majority of seeds, manure, draught and labor was sourced at the farm level. GR technologies shifted the orientation of input access to a greater reliance on markets for seeds and inputs such as chemical fertilizers and pesticides. Initially, State-owned Enterprises (SoEs) played an integral role in the production of inputs. In the late 1980s onward with the liberalization of the Indian economy and post-WTO agreements, private firms have emerged to be significant players in agricultural inputs. The opening up of the economy marked the second stage of the input industry transformation. Table 7.3 shows the changing share in private sector involvement in agricultural inputs. Besides fertilizer production, the private sector dominates the sales of other inputs, namely, seeds and pesticides. Concerning farm implements and machinery such as tractors, the private sector has always been the dominant player.

The current challenges of the Indian food system deviate from what GR technologies were designed to and capable of addressing. Concerning issues

Table 7.3 Changing share of private and public sectors in agricultural inputs (1991–2009)

Industry	1991		2009	
	Public sector	Private sector	Public sector	Private sector
Share of seeds sale	35	65	20	80
Share of pesticides sale	8	92	<1	>99
Share of tractor sales	16	84	1	99
Share of fertilizer sales	60	40	50	50

Source: Pray and Nagarajan (2014)

of diversification and resilience and the inputs that are needed to achieve them, the private sector has emerged as the front-runner. Private sector innovations in the past decade have focused on high-value crops such as fruits and vegetables and also coarse grains such as pearl millets and sorghum (Ferroni & Zhou, 2017). Multinational companies (MNCs) account for 44% of the seed industry R&D and have been responsible for a majority of biotechnology-based research, especially genetic modification (Pray & Nagarajan, 2014). An important aspect relevant in the context of these changes in the input market is the ability of smallholders to access new seed technologies.

Access to capital is essential to increase access to quality inputs. Smallholders have low access to institutional credit and this influences their ability to increase production and diversify through the access to quality inputs and technology. Regions with irrigation and lower climatic risk were able to implement scale-neutral technologies enabling productivity growth during the Green Revolution. The current challenge is to improve agricultural productivity in marginal lands and regions that did not benefit from the Green Revolution. The newer production and seed technologies essential to achieve this requires credit and context-specific information and mechanization. Addressing the issue of scale and access to capital, therefore, remains the two main challenges for smallholder productivity growth in agriculture.

7.4   The Way Forward: Institutional Interventions to Address Production Challenges and Reducing Regional Disparity

The ability of smallholder production to adapt to changing demand and the opportunities for growth depend on increasing marketable surplus and diversifying. As production challenges vary according to regions, addressing regional disparities is needed to reduce yield gaps and improve livelihoods in poorer states that did not benefit from the Green Revolution. In this section, we first look at the scope of institutional interventions such as aggregation models and land reforms in addressing the issue of scale. Second, we assess the potential of bringing the Green Revolution to the eastern states of India. These measures we argue are critical to address issues related to economies of scale disadvantages to small farms and unequal economic and agricultural development.

7.4.1   Institutional Interventions in Smallholder Agriculture-Aggregation Models—Revisiting Land Tenure Systems

In smallholder agricultural systems, the cost of accessing inputs, information and R&D is a challenge for resource-poor small farms. Institutional interventions that can offset disadvantages of small farms and enable effective implementation and uptake of policy targeted at improving production become important. Aggregation models such as producer organizations and cooperatives, where smallholders organize themselves in groups to jointly access resources and market their produce, have shown to reduce transaction cost and form market linkages (Barrett et al., 2012; Bellemare, 2012; Boselie, Henson, & Weatherspoon, 2003; Briones, 2015; Reardon, Barrett, Berdegué, & Swinnen, 2009; Schipmann & Qaim, 2010). Promoting these institutions will help smallholders mitigate some of the transaction costs associated with market entry, as it addresses problems associated with economies of scale.

Cooperatives have been promoted globally to remedy the disadvantages of scale to small farms with differing levels of success (Devaux et al., 2009; Kherallah, Delgado, Gabre-Madhin, Minot, & Johnson, 2002; Stockbridge, Dorward, & Kydd, 2003). In countries like Japan, South Korea and Taiwan that were founded upon small farms,[1] cooperatives were set up, and factors that put small farms at a disadvantage were neutralized through state-provisioned extension services, key inputs, irrigation and market intervention operations (Huang, 2006; Kajita, 1965; Lin, 2006). Aggregation of producers will help reduce the fixed cost of accessing resource and services and once made available these institutions can disseminate it with little additional costs.

---

[1] The average size of landholdings in Japan and Korea in the twenty-first century are 1.2 acres and 1 acre, respectively (Fan & Chan-Kang, 2003) and less than 1 acre in Taiwan (Lam, 2006).

However, in many developing countries and in India, cooperatives in the past have been less successful. Their effectiveness was limited by issues of poor organization and incompetent management, political interference in their functioning, financial irregularities and corruption within the organizations (Akwabi-Ameyaw, 1997; Attwood, 1982, 1987; Baviskar, 1987; Holloway, Nicholson, Delgado, Staal, & Ehui, 2000; Lalvani, 2008). In India, the significant challenges the cooperatives faced were structural and incentive based. The structural problems were political and bureaucratic interference, poor management and governance, and elite capture of the activities to their benefit. Cooperatives also faced incentive problems characterized by dormant membership and poor participation of members, hindering the growth of these organizations. These incentive problems were due to non-percolation of benefits to members, especially the demography the cooperatives meant to empower.

Since the early 2000s, there has been a significant drive in India to promote producer organizations in the agricultural sector. The amendment of the Companies Act in 2003 that enabled the formation of Producer Companies (PCs) was a vital step in this direction. The producer-owner system increases the agency of members and reduces the role of the state and bureaucracy, preventing exogenous power capture. More agency for these organizations may prove to be a crucial step in addressing some of the structural issues that hindered the effectiveness of cooperatives. State support to set up aggregation models and capacity building to help producers manage these organizations and help in forming linkages to input and output markets will be important. These institutions can rectify scale-related disadvantages for smallholders in accessing technology, credit, information and inputs while reducing transaction costs to enable commercialization.

7.4.1.1 Land Tenure and the Question of Access to Land
Unequal access to land has persisted in India due to the failure to implement land reforms post-independence. Although land reforms failed to redistribute land among cultivators, it did to an extent limit land tenure practices and made them in illegal in many states. The two central tenure practices are fixed rent contracts and sharecropping contracts (Chaudhuri & Maitra, 1997). In a fixed rent contract, the tenant cultivates the land leased from the owner for a fixed share of the produce. The tenant bears the production risks and may not have the incentive to increase production over a certain level due to perceived risks. In a sharecropping contract,

the tenant leases land from the owner and the rent is a percentage share of the total output. Here the owner and the tenant share the risk, and the tenant has a higher incentive to make investments on the farm.

According to the latest census data (2010–11), 86% of agricultural land in India is less than two hectares in size. The number of small farms has increased by about 6% since 1991–92. Because of increasing fragmentation of land holdings, land leasing is an essential practice for improving access to land (Ballabh & Walker, 1992; Bell, 1990; Melmed-Sanjak, 1998; Sadoulet, Murgai, & de Janvry, 1998; Vaidyanathan, 1994). Although land tenancy has fallen considerably since the land reforms, according to the 2010–11 census of the Government of India, 10.4% of rural households lease land. This figure ranges from 5% in Madhya Pradesh to 36% in the erstwhile Andhra Pradesh. The Government of India in 2016 proposed a model land leasing act to enable the leasing of land. According to the Expert Committee report on land leasing (GOI, 2016), legalizing land leasing can encourage larger landowners and small and marginal farms alike. Larger landowners can lease out land through sharecropping when agricultural wages and monitoring costs are high without fear of losing ownership, while smallholders can lease out land and seek employment outside agriculture when non-farm wages increase, supplementing wages with land rent.

Legalizing land leasing can improve access to land. However, issues of how tenant farmers can access credit, as leased-in land is insufficient collateral, will need to be addressed. A study by Haque and Nair (2014) on the Kudumbashree Mission, a women's collective in Kerala, shows that women's collectives (of 2–10 members) jointly leasing in land to cultivate fruits and vegetables and tapioca earned on an average 42,000 rupees per acre. These women's groups also had access to collateral-free credit through Joint Liability Groups (JLGs), where the groups were jointly liable for the loans they took. Valuable lessons can be learned from such experiences.

7.4.2   Agricultural Development in Eastern India—Rectifying Regional Disparities

Improving agricultural production in regions that the Green Revolution did not benefit will be important to rectify regional disparity through agricultural development and improved incomes. Agriculture's share in state GDP of the eastern states of Bihar, Chhattisgarh, Jharkhand, Odisha, eastern Uttar Pradesh, West Bengal and Assam is high, while productivity remains low. Improving agricultural production in regions that did not reap the benefits of the Green Revolution is important to rectify regional disparity in agricultural development and incomes. According to the National Bureau of Soil Survey and Land Use Planning (NBSS&LUP), the LGP in these regions is 240 days and the annual rainfall range from 1000 to 2500 mm per annum (GOI, 2015). The availability of groundwater in these regions is also high but remains untapped for agricultural development.

Despite these advantages, the exposure to abiotic stress resulting from droughts, floods and submergence is high due to poor access to irrigation and infrastructure of flood control. In many states such as Odisha, Assam, Jharkhand and Chhattisgarh, households only have a single sowing season. Eighty-two percent of the fallowed land is in the eastern part of India (Singh, Praharaj, & Sandhu, 2016). In the post paddy season, the land is often left fallow although there is potential to grow crops such as pulses using the residual moisture of the previous season. Practices of open grazing and labor outmigration during this season also make the adoption of second sowing problematic. In these states mentioned above, the rate of migration to urban areas and *urbanizing states* are high as off-farm wages have increased in recent years resulting in the pull of labor from the agricultural sector.

Getting agricultural productivity going in these regions requires infrastructural development and institutional interventions. Development of irrigation in these regions is vital to reduce abiotic stress during the growing seasons. Micro-irrigation and communal irrigation facilities such as water user groups can help reduce overuse of water and promote judicious use of water resources. Improved access to irrigation and reduced abiotic stress resulting from late rainfall and drought, increase the scope for diversification and may improve access to credit as risks reduce. Improving access to cold chains and specific value chains for perishables will also improve connectivity to markets and marketing opportunities (this is discussed in detail in the next chapter). Institutional interventions such as good extension services, R&D focused on the advantages of these regions and aggregation models to reduce the disadvantages of scale are especially relevant in the eastern states. This region may not have the same potential as Punjab, Haryana and the southern Delta regions in reaching yield potential in paddy, but have the scope to develop a comparative advantage in growing crops such as pulses and certain fruits and vegetables.

Development of extension services to help with cropping transitions is essential. Traditionally, R&D has focused on significant cereals, and extending this to other crops will disproportionately benefit these regions. Technologies in increasing yields in pulses and coarse grains, short duration crops to adjust to climatic conditions, and crops with improved resilience to abiotic stresses will be crucial to this region. These technologies along with mechanization can offset the effects of migration by reducing the drudgery of women and improving productivity. Lastly, aggregation models can remedy the disadvantages of scale in accessing resources and technology and will prove essential for the development of the agricultural sector in this region.

7.5   CONCLUSION

Growing population and changing demand have brought about opportunities for growth and challenges to the Indian agricultural sector. At the farm level, the ability of small farms to commercialize (increase engagement with input and output markets) and diversify will determine their scope to increase production and diversify in line with changing demand. However, the institutional challenges for small farms are their ability to access capital, technology and mechanization that are essential for commercialization. The Green Revolution was successful in India because the technologies that it brought were scale-neutral and small farms were able to take advantage of the higher productivity of family labor. Institutional support in the form of direct procurement of food grains, minimum support prices and input subsidies complemented technological measures to incentivize adoption. However, these GR technologies were concentrated on major food grains, were not resource-neutral and therefore were successful only in regions that had access to irrigation or had low agroclimatic risks.

Agricultural sector growth depends on rectifying interregional disparities and improving access to capital, mechanization and quality inputs such as yield increasing seed technologies to enable commercialization and diversification. As newer technologies are not scale-neutral and the advantages of family labor utilization are being eroded due to rising off-farm wages, access to capital and addressing the issues of economies of scale is critical. In this chapter, we looked at the scope of institutional interventions to rectify small farm disadvantages. We assessed the scope of aggregation models such as cooperatives and FPOs in rectifying the scale disadvantages of accessing capital and technology and suggested their widespread promotion in different parts of the country. We touched upon the need to revisit the issue of land reforms, not from the point of view of redistribution, but concerning reforming land tenure systems to improve access to land and better enable access to mechanization and credit. We also suggested that special attention be paid to agricultural development in eastern India that has a high potential for commercialization and diversification. Measures to improve access to yield increasing technologies and corresponding institutional support in the form of increased access to credit, R&D and information will be essential. Interventions on these lines can help align supply conditions to changing demand to utilize the opportunities for growth for smallholder agriculture.

References

Abraham, M., & Pingali, P. (2019). Shortage of pulses in India: Understanding how markets incentivize supply response. *Journal of Agribusiness in Developing and Emerging Economies*, forthcoming.

Agarwal, B. (2010). Rethinking agricultural production collectivities. *Economic and Political Weekly, 45*(9), 64–78.

Akwabi-Ameyaw, K. (1997). Producer cooperative resettlement projects in Zimbabwe: Lessons from a failed agricultural strategy. *World Development, 25*, 437–456.

Attwood, D. W. (1982). *Class interests and changes in the organisation of production in the Indian sugar industry*. Paper presented at the annual meeting of the Social Science History Association (Vol. Bloomington).

Attwood, D. W. (1987). Social and political preconditions for successful cooperatives: The cooperative sugar factories of western India. In D. W. Attwood & B. S. Baviskar (Eds.), *Cooperatives and rural development*. New Delhi and Oxford: Oxford University Press.

Ballabh, V., & Walker, T. S. (1992). Land fragmentation and consolidation in dry semi-arid tropics of India. *Artha Vijnana, 34*(4), 363–387.

Bardhan, P. (1973). Size, productivity and returns to scale: An analysis of farmlevel data in Indian agriculture. *Journal of Political Economy, 81*(6), 1370–1386.

Bardhan, P. (1996). The nature of institutional impediments to economic development. Mimeo. Retrieved from https://ageconsearch.umn.edu/record/233429/files/cal-cider-c096-066.pdf

Barrett, C. B., Bachke, M. E., Bellemare, M. F., Michelson, H. C., Narayanan, S., & Walker, T. F. (2012). Smallholder participation in contract farming: Comparative evidence from five countries. *World Development, 40*(4), 715–730. https://doi.org/10.1016/j.worlddev.2011.09.006

Baviskar, B. S. (1987). Cooperatives and rural development in India. *Current Anthropology, 28*(4), 564–565.

Bell, C. (1990). Reforming property rights in land and tenancy. *World Bank Research Observer, 5*(2), 143–166.

Bellemare, M. F. (2012). As you sow, so shall you reap: The welfare impacts of contract farming. *World Development, 40*(7), 1418–1434. https://doi.org/10.1016/j.worlddev.2011.12.008

Benjamin, D. (1995). Can unobserved land quality explain the inverse productivity relationship? *Journal of Development Economics, 46*, 51–84.

Bernstein, H. (2010). *Class dynamics of agrarian change*. West Hartford, CT: Kumarian Press.

Besley, T. (1995a). Property rights and investment incentives: Theory and evidence from Ghana. *Journal of Political Economy, 103*(5), 903–937.

Besley, T. (1995b). Savings, credit and insurance. In J. Behrman & T. N. Srinivasan (Eds.), *The handbook of developmental economics* (pp. 2124–2207). Amsterdam: Elsevier Science Publishers, B.V.

Bhaduri, A. (1977). On the formation of usurious interest rates in backward agriculture. *Cambridge Journal of Economics, 1*(4), 341–352.

Bhalla, G. S., & Singh, G. (2010). *Growth of Indian agriculture: A district level study*. Final report submitted to Planning Commission, Government of India, New Delhi.

Bhalla, S. S., & Roy, P. (1988). Mis-specification in farm productivity analysis: The role of land quality. *Oxford Economic Papers, 40*(1), 55–73.

Binswanger-Mkhize, H. P. (2013). The stunted structural transformation of the Indian economy: Agriculture, manufacturing and the rural non-farm sector. *Economic and Political Weekly, 48*, 5–13. Retrieved from https://www.epw.in/journal/2013/26-27/review-rural-affairs-review-issues/stuntedstructural-transformation-indian

Binswanger, H. P., & Khandker, S. (1992). *The impact of formal finance on the rural economy of India* (No. 949). Washington, DC.

Binswanger, H. P., & Rosenzweig, M. R. (1986). Behavioural and material determinants of production relations in agriculture. *Journal of Development Studies, 22*, 503–539.

Binswanger, H. P., & Singh, S. K. (2017). Wages, prices and agriculture: How can Indian agriculture cope with rising wages? *Journal of Agricultural Economics, 69*(2), 281–305. https://doi.org/10.1111/1477-9552.12234

Birner, R., & Resnick, D. (2010). The political economy of policies for smallholder agriculture. *World Development, 38*(10), 1442–1452. https://doi.org/10.1016/j.worlddev.2010.06.001

Boselie, D., Henson, S., & Weatherspoon, D. (2003). Supermarket procurement practices in developing countries: Redefining the roles of the public and private sectors. *American Journal of Agricultural Economics, 85*(5), 1155–1161.

Briones, R. M. (2015). Small farmers in high-value chains: Binding or relaxing constraints to inclusive growth? *World Development*, *72*, 43–52. https://doi.org/10.1016/j.worlddev.2015.01.005

Carletto, C., Corral, P., & Guelfi, A. (2017). Agricultural commercialization and nutrition revisited: Empirical evidence from three African countries. *Food Policy*, *67*, 106–118. https://doi.org/10.1016/j.foodpol.2016.09.020

Chaudhuri, A., & Maitra, P. (1997). *Determinants of land tenure contracts; Theory and evidence from rural India*. Department of Economics—Departmental Working Papers.

de Janvry, A., & Subbarao, K. (1986). *Agricultural price policy and income distribution in India*. New Delhi: Oxford University Press.

Devaux, A., Horton, D., Velasco, C., Thiele, G., López, G., Bernet, T., ... Ordinola, M. (2009). Collective action for market chain innovation in the Andes. *Collective Action for Smallholder Market Access*, *34*(1), 31–38. https://doi.org/10.1016/j.foodpol.2008.10.007

Dorward, A., Kydd, J., Morrison, J., & Urey, I. (2004). A policy agenda for pro-poor agricultural growth. *World Development*, *32*(1), 73–89.

Eastwood, R., Lipton, M., & Newell, A. (2010). Farm size. *Handbook of Agricultural Economics*, *4*, 3323–3397. https://doi.org/10.1016/S1574-0072(09)04065-1

Eswaran, M., & Kotwal, A. (1986). Access to capital and agrarian production organisation. *Economic Journal*, *96*(382), 482–498.

Fan, S., & Chan-Kang, C. (2003). Is small beautiful? Farm size, productivity and poverty in Asian agriculture. In *Proceedings of the 25th International Conference of Agricultural Economists*, Durban, South Africa.

Feder, G. (1985). The relation between farm size and farm productivity. *Journal of Development Economics*, *18*, 297–313.

Feder, G., Just, R. E., & Zilberman, D. (1985). Adoption of agricultural innovations in developing countries: A survey. *Economic Development and Cultural Change*, *33*(2), 255–298. https://doi.org/10.1086/451461

Ferroni, M., & Zhou, Y. (2017). The private sector and India's agricultural transformation. *Global Journal of Emerging Market Economies*, *9*(1–3), 28–37. https://doi.org/10.1177/0974910117716406

Freebairn, D. K. (1995). Did the green revolution concentrate incomes? A quantitative study of research reports. *World Development*, *23*(2), 265–279. https://doi.org/10.1016/0305-750X(94)00116-G

Ghosh, J. (2013). Microfinance and the challenge of financial inclusion for development. *Cambridge Journal of Economics*, *37*(6), 1203–1219.

Ghosh, P., Mookherjee, D., & Ray, D. (2001). Credit rationing in developing countries: An overview of the theory. In D. Mookherjee & D. Ray (Eds.), *Readings in the theory of economic development* (pp. 283–301). Malden, MA: Blackwell Publishing Ltd.

GOI. (2015). *Raising agricultural productivity and making farming remunerative for farmers*. New Delhi.

GOI. (2016). *Report of the expert committee on land leasing*. New Delhi.

Goldman, A., & Smith, J. (1995). Agricultural transformations in India and Northern Nigeria: Exploring the nature of Green Revolutions. *World Development, 23*(2), 243–263. https://doi.org/10.1016/0305-750X(94)00115-F

Gulati, A., Jain, S., & Satija, N. (2014). Rising farm wages in India—The 'pull' and 'push' factors. *Journal of Land and Rural Studies, 2*(2), 261–286. https://doi.org/10.1177/2321024914534045

Haque, T., & Nair, J. L. (2014). *Ensuring and protecting the land leasing right of poor women in India*. Paper prepared for presentation at the "2014 World Bank Conference on Land and Poverty", The World Bank.

Hazell, P. (2018). Urbanization, agriculture and smallholder farming. In R. Serraj & P. Pingali (Eds.), *Agriculture and food systems to 2050: Global trend, challenges and opportunities* (pp. 137–160). Singapore: World Scientific.

Hazell, P., Poulton, C., Wiggins, S., & Dorward, A. (2010). The future of small farms: Trajectories and policy priorities. *World Development, 38*(10), 1349–1361. https://doi.org/10.1016/j.worlddev.2009.06.012

Holloway, G., Nicholson, N., Delgado, C., Staal, S., & Ehui, S. (2000). Agroindustrialization through institutional innovation: Transaction costs, cooperatives and milk-market development in the east-African highlands. *Agricultural Economics, 23*, 279–288.

Huang, J. (2006). *Taiwan in transformation, 1895–2005: The challenge of a new democracy to an old civilization*. New Brunswick, NJ: Transaction Publishers.

Johnson, N. L., & Ruttan, V. W. (1994). Why are farms so small? *World Development, 22*(5), 691–706. https://doi.org/10.1016/0305-750X(94)90044-2

Kajita, M. (1965). Land policy after land reforms in Japan. *Developing Economies, 3*(1), 88–105. https://doi.org/10.1111/j.1746-1049.1965.tb00749.x

Kherallah, M., Delgado, C., Gabre-Madhin, E., Minot, N., & Johnson, M. (2002). *Reforming agricultural markets in Africa*. Baltimore, MD: John Hopkins University.

Kumar, A., Yadav, C., Jee, S., Kumar, S., & Chauhan, S. (2011). Financial innovation in Indian agricultural credit market: Progress and performance of Kisan Credit Card. *Indian Journal of Agricultural Economics, 66*(3), 418–428.

Lalvani, M. (2008). Sugar co-operatives in Maharashtra: A political economy perspective. *Journal of Development Studies, 44*(10), 1474–1505. https://doi.org/10.1080/00220380802265108

Lam, W. F. (2006). Foundations of a robust social-ecological system: Irrigation institutions in Taiwan. *Journal of Institutional Economics, 2*(2), 203–226.

Lin, D. (2006). Agricultural cooperatives in Taiwan. In *2006 FFTC-NACF International Seminar on Agricultural Cooperatives in Asia: Innovations and Opportunities in the 21st Century*. Seoul, Korea.

Mani, G. (2016). *Study on implementation of Kisan Credit Card scheme*. Occasional Paper No. 64.

Mazumdar, D. (1965). Size of farm and productivity—A problem of Indian peasant agriculture. *Economica, 32*(126), 161–173.

Melmed-Sanjak, J. (1998). *A review of the literature on land leasing arrangements in selected Asian countries.* Rome.

Mosley, P. (2002). The African green revolution as a pro-poor policy instrument. *Journal of International Development, 14*(6), 695–724. https://doi.org/10.1002/jid.912

National Sample Survey Organisation (NSSO). (2014). *Key indicators of situation of agricultural households in India.* National Sample Survey 70th Round, Ministry of Statistics and Programme Implementation, Government of India, New Delhi.

Pattnaik, I., Lahiri-Dutt, K., Lockie, S., & Pritchard, B. (2018). The feminization of agriculture or the feminization of agrarian distress? Tracking the trajectory of women in agriculture in India. *Journal of the Asia Pacific Economy, 23*(1), 138–155. https://doi.org/10.1080/13547860.2017.1394569

Pingali, P. (2012). Green revolution: Impacts, limits, and the path ahead. *Proceedings of the National Academy of Science, 109*(31), 12302–12308. https://doi.org/10.1073/pnas.0912953109

Pingali, P. (2015). Agricultural policy and nutrition outcomes—Getting beyond the preoccupation with staple grains. *Food Security, 7*(3), 583–591. https://doi.org/10.1007/s12571-015-0461-x

Pingali, P., Khwaja, Y., & Madelon, M. (2005). *Commercializing small farms: Reducing transaction cost.* ESA Working Paper (No.), 05-08.

Pingali, P., & Rosegrant, M. W. (1995). Agricultural commercialization and diversification: Processes and policies. *Food Policy, 20*(3), 171–185. https://doi.org/10.1016/0306-9192(95)00012-4

Poulton, C., Dorward, A., & Kydd, J. (2010). The future of small farms: New directions for services, institutions, and intermediation. *World Development, 38*(10), 1413–1428. https://doi.org/10.1016/j.worlddev.2009.06.009

Prakash, P., & Kumar, P. (2016). Performance of Kisan Credit Card scheme in Tamil Nadu. *Indian Journal of Agricultural Economics, 71*(2), 191–211.

Pray, C. E., & Nagarajan, L. (2014). The transformation of the Indian agricultural input industry: Has it increased agricultural R&D? *Agricultural Economics, 45*(S1), 145–156. https://doi.org/10.1111/agec.12138

Reardon, T., Barrett, C. B., Berdegué, J. A., & Swinnen, J. F. M. (2009). Agrifood industry transformation and small farmers in developing countries. *World Development, 37*(11), 1717–1727. https://doi.org/10.1016/j.worlddev.2008.08.023

Reardon, T., & Timmer, P. C. (2007). Chapter 55 Transformation of markets for agricultural output in developing countries since 1950: How has thinking changed? In *Handbook of agricultural economics* (Vol. 3, pp. 2807–2855). Elsevier. https://doi.org/10.1016/S1574-0072(06)03055-6

Sadoulet, E., Murgai, R., & de Janvry, A. (1998). *Access to land via land rental markets.*

Schaffner, D. J., Schroder, W. R., & Earle, M. D. (1998). *Food marketing: An international perspective.* Boston, MA: WCB McGraw-Hill.

Schipmann, C., & Qaim, M. (2010). Spillovers from modern supply chains to traditional markets: Product innovation and adoption by smallholders. *Agricultural Economics, 41*(3–4), 361–371. https://doi.org/10.1111/j.1574-0862.2010.00438.x

Sen, A. K. (1962). An aspect of Indian agriculture. *The Economic Weekly, 14*(46), 243–246.

Sen, A. K. (1966). Peasants and dualism with or without surplus labor. *Journal of Political Economy, 74,* 425–450.

Singh, N., Praharaj, C., & Sandhu, J. (2016). Utilizing untapped potential of rice fallow of East and North-east India through pulse production. *Indian Journal of Genetics and Plant Breeding, 76*(4), 388–398.

Stockbridge, M., Dorward, A., & Kydd, J. (2003). *Farmer organizations for market access: Learning from success.* Volume Briefing Paper. London, UK: Wye College, University of London.

Vaidyanathan, A. (1994). Agrarian relations in the context of new agricultural technology: An issues paper. *Indian Journal of Agricultural Economics, 49*(3), 317–329.

Varshney, A. (1998). *Democracy, development, and the countryside: Urban-rural struggles in India.* https://doi.org/10.1017/CBO9780511609367

von Braun, J. (1995). Agricultural commercialization: Impacts on income and nutrition and implications for policy. *Food Policy, 20*(3), 187–202. https://doi.org/10.1016/0306-9192(95)00013-5

CHAPTER 8

Linking Farms to Markets: Reducing Transaction Costs and Enhancing Bargaining Power

8.1 Introduction

For commercialization, along with increased linkages to factor markets, the link to agricultural output markets is also essential. Access to output or commodity markets determines price realization, incentivizing small farms to diversify production in line with the changing demands of the market. Rising demand for diversified foods has led to a growing emphasis on grades and standards to ensure quality, health, safety and differentiation of products based on tastes and preferences. In response, rapid technological changes to improve the quantity, quality and efficiency of production and marketing are becoming increasingly relevant (Eaton, Meijerink, & Bijman, 2008; Narayanan, 2014; Poulton, Dorward, & Kydd, 2010; Roy & Thorat, 2008; Swinnen & Maertens, 2007). A majority of agricultural marketing in India takes place through traditional spot markets. These predominantly unorganized markets with limited infrastructure cannot meet the quality requirements and specifications of changing demand and this has increased the importance of organized retail for agricultural products (McCullough, Pingali, & Stamoulis, 2008). Parallel to traditional markets, because of changing demand, the organized value chains for food is also growing. In 2017, India's retail sector was valued at 641 billion USD. The share of food and grocery retail in this share was about 60% (or about 380 billion USD), and the percentage of organized retail in this

© The Author(s) 2019

P. Pingali et al., *Transforming Food Systems for a Rising India*,
Palgrave Studies in Agricultural Economics and Food Policy,
https://doi.org/10.1007/978-3-030-14409-8_8

share was roughly 2% (about 7.6 billion USD).[1] The retail food segment in India is therefore significant and unorganized, and the share of organized retail is in comparison small.

Although the current share of organized retail is small, projections expect its share to double by the year 2020. The scope of organized retail in food and groceries is vast. Along with organized retail outlets such as Hypermarket, DMart, More, Big Bazaar, Godrej Nature's Market, Walmart, among others, the growth of e-retail in food is also increasing. Companies such as Amazon Pantry, Big Basket, Grofers and Flipkart (after its purchase by Walmart) are expected to show a high level of growth. Developments in organized retail in food are dependent on effective linkages between farm and retail. This farm-retail linkage is essential for income growth at the farm level, the creation of non-farm employment both in rural and urban areas and also improving efficiency and reducing wastage. Therefore, it will have an impact on economic growth, agricultural development and nutrition and access to food. The ability of small farms to effectively link to value chains that take into consideration new requirements of quality, quantity and efficiency is a significant challenge for the agricultural sector. This chapter is divided into three parts. First, we look at the characteristics and features of traditional marketing chains in India in the context of transaction costs to determine the challenges of market participation to small farms. Second, we assess existing forms and newer market linkages that have emerged in agriculture to identify their potential and problems. Last, we determine the need for institutional interventions to improve small farm-market linkages to bring about an inclusive, nutrition-sensitive value chain.

8.2   AGRICULTURAL MARKETS, SMALL PRODUCERS AND TRANSACTION COSTS

The three agricultural marketing channels in India are state-trading, cooperative marketing and private trade (GOI, 2007). Governmental organizations, such as the Food Corporation of India (FCI), Cotton Corporation of India, Jute Corporation of India and National Agricultural Cooperative Marketing Federation (NAFED), along with specialized commodity boards,

[1] Global Agricultural Information Report (GAIN) (2017): https://gain.fas.usda.gov/Recent%20GAIN%20Publications/Retail%20Foods_New%20Delhi_India_6-28-2018.pdf (Accessed on 24/10/2018).

which were crop-specific to rubber, tea, coffee, tobacco and spices carry out state-trading, where the state is involved in the procurement. Cooperative marketing exists for commodities with high-asset fixity such as milk and fruits like grapes and bananas. Here, members belonging to cooperatives sell their produce by way of specialized supply/value chains. A significant part of agricultural marketing happens through private trade. The Agriculture Produce Marketing Committee (APMC) often referred to as the *mandi* is the primary market infrastructure found in all states (except Jammu and Kashmir, Bihar, Kerala and Manipur). Their primary function is to regulate market practices such as weighing, methods of sale, methods of grading and methods of payment. To date, there are 7246 functioning *mandis* in India.

Although the APMC aims to provide a platform for marketing activities and reducing exploitation by traders and mercantile capital, much of the transactions that take place is unregulated. Figure 8.1 shows the structure of agricultural markets for non-perishable commodities such as cotton, oilseeds, pulses and grain. The various participants in the market are national agri-businesses, big retailers, agro-processors, traders and their commissioning agents and unlicensed petty commodity producers with different forms of contracts and exchange relations with the primary producer. The fragmented

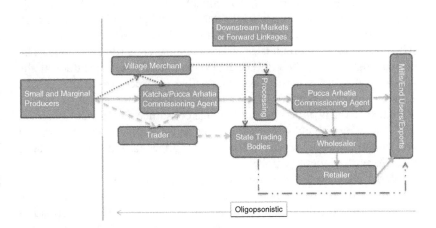

Fig. 8.1 Structure of agricultural markets. Note: The different colored lines denote different channels through which goods are sold and distributed in the market

nature of agricultural markets leads to high transaction costs in its access. The various costs of carrying out marketing activities from price discovery and transportation to searching for buyers and selling are considered market transaction costs.

8.2.1   Transaction Costs in Agricultural Marketing

Higher transaction costs for small and marginal producers are due to low economies of scale, low bargaining power, poor connectivity to markets and information asymmetry resulting from poor price and quality knowledge. The exchange relations in agricultural markets, therefore, are not uniform or equal, nor are they set only in price terms (Bharadwaj, 1985). Transaction costs are household-specific, farm-specific, location-specific and crop-specific (Pingali, Khwaja, & Madelon, 2005). Social categorization such as caste and gender can play an inclusive and exclusionary role concerning access to land, credit and markets (Kumar, 2013; RFST, 2005; Sen, 2000). These household-specific transaction costs can in different situations lead to differences in prices charged/paid for services received or goods sold in market transactions (Thorat, 2009).

Farm and location-specific factors also determine the cost of market access and participation. These costs can be attributed to reduced economies of scale (Poulton et al., 2010). Smallholders with limited marketable surplus may not sell directly in the markets owing to geographical constraints, distance to market and poor connectivity. In such situations, they sell their produce to traders or village merchants at the farm gate. The primary function of these intermediaries is consolidating produce at the village level before selling to traders, retailers or processors at the APMC. According to Chand (2012), an average of four to six transactions take place before the produce reaches the final consumer. In the wake of social, scale and geographic disadvantages, intermediaries play an essential role in providing for missing services, although the price realized at the farm level is the lowest competitive price.

Marketing costs to farms are also crop-specific and vary with commodities and high-value products. Higher value perishable crops have more stringent quality requirement making market connectivity, information and infrastructure such as storage important. Initial costs of creating value chains may also be high mainly due to asset specificity. Table 8.1 highlights the various characteristics that influence marketing conditions of agricultural goods. In the wake of higher costs, smallholders may find it hard to

Table 8.1   Characteristics influencing the marketing of commodities and high-value products

Characteristics	Commodities	High-value products
Market information	Not highly differentiated	Highly differentiated—varieties, nutrient characteristics and value—making information important
Price stability	Prices are relatively stable and are often supported by minimum support price (MSP)	Prices can be volatile with huge seasonal variations
Asset specificity	Lower capital investments and better transferability of capital	Higher capital investment in value chains, storage and so on with limited transferability
Perishability	Can be stored for long periods and may not perish quickly	Products are highly perishable, making the timing of supply important
Quality, grades and standards	Low differentiation leads to minimum grades and standards variation	Highly differentiated with large quality, grades and standard differences

diversify from commodities to high-value products. Addressing these market-level costs is central to enable diversification through price incentives to farmers growing them.

Agricultural markets in India are complex institutional arrangements with many forms of exchange relations and transaction costs. The prominent features of these markets are that (a) participants have low economies of scale; (b) the supply chains are highly fragmented with a large number of intermediaries leading to marketing malpractices (e.g., poor weighing practices, no grades and standards), poor price realization and poor signaling; and (c) the nature of agricultural produce (commodity or product) determine the challenges in marketing. Existing markets, therefore, may not be conducive for the marketing of higher value, grades and standard oriented products. Also, private trade through the APMCs with these limitations have made it difficult for direct linkages between farms and retailers to emerge, limiting the potential to diversify production at the farm level to meet the growing demand for higher value products. Until 2003, before the Inter-Ministerial Task Force on Agricultural Marketing Reforms (2002), APMCs had the exclusive right to function as a market (GOI, 2002). The task force suggested reforms that allowed private agencies and cooperatives to trade in markets, contract farming initiatives to purchase goods directly from farmers and processors and bulk buyers to procure products directly from the farmers bypassing the APMC (ibid). The next section evaluates the changes in value chain arrangements that emerged in the twenty-first century following these changes and its impact on agricultural value chains.

8.3   EXPERIENCE OF LINKING FARMS TO MARKET

The inefficiencies of agricultural markets in India pose challenges for the organized retail sector to participate effectively. The need for vertically coordinated markets where the intermediaries are bypassed and transaction costs are reduced is necessary for the signaling price and quality information, contract formation to mitigate supply risks and to establish of grades and standards (Birthal, Joshi, & Gulati, 2005; Pingali et al., 2005). The existing marketing system cannot accommodate these specific requirements essential for retail chains to emerge (McCullough, Pingali, & Stamoulis, 2008). Changes in marketing laws and newer platforms of transactions such as eMarkets, warehousing and commodity futures have developed slowly to rectify this mismatch. The Model APMC Act of 2003 amended the existing marketing law in India to allow direct purchase from primary producers and growers, previously not recognized. This led to the emergence of "contract farming" initiatives in India through which retailers or wholesalers could purchase products of specific grades, standards and other requirements that could not be delivered by the existing markets. Newer marketing initiatives and platforms have also been set in place to align traditional marketing with changing markets. The initiatives using electronic platforms have been the eNAM online trading platforms and online commodity exchanges providing platforms for agricultural commodity derivatives. In this section, we look at the role of vertical coordination and online transactions to assess the potential and challenges for small farm linkages to markets.

8.3.1   *Vertical Coordination in Value Chains—Challenges and Limitations*

Vertical coordination (VC) are modes of exchange in which producers and buyers bypass existing marketing channels to assure the supply of quality agricultural goods, in demanded quality at a stipulated time. VC organizes and orders together activities and information flow to reduce transaction costs and control for quality and standards specifications (Buvik & John, 2000). They are enforced by formal or informal contracts and arise when existing markets and supply chains are rigid to adapt to changes in demand for agricultural goods. Under vertical coordination the terms of sale based on prices, quantity and quality are fixed by contracts ex ante between the producer and buyer to reduce uncertainty. Contract farming (CF) is one form of vertical coordination mechanisms that have been implemented in many developing countries to address the changing demand requirements and inefficiencies of existing markets (Barrett et al., 2012; Glover, 1987; Kumar, 2006; Narayanan, 2014; Singh, 2002).

This model is especially prevalent in highly perishable commodities such as fresh fruits and vegetables (FFV), milk and meat (Birthal, Jha, Tiongco, & Narrod, 2009; Chu-Ping, 2010; Swinnen & Maertens, 2007). Under contract farming, farmers directly supply produce to retailers and wholesalers under advanced contracts that stipulate time of delivery, quantity, quality and variety (Benziger, 1996; S. Singh, 2011). Early examples of CF in Spain and Japan in the 1950s indicate a reduction of production cost, leading to its widespread promotion in these countries (Asano-Tamanoi, 1988). Empirical evidence has shown contract farming to address market failures and improve access to commodity markets and inputs such as seeds, credit, fertilizer and pesticides, technology and extension services (Bellemare, 2012; Birthal et al., 2005; Eaton & Shepherd, 2001; Glover, 1987; Narayanan, 2014; Wang, Wang, & Delgado, 2014). However, whether these institutions have benefited small and marginal farmers have been widely debated. The emergence of supermarkets has led to the widespread use of such contracts to assure the supply of vegetables from producers in China (Hu, Reardon, Rozelle, Timmer, & Wang, 2004), Thailand (Boselie, 2002) and Central America (Berdegué, Balsevich, Flores, & Reardon, 2005) with some success. In India, the contract farming experiences have been varied. The two major challenges in India and many developing countries with small farm-based agricultural systems have been the exclusion of small farmers and the cost of organizing value chains. This has limited the impact contract farming has had in linking small farms to value chains.

8.3.1.1 Size, Crop Type and Geography as Influence of Vertical Coordination

Exclusion of farmers in VC initiatives or the high entry cost of participating in them is a concern for small producers. Size of farms and location are shown to be decisive factors in forming linkages with farms. Some studies have pointed out that because of high transaction and management costs, small farms are discriminated against as it is less costly to make a small number of contracts with large farmers than a large number of contracts with small farmers (Dolan & Humphrey, 2000; Hazell, Poulton, Wiggins, & Dorward, 2010; Reardon & Berdegué, 2002; Reardon, Timmer, Barrett, & Berdegué, 2003; Swinnen & Maertens, 2007). Others have noted that small producers have successfully formed contracts in particular crops such as papaya (Narayanan, 2014), poultry (Chu-Ping, 2010; Nguyen, Dzator, & Nadolny, 2015; Ramaswami, Birthal, & Joshi, 2009), gherkins (Narayanan, 2014; Swain, 2011), milk (Birthal et al., 2005; Holloway, Nicholson, Delgado, Staal, & Ehui, 2000), fresh fruits and vegetables (Ito, Bao, & Su, 2012; Rao, Brümmer, & Qaim, 2012; Trebbin, 2014; H. Wang, Moustier, & Loc, 2014), among others. In perishable commodities with higher asset fixity, contract farm seems to work better, due to sunk costs, investment in infrastructure and limited hold-up costs.

Geographical location and levels of infrastructure can also influence firms' choice of farms for procuring agricultural goods. Geography influences agro-climatic conditions (that determine the levels of risks, type of crops) and distance to markets. Infrastructure such as irrigation systems and good roads with this can mitigate the disadvantages of climatic risks and poor connectivity of farms. Therefore locations with better connectivity, infrastructure and market connectivity are termed as high potential areas and others as low potential areas (Pingali, Khwaja, & Madelon, 2007). Contracts with farms in high potential areas are therefore preferred and there is evidence from India that shows this. A study by Mangala and Chengappa (2008) in Karnataka reveals that farmers in contract with food retail chains had higher land holding sizes and irrigated land (6 acres and 4.5 acres) compared to traditional market farmers (2 acres and 1.5 acres). Trebbin and Franz (2010) highlight that a Food Chain Partnership (FCP) program[2] initiated by Bayer Crop Science in India was highly selective about the farmers' eligibility (larger farms), the location of farms (areas where retail and processing infrastructure was good) and the crops they grew (high-value crops). Public goods complementarity of a location may also influence the potential of backward linkages to the farms. Due to higher transaction and administrative costs, higher risks in production, smallholders may not be preferred for vertical coordination in low potential areas. Enabling VC and even market linkages for private trade in low potential areas remains a big challenge.

---

[2] FCP is a program launched by Bayer Crop Science in many developing countries for sustainable production of vegetables.

8.3.1.2 The High Cost of Organizing Value Chains and Incentives to Form Linkages

Coordination of production and marketing activities in the value chains has costs to it. Some of these costs are organizational costs and not transaction costs and may be higher in certain conditions. Reducing these costs is essential to enable and maintain vertical coordination. In agricultural value chains, buyers use contracts to stipulate ex ante price, quality and time of delivery of products to producers. Forming contracts and managing them are fundamentally new costs that may potentially offset the gains made at the production stages (Pingali et al., 2007). Therefore managing organizational costs at the contracting stages becomes important in VC. Owing to the small size of farms in India, aggregation of farmers is essential to enable contract farming. Here the significant cost to firms are (a) political costs or cost of collaborating with the state to set up initiatives; (b) bureaucratic costs or the cost of identifying farmers, coordinating intentions, formation of groups and establishing systems of governance; (c) management costs or the costs of governing day-to-day functions of the groups, establishing feedback mechanisms and monitoring to reduce free-rider problems; (d) screening costs that entails cost of identifying potential buyers (of produce), sellers (of inputs), institutions (banks, R&D outfits, agricultural universities); and (e) transfer costs of movement of goods to retailers or processors, providing collective goods such as inputs, credit, technology and extension services to producers. Table 8.2 lists the various coordination costs in forming VCs and their effects and influences. Addressing these costs is central to the ability of small farms to make effective linkages to value chains. High costs of coordinating production and contracts with small farms often limit the potential of VC to emerge. Therefore, VC is just one mechanism to rectify the challenges of the markets and the effective functioning of traditional agricultural markets is essential for farm-market linkages.

8.3.2 Alternative Marketing Platforms—eMarkets, Future Markets and Warehousing

The Planning Commission (2011) working group on agricultural marketing stated that the significant challenges for markets were the large number of intermediaries, inadequate infrastructure for storage and grading, poor price setting mechanisms and poor competence of market staff. Agricultural markets and their functioning differ from state to state, as market reforms

Table 8.2 Coordination costs and effects at the firm level

Costs	Characteristics	Effects at firm level
Political cost	Cost of collaboration with the state for support and subsidies	Agency of coordinating organization, social features of groups. Costs may reduce overtime
Bureaucratic cost	Initiating groups, formulating functions and duties	Group leadership, incentive structures, management expertise. Costs may reduce overtime
Management cost	Governing day-to-day tasks of the groups, establishing feedback mechanisms, monitoring	Level of benefits provided, type of goods and services, social capital. Recurring cost
Screening costs	Cost of identifying potential buyers (of produce), sellers (of inputs), institutions (banks, R&D outfits, agricultural universities)	Agency of coordinating organization, ability to form contracts, level of linkages to state and markets. Costs may reduce overtime
Transfer costs	Cost of movement of goods, providing collective goods such as inputs, credit, technology and extension services	Location of farms, crops are grown, level of infrastructure. Recurring cost

and governance are state subjects or under the jurisdiction of individual states rather than the center. Although suggestions for making agricultural markets a center or a concurrent subject to bring uniformity in the transaction have met with many challenges, the electronic portal for agricultural marketing has been operationalized (Narayanamoorthy & Alli, 2018). eNAM is an online trading platform formed in 2016 that intends to link APMCs to create a unified market. The platform has connected 585 APMCs (9% of markets) in 14 states. The electronic portal aims to help price discovery across markets in India enable a harmonized grading and standards system for a transparent transaction, bypassing intermediaries. Figure 8.2 shows the schematics of the functioning of an e-portal depicting the entry, sampling and grading of agricultural produce before being put on an electronic platform. Here traders from across the country can bid for the produce and when the bids are finalized, they are weighed and stored for collection. The payment is then made electronically to the farmer.

Although in principle a unified market is essential for price discovery, standardizing practices and reducing transaction costs, the uptake and integration to a virtual platform have been slow. The challenges are poor infrastructure and systems in the market. The lack of testing machines and

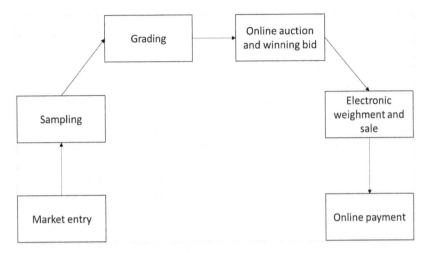

Fig. 8.2   Functioning of the electronic portal (ReMS model) in India

technicians for grades and standards determination, poor internet connectivity, poor storage facilities, low stakeholder participation and malpractices in the form of misreporting physical auction as online auctions (Nirmal, 2017). Online marketing platforms are not without success and the eNAM model is based on Karnataka's Rashtriya eMarkets Services Pvt. Ltd., (ReMS). This joint venture between the Karnataka government and the National Commodity & Derivatives Exchange (NCDEX) eMarkets Limited. Currently, 157 of the 162 APMCs in Karnataka come under this unified platform. The success of this platform can be seen in increased market bids in auctions, reduced collusion among traders and cartels, increased transparency in transactions and reduced delays in payments compared to non-eMarkets (Reddy, 2016). Effective functioning of online marketing platforms can also encourage increased private sector participation, and low potential areas that do not have the advantage for vertical coordination can greatly benefit from such models.

Commodity futures markets and warehousing of agricultural commodities are provisions that exist in the agricultural commodity space that is not widely accessed. The reason for this is mainly due to low economies of scale for smallholders. Although the government comprehensively banned futures trading in 1966, based on the recommendations of various committees, commodity derivatives trading was reintroduced in 2002–03. Through commodity exchanges, a producer or aggregator can agree to sell agricultural produce at a pre-determined fixed price at a fixed location to a buyer. The position can be a short or long position and the buyer can sell the commodity in the spot market. Profit and loss from the commodity increasing or decreasing in value is borne by the buyer, while the seller remains protected. Currently the major commodity exchanges are the National Spot Exchange Limited (NSEL), Indian Commodity Exchange Limited (ICEX), Multi-Commodity Exchange (MCX), National Commodity & Derivatives Exchange Limited (NCDEX), National Multi-Commodity Exchange of India Ltd. (NMCE), Ace Derivatives & Commodity Exchange Ltd. and Universal Commodity Exchange (UCX) among others. Future markets, which are private platforms, help in reducing price risks and in price discovery.

Warehousing systems are essential instruments for agricultural marketing especially in the wake of high price volatility in agricultural commodities. Even when market prices are low, farmers sell their produce due to cash constraints. In principle, under the warehouse receipt system, farmers can store their produce in warehouses when the prices are low and sell in the markets when prices pick up. When storing their produce, they are issued with a warehouse receipt, which functions as a derivative, which can be traded or put up as collateral with banks for immediate cash needs. The advantages of warehousing are reduced handling costs, higher price realization and the ability to buy and sell without physical transfer. Warehouses can be public such as Food Corporation of India, Central Warehousing Corporation, State Warehousing Corporation and State Civil Supplies, cooperative or private.

Alternative markets are spaces where there is increased private sector participation. A majority of the commodity futures platforms are private sector driven, the successful ReMS model in Karnataka is a public-private partnership and both public and private warehousing systems issue the warehouse receipts. Companies such as ITC ABD one of the largest non-state procurers of wheat in India uses futures platforms to buy and sell wheat and soybean (Rajib, 2015). The private sector players also provide essential services to spot markets. For example, NCDEX works with state procurement agencies such as National Agricultural Cooperative Marketing Federation of India Limited (NAFED) and Small Farmers' Agribusiness Consortium (SFAC) to provide grading and testing services before transactions. The significant challenges for smallholder participation in these platforms are infrastructure based and related to scale. Access and connectivity to warehouses and collection points is a concern for producers in low potential areas. Public goods such as roads and storage infrastructures are needed for improved participation. Low volumes of produce is again a concern as agricultural output is highly differentiated and in small quantities. This often means the crops produced may not be of the accepted variety or grades and standards. Additional fixed costs for grading, weighing and storage insurance further dissuade smallholder participation in these platforms.

The scope of different forms of marketing is limited to the type of crops, location and the levels of risks associated with production. In high potential areas with irrigation and good access to markets, the scope for producing high-value crops is strong. In these scenarios, the favorability of vertical coordination emerging is strong. In lower potential areas where there are higher production risks and locational advantages are weak, the effective functioning of APMCs remains crucial. In these locations, the scope of eMarkets, commodity futures and warehousing are also high. Also, with non-perishable agricultural commodities, the development of these alternative markets can help remedy some of the potential challenges of the APMCs such as intermediaries, lack of grades and standards and better price discovery and realization. However, for the emergence of newer forms of value chain linkages, there is still a need to remedy the issue of economies of scale, access to capital for both producers and value chain actors and effective governance of value chains and markets. For this, effective institutions and policy to enable farm-market linkages are necessary.

8.4   INSTITUTIONS AND POLICY—VALUE CHAINS AND THE FUTURE OF FOOD SYSTEMS

Linking smallholders to markets is essential for commercialization, to improve household level incomes and provide the incentive for diversification. Well-functioning value chains are also critical to improving the efficiency of bringing food from farm to table by minimizing food loss and waste, thus improving access and availability of food. With changing demand, we see newer channels and platforms of marketing emerging to cater to the changing need. However for small producers to connect to markets through these requires policy support, interventions like aggregation models, infrastructural development and reform of existing marketing practices that have led to increasing transaction costs in the market. These measures are essential for making value chains sustainable and improving welfare.

8.4.1   Vertical Coordination and Linkages to Alternative Marketing Platforms

In a predominantly smallholder-based agricultural sector, aggregation of farms and effective legislature to enable and enforce contracts are essential for VC. In Chap. 7, we looked at how aggregation models have the potential to address issues of scale with accessing factor markets such as credit, inputs and technology. These models in the form of cooperative and FPOs can also enable better farm-market linkages. Larger farms are preferred to smaller farms as they incur higher costs in contacting and operations. However, in the case of many developing countries, buyers often have no choice but to engage with small and marginal producers due to their predominance in the agricultural sector (Narrod et al., 2007). The role of producer organizations in this regard becomes crucial.

Aggregation models and vertical coordination mechanisms such as contract farming go hand in hand in small farm-based economies as they address the various challenges of the value chain. Although the provisions for contract farming and formation of FPOs were around since 2003, both initiatives have had limited success. Contract farming has been limited to few crops in select locations, and currently, there are few, if any, examples of self-sustaining FPOs. Linkages between these two institutional arrangements are also now few. However, the main factors affecting the uptake of contract farming such as locational disadvantages, costs of selecting farmers, contracting and monitoring and enforcement are potentially remediable through FPOs. Table 8.3 summarizes the various cost characteristics of selection barriers of choosing location and farmers and adherence problems of contract formation and implementation along with costs to both firm and individuals/FPO and the incentives to firms to backward integrate. Aggregation models can reduce search costs (farms and locations) and contracting and monitoring costs (compliance and enforcement) and address some of the disadvantages smallholders have in vertical coordination. In 2018, the government of India introduced the Model Agriculture Produce and Livestock Contract Farming and Services (Promotion & Facilitation) Act, to better facilitate contracts between

Table 8.3   Cost and incentives of firm FPO linkages

Features	Cost characteristics	Cost to firm	The cost to individuals/FPO	Incentives to firms
Choosing a location	Identifying location specific to need	One time: Search and opportunity cost	Location-specific transaction costs	Bypass markets, stable price and supply, control grades and standards requirements
Selecting farmers	Identifying farmers with specific characteristics	One time: Search and opportunity cost	Household-specific transaction costs, opportunity costs	Minimize search costs, screening costs, household-specific transaction costs
Contract	Forming contacts specific to a context	Recurring: The cost of specifying contracts—terms, timing, volume and so on	Bureaucratic costs, screening costs, management costs (esp. monitoring)	Reduced bureaucratic and management costs
Compliance and enforcement	Monitoring and enforcing of contracts by stakeholders	Recurring: Coordination cost of ensuring compliance	Monitoring costs	Reduced enforcement and monitoring costs

farmers and buyers. This new law remains outside the jurisdiction of the APMC act and emphasizes the role of FPOs in contract farming. In the traditional contract farming model, contracts were mostly informal and breach of agreements have been common (Dileep, Grover, & Rai, 2002; S. Singh, 2002; Swain, 2011). The new act now promotes enforceable legal agreements, with dispute settling mechanisms to enable contract adherence by producer and buyer.

In alternative eMarket platforms, future markets and warehousing, economies of scale, information and standardized commodities are essential. Aggregating can help in reducing fixed costs of quality determination, transportation to physical locations of transactions and enable better linkages to financial services. There are examples of FPOs trading on the NCDEX and warehousing their products with them. In 2018, NCDEX has opened accounts with over 151 FPOs in 12 states trading in around 16 mostly non-perishable commodities. These platforms also form the space for private sector linkages with small farms. Aggregation models, therefore, have the potential to develop a tie to both VC and alternative marketing platforms.

8.4.2   Market Reforms and Infrastructure

Although vertical coordination and alternative markets are essential platforms and strategies for improving market access in small farm-based economies, enabling efficient access to agricultural spot markets is also necessary. Agricultural markets are fragmented with a large number of intermediaries functioning in them. These intermediaries, however, perform important aggregation roles when agricultural markets are thin and standardization roles in the absence of established grades and standards. Better access to markets would require infrastructure to improve connectivity through roads to enable better transportation of goods, cold chains and goods storage facilities to reduce wastage and proper communication channels through which price and quality information can be transferred. These changes will also allow for better functioning of alternative marketing platforms, especially eMarkets and warehousing. The role of public sector investment is essential to create public goods in this sector. Effective infrastructural development is also vital to elicit a private sector investment response in the value chain. Despite policy mandating the creation of backend infrastructure in organized retail, this has not been the case due to uncertainty about policy regarding FDI in organized retail. Introduction of grades and standards along with infrastructure and methods to determine this at markets is essential to bring about objective grade-based price determination. Policy to enable market reforms, institutions for the enforcement of enacted policy and infrastructure to improve physical access to markets are therefore critical for sustainable value chains.

Ethics in value chains is essential for sustainable development of the agricultural sector. This involves elements of livelihood rights, food and environmental safety, reduction of ecological externalities and human and animal rights. Therefore, ethical supply chains essentially comprise three significant components: profitability, local development and the environment. Profitability takes into consideration how revenue and profits are shared within a value chain, where every stakeholder stands to benefit. Local development considers public and consumer health, welfare and labor standards while environment ascertains the environmental impact of the value chain from farm to fork. Another aspect associated with sustainable value chains is the issue of food loss. Reduction of food loss in the value chain will ease production pressures when economical, improving access and availability and reducing environmental externalities from the need to produce more. Compared to developed economies where a significant portion of food loss happens at the retail and household levels, in emerging economies, food loss often takes place at the post-harvest stages of storage and transportation. This is usually due to inadequate information regarding best practices or poor or inadequate infrastructure. Food loss often means loss of macronutrients such as fat, calories or proteins, or micronutrient loss such as vitamins and minerals. Reducing wastage and loss are crucial for food security through nutrition-sensitive food systems and sustainability as this would help reduce the strain of population increase and environmental degradation.

8.5   Conclusion

Smallholder linkages to commodity markets are essential for agricultural development and commercialization. These linkages help improve household level welfare through income growth when commodity prices are realized in the market. However, the ability of smallholders to access markets that are characterized by changing demand for higher value and quality goods is problematic due to farm and market level challenges. The primary farm level challenge has been rectifying economies of scale problems, while the main market level problem has been high transaction costs resulting from poor infrastructure and institutions to regulate and stipulate exchange (commodities price being determined by non-price factors and lack of enforced grades and standards-based transactions is a good example). Aiding smallholders to address these problems will help improve market linkages and incentivize production corresponding to changing demand.

Vertical coordination, alternative private markets such as commodity futures markets and warehousing and private-public venture markets have emerged to rectify what traditional spot markets have had limited success in addressing. Vertical coordination has improved market access in perishables such as fruits and vegetables, while alternative markets have helped in the marketing of non-perishables such as oilseeds, cereals, pulses, spices and plantation crops. While these linkages play an essential role, effective functioning of spot markets remains crucial. Reducing transaction costs through improved connectivity, development of market infrastructure, reducing the influence of intermediaries will be central to this. Aggregation models to rectify scale disadvantages will enable better participation of smallholders in different marketing arrangements. The emergence of different marketing platforms are essential as they can address various kinds of institutional, access and marketing problems. Formulating policy to better link smallholders to these platforms will prove critical.

References

Asano-Tamanoi, M. (1988). Farmers, industries, and the state: The culture of contract farming in Spain and Japan. *Comparative Studies in Society and History, 30*(3), 432–452.

Barrett, C. B., Bachke, M. E., Bellemare, M. F., Michelson, H. C., Narayanan, S., & Walker, T. F. (2012). Smallholder participation in contract farming: Comparative evidence from five countries. *World Development, 40*(4), 715–730. https://doi.org/10.1016/j.worlddev.2011.09.006

Bellemare, M. F. (2012). As you sow, so shall you reap: The welfare impacts of contract farming. *World Development, 40*(7), 1418–1434. https://doi.org/10.1016/j.worlddev.2011.12.008

Benziger, V. (1996). Helping small farmers make transition to high value added crops. *World Development, 24*(11), 1681–1693.

Berdegué, J. A., Balsevich, F., Flores, L., & Reardon, T. (2005). Central American supermarkets' private standards of quality and safety in procurement of fresh fruits and vegetables. *Food Policy, 30*(3), 254–269.

Bharadwaj, K. (1985). A view on commercialisation in Indian agriculture and the development of capitalism. *Journal of Peasant Studies, 12*(4), 7–25.

Birthal, P. S., Jha, A. K., Tiongco, M. M., & Narrod, C. (2009). Farm-level impacts of vertical coordination of the food supply chain: Evidence from contract farming of milk in India. *Indian Journal of Agricultural Economics, 64*(3), 481–496.

Birthal, P. S., Joshi, P. K., & Gulati, A. (2005). *Vertical coordination in high value commodities: Implications for the smallholders*. Washington, DC: IFPRI.

Boselie, D. (2002). *Business case description: TOPS supply chain project, Thailand*. Den Bosch: Agri Supply Chain Development Program, Agrichain Competence Center, KLICT International.

Buvik, A., & John, G. (2000). When does vertical coordination improve industrial purchasing relationships? *Journal of Marketing, 64*(4), 52–64.

Chand, R. (2012). Development policies and agricultural markets. *Economic and Political Weekly, 47*(52), 53–63.

Chu-Ping, L. (2010). Perishability as a determinant of vertical coordination. *China Agricultural Economic Review, 2*(1), 49–62. https://doi.org/10.1108/17561371011017496

Dileep, B. K., Grover, R. K., & Rai, K. N. (2002). Contract farming in tomato: An economic analysis. *Indian Journal of Agricultural Economics, 52*(7), 197–210.

Dolan, C., & Humphrey, J. (2000). Governance and trade in fresh vegetables: The impact of UK supermarkets on the African horticulture industry. *Journal of Development Studies, 37*(2), 147–176.

Eaton, C., & Shepherd, A. W. (2001). *Contract farming: Partnerships for growth*. Rome: FAO.

Eaton, D., Meijerink, G., & Bijman, J. (2008). *Understanding institutional arrangements—Fresh fruit and vegetable value chains in East Africa*. Markets, Chains and Sustainable Development Strategy and Policy Paper No. XX.

Glover, D. J. (1987). Increasing the benefits to smallholders from contract farming: Problems for farmers' organizations and policy makers. *World Development, 15*(4), 441–448.

GOI. (2002). *Report of Inter-Ministerial Task Force on Agricultural Marketing Reforms, Department of Agriculture and Cooperation*. Retrieved from https://dmi.gov.in/Documents/ReportTaskForceAMR.pdf

GOI. (2007). *Report of the Steering Committee on Agriculture for 11th Five Year Plan*. Yojana Bhavan, New Delhi.

GOI. (2012). *Report of Task Force on Agricultural Marketing Reforms*. Directorate of Marketing and Inspection, Ministry of Agriculture and Farmers Welfare, Delhi. Retrieved from http://dmi.gov.in/Documents/ReportTaskForceAMR.pdf

Hazell, P., Poulton, C., Wiggins, S., & Dorward, A. (2010). The future of small farms: Trajectories and policy priorities. *World Development, 38*(10), 1349–1361. https://doi.org/10.1016/j.worlddev.2009.06.012

Holloway, G., Nicholson, N., Delgado, C., Staal, S., & Ehui, S. (2000). Agroindustrialization through institutional innovation: Transaction costs, cooperatives and milk-market development in the east-African highlands. *Agricultural Economics, 23*, 279–288.

Hu, D., Reardon, T., Rozelle, S., Timmer, P. C., & Wang, H. H. (2004). The emergence of supermarkets with Chinese characteristics: Challenges and opportunities for China's agricultural development. *Development Policy Review, 22*(4), 557–586.

Ito, J., Bao, Z., & Su, Q. (2012). Distribution effects of agricultural cooperatives in China: Exclusion of smallholders and potential gains in participation. *Food Policy, 37*(6), 700–709.

Kumar, P. (2006). Contract farming through agribusiness firms and state corporation: A case study in Punjab. *Economic and Political Weekly, 52*(30), A5367–A5375.

Kumar, S. M. (2013). Does access to formal agricultural credit depend on caste? *World Development, 43*, 315–328.

Mangala, K. P., & Chengappa, P. G. (2008). A novel agribusiness model for backward linkages with farmers: A case of food retail chain. *Agricultural Economics Research Review, 21*, 363–370.

McCullough, E. B., Pingali, P., & Stamoulis, K. G. (2008). Small farms and the transformation of food systems: An overview. In E. B. McCullough, P. L. Pingali, & K. G. Stamoulis (Eds.), *The transformation of agri-food systems: Globalisation, supply chains, and smallholder farmers* (pp. 3–46). Rome: FAO.

Narayanamoorthy, A., & Alli, P. (2018, January). Agriculture market reforms are a must. *The Hindu Business Line.*

Narayanan, S. (2014a). Profits from participation in high value agriculture: Evidence of heterogeneous benefits in contract farming schemes in Southern India. *Food Policy, 44,* 142–157. https://doi.org/10.1016/j.foodpol.2013.10.010

Narrod, C., Roy, D., Okello, J., Avendaño, B., Rich, K., & Thorat, A. (2007). *The role of public–private partnerships and collective action in ensuring smallholder participation in high value fruit and vegetable supply chains.* CAPRi Working Paper, Washington, DC.

Nirmal, R. (2017, July). Why the eNAM platform hasn't taken off despite all the fanfare. *The Hindu Business Line.*

Pingali, P., Khwaja, Y., & Madelon, M. (2005). *Commercializing small farms: Reducing transaction cost.* ESA Working Paper (No.), 05-08.

Pingali, P., Khwaja, Y., & Madelon, M. (2007). The role of the public and private sectors in commercializing small farms and reducing transaction costs. In J. F. M. Swinnen (Ed.), *Global supply chains, standards and the poor* (pp. 260–267). Oxford, UK: CABI International.

Planning Commission. (2011). *Report of the working group on agricultural marketing infrastructure, secondary agriculture and policy required for internal and external trade for the XII five-year plan 2012–17.* New Delhi.

Poulton, C., Dorward, A., & Kydd, J. (2010). The future of small farms: New directions for services, institutions, and intermediation. *World Development, 38*(10), 1413–1428. https://doi.org/10.1016/j.worlddev.2009.06.009

Rajib, P. (2015). Indian agricultural commodity derivatives market—In conversation with S Sivakumar, Divisional Chief Executive, Agri Business Division, ITC Ltd. *IIMB Management Review, 27*(2), 118–128. https://doi.org/10.1016/j.iimb.2015.02.002

Rao, E. J. O., Brümmer, B., & Qaim, M. (2012). Farmer participation in supermarket channels, production technology, and efficiency: The case of vegetables in Kenya. *American Journal of Agricultural Economics, 23*(3), 784–796.

Reardon, T., & Berdegué, J. A. (2002). The rapid rise of supermarkets in Latin America: Challenges and opportunities for development. *Development Policy Review, 20*(4), 371–388.

Reardon, T., Timmer, P. C., Barrett, C. B., & Berdegué, J. A. (2003). The rise of supermarkets in Africa, Asia, and Latin America. *American Journal of Agricultural Economics, 85*(5), 1140–1146.

Reddy, A. (2016). Impact of e-markets in Karnataka, India. *Indian Journal of Agricultural Marketing, 30*(2), 31–44.

RFST. (2005). *Impact of WTO on women in agriculture*. New Delhi.

Roy, D., & Thorat, A. (2008). Success in high value horticultural export markets for the small farmers: The case of Mahagrapes in India. *World Development, 36*, 1874–1890.

Sen, A. K. (2000). *Social exclusion: Concept, application, and scrutiny*. Social Development Paper No. 1, Bangkok.

Singh, S. (2002). Contracting out solutions: Political economy of contract farming in the Indian Punjab. *World Development, 30*(9), 1621–1638.

Singh, S. (2011). FDI in retail: Misplaced expectations and half-truths. *Economic and Political Weekly, 47*(51), 13–16.

Swain, B. B. (2011). Contract farming in Andhra Pradesh: A case of rice seed and gherkin. *Economic and Political Weekly, 46*(42), 60–68.

Swinnen, J. F. M., & Maertens, M. (2007). Globalization, privatization, and vertical coordination in food value chains in developing and transition countries. *Agricultural Economics, 37*, 89–102. https://doi.org/10.1111/j.1574-0862.2007.00237.x

Thorat, S. (2009). Economic exclusion and poverty linkages: A reflection on concept, consequences, and remedies in an Asian context. In J. von Braun, R. V. Hill, & R. Pandya-Lorch (Eds.), *The poorest and hungry assessments, analyses, and actions*. Washington, DC: International Food Policy Research Institute.

Trebbin, A. (2014). Linking small farmers to modern retail through producer organizations—Experiences with producer companies in India. *Food Policy, 45*, 35–44. https://doi.org/10.1016/j.foodpol.2013.12.007

Trebbin, A., & Franz, M. (2010). Exclusivity of private governance structures in agrofood networks: Bayer and the food retailing and processing sector in India. *Environment and Planning, 42*, 2043–2057.

Wang, H., Moustier, P., & Loc, N. T. T. (2014b). Economic impact of direct marketing and contracts: The case of safe vegetable chains in northern Vietnam. *Food Policy, 47*, 13–23.

Wang, H. H., Wang, Y., & Delgado, M. S. (2014a). The transition to modern agriculture: Contract farming in developing economies. *American Journal of Agricultural Economics, 96*(5), 1257–1271.

CHAPTER 9

Agricultural Technology for Increasing Competitiveness of Small Holders

9.1 INTRODUCTION

Agricultural technology plays a vital role in building viable and sustainable food systems. The Green Revolution (GR) is a landmark example of how scale-neutral technology transformed agricultural production, leading to increased productivity of staple grains, poverty reduction, increased availability of food grains and lower food prices (Pingali, 2012). It played an integral part in making many parts of the developing world food secure regarding calorific access and put to rest concerns of having reached the carrying capacity where the population exceeds what the agricultural sector can support. However, as India moves towards becoming the most populous nation in the world by 2050, concerns of agricultural productivity are being revisited. The limitations of GR technologies were that it was concentrated to high potential regions where irrigation was readily available, it was limited to wheat and rice and that it has had environmental consequences due to injudicious use of inputs leading to reduced soil fertility and water table depletion in some regions. In Chap. 7, we looked at the institutional factors such as land size and access to land, credit, technology and infrastructure such as irrigation that influences the ability of smallholders to commercialize and diversify. In the wake of challenges of growing population and climate change along with improving productivity and profitability, sustainability through reduced impact

© The Author(s) 2019
P. Pingali et al., *Transforming Food Systems for a Rising India*,
Palgrave Studies in Agricultural Economics and Food Policy,
https://doi.org/10.1007/978-3-030-14409-8_9

on the environment is central for the future of agricultural development. Therefore, while technology remains crucial to boosting agricultural yields and growth, newer approaches to technological interventions need to help limit environmental externalities such as land and water degradation and emission of greenhouse gases, expand to low potential areas of eastern India bypassed by the Green Revolution and bring yield increases to a more diverse group of crops.

Sustainable intensification is a process by which agricultural outputs can be increased without increasing inputs such as land, through the judicious use of agricultural inputs such as water and fertilizers and reducing externalities such as greenhouse gas (GHG) emissions and land and water degradation (Pingali, 2012; Pretty, Toulmin, & Williams, 2011). Technology or the use of scientific knowledge and management of inputs are the two main components of this approach. Technology is essential to improve yields and increase resistance to climatic risks such as droughts and floods and mechanization to reduce drudgery and improve efficiency, while management practices are necessary to improve resource utilization and reduce emissions of greenhouse gases from agricultural production. In this chapter, we highlight the significant challenges of agricultural production and the technological and input management interventions that are required to address them in the context of the Indian food system. The chapter is divided into three parts. In the first part, we look at the significant post-Green Revolution production and environmental challenges of the agricultural sector in different agro-climatic regions of the country to highlight the various challenges. In the second part, we assess the nature of technological interventions, specific to the region, that are needed to increase productivity, while limiting environmental externalities and assuring equitable growth. In this section, we look at the shift from conventional plant-breeding technologies to first- and second-generation genetically modified (GM) technologies and the promise they hold for the agricultural sector and the future of food security. Here we also look at the need for the collation and dissemination of information about the environment, economy and good practices to enable better decision making at the farm level to complement technology with effective use of scarce resources. The last part looks at the policy and institutional support that is required to enable technological interventions and adoption, especially by smallholder farmers as we look ahead to 2050.

9.2 THE POST-GREEN REVOLUTION CHALLENGES TO INDIAN AGRICULTURE—FROM ENVIRONMENTAL EXTERNALITIES TO CLIMATE CHANGE

India's grain production alone needs to grow by about 42% from the 2015 levels (or by 377 million tons) to meet the projected demand of 2050.[1] The rising demand for higher value food products such as fruits and vegetables and animal products has pressured food systems to increase yields and to diversify. The Green Revolution (GR) by tripling grain production with only a 30% increase in land under cultivation (Pingali, 2012) in the 1970s was able to offset potential shortages arising from population growth. As India moves towards becoming the most populous nation, technology is again being sought out for solutions. However, the challenges going forward are different and there is a need to develop technological interventions to address them. In this section, we look at the main challenges that sustainable intensification needs to address to emerge as a solution to boosting agricultural productivity and growth. First, we discuss the limitations of GR technologies concerning their environmental externalities and not being resource-neutral, and second we look at the challenges of climate change as a dominant variable in its influence on food production.

9.2.1   Going Beyond Green Revolution Technologies

Although GR technologies were scale-neutral allowing small farms to adopt them, they were not resource-neutral that led to sizeable regional inequality and low diversification (Chap. 7 details this discussion). Rainfed regions, which could not adopt these technologies, did not benefit from productivity growth and development of the agricultural sector. The focus on wheat and rice led to food self-sufficiency and calorie availability, but crowding out of coarse cereals led to low micronutrient availability in the food system. The lopsided production incentives in some crops led to the emergence of intensive mono-cropping in irrigated tracts of India (Abraham & Pingali, 2019; Pingali, 2012). The environmental impact of the GR was also mixed. Although it limited conversion of new land for agriculture, excessive use of inputs led to chemical runoffs, soil degradation

---

[1] http://www.icrisat.org/yield-gap-and-water-productivity-atlas-launched-for-india/ (Accessed on 10/01/2018).

and water table depletion (Pingali, 2012). India has one of the world's highest rates of water depletion (Aeschbach-Hertig & Gleeson, 2012). According to the World Resources Institute, 54% of India's total area faces high water stress concentrated in the northwestern regions and the eastern coastal regions (Shiao, Maddocks, Carson, & Loizeaux, 2015), where GR technologies were most successfully adopted. Much of the eastern part of India where farm level access to irrigation is low, water stress remains low to medium.

About 64% of land degradation in India is caused by water erosion (Mythili & Goedecke, 2016), while the remaining can be attributed to human-induced and natural soil degradation resulting from deforestation, pollution, poor agricultural practices, over-grazing and wind and water erosion. Table 9.1 shows that the northwestern and southern regions have the largest degraded land area; these are also the regions with high water stress. GR technologies, therefore, came at an environmental cost and as India looks to increase yields and diversify production, it is important to consider measures to reduce environmental externalities of technological intervention and adopt technologies that may require resource use in line with regional endowments. The potential of eastern India for agricultural growth will shift the development focus to the region, and the adoption of technology along with good management practices will be necessary to reduce environmental stress and keep agricultural production sustainable.

9.2.2   Climate Change, Environmental Degradation and Production Risks

Climate change and its effect of agricultural production was not a variable considered during the GR era, but productivity growth requires higher energy utilization that inevitably leads to higher emissions. Today there is ample evidence that high emissions leading to climate change have an impact on the production conditions of crops and livestock. Agricultural production, therefore, influences and is influenced by climate change. It is a large emitter of carbon dioxide (CO_2)-based and non-CO_2-based greenhouse gases (GHGs) such as methane (CH_4) and nitrous oxide (N_2O), contributing to changes in temperature. The Indian agricultural sector contributes 18% of the total emissions of India.[2] Rice and livestock

---

[2] A detailed discussion on the role of climate change and food systems will be discussed in Chap. 10.

Table 9.1 Classification of land degradation in India by regions (in '000 hectares)

Region	Water erosion	Wind erosion	Waterlogging	Salinity/ alkalinity	Several degradation types combined	Total degraded area	Area	Degraded area (%)
North	23,449	9,040	4,396	3,342	335	40,562	101,061	40
Northeast	4,136	–	522	5,534	2,422	12,614	26,219	48
Central	17,883	–	359	6,842	1,126	26,210	44,345	59
East	9,249	–	3,392	2,322	194	15,157	41,833	36
West	16,446	443	599	1,869	1,993	21,350	50,743	42
South	22,330	–	5,031	1,902	1,302	30,565	63,576	48
Union territories	187	–	–	9	9	205	825	25
India	93,680 (64%)	9483 (6%)	14,299 (10%)	21,820 (15%)	7,381 (5%)	146,663 (100%)	328,602	45

Source: Mythili and Goedecke (2016)

production are the largest contributors emitting 36.9% and 38.9% of GHGs respectively by way of anaerobic and enteric fermentations (Vetter et al., 2017). Simultaneously, changing weather patterns and extreme weather events influence production conditions and the risks under which agricultural production takes place.

Yield increasing technology interventions in agriculture were also supported by policies providing input subsidies to improve and incentivize adoption. Over time, however, continued subsidization of technologies has led to their overuse. Subsidized electricity for water use made the agricultural sector energy intensive, and fertilizer subsidies made agriculture GHG intensive, especially N_2O (Vetter et al., 2017). Urea subsidies have been higher than phosphate and potash-based fertilizers, and this has led to over-application of nitrogenous fertilizers resulting in lower efficiency and soil health (Prasad, 2009). Subsidized electricity has also shown to lead to over irrigation, severely depleting groundwater levels (Bhanja et al., 2017; Jacoby, 2017; Raman et al., 2015). Agricultural practices such as excessive tillage and overuse of machinery, heavy use of inorganic fertilizers, poor irrigation and water management techniques, pesticide overuse, low carbon inputs, and reduced crop cycle planning are significant contributors to degradation (R. Bhattacharyya et al., 2015).

The effects of climate change from temperature increase and land and water degradation will have different effects in various agro-ecological regions. In marginal areas constrained by water-related challenges, the impact of droughts and water shortages will have a significant impact on productivity through increased agro-climatic risks. In high agricultural productivity areas, water shortages due to depleting groundwater levels, water contamination due to runoffs and soil degradation due to over-application of fertilizers will be detrimental to production. Diversification to higher value agriculture may also require higher inputs in the form of water, fertilizer and feed, and with it will come increased emissions. Technology interventions, therefore, have the twin task of improving productivity while reducing and managing externalities. However, technology interventions come at an energy cost (Soby, 2013), and as agricultural production moves towards higher commercialization, emissions are bound to increase. Coupling technology with good management practices to reduce externalities, efficiently utilize water and land resources and chemical and fuel inputs are essential to mitigate climate change and reduce its impact on agriculture.

9.3   THE NEW ROLE OF TECHNOLOGY
AND MANAGEMENT FOR SUSTAINABLE AGRICULTURE

The biggest technological challenge in agriculture is to increase yields through intensification, without increasing negative externalities of diminishing biodiversity, greenhouse emissions and land and water degradation, among others—this is often referred to as sustainable agricultural intensification (FAO, 2016; Matson, Parton, Power, & Swift, 1997; Pretty et al., 2011). With a majority of production taking place on small and marginal farms, making technology accessible is crucial for income growth, poverty reduction, food security, gender empowerment and environmental sustainability (Byerlee, de Janvry, & Sadoulet, 2009; Pingali, 2010). However, the limited capacity of smallholders to manage climatic risks, especially during adverse events is limited, and this can trap them in chronic poverty (Carter & Barrett, 2006; Fafchamps, 2003; Kebede, 1992).

Technology, therefore, needs to focus on three aspects: One, technology needs to be accessible by often resource-poor small and marginal producers. Two, it should help increase productivity for a growing population keeping in mind limitations of land and water resource availability. Three, technology should enable and better manage resource utilization and externalities from agricultural production to prevent accentuation of climate change. The impacts of climate change will be felt disproportionately across India with sub-humid and semi-arid regions prone to droughts, the delta and coastal regions prone to flooding and storms. Strategies tailored to regions depending on current agricultural development and climatic risks are essential to address specific risks. In this section, we look at the role of plant technology interventions in increasing production and management practices that make up the core of sustainable intensification and technology approaches to improve efficiency in the context of Indian agriculture. We specifically look at the increasingly important role of biotechnology in the form of genetic modification supplementing GR technologies that were predominantly based on conventional plant-breeding (CBP).

9.3.1   *Yield Gaps and Resilience—The Role of Plant Technologies*

India has 20 agro-ecological zones (AEZs)[3] with varying physiography, precipitation, temperature and soil type determining conditions under which agricultural production takes place (L. Ahmad, Habib, Parvaze, &

---

[3] This classification is used by the National Bureau of Soil Survey & Land Use Planning (NBSS&LUP). These 20 AEZs are further divided into 60 sub-zones.

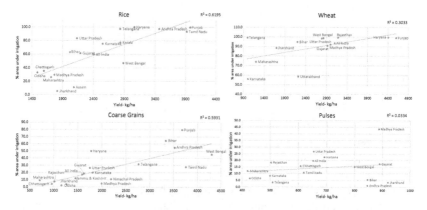

Fig. 9.1 Relationship between yield and area under irrigation in selected crops in India (2015–16). Source: Department of Agriculture, Cooperation & Farmers Welfare, Government of India; based on authors calculations

Sheraz, 2017). In the sub-humid and semi-arid regions of central and the eastern parts of the country, agro-climatic risks and availability of water are significant challenges to agricultural production. Ninety-four percent of wheat production and 95% of sugar production takes place under irrigated conditions. Sixty percent of the area under rice is irrigated while less than 10% of coarse grains and 20% of pulses are grown under irrigated conditions. Figure 9.1 shows the relationship between yield and irrigation in various states for rice, wheat and coarse grains. In the case of rice, wheat and coarse grains, there is a strong relationship between yields and irrigation, with states with higher access to irrigation having higher yields. In pulses, this relationship does not hold as the average yield in Jharkhand and Madhya Pradesh is the same despite a 40% difference in access to irrigation for pulses cultivation.

In Punjab, the wheat yields are 2 to 2.4 times higher than in other states, and rice yields are 1.5 to 2 times that of states such as Odisha, Maharashtra, Madhya Pradesh and Bihar. Increasing production of major staples sustainably would mean closing this yield gap between regions. Figure 9.2 also shows differences levels of irrigation within a state for different crops. While close to 90% of wheat cultivation in Madhya Pradesh is under irrigation, less than 10% of coarse grains come under irrigated conditions. In coarse grains such as millets and sorghum and pulses, the Indian yields are low in

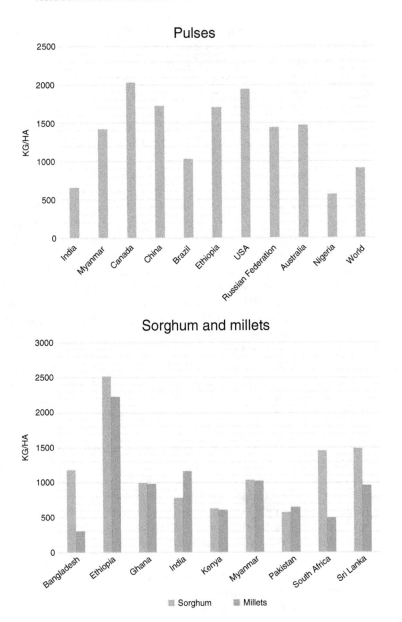

Fig. 9.2 Global variations in yield. Source: FAOSTAT; based on authors calculations

comparison to other developing countries (Fig. 9.2). Low level of R&D and limited access to irrigation for coarse grains and pulses restricts the availability of marketable surplus and increases risks of production, disincentivizing production. Increasing the yield of pulses will incentivize their adoption in the fallows of eastern India helping improve availability and incomes. Higher yields from pulses that are grown mostly in regions where access to irrigation is low will enable income growths and incentivize production. Increasing coarse grain yields and breeding more climate resilient varieties will enable its adoption more widely.

Evidence of climate change affecting agriculture is strong. The challenges agricultural production faces from temperature increases are decreased yields (Lobell, Schlenker, & Costa-Roberts, 2011; Nelson, Valin, et al., 2014), higher risks of pest attacks and disease outbreaks (O'Brien et al., 2004), lower quality and quantity of feed and forage and water availability depletion. These changes would not only affect the production of crops, but also impact the production of livestock and complementary products such as milk availability (Rojas-Downing, Nejadhashemi, Harrigan, & Woznicki, 2017). Also, heat stress impacts animal health, increases parasites and pathogens (Niang et al., 2014; Thornton, van de Steeg, Notenbaert, & Herrero, 2009) and increases the risk of mycotoxin contamination in cereals and pulses (Paterson & Lima, 2010). The latter increases safety concerns in the food supply chains as products move from farm to plate. Closing existing yield gaps and regional disparities in agricultural production, while simultaneously dealing with concerns of climate change, will be the significant aim and challenge of technological interventions as we look ahead.

Although the role of conventional plant-breeding to improve yields in coarse grains and pulses remain significant, genetic engineering advances have led to opportunities in developing plants that can improve yields, remain resilient to climate change impacts and also reduce environmental externalities. Genetically modified organisms (GMOs) can be more precise, productive and faster than conventional plant-breeding (CPB) and have found use in biofuels, food, cash and fodder crops, livestock, fisheries and forestry. The primary difference between GM biotechnology and CPB is that biotechnology transcends species and uses gene manipulation, gene transfer between species, DNA typing and cloning to develop new plant varieties (C. N. Rao, Pray, & Herring, 2018). The first-generation of GM crops was engineered to have tolerance or resistance to insects, pesticides and herbicides, and examples of these were Bt maize, Bt cotton,

Pat-maize and GT soybeans, among others. In India, Bt cotton was the only first-generation GMO that was introduced to the agricultural sector. Second-generation GMOs are characterized by increased tolerance to abiotic stress (drought, flood salinity) and substantial changes in content of nutrients (protein, amino acids, fatty acids, starch, vitamins, minerals and enzymes), enabling the creation of resilient and more nutritive crops (Buiatti, Christou, & Pastore, 2013; Flachowsky & Aulrich, 2001; C. N. Rao et al., 2018). So far, no second-generation GMOs have been allowed in the Indian agricultural sector.

Enabling yield increases in coarse grains such as millets and sorghum and pulses and developing crop varieties specific to sub-humid and semi-arid agro-ecologies will be the role of technology in production increase. R&D through CPB to introduce high-yielding varieties (HYVs) of coarse grains and pulses will help productivity growth in regions of eastern India where they have an advantage in growing, enabling income growths and increasing per capita availability of these crops that have been decreasing over the past few decades. Adoption and growth of Bt cotton production in India is an example of a first-generation GMO that has been widely adopted and has had a significant impact on pesticide reduction, yield gains and income increase contributing to poverty reduction and rural development (Qaim, Subramanian, Naik, & Zilberman, 2006; A. Subramanian & Qaim, 2011). Bt cotton, a genetically modified organism (GMO) using *Bacillus thuringiensis*, a naturally occurring bacterium that protects from bollworm infestation, was first introduced in India in 2002. Since then, cotton yields have gone up almost four times and the total cotton production increased from 11.53 million tons in 1999–2000 to 32.58 million tons (Fig. 9.3).

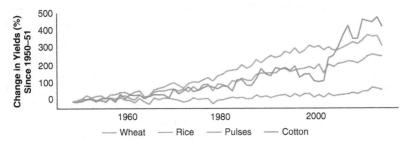

Fig. 9.3 Yield trends in selected crops in India from 1950–51 to 2016–17. Source: Department of Agriculture, Cooperation & Farmers Welfare, Government of India; based on authors calculations

Due to the reduced use of pesticides, it has been found that the environmental impact quotient of Bt cotton was lower than conventional cotton breeds (Ashok, Uma, Prahadeeswaran, & Jeyanthi, 2018).

In the wake of climate change, development of second-generation GMOs that can withstand agro-climatic risks is essential. Development of heat-tolerant and drought-resistant crops will allow for productivity growth in regions that were bypassed by the Green Revolution and in temperate regions susceptible to weather-related risks. Drought tolerant varieties in staples such as maize, rice and wheat have been in development and are in various stages of implementation or trials. The International Maize and Wheat Improvement Center (CIMMYT) and the International Rice Research Institute (IRRI) have been front-runners in this research. Research on developing heat-resistant wheat, rice and maize are still ongoing, and they are not yet commercially available (Rosegrant et al., 2014). Like drought resistance, heat resistance in a plant is an essential trait in the wake of climate change. In the semi-arid regions, this may prove crucial for agricultural production. Chapter 10 discusses the effects of climate change on the nutritive value of crops as there is ample lab-based evidence to show that rising temperatures can reduce the nutrient contents such as proteins and vitamins in crops. GMOs allow for the biofortification of crops that would increase nutrient content, compensating for reduced availability.

Technology to reduce emissions from growing various crops is also important. Plants with traits such as Biological Nitrification Inhibition (BNI) that suppresses the loss of nitrogen from the soil can improve uptake efficiency and boost crop productivity (Subbarao et al., 2017). These technologies coupled with management practices such as zero tillage can reduce emissions significantly. The IMPACT models of the International Food Policy Research Institute (IFPRI) that assesses the long terms challenges in addressing hunger and poverty forecasts that the number of undernourished people can be reduced by 12% or 124 million in developing countries through nitrogen-efficient crops. Further, the model also predicts that 9% or 91 million and 8% or 80 million of the worlds under nourished can be reduced though adopting zero tillage and heat tolerant and precision agriculture methods respectively (FAO, 2016; Rosegrant et al., 2014). These changes might be significant in the Indian agricultural sector. Technological intervention, however, needs to be coupled with management practices for efficient implementation and reducing environmental externalities as witnessed under the Green Revolution.

9.3.2 Information, Management Practices, Production and Consumption Efficiency for Sustainable Intensification

The accessibility and availability of information are crucial to making agricultural production and marketing decisions needed for agricultural growth and development. As farms increase their engagement with markets, information systems are essential to enable them to make proper planting, harvest and marketing decisions (Aker, 2011; Ogutu, Okello, & Otieno, 2014). Information communication technologies (ICTs) have been shown to have great potential in reducing information asymmetries and improving the efficiency of production and marketing. Management of resources, especially inputs, is essential to bring about sustainable intensification. Technological measures to increase productivity need to be coupled with management of resources to reduce externalities such as emissions and overuse of natural resources. Management practices in agriculture and availability of information are inextricably linked as one complements the other. In this section, we look at the importance of improving access to information, the role technology plays in enabling this and how information access and good management practices go hand in hand.

ICTs are any medium or device that allows for the collation and dissemination of information. The advantages of ICTs are that they can enable quick dissemination of accurate information in an information-intensive activity like agriculture. Table 9.2 shows the different stages of production and the nature of the information that is essential to make significant production and marketing decisions. The major types of information and services producers require are market and price information, weather information, technical extension services-based information or the combination of the three (Aker, Ghosh, & Burrell, 2016). The traditional ICTs were the television, radio and newspapers, and in the last decade or so, mobile phones have emerged to be the dominant medium. Between 2003 and 2016, the number of mobile phones grew at a CAGR of 40% from 13.29 million to 1027 million. Mobile phone penetration and easy access to data plans make ICTs more effective in making information accessible. There is evidence to show that ICTs can play a role in the early adoption of technologies such as GM crops and practices such as zero tillage (Fischer, Byerlee, & Edmeades, 2009). Studies have also shown that ICTs help in acquiring information about

Table 9.2   Stages of production and marketing and type and source of information

Stages	Information	Source
Pre-cultivation	Crop selection	Input and output market, technical extension and meteorological
	Land selection	Input market
	Commodity price	Output market
	Weather	Meteorological
Cultivation	Land preparation	Technical extension
	Access to credit	Financial
	Access to inputs	Input market
	Planting	Technical extension
	Weather	Meteorological
	Water, fertilizer, pest management	Technical extension
	Labor	Labor market
Harvest	Labor	Labor market
	Mechanization	Technical extension
Post-harvest	Processing	Output market
	Storage	Output market
	Transportation	Output market
	Marketing	Output market
	Commodity price	Output market
	Grades and standards/quality	Output market

Source: Adapted from Aker et al. (2016)

seed varieties, weather-related information and diseases (S. Mittal & Mehar, 2012) and better price realization and less wastage (Aker & Fafchamps, 2015; Muto & Yamano, 2009; J. Robert, 2007).

ICTs often rely on platforms on which information can be collated. These platforms would bring together information regarding weather, technical extension and markets. Creating and maintaining these platforms can be costly. Information platforms need to have a sufficient user strength and a steady revenue stream in order to be financially viable. Information also needs to be reliable, accessible and affordable for it to have an impact on agricultural production and marketing.

Management of resources that goes into agricultural production needs to complement technology adoption for sustainable intensification and reduced environmental externalities. The FAO (2010) describes conservation agriculture (CA) technologies as resource-saving agricultural practices that consider sustainable productivity and profits in enabling conservation. Climate-smart agriculture as "agriculture that sustainably increases productivity enhances resilience (adaptation), reduces/removes greenhouse gases (mitigation), and enhances achievement of national food security and development goals" (FAO, 2010; Lipper et al., 2014). Supplementing agricultural programs with agroforestry for carbon sequestering, soil conservation and watershed management programs is crucial for sustainable intensification (Lipper, Pingali, & Zurek, 2006; Pretty et al., 2011).

As soils hold the second largest pool of carbon (after the oceans), changes in the stock of organic carbon in them can affect atmospheric CO_2 to a great extent (Chappell, Baldock, & Sanderman, 2015). The type of soil, nutrient and water management practices adopted by farmers during agricultural production influences these cycles. Maintaining the balances in the carbon and nitrogen cycles plays a vital role in the reduction of GHGs and is an integral part of soil management (J. A. Burney, Davis, & Lobell, 2010; Wollenberg et al., 2016). In India, the use of nitrogenous fertilizers (urea) is disproportionately higher than phosphate and potash due to high subsidies, and the use varies from state to state. In irrigated tracts application rates are much higher, and in states like Punjab, Haryana and Telangana, urea use ranges between 169 and 185 kg/hectare, while in Madhya Pradesh, Rajasthan and Odisha, the application rates range between 24 and 53 kg/hectare. The amount of fertilizer applied to the soil, fallowing practices, nitrogen-fixing crop cover and tilling practices are the main determinants of these cycles and the amount of CO_2 and N_2O released into the atmosphere. Judicious use of nitrogen fertilizers and fallowing and tilling practices are critical to limiting N_2O emissions and prevent soil erosion and loss of organic matter from the soil. Also, integrated soil fertility management (ISFM) that involves balancing organic and synthetic fertilizer to maintain a balanced supply of nutrients and good land management practices need to be put in place to ensure the sustainable increase of yields.

Increasing water use efficiency is essential to ensure the availability of water and mitigate the effects of prolonged drought scenarios. This requires an institutional and technical change at the farm and national level that enables conservation, replenishment and effective allocation. In rain-fed regions of the country, investment in irrigation infrastructure, especially drip irrigation, and promotion of activities such as water harvesting will be critical to improving water availability. Water stress and drought are often exacerbated by land degradation in sub-humid and semi-arid conditions to a higher degree than purely arid conditions (Adhikari, 2013). The sensitivity of a particular food system to climate change increases with scarcity and degradation of these natural resources. Therefore, systems by which resources are used and replenished will help manage the impact of agricultural production on the environment. Watershed and aquifer management in semi-arid regions along with informational services on climatic variability need to be built into water management practices to help regions cope or manage water stresses.

Effective management of common-pool resources is critical to conservation agriculture, and this cannot be done without community-based initiatives that disseminate and implement location-specific interventions in different agro-climatic zones. Conservation and climate-smart agriculture are methods of sustainable intervention that works in tandem with technological intervention. Extension services to improve agronomic practices, infrastructure and access to technology are essential interventions for smallholders. However, institutional interventions are required to enable adaptation by small farms.

9.4   The Way Forward: Institutional Support for Technology Adoption

The role of the state and institutions in areas such as biotech policies, infrastructure and credit systems that can improve smallholder access to technology is critical to enable sustainable intensification. The successful diffusion of GR technologies was a result of scale-neutrality of technologies and state and policy support. State involvement resulted in subsidies for inputs and their effective distribution along with extension services at the production stages and assured prices and procurement by the state to create buffers incentivized their adoption in a big way (Pingali, 2012). The Indian Council of Agricultural Research (ICAR) and the State Agricultural Universities (SAUs) adapted the technology that came from the International Maize and Wheat Improvement Center (CIMMYT) and the International Rice Research Institute (IRRI) for Indian conditions. The National Chemical Laboratory in Pune helped with developing efficient methods for pesticide production, the Projects and Development India Ltd. (PDIL) designed and built fertilizer factories and the Central Mechanical Engineering Research Institute (CMERI) was instrumental in designing the economic Swaraj tractors (Pray & Nagarajan, 2014).

The fundamental platform of GR technology was hybrid seeds through conventional plant-breeding that could improve the yield of crops. Since GR, there has been a significant paradigm shift in agricultural R&D, and newer agricultural technological interventions that have emerged are based on genetic modification, relying on changing the fundamental traits of plants (Ramani & Thutupalli, 2015). This brings to the forefront three concerns of affordability, adaptability and safety. Newer technologies may require a higher amount of capital, expertise and infrastructure to be accessed and implemented. For mechanization of farms the issues of economies of scale and with reference to GM technologies, issues of public health and safety need to be addressed. Institutional intervention such as improved access to credit, smallholder aggregation and platforms for debate and deliberation regarding GMOs need to evolve.

9.4.1 Cost of Technology—Affordability, Adaptability and Economies of Scale

In the last decade, funds for public sector R&D have reduced globally and private sector involvement in this space has been growing (Jaruzelski, Staack, & Johnson, 2017). In the case of China, India and Brazil, however, public sector investments have been increasing, although not at the pace of private sector investments. Significant investments are being made in seed and plant biotechnology, agricultural machinery, pesticides and fertilizers (Pray & Nagarajan, 2014). In India, the public sector is a significant player in R&D with regard to self-pollinated crops such as rice, wheat, pulses and oilseeds (Ferroni & Zhou, 2017). The public sector has a 50% share in fertilizer and 20% share in seed production and sales. As the majority of seed production and sale and mechanization and pesticides take place through the private sector, it has come to play a significant role in agricultural inputs since the 1980s. At the same time, public sector R&D under the ambit of the ICAR has been under considerable stress due to lack of financial resource, research clarity and collaboration between different public research institutions (GOI, 2015).

Smallholder access to seed technologies, mechanization, information and extension services will determine their ability to be economically viable and sustainable. Traditionally the state has played an enabling role in agricultural production as policies and R&D institutions have determined smallholder access to credit, information and extension services, subsidies and price support. These measures favored the major staple grains such as wheat and rice, incentivizing their widespread adoption at the cost of other crops such as pulses and coarse grains. Leveling the policy playing field by removing distorted support and improving marketing infrastructure can encourage the emergence of R&D in other crops such as coarse grains and pulses and enable diversification. The state support and encouragement in the formation of community-based development programs such as water user groups, agroforestry and aggregation models are needed and essential to enable smallholders to better adapt and implement newer interventions for conservation agriculture and to rectify economies of scale disadvantages.

The role of aggregation models in smallholder agricultural systems like India is vital in accessing credit and mechanization. This is discussed in more detail in Chap. 7. Mechanization is emerging to be an essential aspect of production, especially concerning rising farm and non-farm wages. It plays a crucial role in improving the efficiency of labor by reducing drudgery, time savings (Ibarrola-Rivas, Kastner, & Nonhebel, 2016) and also improving the nutritional status of individuals by diversifying household level time use (D. Johnston, Stevano, Malapit, Hull, & Kadiyala, 2018). Women face significant labor productivity constraints, and often conservation agriculture may increase women's workload (from weeding and other labor-intensive activities) and reduce the burden on men (Kaczan, Arslan, & Lipper, 2013). Rental market for farm machinery is a fast growing service (Binswanger & Singh, 2017), and women's self-help groups (SHGs) jointly owning and leasing out machines are successful models that can be seen in many locations. Therefore, productivity-enhancing technologies and interventions need to be gender-neutral and in some cases gender-specific (Carrand & Hartl, 2010). The policy challenge we highlight here is how to promote (a) context-specific, (b) environmentally sustainable, (c) affordable and (d) gender-neutral technologies.

9.4.2   The GM Debate

Genetic modification entails the creation of crops with desired characteristics such as herbicide tolerance, disease and pest tolerance, quality improvements, reduced emissions, tolerance to biotic stress and quality enhancements (Nelson, 2001). The process often involves moving genes between (sexually incompatible) organisms to create 'transgenic' crop species that can be conducive to resilient agricultural development. In the wake of climate change, natural resource degradation and the need to increase food production, the potential of biotechnology is promising. However, the longer-term side effects of technology can seldom be predicted with accuracy. Even with GR technologies, externalities such as environmental degradation and erosion of biodiversity, among others, emerged only later, making GMO a contentious topic in India as around the world. Despite no verifiable evidence of adverse effects on the environment, human or animal health, there has been a strong opposition to GM technology in India (C. N. Rao et al., 2018). Bt cotton, the only GM crop allowed in India, is a cash crop, and the lines of the debate were soft. However, resistance by civil society to introducing GM crops for human consumption has been influential within India. Although the biosafety regulatory mechanism in India is robust with every organization involved with recombinant DNA research requiring Institutional Biosafety Committees (IBSCs) and having the Department of Biotechnology under the Ministry of Science approving any new technology, the debate on GM crops is still polarizing.

The existing and future challenges of the Indian and global agricultural systems to increase production and adapt to climate change require technological interventions in both the first- and second-generation GM crops. As discussed earlier in this chapter, the impact of Bt cotton on incomes and the environment in India have been positive as a result of lower cost of production from reduced pesticide use and higher yields. In 2009, an attempt to introduce Bt brinjal in India failed due to pressure from civil society organizations despite being approved by the Genetic Engineering Approval Committee (GEAC) under the Ministry of Science (Herring, 2015). The government has since introduced a moratorium on GMOs until sufficient evidence proved they were safe. In 2014, the government proclaimed GM crops to be in the national interest which approved further field trials for GM rice, mustard, cotton, chickpea and brinjal (Ramani & Thutupalli, 2015). Categorization of GM as a special risk has created an uncertain investment climate that has driven out small players in the biotechnology sector (C. N. Rao et al., 2018).

The NITI Aayog in the Economic Survey of 2015–16 came out in favor of GMOs and in the years to come India can expect a shift to GMOs in food crops. However, there are significant issues that still need to be addressed regarding trust in regulatory mechanisms, platforms for dialogue and information dissemination and reporting. With the deviation from the state being the center of R&D in agriculture, its approaches to regulating biotechnology to assure biosafety are essential. Central to this regulation is building trust in these institutional processes. For this, in India, there is a need for platforms for debate between science communities, civil societies, farmers groups, state and citizens. Misinformation and inadequate translation of scientific research impact on society can often skew or polarize debates of such kind. The need to promote translation services to inform debates is also vital as we move ahead. Effective platforms of addressing such concerns are central to encourage R&D and innovations especially in the private sector that can address specific problems related to crop yield, resilience and quality to meet the food security challenges of the future.

9.5   CONCLUSION

Technology in the past has played a critical role in enabling food security in the developing world. The Green Revolution helped in increasing yields of wheat and rice, making many countries like India self-sufficient in these grains. One main reason the Green Revolution was successfully implemented was that it was scale-neutral, allowing small and marginal producers to adopt them. However, as these technologies were not resource-neutral, only regions with access to irrigation and rainfall were able to adopt them. The limitation of these technologies was that they were limited to significant staple grains and in regions where irrigation resources were available, leading to inter-regional and intercrop disparities. The impact these technologies had on the environment because of poor management was also high, leading to depletion of water tables and land degradation.

Technology remains critical for the new food security challenges India will face as we move towards becoming the most populous country in the world. Adding to production challenges is the issue of climate change. As agriculture influences and is influenced by climate change, the need to reduce emissions and other environmental externalities as the sector grows become essential. Therefore, the new role of technology is sustainable intensification—or increasing productivity by limiting or reducing externalities such as land and water degradation and emissions. First- and second-generation GM technologies hold promise in improving returns to farming through reduced cost of production and increasing resilience and the nutritive value of crops in the wake of global warming and climate change. Coupled with the effective management of resources (nutrient, water, natural resources) to improve efficiency and reduce their overuse is necessary in India.

However, assuring access and availability of technology to smallholders is vital to ensure sustainable intensification. Unlike Green Revolution technologies, newer technologies are private goods, and access to capital and scale to implement are essential. Institutional interventions to promote aggregation models and improve access to credit are essential to enable adoption by smallholders. There has been much debate about the safety of GM crops in India and around the world. Despite no evidence being found that GMOs are detrimental to human, animal and environmental health there has been much opposition to it, discouraging investments and innovation in agricultural R&D. India needs to have more forward-looking biotechnology policies and institutions that can address some of the concerns regarding the safety of GMOs and lay to rest misinformation. This is essential to bolster innovation and investment from the private sector and also enable institutional support for the adoption of biotechnology in agriculture.

REFERENCES

Abraham, M., & Pingali, P. (2019). Shortage of pulses in India: Understanding how markets incentivize supply response. *Journal of Agribusiness in Developing and Emerging Economies*, forthcoming.

Adhikari, B. (2013). Poverty reduction through promoting alternative livelihoods: Implications for marginal drylands. *Journal of International Development*, 25(7), 947–967. https://doi.org/10.1002/jid.1820

Aeschbach-Hertig, W., & Gleeson, T. (2012). Regional strategies for the accelerating global problem of groundwater depletion. *Nature Geoscience, 5*, 853. https://doi.org/10.1038/ngeo1617

Ahmad, L., Habib, R. K., Parvaze, S., & Sheraz, S. M. (2017). Agro-climatic and agro-ecological zones of India BT. In L. Ahmad, R. Habib Kanth, S. Parvaze, & S. Sheraz Mahdi (Eds.), *Experimental agrometeorology: A practical manual* (pp. 99–118). Cham: Springer International Publishing. https://doi.org/10.1007/978-3-319-69185-5_15

Aker, J. C. (2011). Dial "A" for agriculture: A review of information and communication technologies for agricultural extension in developing countries. *Agricultural Economics, 42*(6), 631–647. https://doi.org/10.1111/j.1574-0862.2011.00545.x

Aker, J. C., & Fafchamps, M. (2015). Mobile phone coverage and producer markets: Evidence from West Africa. *The World Bank Economic Review, 29*(2), 262–292.

Aker, J. C., Ghosh, I., & Burrell, J. (2016). The promise (and pitfalls) of ICT for agriculture initiatives. *Agricultural Economics, 47*(S1), 35–48. https://doi.org/10.1111/agec.12301

Ashok, K., Uma, K., Prahadeeswaran, M., & Jeyanthi, H. (2018). Economic and environmental performance of Bt cotton in India. In C. N. Rao, C. E. Pray, & R. J. Herring (Eds.), *Biotechnology for a second green revolution in India* (pp. 325–350). Academic Foundation.

Bhanja, S. N., Mukherjee, A., Rodell, M., Wada, Y., Chattopadhyay, S., Velicogna, I., ... Famiglietti, J. S. (2017). Groundwater rejuvenation in parts of India influenced by water-policy change implementation. *Scientific Reports, 7*(1), 7453. https://doi.org/10.1038/s41598-017-07058-2

Bhattacharyya, R., Ghosh, B. N., Mishra, P. K., Mandal, B., Rao, C. S., Sarkar, D., ... Franzluebbers, A. J. (2015). Soil degradation in India: Challenges and potential solutions. *Sustainability, 7*(4), 3528–3570. https://doi.org/10.3390/su7043528

Binswanger, H. P., & Singh, S. K. (2017). Wages, prices and agriculture: How can Indian agriculture cope with rising wages? *Journal of Agricultural Economics, 69*(2), 281–305. https://doi.org/10.1111/1477-9552.12234

Buiatti, M., Christou, P., & Pastore, G. (2013). The application of GMOs in agriculture and in food production for a better nutrition: Two different scientific points of view. *Genes & Nutrition, 8*(3), 255–270. https://doi.org/10.1007/s12263-012-0316-4

Burney, J. A., Davis, S. J., & Lobell, D. B. (2010). Greenhouse gas mitigation by agricultural intensification. *Proceedings of the National Academy of Sciences, 107*(26), 12052–12057.

Byerlee, D., de Janvry, A., & Sadoulet, E. (2009). Agriculture for development: Toward a new paradigm. *Annual Review of Resource Economics, 1*, 15–31.

Carrand, M., & Hartl, M. (2010). *Lightening the load: Labor-saving technologies and practices for rural women.* International Fund for Agricultural Development (IFAD)/Practical Action Publishing Ltd.

Carter, M. R., & Barrett, C. B. (2006). The economics of poverty traps and persistent poverty: An asset-based approach. *The Journal of Development Studies, 42*(2), 178–199. https://doi.org/10.1080/00220380500405261

Chappell, A., Baldock, J., & Sanderman, J. (2015). The global significance of omitting soil erosion from soil organic carbon cycling schemes. *Nature Climate Change, 6*, 187.

Fafchamps, M. (2003). *Rural poverty, risk and development.* Cheltenham, UK: Edward Elgar Publishing.

FAO. (2010). *The status of conservation agriculture in Southern Africa: Challenges and opportunities for expansion.* Johannesburg, South Africa.

FAO. (2016). *The state of food and agriculture—Climate change, agriculture and food security.* Rome.

Ferroni, M., & Zhou, Y. (2017). The private sector and India's agricultural transformation. *Global Journal of Emerging Market Economies, 9*(1–3), 28–37. https://doi.org/10.1177/0974910117716406

Fischer, R., Byerlee, D., & Edmeades, G. (2009). Can technology deliver on the yield challenge to 2050? In *How to feed the world in 2050*. Rome: FAO and Economic and Social Development Department.

Flachowsky, G., & Aulrich, K. (2001). Nutritional assessment of feeds from genetically modified organism. *Journal of Animal and Feed Sciences, 10*(Suppl. 1), 181–194. https://doi.org/10.22358/jafs/70020/2001

GOI. (2015). *Raising agricultural productivity and making farming remunerative for farmers*. New Delhi.

Herring, R. J. (2015). State science, risk and agricultural biotechnology: Bt cotton to Bt Brinjal in India. *The Journal of Peasant Studies, 42*(1), 159–186. https://doi.org/10.1080/03066150.2014.951835

Ibarrola-Rivas, J. M., Kastner, T., & Nonhebel, S. (2016). How much time does a farmer spend to produce my food? An international comparison of the impact of diets and mechanization. *Resources*. https://doi.org/10.3390/resources5040047

Jacoby, H. G. (2017). "Well-fare" economics of groundwater in South Asia. *The World Bank Research Observer, 32*(1), 1–20.

Jaruzelski, B., Staack, V., & Johnson, T. (2017). The role of private-sector R&D in agricultural innovation: Improving yields, equipment productivity, and sustainability. In S. Dutta, B. Lanvin, & S. Wunsch-Vincent (Eds.), *The global innovation index*. Ithaca, Fontainebleau, and Geneva: Cornell University, INSEAD, and WIPO.

Johnston, D., Stevano, S., Malapit, H. J., Hull, E., & Kadiyala, S. (2018). Review: Time use as an explanation for the agri-nutrition disconnect: Evidence from rural areas in low and middle-income countries. *Food Policy, 76*, 8–18. https://doi.org/10.1016/j.foodpol.2017.12.011

Kaczan, D., Arslan, A., & Lipper, L. (2013). *Climate-smart agriculture? A review of current practice of agroforestry and conservation agriculture in Malawi and Zambia*. ESA Working Paper No. 13-07, Rome.

Kebede, Y. (1992). Risk taking behaviour & new technologies: The case of producers in the Central Highlands of Ethiopia. *Quarterly Journal of International Agriculture, 31*, 269–289.

Lipper, L., Pingali, P., & Zurek, M. (2006). Less-favoured areas: Looking beyond agriculture towards ecosystem services. In R. Ruben, J. Pender, & A. Kuyvenhoven (Eds.), *Sustainable poverty reduction in less-favoured areas: Problems, options and strategies* (pp. 442–460). Wallingford, UK: CABI.

Lipper, L., Thornton, P., Campbell, B. M., Baedeker, T., Braimoh, A., Bwalya, M., … Torquebiau, E. F. (2014). Climate-smart agriculture for food security. *Nature Climate Change, 4*(12), 1068–1072. https://doi.org/10.1038/nclimate2437

Lobell, D. B., Schlenker, W., & Costa-Roberts, J. (2011). Climate trends and global crop production since 1980. *Science, 333*(6042), 616–620.

Matson, P. A., Parton, W. J., Power, A. G., & Swift, M. J. (1997). Agricultural intensification and ecosystem properties. *Science, 277*(5325), 504–509. https://doi.org/10.1126/science.277.5325.504

Mittal, S., & Mehar, M. (2012). How mobile phones contribute to growth of small farmers? Evidence from India. *Quarterly Journal of International Agriculture, 51*(3), 227–244.

Muto, M., & Yamano, T. (2009). The impact of mobile phone coverage expansion on market participation: Panel data evidence from Uganda. *World Development, 37*(12), 1887–1896. https://doi.org/10.1016/j.worlddev.2009.05.004

Mythili, G., & Goedecke, J. (2016). Economics of land degradation in India. In E. Nkonya, A. Mirzabaev, & J. von Braun (Eds.), *Economics of land degradation and improvement—A global assessment for sustainable development* (pp. 431–469). Cham: Springer.

Nelson, G. C. (2001). Traits and techniques of GMOs. In A. Nelson (Ed.), *Genetically modified organisms in agriculture, economics and politics* (pp. 7–13). London: Academic Press. https://doi.org/10.1016/B978-012515422-2/50005-9

Nelson, G. C., Valin, H., Sands, R. D., Havlík, P., Ahammad, H., Deryng, D., ... Willenbockel, D. (2014b). Climate change effects on agriculture: Economic responses to biophysical shocks. *Proceedings of the National Academy of Sciences, 111*(9), 3274–3279. https://doi.org/10.1073/pnas.1222465110

Niang, I., Ruppel, O. C., Abdrabo, M. A., Essel, A., Lennard, C., Padgham, J., & Urquhart, P. (2014). Africa. In *Regional aspects. Contribution of Working Group II to the Fifth Assessment Report of the Intergovernmental Panel on Climate Change*. Cambridge, UK: Cambridge University Press.

O'Brien, K., Leichenko, R., Kelkar, U., Venema, H., Aandahl, G., Tompkins, H., ... West, J. (2004). Mapping vulnerability to multiple stressors: Climate change and globalization in India. *Global Environmental Change, 14*(4), 303–313. https://doi.org/10.1016/j.gloenvcha.2004.01.001

Ogutu, S. O., Okello, J. J., & Otieno, D. J. (2014). Impact of information and communication technology-based market information services on smallholder farm input use and productivity: The case of Kenya. *World Development, 64*, 311–321. https://doi.org/10.1016/j.worlddev.2014.06.011

Paterson, R. R. M., & Lima, N. (2010). How will climate change affect mycotoxins in food? *Food Research International, 43*(7), 1902–1914. https://doi.org/10.1016/j.foodres.2009.07.010

Pingali, P. (2010). Chapter 74 Agriculture renaissance: Making 'agriculture for development' work in the 21st century. In P. Pingali & R. Evenson (Eds.), *Handbook of agricultural economics* (pp. 3867–3894). Elsevier. Retrieved from http://www.sciencedirect.com/science/article/pii/S1574007209040742

Pingali, P. (2012). Green revolution: Impacts, limits, and the path ahead. *Proceedings of the National Academy of Science, 109*(31), 12302–12308. https://doi.org/10.1073/pnas.0912953109

Prasad, R. (2009). Efficient fertilizer use: The key to food security and better environment. *Journal of Tropical Agriculture, 47*(1–2), 1–17.

Pray, C. E., & Nagarajan, L. (2014). The transformation of the Indian agricultural input industry: Has it increased agricultural R&D? *Agricultural Economics, 45*(S1), 145–156. https://doi.org/10.1111/agec.12138

Pretty, J., Toulmin, C., & Williams, S. (2011). Sustainable intensification in African agriculture. *International Journal of Agricultural Sustainability, 9*(1), 5–24. https://doi.org/10.3763/ijas.2010.0583

Qaim, M., Subramanian, A., Naik, G., & Zilberman, D. (2006). Adoption of Bt cotton and impact variability: Insights from India. *Applied Economic Perspectives and Policy, 28*(1), 48–58.

Raman, S., Devineni, N., & Fishman, R. (2015). Can improved agricultural water use efficiency save India's groundwater? *Environmental Research Letters, 10*(8), 84022.

Ramani, S. V., & Thutupalli, A. (2015). Emergence of controversy in technology transitions: Green Revolution and Bt cotton in India. *Technological Forecasting and Social Change, 100*, 198–212. https://doi.org/10.1016/j.techfore.2015.06.018

Rao, C. N., Pray, C. E., & Herring, R. J. (2018). Biotechnology for second green revolution in India: Overview of issues. In R. N. Chandrashekhar, C. E. Pray, & R. J. Herring (Eds.), *Biotechnology for a second green revolution in India* (pp. 45–74). New Delhi: Academic Foundation.

Robert, J. (2007). The digital provide: Information (technology), market performance and welfare in the South Indian fisheries sector. *Quarterly Journal of Economics, 121*(2), 879–924.

Rojas-Downing, M. M., Nejadhashemi, A. P., Harrigan, T., & Woznicki, S. A. (2017). Climate change and livestock: Impacts, adaptation, and mitigation. *Climate Risk Management, 16*, 145–163. Retrieved from http://www.sciencedirect.com/science/article/pii/S221209631730027X

Rosegrant, M. W., Koo, J., Cenacchi, N., Ringler, C., Robertson, R., Fisher, M., … Sabbagh, P. (2014). *Food security in a world of natural resource scarcity: The role of agricultural technologies.* Washington, DC: International Food Policy Research Institute.

Shiao, T., Maddocks, A., Carson, C., & Loizeaux, E. (2015). 3 maps explain India's growing water risks. Washington, DC. Retrieved from https://www.wri.org/blog/2015/02/3-maps-explain-india-s-growing-water-risks

Soby, S. D. (2013). The end of the Green Revolution. *Journal of Agricultural and Environmental Ethics, 26*(3), 537–546. https://doi.org/10.1007/s10806-012-9393-z

Subbarao, G. V., Arango, J., Masahiro, K., Hooper, A. M., Yoshihashi, T., Ando, Y., ... Iwanaga, M. (2017). Genetic mitigation strategies to tackle agricultural GHG emissions: The case for biological nitrification inhibition technology. *Plant Science, 262*, 165–168. https://doi.org/10.1016/j.plantsci.2017.05.004

Subramanian, A., & Qaim, M. (2011). Interlocked village markets and trader idiosyncrasy in rural India. *Journal of Agricultural Economics, 62*(3), 690–709. https://doi.org/10.1111/j.1477-9552.2011.00309.x

Thornton, P. K., van de Steeg, J., Notenbaert, A., & Herrero, M. (2009). The impacts of climate change on livestock and livestock systems in developing countries: A review of what we know and what we need to know. *Agricultural Systems, 101*(3), 113–127. https://doi.org/10.1016/j.agsy.2009.05.002

Vetter, S. H., Sapkota, T. B., Hillier, J., Stirling, C. M., Macdiarmid, J. I., Aleksandrowicz, L., ... Smith, P. (2017). Greenhouse gas emissions from agricultural food production to supply Indian diets: Implications for climate change mitigation. *Agriculture, Ecosystems & Environment, 237*(Suppl. C), 234–241. https://doi.org/10.1016/j.agee.2016.12.024

Wollenberg, E., Richards, M., Smith, P., Havlík, P., Obersteiner, M., Tubiello, F. N., ... Campbell, B. M. (2016). Reducing emissions from agriculture to meet the 2 °C target. *Global Change Biology, 22*(12), 3859–3864. https://doi.org/10.1111/gcb.13340

CHAPTER 10

Managing Climate Change Risks in Food Systems

10.1 Introduction

Through this book, we have presented arguments for developing a robust and equitable food system which is anchored on the goal that all individuals who depend on it have to be able to secure food and nutrition for greater welfare. Food and nutrition security in its broadest definition refers to the ability of individuals to access good quality, nutritious foods that are affordable and available at all times. In addition to providing access to nutritious foods, food systems have to account for external conditions, such as vagaries of the weather, and political stability, which moderate the ability of individuals to access nutrition. In this context, climate change has been identified as one of the greatest threats to food and nutrition security. This complex phenomenon, which involves changing weather patterns, increased incidence of extreme weather events and the reduction in the quality of natural resources, is expected to impact food systems through multiple channels. One, by changing optimal growing conditions for crops and increasing uncertainty in extreme weather events, climate change is expected to impact the availability of food and nutrients. Two, at the current level of technology, climate change will increase uncertainty in production. This can lower access to nutrients and nutrition in the food that is already available for consumption. In combination with its effects on overall health quality of individuals, climate change will reduce the ability of individuals to absorb nutrients,

© The Author(s) 2019   241
P. Pingali et al., *Transforming Food Systems for a Rising India*,
Palgrave Studies in Agricultural Economics and Food Policy,
https://doi.org/10.1007/978-3-030-14409-8_10

thus impacting labor productivity. This, in turn, would reduce future economic growth prospects. Finally, climate change is expected to negatively impact economic development by increasing the vulnerability of different regions and different population groups. For example, for those with social disadvantages, lower ability to cope with climate changes will further increase their risk of hunger and food insecurity. Similarly, regions with low rural development and high poverty rates will be less capable of adapting to climate change.

In this chapter, we review climate change related risks on food systems. We outline the various pathways through which climate change impacts food systems and emphasize evidence from India. We discuss policy and institutional measures that are currently in place to mitigate and manage these risks. Keeping in sight the food security needs of the future, we also discuss some guiding principles for mitigation and adaptation strategies that can be included in these policies that can help in creating robust food systems.

10.2   WHAT IS INDIA'S EXPERIENCE OF CLIMATE CHANGE THUS FAR?

At its core, climate change refers to the fallout of the phenomenon of increasing global temperatures, due to increased greenhouse gas (GHG) emissions,[1] on human welfare. Increase in global temperature has been associated with the melting of glaciers, changing intensity of precipitation cycles, melting of permafrost in the arctic, depletion of the ozone layers and the acidification of oceans (Cruz et al., 2007; IPCC, 2014; Schuur et al., 2015; Shrestha, Gautam, & Bawa, 2012; Speers, Besedin, Palardy, & Moore, 2016). Extreme events such as high-intensity hurricanes,

---

[1] GHG contributes to warming of temperatures by their ability to absorb and emit radiant energy from thermal infrared radiations. The primary GHGs in the earth's atmosphere are carbon dioxide (CO_2), ozone, nitrous oxide methane and water vapor. Human activity in the post-industrial era is the prime contributor to CO_2 increasing from 280 ppm in the early 1800s to around 400 ppm in 2014 (ppm—parts per million). This is a 40% increase over the 250 years, the highest ever in the paleo experience of the earth. Nearly 80% of these CO_2 emissions come from industrial processes and the burning of fossil fuels while the rest of the 20% comes from deforestation, land clearing and degradation of soils. Increase in global GHG emissions have increased average global temperatures by around 1 degree Celsius (IPCC, 2014).

flooding, droughts, forest fires, extreme heating of lakes, changing coast-lines and so on are perceivable and measureable outcomes of climate change. These have been increasing in both frequency and intensity over the last decade, and the distress caused to human health, economic devel-opment and agricultural systems has been well documented across the globe (IPCC, 2014).

Experts have also brought to the fore the more immediate impacts of global warming in the Indian subcontinent. In the last 50 years, satellite data suggest that maximum temperature increases have been around 1 degree Celsius across the country (Fig. 10.1). Current projections estimate further increases by around 2 to 4 degree Celsius by the end of the century. Also, projections also show regional variation in the impacts of tempera-ture. For example, the western and the southern parts of the country are expected to see the greatest increases with regard to temperature. Increase in the mean temperature and increases in the number of hot days have been documented across the country as well (IMD, 2018; K. R. Kumar, Kumar, & Pant, 1994). Changes in precipitation patterns such as increased floods, increased incidences of severe droughts, changing optimal growing seasons and changes in rainy period start dates have created already increased

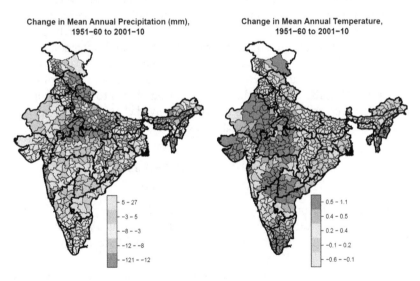

Fig. 10.1 Temperature (degree Celsius) and rainfall (mm) change. Source: AidGeo Data; based on authors calculations

uncertainty for agricultural systems (Kothawale & Rupa Kumar, 2005; K. S. K. Kumar & Parikh, 2001; S. N. Kumar, Yadav, Jee, Kumar, & Chauhan, 2011; A. K. Misra, 2014; O'Brien et al., 2004; A. Sharma & Pingali, 2016). Figure 10.1 also shows us some of these significant changes in the rainfall pattern across the country.[2] Here we see that parts of the north and northwest have seen a decline in precipitation while southern, eastern and northeastern regions have seen an increase in precipitation over time. There is also evidence that increase in the rate of glaciers melting in the Himalayas has increased downstream flooding thus impacting the productivity of lowlands (Kattelmann, 2003; Shrestha et al., 2012; Vedwan & Rhoades, 2001; Watanabe, Ives, & Hammond, 1994). Excessive deforestation and indiscriminate land clearing have also contributed to flooding and have increased air pollution (Sinha & Swaminathan, 1992; E. Somanathan, Prabhakar, & Mehta, 2009). Increased traffic, urban congestion, poor waste management and land degradation have also been linked with increasing pollution and higher carbon emission rates across the country's landscape (Auffhammer, Ramanathan, & Vincent, 2006; J. Burney & Ramanathan, 2014; R. Gupta, Somanathan, & Dey, 2017; O'Brien et al., 2004). Even in current folklore, the urban rich complain about buying new air conditioners since summers have become too hot and also complain that pollution prevents them from enjoying the cool winter breeze. In rural areas, farmers now concede that they can no longer accurately predict changing rainfall patterns and intensity and their ground water sources are drying up. These anecdotal conversations find themselves validated in journalistic articles that further reinforce the importance of both accepting and also addressing the problem that climate change poses to us as a population. However, aside from these directly perceived changes to welfare, climate change creates additional challenges to food systems as we look ahead.

10.3   PATHWAYS THROUGH WHICH CLIMATE CHANGES IMPACT FOOD SYSTEMS

By increasing the probability and frequency of extreme weather events, climate change can impact food systems in the following ways (Fig. 10.2). First, by reducing access to water,[3] increasing unpredictability of weather

[2] In the paper by (Mall et al., 2006), authors show evidence that changes to temperature and rainfall will become evident by 2040 in India.

[3] In Chap. 8, we discussed the problem of lack of water access in more detail. Hence we do not delve further into the topic in this chapter.

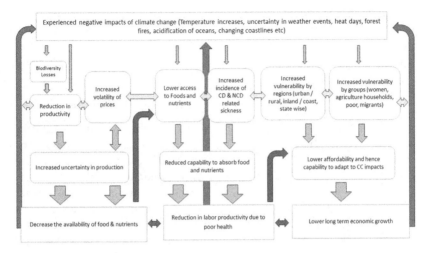

Fig. 10.2   Pathways: Impact of climate change on food systems

conditions and reducing the quality of natural resources on which crops depend, climate change can increase uncertainty with regard to food production. This, in turn, can reduce food and nutrition availability and increase food price volatility. Two, climate change can reduce labor productivity by affecting individual's health both directly and indirectly. By increasing morbidity and the severity of communicable and non- communicable diseases, climate change can reduce an individual's capability to absorb nutrients from food, thus reducing health. Through the channel of increased volatility of food prices and decreased food and nutrient availability, climate change reduces access to food. This too impacts the health of individuals and hence their labor productivity. In the absence of safety nets, lower labor productivity reduces the affordability of individuals and hence reduces their economic growth prospects for the future. Finally, climate change can directly reduce economic opportunities by increasing the vulnerability of certain regions and population groups. Vulnerable groups such as people living in coastal areas, poor rural agricultural households and women and older individuals may experience the negative effects of climate change by more if they do not have the appropriate capabilities to adapt to its negative effects. This, in turn, lowers long-term economic growth prospects for both individuals and food systems. Decrease in food availability, labor productivity and lower long-term economic growth may create a vicious cycle of low adaptation capability towards climate change which can worsen its impacts on individuals. In the next section, we present evidence on these pathways and we bring forth evidence from India on the same.

10.3.1   Impacts on Food and Nutrient Availability

Climate change impacts food and nutrient availability by reducing agricultural productivity both directly and indirectly. In the absence of crop technologies to tide over the vagaries of weather, climate change can increase production uncertainty as well as decrease crop and livestock productivity. With lower amounts of foods available, climate change can directly impact total nutrient availability within a food system. Climate change can also impact the quality of natural resources on which human food production depends. Soil degradation and acidification of oceans can reduce the quality of nutrients by impacting the health of crops, livestock and fisheries. Finally, an indirect method through which climate change can impact food and nutrient availability is through increasing price volatility. As food and nutrient availability decreases and extreme events threaten their production, increasing prices and increased price volatility will reduce access if income increases cannot keep pace with these changes. Also, if actors along the food supply chain do not store food properly or distribute surpluses across times of shortages, this can further reduce the availability of foods and nutrients for individuals. In this section, we highlight some of the research on this pathway.

10.3.1.1 Impact on Agricultural Productivity

Plant scientists agree that quantifying the impact of increasing temperatures on crop yield is not straightforward. For example, temperature increases have been found to have beneficial impacts if it combined with other optimal growing conditions. Increase in atmospheric CO_2 (a GHG) too, can improve crop growth performance by increasing the rate of photosynthesis and water use efficiency (Challinor et al., 2014; Lobell & Burke, 2010; Nelson, Mensbrugghe et al., 2014). However, there few important caveats that need to hold for the conclusion that yield changes can be positive. One, agricultural systems require adequate ground water management systems and enough access to irrigation to tide over changes in precipitation patterns that come with climate change (A. K. Misra, 2014; Qadir et al., 2008; R. G. Taylor et al., 2013). Two, temperature need to remain increase below 30 degree Celsius during the growing season. After this threshold, temperature increases are considered to be extremely damaging to yields for crops that are rain fed (IPCC, 2014). Even across crop groups, total impacts on yields are found to differ. For example, climate model projections find that with adequate irrigation, rice crops may actually benefit but crops such as wheat and maize will lose out (Challinor et al., 2014; Nelson, Mensbrugghe et al., 2014). Also, much of the research on the impacts of climate has been conducted in developed countries, which are located in temperature zones where increases in temperature will be beneficial. However, many developing and emerging countries are in tropical zones. Due to their geographical locations, these areas are expecting to see an unfavorable increase in temperature which has greater impacts on food production and hence food security. Three, scientists have also established that even if there may be net benefits to calorie availability through greater yields, a major fallout of climate change will be lower bioavailability of protein and micronutrients such as iron and zinc which are more sensitive to changes in plant physiology due to climate change (Dietterich et al., 2014; Müller, Elliott, & Levermann, 2014).

In India too, projections of climate impact on yields and production have shown there are differences in outcomes both by crops and by region. Table 10.1 summarizes the more recent projections for different crops in India. Overall, we see that by 2050, projections estimate between 4% to 8% decrease in yields of crops at the minimum and around 25% decrease at the maximum. Regarding staple crops, we see that rice yields are expected to decrease by 4% and the productivity in the northwestern region, which is currently the high productivity belt for rice production, is extremely vulnerable to temperature changes. For wheat and sorghum too, experts estimate 6–7% decrease in overall productivity by 2050 due to increases in temperatures. Due to low adaptation capability of agricultural systems in the east, there are expected decreases in the productivity of horticultural crops such as coconut, potato and mustard. On the positive side, these productivity decreases may be offset by increases in productivity of the same crop groups in the south. Regarding staples, production and yields of wheat, maize and chick pea are thought to be most vulnerable especially in areas where crops are rain fed (Mall, Singh, Gupta, Srinivasan, & Rathore, 2006; A. Sharma & Pingali, 2016, 2018). However, for some non-staple crops such as pearl and finger millets, A. Sharma and Pingali (2018) find that climate change may be more detrimental due to the lack of availability of heat- and drought-resistant crop technology. Threats to

Table 10.1 Climate change impacts on yields in India

Literature	Crops	Temp threshold	Projections (2020, 2050, 2080)	Strategies for adaptation	Regional disparities
S. N. Kumar et al. (2015)	Potato	17 degree Celsius	Declines by 2.5%, 6%, 11%	Changing planting period & nitrogen application	Northwest + East –
Boomiraj, Chakrabarti, Aggarwal, Choudhary, and Chander (2010)	Mustard	25 degree Celsius	Declines by 2%, 7.9%, 15%	Changing planting period & fertilizer application	Punjab + Central – East –
P. Singh et al. (2014)	Groundnut		Yield gains to be expected	Drought-resistant variety	Project site Anantapur, Junagadh
S. N. Kumar and Aggarwal (2013)	Coconut		4% to 5% increase by 2050 1% to 4% increase by 2080	Soil moisture conservation, summer irrigation, drip irrigation	South + Northeast + East –
Hebbar, Venugopalan, Prakash, and Aggarwal (2013)	Cotton	Regional increases in temperature	No changes for A1B Reduction in yield for other scenarios	Water management	North – Central + or same South + or same
S. N. Kumar et al. (2014)	Wheat	27 degree Celsius	Declines by 6% to 23% by 2050, 15% to 25% by 2080	Timely planting, heat-tolerant varieties, input efficiency	Central – South –

Soora et al. (2013)	Rice	Sensitive to min temp> 19 degree Celsius	Declines by 4%, 7%, 10%	Heat-resistant variety, irrigation	All India – Northwest large decrease
A. Srivastava, Kumar, and Aggarwal (2010)	Sorghum	Sensitivity increases after 2 deg. Celsius temp increase	Decreases by 7%, 11%, 32%	Changing sowing dates of monsoon-dependent varieties	South Central – Central – Southwest zone –
Byjesh, Kumar, and Aggarwal (2010)	Maize	Temperature increases can be offset by rainfall	In some areas, it is expected to increase		South – Central – Upper Indo-Gangetic Plains +

their production will have important implications for nutrient security as these crops (millets) are known to be the most important source of proteins and micronutrients in the diets of the poor.

The other caveats to keep in mind while talking about the benefits from climate change are the following. One, while many of the climate models used to make projections based on estimates to changes in seed technology and water availability, they do not account for increases in temperature that will make environmental conditions favorable for new pests, weeds and pathogens to thrive. The increased pestilence and pests resistant to current treatment options can have a major negative impact on crop productivity. The productivity impact of heat stress on agricultural inputs such as labor and livestock are also not accounted for in the projections. Two, in India, nearly 60% of all agricultural land continues to remain rain fed (Mall et al., 2006). Without appropriate groundwater management practices such as construction of aquifers, improvement of irrigation channels and prevention of acidification of soils, the impact of the changes on crops yields may be more devastating than what the models predict (Abraham & Pingali, 2017; Brenkert & Malone, 2005; Guhathakurta, Sreejith, & Menon, 2011; O'Brien et al., 2004; Sinha & Swaminathan, 1992). Three, while a large part of the scientific discourse has been focused on calorie security through investments in staple grains, the impacts of climate on the yields of non-staples and hence impacts on protein and micronutrient availability is less understood (A. Sharma & Pingali, 2018). Many of the poor (and vegetarians) in India rely on non-staple crops for enhancing their nutritional diversity. Given the lack of technologies currently available to safeguard productivity and the lack of information about climate impacts on these types of crops, the vulnerability of non-staple crop production becomes a major food security concern for the future. Safeguarding the production of these crops will be important in the goal of achieving nutrition security. This argument also extends towards yields of non-staple crops as well as yields of livestock and fisheries. For example, increasing sea temperatures are known to decrease yields of small fishes and increase the incidence of harmful cyanobacteria that will impact nutrition availability from these sources (Brenkert & Malone, 2005; Paerl & Paul, 2012). Changes in temperature are also expected to bring forth new pathogens that will affect zoonotic pathways within which human and livestock interact with each other, thus further impacting yields and productivity of livestock (Myers et al., 2017). These factors too may impact nutrient availability and hence the quality of food.

10.3.1.2 Impact on Biodiversity

Forests, grasslands, marshes and their related ecological species play an important role in protecting food systems. The most important is their ability to mitigate some effects of climate change through carbon sequestration. For example, even though agriculture is thought to contribute to nearly 25% of the world's GHGs, nearly 20% of these emissions are reabsorbed by the bio-ecosystems around them (IPCC, 2014). Mature ecological systems are thus key to reducing the GHGs in the atmosphere and reducing the intensity of climate change on inputs in the food systems. Regarding benefits to agriculture and food production, bio-ecosystems play a major role in soil conservation. Forests prevent soil erosion and produce organic matter that can improve nutrient content in soils around them (R. R. Banerjee, 2015; Steiner, Briske, Brown, & Rottler, 2018). Coastal marshes are also known to prevent excess flooding and acidification of soils in areas around them (Wigand et al., 2017). However, there are currently no market tools that can value the contributions of ecological systems services towards climate health and hence their value in food systems is underestimated. Even climate scientists do not account for the role of these systems in mitigation and adaptations strategies for global climate change, thus reducing global discussion on their preservation. This increases the vulnerability of bio-ecosystems to climate change which spills over as a greater vulnerability for food security.

10.3.1.3 Impact on Price Volatility and Food Access

In a country like India, having access to food is complicated by food price volatility (from production uncertainty) and inefficient food distribution systems. The former reduces the affordability of foods and the latter reduces access due to high rates of food loss and waste. Both these factors reduce access to nutrition in diets. With regard to the former, in combination with rising per capita demand for food, changing preferences towards more diverse diets and shrinking productivity and (or) food production, climate change increases uncertainty in the food supply and hence increases volatility in associated food prices. While a trend of rising prices may reflect increasing demand for food, increase in price volatility in the short run (due to shortfalls in production from extreme weather events) additionally widen the gap of access for the poor who have limited abilities to smooth consumption in times of price volatility. Another major contributor to price volatility is inefficient supply chains that are associated with high levels of food and nutrient loss as food moves from farm to plate.

In a report by the FAO in 2011 on food loss and waste, it was estimated that nearly 90% of all food losses occurs in the supply chain process between the farms and the urban markets in South Asia. These losses contribute to the reduction in food and nutrient availability, thus exacerbating production shortfalls. Even as late as 2014, inefficient supply chain processes of the PDS that were meant to supply adequate calories to individuals could not reach 194 million hungry people in India.[4] This was in a year where the country produced a surplus of 40 million tons of staples.

Unexpected spikes in prices of food have been associated with increased incidence of conflicts (Bellemare, 2015; D'Souza & Jolliffe, 2013; Hossain & Green, 2011; J. Swinnen & Squicciarini, 2012; C. P. Timmer, 1989), reduction in welfare of net consumers of food (Wodon & Zaman, 2010) and lower diet quality in households (D'Souza & Jolliffe, 2013). The unprecedented spikes in world food prices in 2008 due to energy related constraints was thought to have been an underlying factor in food riots across 23 countries. India, too, is also not a stranger to food inflation risks. Research has documented that food price volatility can impact an incumbent's political position during election cycles (Besley & Burgess, 2002). In the past, when there have been production shortages, either locally or globally, the government of India has smoothened prices through the release of its own stocks as well as procuring from international markets to avoid such political upheavals (Besley & Burgess, 2002; C. P. Timmer, 1989).

10.3.2   Impacts on Health and Thus Future Labor Productivity

Having good health has been linked to better educational outcomes, wages and labor productivity. More healthy individuals are more productive and can access opportunities to better their own and their family's circumstances. Climate change can affect the health of individuals, and hence labor productivity, by (1) increasing risks for malnutrition and by (2) increasing morbidity that spills over into poor health through the same channel. With regard to its direct effects, by reducing access to good quality food and foods with micronutrients, climate change can increase undernutrition, hidden hunger and obesity risks. Indirectly as well, by increasing risks of

---

[4] https://www.reuters.com/article/us-india-food-hunger/as-millions-go-hungry-india-eyes-ways-to-stop-wasting-14-billion-of-food-a-year-idUSKBN1ET07Y (Accessed February 2018).

vector-borne diseases (due to changes in temperature or precipitation) and non-communicable diseases (due to the changing health environment), climate change can increase risk factors related to malnutrition. These changes can lead to a vicious cycle of poor health and increased exposure to climate risks. As the health of individuals deteriorates, labor productivity of individuals will fall and this increases their exposure to income shocks that climate change may pose.

10.3.2.1 Direct Impact on Malnutrition

A more nuanced assessment of the impact of climate on food and nutrition security involves unpacking its implications on food quality. Quality, here, refers to access to a diet that reduces the incidence of the triple burden of malnutrition. Food system related interventions in the past have focused singularly on increasing the access to calories in order to reduce hunger and undernutrition. However, even as we have had some successes towards meeting the SDG targets of reducing calorie-related undernutrition, climate change has brought new problems to the center stage. First is the impact of climate change on undernutrition and hidden hunger. The majority of the poor in India depend on plant-based foods for proteins and micronutrients. With lower bio-availability of protein due to climate change, this can adversely affect protein related undernourishment (Myers et al., 2014). Lower micronutrient content in plants too will manifest itself in higher rates of anemia (Brabin, Hakimi, & Pelletier, 2001; Kalaivani, 2009; Rasmussen, 2001; Yip, 2000). Two, prices of foods generally reflect calorie availability and not value from its nutrition content. Without an appropriate way to signal the value of nutrient diversity, prices of food will never reflect nutrition scarcity. Without this information, the research and business community may continue to focus on developing adaptive strategies to maintain calorie content for foods rather than developing nutrient rich crops. Lack of support for increasing diversity in diets by incentivizing greater production and consumption of non-staple foods (such as livestock, fisheries and non-staple crops) may lead to further degradation of diet diversity within households (P. Pingali, 2012, 2015; P. L. Pingali, Spielman, & Zaidi, 2014). Three, without the proper incentives to develop nutrient rich food, individuals may face increases in obesity due to over-consumption of nutrient poor foods. All these factors would, in turn, impact nutrient absorption capability of individuals and hence affect the health of individuals.

10.3.2.2 Other Impacts on Health and Nutrition Access

In addition to the direct climate impacts on nutrition availability, accessibility and quality, there are some indirect pathways through which climate can impact food security. With temperature increases across the globe, experts have predicted that there will be a spatial redistribution in the incidence of vector-borne diseases. Zoonotic diseases, diseases transmitted from animals to humans, that were traditionally found in warmer climates will become more common in colder areas (Patz, Campbell-Lendrum, Holloway, & Foley, 2005). This includes the incidence of diseases such as malaria and other vector-borne diseases that are dependent on temperature, water, humidity and so on (Dhiman, Pahwa, Dhillon, & Dash, 2010; Lindblade, Walker, Onapa, Katungu, & Wilson, 2000; Paaijmans et al., 2010; Sutherst, 2004; Tanser, Sharp, & le Sueur, 2003). Increase in morbidity from these diseases tends to affect the nutrition absorption capacity of individuals, thus impacting access to nutrition. In addition to the associated mortality risks, these diseases are also known to impact the health and productivity of individuals and thus economic development and food security (Watts et al., 2015). Climate stressors such as fires, heat waves, droughts and floods may bring with them heat stress, more particulate pollution, pollen allergens and change the composition of the ozone. These changes have been associated with increased risk of diseases of the respiratory systems, cardiovascular system and chronic and acute diseases such as cancer (Ebi & McGregor, 2008; McMichael, Woodruff, & Hales, 2006; Watts et al., 2015; Ziska et al., 2003). It has also been established in the literature that heat stress is a major cause for reduction in productivity (Ciais et al., 2005; Kjellstrom, Holmer, & Lemke, 2009; Xiang, Bi, Pisaniello, & Hansen, 2014). In the current research from India, air pollution and heat stress have been associated with reductions in crop yields (Auffhammer et al., 2006; J. Burney & Ramanathan, 2014; R. Gupta et al., 2017), health effects such as increase in respiratory disorders and increases in mortality (Greenstone & Hanna, 2014; Majra & Gur, 2009; Ziska et al., 2003) as well as reduction in labor productivity (E. Somanathan, Somanathan, Sudarshan, & Tewari, 2015). All these factors may contribute to affecting the health of individuals which may spill over as lower labor productivity.

10.3.3   Impacts on Long-Term GDP Growth

In the previous two sections, we have presented evidence that climate change can have negative impacts on health and agriculture. In the short term, labor productivity losses from poor health and poor access to food reduce an individual's ability to access opportunities for enhancing their welfare. In the long term, by reducing the labor dividend from young populations, GDP growth prospects that depend on this resource will be negatively affected. Also, when agricultural systems perform poorly, structural transformation (ST) processes may be stunted as well. This, in turn, leads to some areas lagging behind and makes catch-up growth in the long term difficult. These spillovers aside, climate change can directly impact GDP growth. From a regional perspective, by changing comparative advantages of resources (land quality, labor quality, etc), climate change poses a major threat to ST prospects within the country. In the absence of access to appropriate adaptation technologies, some households may be more vulnerable than others. For example, households that are poor, households that depend on low-skilled labor for income generation and households headed by women may be more vulnerable to climate change if they cannot cope with its impacts. Within households as well, women and girl children may be more vulnerable if their human capital investments depended on good weather outcomes. These factors contribute to increasing income inequality across the country, thus reducing prospects for equitable growth. Further, as GDP growth stagnates, lower capacity to tide over events related to climate change may be reinforced. In this section, we bring together evidence with regard to climate impacts on economic growth prospects.

10.3.3.1 Regional Losses from Climate Change on GDP

From a global perspective, changes in climate have been linked to decreasing GDP growth rates under all scenarios of climate change. In some regions in the tropical South—such as countries in Africa—the effects are likely to be more severe. In scenarios of high adaptation to climate change, these growth rate declines are expected to be smaller, but overall, the climate community is of the opinion that the decreasing GDP growth rates are the reality of the future (Burke, Hsiang, & Miguel, 2015; Dell, Jones, & Olken, 2012; Lobell & Burke, 2010; Nelson, Mensbrugghe et al., 2014). In India, vulnerability studies that assess the impact of climate change find that the northwest regions, the southern coastlines and hilly regions are especially vulnerable to climate change. Even though these

regions are thought to have better adaptive capacity due to better education and higher incomes of the individuals living in these areas, changing
weather patterns and increases in the sea levels are expected to negatively
impact these regions more than the rest of the country (Jacoby, Rabassa,
& Skouas, 2011; Skoufias, Rabassa, & Olivieri, 2011; E. Somanathan &
Somanathan, 2009). A regression of GDP on climate variables, controlling
for the structural transformation experiences across states as well as historical advantages in development, shows us that increases in temperature of
about one degree Celsius may have reduced GDP growth by more than 19
percentage points over the last four decades (Table 10.2). There are also
differences across regions. For example, for states that are poor, increases
in temperature and precipitation may have been beneficial for growth. For
agricultural states, increases in precipitation may have reduced growth, and
for urbanized states, temperature increases may have been beneficial.

10.3.3.2 Impact on Communities and Households
Even though the prospects for economic growth are dire for the future, the
literature on the impact of climate change on poverty rates has shown that
climate change may come with heterogeneous impacts for different groups.
The two main channels through which climate is expected to impact
household incomes is through prices and cost of production (Hertel,
Burke, & Lobell, 2010). If climate change increases the earning potential
of the household relative to their costs, then some models do find that
poverty rates of certain groups of individuals may decrease. In a paper by
Hertel et al. (2010), the authors integrate household survey data into economic and climate change models to estimate the future impact on poverty. They find that in scenarios of low productivity where prices of food
increase, poverty rates of farmers who are net sellers of food may reduce.
Even in cases low prices, appropriate adaptation strategies may lower the
burden of climate change on the agriculture community if agricultural productivity is high. For agricultural laborers, the results from the literature
are mixed. L. Banerjee (2007) and E. Somanathan and Somanathan (2009)
find that in times of flood, wages of hired help tended to increase in
Bangladesh and India in the short term. However, E. Somanathan and
Somanathan (2009) also found that in the medium term, these benefits are
eroded as unemployment increases in these areas. In India, the impacts of
increasing vagaries of the weather are known to negatively impact incomes
and increase the vulnerability of those depending on the natural environment for their food security. Subsistence farmers or fisher folk with little
financial capabilities to smooth over the production shortfalls created by

Table 10.2   Regional impacts of climate change between 1970 and 2014

Variables	(1)	(2)	(3)	(4)
	Mod1	Mod2	Mod3	Mod4
Mean_temperature	−6.309e+06***	−6.309e+06***	−0.193***	−0.193***
	(1.117e+06)	(1.117e+06)	(0.043)	(0.043)
Poor × Temp	1.946e+06	1.946e+06	0.131*	0.131*
	(1.868e+06)	(1.868e+06)	(0.071)	(0.071)
Ag × Temp	6.982e+06***	6.982e+06***	0.0350	0.035
	(1.368e+06)	(1.368e+06)	(0.053)	(0.053)
Urb × Temp	1.063e+07***	1.063e+07***	0.109*	0.109*
	(1.786e+06)	(1.786e+06)	(0.063)	(0.063)
Mean_precipitation	−2,859	−2,859	−0.001	−0.001
	(7,489)	(7,489)	(0.00)	(0.00)
Poor × Precip	−13,884	−13,884	0.002***	0.002***
	(19,517)	(19,517)	(0.001)	(0.001)
Ag × Precip	−27,257**	−27,257**	−0.001**	−0.001**
	(12,511)	(12,511)	(0.001)	(0.001)
Urb × Precip	50,569**	50,569**	0.000	0.000
	(25,584)	(25,584)	(0.001)	(0.001)
Constant	−1.310e+08***	6.459e+07	16.51***	21.58***
	(4.949e+07)	(5.418e+07)	(1.402)	(1.617)
Observations	1,340	1,340	1,340	1,340
R-squared	0.818	0.818	0.992	0.992
State FE	Yes	Yes	Yes	Yes
Region year FE	Yes	Yes	Yes	Yes
Poor state year FE	Yes	Yes	Yes	Yes
Robust SE	Yes	Yes	Yes	Yes
HAP dummy	No	Yes	No	Yes
URB dummy	No	Yes	No	Yes
Poor dummy	No	Yes	No	Yes

Robust standard errors are in parentheses. Models are panel fixed effects with the state being the key cross-sectional variation while year being the time series variation. Stars indicate the following: ***$p < 0.01$, **$p < 0.05$, *$p < 0.1$

This table uses a panel of information on state-wise climate and GDP data (annual) between 1970 and 2013 coming from multiple sources. [This dataset includes all years for which there is complete information for constructing the panel. Union territories of Dadra and Nagar Haveli, Lakshadweep and Daman and Diu did not have GDP data. For states formed only after 2000, the GDP of the parent state was assigned before it was formed. The climate data has already accounted for this transition of the state.] Temperature and precipitation data were downloaded using the AidGeo dataset available at http://geo. aiddata.org/query/#!/. For state GDP data, I have used the information collated from the EPW Research Foundation. [http://www.epwrfits.in/index.aspx GDP values have been converted to constant prices in 2004–05 rupees for comparability across years.] State FE captures within state variation. Region year FE captures changes across regions and years. Here states are coded as being in north, south, northeast, northwest and west based on their geographical location. Poor state year fixed effects control for the differential experience of states which have had low ST experience (also referred to as *lagging states*) due to their inherent disadvantages. The Ag dummy captures the experience of states which have highly productive agricultural systems (as defined in Chap. 2), URB dummy captures those states with high levels of ST

weather-related risks are often forced into debt when they borrow high interest loans from the informal sectors (R. M. Townsend, 1994). The recent protests in Delhi that were organized by farmers to discuss relief packages for extended drought cycles in Tamil Nadu reflect on the intensity of this problem.[5] Among the class of individuals who are expected to be the most vulnerable to climate change are the urban wage laborers. Regardless of whether the world realizes high or low adaptation scenarios, authors have found that this group will be negatively impacted both in terms of their earning shares and cost of living (Ahmed, Diffenbaugh, & Hertel, 2009; Hertel et al., 2010; Pettengell, 2010; Skoufias et al., 2011).

Most estimates of the impacts of climate change, however, tend to underestimate the negative impacts. There are many reasons for this. For one, many of these models assume too simply that the poverty line of today is a good representation of the poverty line for the future. Reducing poverty rates by moving people above the current poverty line does not account for their increased vulnerability to extreme events and the increasing costs that are associated with the same. Two, these models have simplistic assumptions on the nature of the damage functions and assume the low probability of catastrophic events. This leads them to underestimate the risks involved (Pindyck, 2013; Pindyck & Wang, 2013; Weitzman, 2014). Three, climate models do not account for changing urbanization patterns and thus tend to underestimate how many people will actually be vulnerable and poor in the future and hence the depth of the problem. Four, effects of climate changes are believed to impact different areas with different intensity. For example, many of the studies have shown that the northwest of India, that is traditionally associated with high agricultural productivity, may be more vulnerable to climate changes than the east (Jacoby et al., 2011; O'Brien et al., 2004; E. Somanathan & Somanathan, 2009). Hence, agricultural households in these areas may be more vulnerable. Also, the southern states are more vulnerable to changes in sea levels which will affect the livelihoods and poverty rates of populations subsisting on the coastlines (Brenkert & Malone, 2005). These differences in experiences will complicate the policy landscape on how to bolster the livelihoods of groups who are impacted by climate change.

10.3.3.3 Impact on Individuals Within Households

Within households, gender, age, cultural norms and social and economic constraints tend to exacerbate the problem of food access in the face of climate change. Women in households are particularly disadvantaged in

[5] http://www.bbc.com/news/world-asia-india-39650496

these situations since inaccurate economic values associated with their contributions to the household, cultural norms and social expectations tend to exacerbate the problem of poor access. Without appropriate safety nets such as conditional cash transfers and so on in the event of major weather shocks, such as rainfall shocks, women of the household often bear the brunt of the reduction in food security of households (Demeke, Keil, & Zeller, 2011; Gladwin, Thomson, Peterson, & Anderson, 2001). For those women who survive through tough times such as droughts and famines with limited access to resources, the intergenerational impacts of poor health are transmitted to their children, thus perpetuating disadvantages of these events (Dyson & Maharatna, 1992; J. Hoddinott & Kinsey, 2001; Shah & Steinberg, 2012). Microeconomic analysis of households shows that nutrition outcomes of children too tend to be drastically affected during times of droughts and famines. These poor outcomes tend to persist into adulthood, where children who have been through famines have lower educational outcomes, wages and health (Chen & Zhou, 2007; C. Huang, Li, Wang, & Martorell, 2010; Luo, Mu, & Zhang, 2006; T. Roseboom, de Rooij, & Painter, 2006; T. J. Roseboom et al., 2001). Girls are often at higher risks to these shocks. The literature has shown, for example, that only when there are good years for rain, farming households increase investments in education and health for female children. In times of drought, authors find that household members reallocate scarce human capital resources away from female children towards male children within households (Baird, McIntosh, & Özler, 2011; Bonesrønning, 2010; J. Hoddinott & Kinsey, 2001; Maccini & Yang, 2009; Verwimp, 2012). This is often reflected in poorer health outcomes of girl children regarding malnutrition indicators. Thus, these groups tend to be more vulnerable to climate change.

10.4   MANAGING CURRENT AND FUTURE CLIMATE RISKS FOR INDIA

Looking ahead, we see that climate change risks pose a major threat to current and future food systems in India. Evidence documented on its risks on health, agriculture and economic development suggests that it is important to take this threat seriously as we envision food systems of the future. Also, the Indian subcontinent has seen a rapid increase in extreme weather events and unprecedented changes to weather and pollution rates. These events call upon the urgency to address the impacts of climate change.

In this section, we outline India's commitment to climate change mitigation and provide some recommendations on how climate policies can be focused towards enabling nutrition-secure food systems. In the next chapter, we provide a more detailed discussion on policy options in this regard.

10.4.1   *Quantifying India's Contribution Towards Climate Change*

Based on data from the World Bank DataBank, India was the third largest emitter of carbon dioxide, following China and the United States in 2014 (Fig. 10.3). Within India, the MoEF (2010) report[6] concluded that the energy sector contributed to around 60% of the total emissions with nearly two-thirds of the emissions coming from electricity generation through the use of coal. Emissions from the transport and residential sector made up around one-fourth of total emissions from the same sector. While the

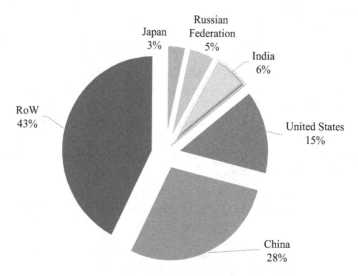

Fig. 10.3 Share of CO_2 (total) emissions by country in 2014. Source: World Bank DataBank; based on authors calculations

---

[6]Note that there have been no updates to these numbers since then. All the new MoEF reports continue to refer to these numbers.

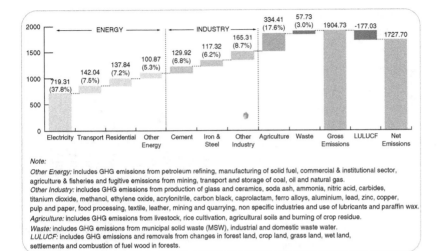

Note:

Other Energy: includes GHG emissions from petroleum refining, manufacturing of solid fuel, commercial & institutional sector, agriculture & fisheries and fugitive emissions from mining, transport and storage of coal, oil and natural gas.
Other Industry: includes GHG emissions from production of glass and ceramics, soda ash, ammonia, nitric acid, carbides, titanium dioxide, methanol, ethylene oxide, acrylonitrile, carbon black, caprolactam, ferro alloys, aluminium, lead, zinc, copper, pulp and paper, food processing, textile, leather, mining and quarrying, non specific industries and use of lubricants and paraffin wax.
Agriculture: includes GHG emissions from livestock, rice cultivation, agricultural soils and burning of crop residue.
Waste: includes GHG emissions from municipal solid waste (MSW), industrial and domestic waste water.
LULUCF: includes GHG emissions and removals from changes in forest land, crop land, grass land, wet land, settlements and combustion of fuel wood in forests.

Figure ES1: GHG emissions by sector in 2007 (million tons of CO_2 eq). Figures on top indicate the emissions by sectors and in brackets indicate % of emission of the category with respect to the net CO_2 equivalent emissions. See glossary for definition of CO_2 equivalent.

Fig. 10.4   Emission by sectors. Source: Ministry of Environment & Forestry report, 2009

agricultural sector contributed to around 18% of the emissions, nearly 64% of the emissions came from the livestock sector and 21% from rice cultivation (Fig. 10.4). Construction materials accounted for nearly 60% of the total industrial emission. Municipal, domestic and industrial waste made up around one-third of the emissions from waste. Among other factors that have contributed to GHGs are excessive deforestation and land clearing that have reduced the number of carbon sinks[7] across the country. In 2009, less than 10% of all emissions from the country were reabsorbed by these carbon sinks. This rapid growth of emissions is documented in Fig. 10.5, where one sees that both total emissions and per capita emissions have been increasing over time. In a projection exercise conducted by the Ministry of Environment, Forests and Climate Change (MoEF, 2008), it was estimated that per capita emissions in India would be around 4–5 tons per capita by 2030, a threefold increase after 2009. This would

---

[7] Carbon sinks are natural or artificial reservoirs that absorb and store atmospheric carbon with physical and biological mechanisms. Forests and land covered with vegetation are one type of carbon sink.

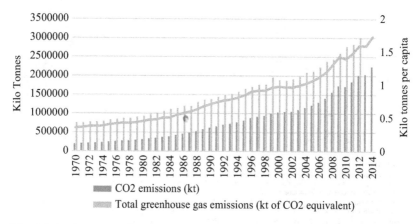

Fig. 10.5 Overview of GHG emissions in India. Source: World Bank DataBank; based on authors calculations

imply that global emissions from India would be around 6 billion tons (higher than United States emissions for 2014). Given the climate sensitivity to these irreversible emissions, Indian and global food systems face a major threat from the current Indian economic growth experience.

10.4.2   Overview of India's Commitment Towards Mitigation and Reduction of GHG Emissions

In recognition of the local and global impacts of climate change and the role of India as one of the largest emitters of GHGs, policy makers have been working towards creating policies to reduce GHG emissions across its economic sectors. After ratifying its commitment towards climate change mitigation in the Paris agreement, the central government and the state governments have put forth comprehensive action plans that outline strategies, goals and priorities towards reducing GHG emissions to cut India's emissions by 25% in 2020. To do so, policy makers have committed to promoting clean and efficient energy use in the power sector, industrial sectors and urban housing, increasing a number of carbon sinks and investing in sustainable agricultural practices. With regard to the power sector, replacing the current capacity for coal-generated power with solar energy and renewable energy provision has become a national priority. Large investments have been made in the wind and solar energy sector, which now provides around 14% of all power within the country.[8] With regard to household level clean energy production, the government has taken important steps to reduce firewood dependence by introducing alternative cost-effective clean energy technologies such as biogas fuels and solar-dependent cooking stoves in rural areas. Urban-focused initiatives that seek to reduce emissions through investments in green infrastructure housing projects and reduce solid waste in cities through investments proper disposal infrastructure are under way in many areas.[9] There have been efforts made towards fully converting public transport vehicles to using low emissions fuels, and subsidies towards adopting clean energy private vehicles are in place. The government has also introduced a program called the "Perform, Achieve and Trade" that sets caps on GHGs and particulate emissions on industries across the country. Industries can trade their E-Certificates through a regulated exchange to achieve compliance obligations and reduce non-compliance penalties. In states where health-related concerns from communicable diseases are a threat to population health, investments in improving health infrastructure, services and access to health technology have been proposed. Many states have also proposed moving agricultural systems towards organic farming practices, investing in water conservation technologies, improving management practices with regard to livestock and investing in research and development focused on technologies for climate adaptation in the agricultural sector as a means to reduce damages from climate uncertainties. At the national level, improving biodiversity and vegetation cover through initiatives for reforestation, protecting forest areas from exploitation as well as working with communities through decentralized forms of governance of natural resources have been proposed. Also, there have been proposals to develop climate-smart strategies that finance research in developing heat- and drought-resistant varieties of crops, setting up disaster management systems, instituting weather-based insurance programs and desilting irrigation systems to improve water management and to improve management of forest and coastal ecology. These investments are also thought to play a role in GHG reductions from the agricultural sectors as well as help in increasing the

[8] India is one of the largest producers of electricity through wind energy in the world.

[9] Building regulations to construct environment friendly urban infrastructure that are energy efficient have been encouraged and regulations for industrial waste management and recycling of solid waste have been introduced as a part of mitigation strategies (MoEF, 2008). A comprehensive commentary on the policies under the NAPCC and the actions taken by the government can be found in the reference (J. Ahmad, 2013).

capacity to adapt. The commitments made towards various initiatives both at the national and the state level can be found in national and state action plan towards reducing the impact of climate change, respectively. In these comprehensive documents, a summary of these actions proposed and the funds allocated towards each topic can be found. These strong commitments made have put India in a leadership position in talks on tackling climate change on the global stage.

10.4.3   Refocusing Climate Change Policies Towards Tackling Risks for Food Systems

While India's climate mitigation strategies have been extremely progressive, in this chapter, we have highlighted the risks that climate change poses to current and future food systems. Extreme weather events in the country have increased the urgency to design and implement adaptation strategies in response to climate change. The process involves assessing vulnerabilities of different stakeholders in food systems and supporting them to develop capabilities to respond to the uncertainties both in the current time and as we look ahead. The ability to adopt strategies to deal with climate change is known to be a function of an individual's wealth, capabilities, access to market and access to knowledge and technology. These factors determine the individual's vulnerability to climate change, that is, how much they are likely to be affected, and their resilience against uncertainties, that is, how much they can cope with these changes (Hallegatte, 2009; Pettengell, 2010; B. Smit, Burton, Klein, & Wandel, 2000; B. Smit & Wandel, 2006). From a food systems perspective, ensuring food and nutrition security of individuals thus requires strategies that both increase the availability of welfare-enhancing goods and ensure that adequate safety nets exist to improve current levels of access (Campbell et al., 2016; Lobell et al., 2008; Myers et al., 2017; Vermeulen et al., 2012). Investments in reducing production uncertainty, improving labor productivity through investments in health and food access and introducing policies to reduce inequities in access will be important for future adaptation policies meant to reduce the negative impact of climate change. Part of the challenge for adaptation strategies is to prioritize which policies will yield immediate returns and which policies are expected to yield benefits in the long run. This requires consolidating the evidence of adaptation strategies within India currently as well as identifying new ways to evaluate and compare the relative benefits of different strategies. Investing in research and development for technologies that increase productivity while reducing GHG emissions, encouraging participation of local communities in biodiversity preservation, sharing technology and resources across regional and national borders and encouraging investments in climate smart businesses will also be key features of successful mitigation strategies for the future. In the next chapter, we discuss some of the options available for moving the country towards a more nutrition-secure future as climate change increases food systems risk.

10.4.4   Moving Beyond Strategies and Towards Concrete Measureable Actions

A major concern for many intellectuals has been the lack of commitment to pursue these strategies to their full potential. For one, many of these strategies remain top down with the government setting goals without involving the communities affected. This approach has increased inefficiencies in implementation and in many cases caused well-meaning projects to fail. Even despite their best efforts, the government has not been able to reduce the rate of deforestation in the country since it has not involved the forest communities in conservation efforts (J. Ahmad, 2013; E. Somanathan et al., 2009). Two, due to corruption and the lack of transparency, well-designed plans to contain and recycle waste often fall to the wayside. The environmental protection agency in India is often not considered to be reliable in monitoring industries and has been known to turn a blind eye towards health concerns of communities who are affected by the location of the industrial plants (Dutta, Ghosh, Gopalakrishnan, Bijoy, & Yasmin, 2013). This has affected the compliance of industries and increased inefficiency in carbon trading. Three, many of these plans on close reading reveal that there are no measureable outcomes defined in these action plans that would help monitor climate centric efforts and their outcomes. Without metrics to measure mitigation, it becomes difficult to measure progress. This reduces the incentive to commit and participate in the mitigation strategies for both individuals and industries. Four, without property rights, communities that subsist on the environment have no incentive to lobby for better environmental practices in their areas. This has prevented the integration of individuals into trading carbon credits in the climate market, a potentially important channel through which mitigation can be integrated globally (J. Ahmad, 2013; E. Somanathan et al., 2009). Five, there has been very little commitment towards developing technology or investing in business driven solutions that reduce climate dependence. Introducing climate-smart agricultural services that increase yields and reduce environmental degradation has not found their way into mainstream mitigation and adaptation strategies. Developing cost-effective technology or supporting businesses that invest in environment-friendly urban development has not taken off. This has prevented well-conceived strategies for mitigation from becoming self-sustaining (J. Ahmad, 2013; Dutta et al., 2013; Ray, 2011; E. Somanathan et al., 2009).

10.5   CONCLUSION

In this chapter, we identify the pathways through which climate change will impact nutrition security in India. Synthesizing the scientific evidence on climate change and its ongoing and future impacts on food availability, labor productivity and long-term economic growth in India, we highlight its role in reducing the effectiveness of food systems in ensuring nutrition security. For food availability, for example, we present evidence that changing temperature and rainfall patterns have begun to impact crop and livestock productivity across the country. Without adequate adaptation capabilities, future production capacity will decrease and the probability of facing production shocks will increase. Lower availability of food and thus nutrients will increase malnutrition by reducing access to food diversity. Similarly, by increasing susceptibility to communicable and non-communicable diseases, climate change will increase malnutrition by reducing individual's capacity to absorb nutrients from food that may be available for consumption. These factors will combine to reduce the overall health and hence labor productivity. Poor health, low labor productivity and low productive agricultural systems will in turn impact long-term growth prospects by reducing the ability of economies to undergo a structural transformation, thus leading to stunted growth. Finally, we present evidence that climate change will increase vulnerability of regions by changing their comparative advantages, will increase the vulnerability of households by affecting health and will reinforce intra-household inequities in access. Continuing down the current path of development without integrating appropriate adaptation strategies, we argue, will have serious negative repercussions on nutrition security within the country. Side by side with adaptation strategies, integrating mitigation strategies that reduce the overall carbon foot print will not only contribute to the global goals of GHG mitigation, it will thus help reduce food systems risks related to nutrition security.

Currently, India is one of the countries leading discussions on climate change mitigation due to its forward-looking policies that encourage investments in clean energy sources, climate-smart infrastructure, preservation and conservation of biodiversity and ground water management processes. Both the central and state governments have focused attention on addressing this development challenge by increasing investments in renewable sources for energy generation. However, many other policies remain academic and their implementation has been slow. In order to cement India's position as a leader in climate change discussions on the global stage, moving these policies from desk to field will be important. As we look ahead, we also argue that climate policies for the future should allow diversification of the food system in ways that enhance the environment while improving the nutrition content of foods produced and ensuring equity in access. This discussion is currently lacking in the policy circles. To truly create a food system that ensures nutrition security of all individuals, we submit that climate change risks must not be understated and appropriate actions towards its mitigation need to be urgently adopted.

References

Abraham, M., & Pingali, P. (2017). Transforming smallholder agriculture to achieve the SDGs. In L. Riesgo, S. Gomez-Y-Paloma, & K. Louhichi (Eds.), *The role of small farms in food and nutrition security*. Springer.

Ahmad, J. (2013). *Climate change and sustainable development in India*. New Century Publications.

Ahmed, S. A., Diffenbaugh, N. S., & Hertel, T. W. (2009). Climate volatility deepens poverty vulnerability in developing countries. *Environmental Research Letters, 4*(3), 34004.

Auffhammer, M., Ramanathan, V., & Vincent, J. R. (2006). Integrated model shows that atmospheric brown clouds and greenhouse gases have reduced rice harvests in India. *Proceedings of the National Academy of Sciences, 103*(52), 19668–19672.

Baird, S., McIntosh, C., & Özler, B. (2011). Cash or condition? Evidence from a cash transfer experiment. *Quarterly Journal of Economics, 126*(4), 1709–1753. https://doi.org/10.1093/qje/qjr032

Banerjee, L. (2007). Effect of flood on agricultural wages in Bangladesh: An empirical analysis. *World Development, 35*(11), 1989–2009.

Banerjee, R. R. (2015). Farmers' perception of climate change, impact and adaptation strategies: A case study of four villages in the semi-arid regions of India. *Natural Hazards, 75*(3), 2829–2845.

Bellemare, M. F. (2015). Rising food prices, food price volatility, and social unrest. *American Journal of Agricultural Economics, 97*(1), 1–21. https://doi.org/10.1093/ajae/aau038

Besley, T., & Burgess, R. (2002). The political economy of government responsiveness: Theory and evidence from India. *The Quarterly Journal of Economics, 117*(4), 1415–1451.

Bonesrønning, H. (2010). Are parental effort allocations biased by gender? *Education Economics, 18*(3), 253–268. https://doi.org/10.1080/09645290902843514

Boomiraj, K., Chakrabarti, B., Aggarwal, P. K., Choudhary, R., & Chander, S. (2010). Assessing the vulnerability of Indian mustard to climate change. *Agriculture, Ecosystems & Environment, 138*(3–4), 265–273.

Brabin, B. J., Hakimi, M., & Pelletier, D. (2001). An analysis of anemia and pregnancy-related maternal mortality. *The Journal of Nutrition, 131*(2), 604S–615S.

Brenkert, A. L., & Malone, E. L. (2005). Modeling vulnerability and resilience to climate change: A case study of India and Indian states. *Climatic Change, 72*(1), 57–102. https://doi.org/10.1007/s10584-005-5930-3

Burke, M., Hsiang, S. M., & Miguel, E. (2015). Global non-linear effect of temperature on economic production. *Nature, 527*(7577), 235–239.

Burney, J., & Ramanathan, V. (2014). Recent climate and air pollution impacts on Indian agriculture. *Proceedings of the National Academy of Sciences, 111*(46), 16319–16324.

Byjesh, K., Kumar, S. N., & Aggarwal, P. K. (2010). Simulating impacts, potential adaptation and vulnerability of maize to climate change in India. *Mitigation and Adaptation Strategies for Global Change, 15*(5), 413–431.

Campbell, B. M., Vermeulen, S. J., Aggarwal, P. K., Corner-Dolloff, C., Girvetz, E., Loboguerrero, A. M., … Wollenberg, E. (2016). Reducing risks to food security from climate change. *Global Food Security, 11*, 34–43. https://doi.org/10.1016/j.gfs.2016.06.002

Challinor, A. J., Watson, J., Lobell, D. B., Howden, S. M., Smith, D. R., & Chhetri, N. (2014). A meta-analysis of crop yield under climate change and adaptation. *Nature Climate Change, 4*(4), 287.

Chen, Y., & Zhou, L.-A. (2007). The long-term health and economic consequences of the 1959–1961 famine in China. *Journal of Health Economics, 26*(4), 659–681.

Ciais, P., Reichstein, M., Viovy, N., Granier, A., Ogée, J., Allard, V., … Carrara, A. (2005). Europe-wide reduction in primary productivity caused by the heat and drought in 2003. *Nature, 437*(7058), 529–533.

Cruz, R. V., Harasawa, H., Lal, M., Wu, S., Anokhin, Y., Punsalmaa, B., ... Ninh, N. H. (2007). Asia. In M. L. Parry, O. F. Canziani, J. P. Palutikof, P. J. van der Linden, & C. E. Hanson (Eds.), *Climate change 2007: Impacts adaptation and vulnerability. Contribution of Working Group II to the Fourth Assessment Report of the Intergovernmental Panel on Climate Change* (pp. 469–506). Cambridge: Cambridge University Press.

D'Souza, A., & Jolliffe, D. (2013). Conflict, food price shocks, and food insecurity: The experience of Afghan households. *Food Policy, 42*, 32–47. https://doi.org/10.1016/j.foodpol.2013.06.007

Dell, M., Jones, B. F., & Olken, B. A. (2012). Temperature shocks and economic growth: Evidence from the last half century. *American Economic Journal: Macroeconomics, 4*(3), 66–95.

Demeke, A. B., Keil, A., & Zeller, M. (2011). Using panel data to estimate the effect of rainfall shocks on smallholders food security and vulnerability in rural Ethiopia. *Climatic Change, 108*(1–2), 185–206.

Dhiman, R. C., Pahwa, S., Dhillon, G. P. S., & Dash, A. P. (2010). Climate change and threat of vector-borne diseases in India: Are we prepared? *Parasitology Research, 106*(4), 763–773. https://doi.org/10.1007/s00436-010-1767-4

Dietterich, L. H., Zanobetti, A., Kloog, I., Huybers, P., Leakey, A. D. B., Bloom, A. J., ... Hasegawa, T. (2014). Increasing CO_2 threatens human nutrition. *Scientific Data, 2*, 150036.

Dutta, S., Ghosh, S., Gopalakrishnan, S., Bijoy, C. R., & Yasmin, H. (2013). *Climate change in India: Analysis of political economy & impact*. New Delhi: Rosa Luxemburg Stiftung-South Asia.

Dyson, T., & Maharatna, A. (1992). Bihar famine, 1966–67 and Maharashtra drought, 1970–73: The demographic consequences. *Economic and Political Weekly, 27*(26), 1325–1332.

Ebi, K. L., & McGregor, G. (2008). Climate change, tropospheric ozone and particulate matter, and health impacts. *Environmental Health Perspectives, 116*(11), 1449.

Gladwin, C. H., Thomson, A. M., Peterson, J. S., & Anderson, A. S. (2001). Addressing food security in Africa via multiple livelihood strategies of women farmers. *Food Policy, 26*(2), 177–207.

Greenstone, M., & Hanna, R. (2014). Environmental regulations, air and water pollution, and infant mortality in India. *American Economic Review, 104*(10), 3038–3072.

Guhathakurta, P., Sreejith, O. P., & Menon, P. A. (2011). Impact of climate change on extreme rainfall events and flood risk in India. *Journal of Earth System Science, 120*(3), 359. https://doi.org/10.1007/s12040-011-0082-5

Gupta, R., Somanathan, E., & Dey, S. (2017). Global warming and local air pollution have reduced wheat yields in India. *Climatic Change, 140*(3–4), 593–604.

Hallegatte, S. (2009). Strategies to adapt to an uncertain climate change. *Global Environmental Change, 19*(2), 240–247.

Hebbar, K. B., Venugopalan, M. V., Prakash, A. H., & Aggarwal, P. K. (2013). Simulating the impacts of climate change on cotton production in India. *Climatic Change, 118*(3–4), 701–713.

Hertel, T. W., Burke, M. B., & Lobell, D. B. (2010). The poverty implications of climate-induced crop yield changes by 2030. *Global Environmental Change, 20*(4), 577–585.

Hoddinott, J., & Kinsey, B. (2001). Child growth in the time of drought. *Oxford Bulletin of Economics and Statistics, 63*(4), 409–436. https://doi.org/10.1111/1468-0084.t01-1-00227

Hossain, N., & Green, D. (2011). Living on a Spike: How is the 2011 food price crisis affecting poor people? *Oxfam Policy and Practice: Agriculture, Food and Land, 11*(5), 9–56.

Huang, C., Li, Z., Wang, M., & Martorell, R. (2010). Early life exposure to the 1959–1961 Chinese famine has long-term health consequences. *The Journal of Nutrition, 140*(10), 1874–1878.

IMD. (2018). *Seasonal outlook for the temperatures during March to May 2018.* Retrieved from http://www.imd.gov.in/pages/press_release_view.php?ff=20180228_pr_205

IPCC. (2014). *Mitigation of climate change. Contribution of Working Group III to the Fifth Assessment Report of the Intergovernmental Panel on Climate Change.* Cambridge, UK and New York.

Jacoby, H. G., Rabassa, M., & Skouas, E. (2011). Distributional implications of climate change in India.

Kalaivani, K. (2009). Prevalence & consequences of anaemia in pregnancy. *Indian Journal of Medical Research, 130*(5), 627–633.

Kattelmann, R. (2003). Glacial lake outburst floods in the Nepal Himalaya: A manageable hazard? *Natural Hazards, 28*(1), 145–154.

Kjellstrom, T., Holmer, I., & Lemke, B. (2009). Workplace heat stress, health and productivity—An increasing challenge for low and middle-income countries during climate change. *Global Health Action, 2*(1), 2047.

Kothawale, D. R., & Rupa Kumar, K. (2005). On the recent changes in surface temperature trends over India. *Geophysical Research Letters, 32*(18). https://doi.org/10.1029/2005GL023528

Kumar, A., Yadav, C., Jee, S., Kumar, S., & Chauhan, S. (2011). Financial innovation in Indian agricultural credit market: Progress and performance of Kisan Credit Card. *Indian Journal of Agricultural Economics, 66*(3), 418–428.

Kumar, K. R., Kumar, K. K., & Pant, G. B. (1994). Diurnal asymmetry of surface temperature trends over India. *Geophysical Research Letters, 21*(8), 677–680. https://doi.org/10.1029/94GL00007

Kumar, K. S. K., & Parikh, J. (2001). Indian agriculture and climate sensitivity. *Global Environmental Change, 11*(2), 147–154.

Kumar, S. N., & Aggarwal, P. K. (2013). Climate change and coconut plantations in India: Impacts and potential adaptation gains. *Agricultural Systems, 117*, 45–54.

Kumar, S. N., Aggarwal, P. K., Rani, D. N. S., Saxena, R., Chauhan, N., & Jain, S. (2014). Vulnerability of wheat production to climate change in India. *Climate Research, 59*(3), 173–187.

Kumar, S. N., Govindakrishnan, P. M., Swarooparani, D. N., Nitin, C., Surabhi, J., & Aggarwal, P. K. (2015). Assessment of impact of climate change on potato and potential adaptation gains in the Indo-Gangetic Plains of India. *International Journal of Plant Production, 9*(1), 151–170.

Lindblade, K. A., Walker, E. D., Onapa, A. W., Katungu, J., & Wilson, M. L. (2000). Land use change alters malaria transmission parameters by modifying temperature in a highland area of Uganda. *Tropical Medicine & International Health, 5*(4), 263–274.

Lobell, D. B., & Burke, M. B. (2010). On the use of statistical models to predict crop yield responses to climate change. *Agricultural and Forest Meteorology, 150*(11), 1443–1452. https://doi.org/10.1016/j.agrformet.2010.07.008

Lobell, D. B., Burke, M. B., Tebaldi, C., Mastrandrea, M. D., Falcon, W. P., & Naylor, R. L. (2008). Prioritizing climate change adaptation needs for food security in 2030. *Science, 319*(5863), 607–610.

Luo, Z., Mu, R., & Zhang, X. (2006). Famine and overweight in China. *Review of Agricultural Economics, 28*(3), 296–304.

Maccini, S., & Yang, D. (2009). Under the weather: Health, schooling, and economic consequences of early-life rainfall. *American Economic Review, 99*(3), 1006–1026. https://doi.org/10.1257/aer.99.3.1006

Majra, J. P., & Gur, A. (2009). Climate change and health: Why should India be concerned? *Indian Journal of Occupational and Environmental Medicine, 13*(1), 11.

Mall, R. K., Singh, R., Gupta, A., Srinivasan, G., & Rathore, L. S. (2006). Impact of climate change on Indian agriculture: A review. *Climatic Change, 78*(2), 445–478. https://doi.org/10.1007/s10584-005-9042-x

McMichael, A. J., Woodruff, R. E., & Hales, S. (2006). Climate change and human health: Present and future risks. *The Lancet, 367*(9513), 859–869.

Misra, A. K. (2014). Climate change and challenges of water and food security. *International Journal of Sustainable Built Environment, 3*(1), 153–165. https://doi.org/10.1016/j.ijsbe.2014.04.006

MoEF. (2008). *National Action Plan for Climate Change Report.*

MoEF. (2010). *India: Greenhouse Gas Emissions 2007 executive summary.* Retrieved from http://www.moef.nic.in/downloads/public-information/Report_INCCA.pdf

Müller, C., Elliott, J., & Levermann, A. (2014). Food security: Fertilizing hidden hunger. *Nature Climate Change, 4*(7), 540.

Myers, S. S., Smith, M. R., Guth, S., Golden, C. D., Vaitla, B., Mueller, N. D., ... Huybers, P. (2017). Climate change and global food systems: Potential impacts on food security and undernutrition. *Annual Review of Public Health, 38*(1), 259–277. https://doi.org/10.1146/annurev-publhealth-031816-044356

Myers, S. S., Zanobetti, A., Kloog, I., Huybers, P., Leakey, A. D. B., Bloom, A. J., ... Usui, Y. (2014). Increasing CO_2 threatens human nutrition. *Nature, 510*(7503), 139–142.

Nelson, G. C., Mensbrugghe, D., Ahammad, H., Blanc, E., Calvin, K., Hasegawa, T., ... Lotze-Campen, H. (2014a). Agriculture and climate change in global scenarios: Why don't the models agree. *Agricultural Economics, 45*(1), 85–101.

O'Brien, K., Leichenko, R., Kelkar, U., Venema, H., Aandahl, G., Tompkins, H., ... West, J. (2004). Mapping vulnerability to multiple stressors: Climate change and globalization in India. *Global Environmental Change, 14*(4), 303–313. https://doi.org/10.1016/j.gloenvcha.2004.01.001

Paaijmans, K. P., Blanford, S., Bell, A. S., Blanford, J. I., Read, A. F., & Thomas, M. B. (2010). Influence of climate on malaria transmission depends on daily temperature variation. *Proceedings of the National Academy of Sciences, 107*(34), 15135–15139.

Paerl, H. W., & Paul, V. J. (2012). Climate change: Links to global expansion of harmful cyanobacteria. *Water Research, 46*(5), 1349–1363. https://doi.org/10.1016/j.watres.2011.08.002

Patz, J. A., Campbell-Lendrum, D., Holloway, T., & Foley, J. A. (2005). Impact of regional climate change on human health. *Nature, 438*(7066), 310.

Pettengell, C. (2010). Climate change adaptation: Enabling people living in poverty to adapt. *Oxfam Policy and Practice: Climate Change and Resilience, 6*(2), 1–48.

Pindyck, R. S. (2013). Climate change policy: What do the models tell us? *Journal of Economic Literature, 51*(3), 860–872.

Pindyck, R. S., & Wang, N. (2013). The economic and policy consequences of catastrophes. *American Economic Journal: Economic Policy, 5*(4), 306–339.

Pingali, P. (2012). Green revolution: Impacts, limits, and the path ahead. *Proceedings of the National Academy of Science, 109*(31), 12302–12308. https://doi.org/10.1073/pnas.0912953109

Pingali, P. (2015). Wringing food from the world. *Nature Geoscience, 8*(4), 252–252. https://doi.org/10.1038/ngeo2410

Pingali, P. L., Spielman, D., & Zaidi, F. (2014). Changing donor trends in assistance to agricultural research and development in Africa South of the Sahara. *The Future of African Agricultural R&D,* 6:1–6:25. https://doi.org/10.2499/9780896292123_06

Qadir, M., Tubeileh, A., Akhtar, J., Larbi, A., Minhas, P. S., & Khan, M. A. (2008). Productivity enhancement of salt-affected environments through crop diversification. *Land Degradation & Development, 19*(4), 429–453. https://doi.org/10.1002/ldr.853

Rasmussen, K. M. (2001). Is there a causal relationship between iron deficiency or iron-deficiency anemia and weight at birth, length of gestation and perinatal mortality? *The Journal of Nutrition, 131*(2), 590S–603S.

Ray, B. (2011). *Climate change: IPCC, water crisis, and policy riddles with reference to India and her surroundings*. Lexington Books.

Roseboom, T., de Rooij, S., & Painter, R. (2006). The Dutch famine and its long-term consequences for adult health. *Early Human Development, 82*(8), 485–491.

Roseboom, T. J., Van Der Meulen, J. H. P., Ravelli, A. C. J., Osmond, C., Barker, D. J. P., & Bleker, O. P. (2001). Effects of prenatal exposure to the Dutch famine on adult disease in later life: An overview. *Molecular and Cellular Endocrinology, 185*(1–2), 93–98.

Schuur, E. A. G., McGuire, A. D., Schädel, C., Grosse, G., Harden, J. W., Hayes, D. J., ... Lawrence, D. M. (2015). Climate change and the permafrost carbon feedback. *Nature, 520*(7546), 171–179.

Shah, M., & Steinberg, B. (2012). *Could droughts improve human capital? Evidence from India*. Retrieved from http://www.frbsf.org/economic-research/files/Shah_Steinberg.pdf

Sharma, A., & Pingali, P. (2016). *Does the onset of the rainy season affect crop yields in India?* Ithaca, NY: Tata-Cornell Institute for Agriculture & Nutrition.

Sharma, A., & Pingali, P. (2018). Looking beyond rice & wheat: Climate change impacts on food systems and food security in India. *World Food Policy Journal, 4*(2).

Shrestha, U. B., Gautam, S., & Bawa, K. S. (2012). Widespread climate change in the Himalayas and associated changes in local ecosystems. *PLoS One, 7*(5), e36741.

Singh, P., Nedumaran, S., Ntare, B. R., Boote, K. J., Singh, N. P., Srinivas, K., & Bantilan, M. C. S. (2014). Potential benefits of drought and heat tolerance in groundnut for adaptation to climate change in India and West Africa. *Mitigation and Adaptation Strategies for Global Change, 19*(5), 509–529.

Sinha, S. K., & Swaminathan, M. S. (1992). Deforestation, climate change and sustainable nutrition security: A case study of India. In N. Myers (Ed.), *Tropical forests and climate* (pp. 201–209). Dordrecht: Springer Netherlands. https://doi.org/10.1007/978-94-017-3608-4_20

Skoufias, E., Rabassa, M., & Olivieri, S. (2011). *The poverty impacts of climate change: A review of the evidence.*

Smit, B., Burton, I., Klein, R. J. T., & Wandel, J. (2000). An anatomy of adaptation to climate change and variability. In *Climatic change* (Vol. 45, pp. 223–251). Springer. https://doi.org/10.1023/A:1005661622966

Smit, B., & Wandel, J. (2006). Adaptation, adaptive capacity and vulnerability. *Global Environmental Change, 16*(3), 282–292.

Somanathan, E., Prabhakar, R., & Mehta, B. S. (2009). Decentralization for cost-effective conservation. *Proceedings of the National Academy of Sciences, 106*(11), 4143–4147.

Somanathan, E., & Somanathan, R. (2009). Climate change: Challenges facing India's poor. *Economic and Political Weekly, 44*(31), 51–58.

Somanathan, E., Somanathan, R., Sudarshan, A., & Tewari, M. (2015). *The impact of temperature on productivity and labor supply: Evidence from Indian manufacturing.* Working Paper.

Soora, N. K., Aggarwal, P. K., Saxena, R., Rani, S., Jain, S., & Chauhan, N. (2013). An assessment of regional vulnerability of rice to climate change in India. *Climatic Change, 118*(3–4), 683–699.

Speers, A. E., Besedin, E. Y., Palardy, J. E., & Moore, C. (2016). Impacts of climate change and ocean acidification on coral reef fisheries: An integrated ecological–economic model. *Ecological Economics, 128,* 33–43. https://doi.org/10.1016/j.ecolecon.2016.04.012

Srivastava, A., Kumar, S. N., & Aggarwal, P. K. (2010). Assessment on vulnerability of sorghum to climate change in India. *Agriculture, Ecosystems & Environment, 138*(3–4), 160–169.

Steiner, J. L., Briske, D. D., Brown, D. P., & Rottler, C. M. (2018). Vulnerability of Southern Plains agriculture to climate change. *Climatic Change, 146*(1–2), 201–218.

Sutherst, R. W. (2004). Global change and human vulnerability to vector-borne diseases. *Clinical Microbiology Reviews, 17*(1), 136–173.

Swinnen, J., & Squicciarini, P. (2012). Mixed messages on prices and food security. *Science, 335*(6067), 405–406. https://doi.org/10.1126/science.1210806

Tanser, F. C., Sharp, B., & le Sueur, D. (2003). Potential effect of climate change on malaria transmission in Africa. *The Lancet, 362*(9398), 1792–1798. https://doi.org/10.1016/S0140-6736(03)14898-2

Taylor, R. G., Scanlon, B., Döll, P., Rodell, M., Van Beek, R., Wada, Y., … Edmunds, M. (2013). Ground water and climate change. *Nature Climate Change, 3*(4), 322.

Timmer, C. P. (1989). Food price policy. *Food Policy, 14*(1), 17–27. https://doi.org/10.1016/0306-9192(89)90023-7

Townsend, R. M. (1994). Risk and insurance in village India. *Econometrica, 62*(3), 539–591.

Vedwan, N., & Rhoades, R. E. (2001). Climate change in the Western Himalayas of India. *Climate Research, 19*(2), 109–117. Retrieved from http://www.jstor.org/stable/24866773

Vermeulen, S. J., Aggarwal, P. K., Ainslie, A., Angelone, C., Campbell, B. M., Challinor, A. J., … Kristjanson, P. (2012). Options for support to agriculture and food security under climate change. *Environmental Science & Policy, 15*(1), 136–144.

Verwimp, P. (2012). Undernutrition, subsequent risk of mortality and civil war in Burundi. *Economics and Human Biology, 10*(3), 221–231. https://doi.org/10.1016/j.ehb.2011.09.007

Watanabe, T., Ives, J. D., & Hammond, J. E. (1994). Rapid growth of a glacial lake in Khumbu Himal, Himalaya: Prospects for a catastrophic flood. *Mountain Research and Development, 14*(4), 329–340.

Watts, N., Adger, W. N., Agnolucci, P., Blackstock, J., Byass, P., Cai, W., ... Cooper, A. (2015). Health and climate change: Policy responses to protect public health. *The Lancet, 386*(10006), 1861–1914.

Weitzman, M. L. (2014). Fat tails and the social cost of carbon. *American Economic Review, 104*(5), 544–546.

Wigand, C., Ardito, T., Chaffee, C., Ferguson, W., Paton, S., Raposa, K., ... Watson, E. (2017). A climate change adaptation strategy for management of coastal marsh systems. *Estuaries and Coasts, 40*(3), 682–693.

Wodon, Q., & Zaman, H. (2010). Higher food prices in Sub-Saharan Africa: Poverty impact and policy responses. *The World Bank Research Observer, 25*(1), 157–176. https://doi.org/10.1093/wbro/lkp018

Xiang, J., Bi, P., Pisaniello, D., & Hansen, A. (2014). Health impacts of workplace heat exposure: An epidemiological review. *Industrial Health, 52*(2), 91–101.

Yip, R. (2000). Significance of an abnormally low or high hemoglobin concentration during pregnancy: Special consideration of iron nutrition. *The American Journal of Clinical Nutrition, 72*(1), 272S–279S.

Ziska, L. H., Gebhard, D. E., Frenz, D. A., Faulkner, S., Singer, B. D., & Straka, J. G. (2003). Cities as harbingers of climate change: Common ragweed, urbanization, and public health. *Journal of Allergy and Clinical Immunology, 111*(2), 290–295.

CHAPTER 11

The Way Forward: Food Systems for Enabling Rural Prosperity and Nutrition Security

11.1 Introduction

Why is malnutrition so persistent in India despite the country's self-sufficiency in food production? This book explores this policy conundrum through the lens of its food systems. Laying out a formal exposition of the food systems, we flesh out the linkages between achieving equitable economic growth and agricultural development and improving nutrition outcomes: the bedrock of India's malnutrition challenge. This book adds to the literature by stringing together, for the first time, the inter-linkages between these overlapping themes. We highlight the importance of economic growth for the affordability of nutrition, agricultural development for nutrition availability and the role of improved nutrition access. In this chapter, we deliberate upon the importance of the type of regional development in propelling economic growth. We move away from a national framework to highlight variegated subnational development trajectories. We argue that regions which leveraged agriculture as the engine of growth—through commercialized and market-oriented agricultural systems—have fared better in addressing the problem of undernutrition. In this book, we have classified regional development patterns as *lagging*, *agriculture-led* and *urbanizing*. *Agriculture-led growth states* are those where a highly productive agricultural sector leads growth. *Urbanizing states* leveraged agricultural development to kickstart structural transformation (ST). Now their development is driven by non-agricultural growth

© The Author(s) 2019
P. Pingali et al., *Transforming Food Systems for a Rising India*,
Palgrave Studies in Agricultural Economics and Food Policy,
https://doi.org/10.1007/978-3-030-14409-8_11

and urbanization. Urbanized states have largely succeeded in addressing the undernutrition problem, but are increasingly facing the problem of rising obesity and the rise in non-communicable disease incidence. Regions with lower agricultural productivity—*lagging states*—fare worse than the rest of the country and catch-up growth policies are of importance. In these areas, tackling undernutrition continues to remain the dominant nutrition challenge. Thus in this book, we argue that any policy on nutrition should consider these disparate subnational developmental patterns. The food systems approach provides us with an organizing framework to link the goals for economic growth, agricultural development and nutrition.

Taking the food systems approach, this book offers multiple policy recommendations. We bring agricultural sector-led developmental approach at the center of any policy formulation to ensure greater nutrition security and rural prosperity for greater welfare. Our policy recommendations are also tailored to the subnational variations in the process of structural transformation. While the share of agriculture in India's GDP has declined considerably, agriculture still employs a large share of the labor force. In some states, this is more so and those are the ones where developmental outcomes including malnutrition are poorer. National level policy goals were useful while formulating policies in the immediate aftermath of our independence from the British. In the seven decades that followed, states of India have exhibited distinct and disparate developmental patterns because of various factors which include climate, soil, water facilities among other factors. Despite agriculture being under the purview of state government, one unified national policy blind to the geographical variation and differences in resource endowments is likely to further widen these disparities. Our policy recommendations explicitly factor in these subnational contexts. For example (Table 11.1), we recommend that in the *lagging* regions, creating new comparative advantages for catch-up growth in agriculture, encouraging diversification of agricultural production systems and reducing undernutrition and hunger should be the main policy focus. For the states which fall under the category of *agriculture-led*, policy should prioritize agricultural diversification and commercialization and enabling adoption of sustainable agricultural production techniques. These states would continue to focus on their comparative advantage in agriculture but with a shift in emphasis from their traditional strength in staple grains to higher value crop and livestock production systems. In the *urbanizing* regions, the challenge lies in urban planning and developing strategies which support the process of commercialization of agriculture. The government should

Table 11.1 Policies for enabling nutrition security and rural prosperity

Main goal: Enabling nutrition security and rural prosperity by 2050	Lagging states	Agriculture-led states	Urbanizing states
Agricultural development policies: Increasing rural prosperity and nutrient availability	Growing crops based on comparative advantages provided by agro-ecological zones	Sustainable agriculture production to rectify input overuse from staple grain production	Commercialization of agricultural production
Nutrition policies: Improving nutrient access and absorption and labor productivity	Reduction of undernutrition, communicable diseases and hunger	Reduction of over nutrition, non-communicable diseases (NCDs) and hunger	Reduction of over-nutrition, NCDs and urban food insecurity
Economic growth policies: Improving nutrient affordability through the creation of new economic opportunities for catch-up growth	Policies for a Green Revolution 2.0	Diversification to the non-agricultural sectors	Policies for planned urban development and growth

simultaneously enact policies which aim at reducing obesity while addressing the issue of urban food insecurity. Our policy recommendations aim at allowing states to choose policies which address their unique nutritional and agricultural challenge while factoring in their state of structural transformation. The end goal of our policies would be to facilitate to states to move into a structural transformation pathway which addresses the context-specific development challenge while ensuring high growth. In this context, agricultural and economic growth policies grounded in critical regional concerns for nutrition are the key to ensuring greater nutrition security and rural prosperity.

In the past, in recognition of the role of state in facilitating its own development, the Indian constitution allotted the subjects of agriculture, health and industries to states and concurrent subjects, respectively. For all substantive development issues, the state government was envisioned to be the main implementation agency of policy while the central government was assumed to support in funding and providing technical support. Due to the scarcity of resources and a low savings rate after independence from the British, the central government had to play the leadership role in both aggregating fiscal resources nationally as well as in designing and implementing development programs with critical national security concerns. However, over time, we have seen that this approach has led to an inadvertent divergence in economic development across states. States which have been most successful in structural transformation have reduced their dependence on the central government for fiscal transfers and have implemented their own state run initiatives for tackling the most pressing development concerns. This has facilitated greater structural transformation in these regions. Thus, in our approach, we advocate for the greater decentralization of resources to state governments and greater flexibility in designing and implementing policies that best tackle their unique development challenges while also facilitating greater growth based on their comparative advantages. In our model, for example, the central government plays the role of a coordinator in the development process. It is responsible for setting national goals, monitoring progress towards these goals, bolstering financing of the various interventions and programs and creating synergies across the various stakeholders including the private sector, the federal government and the farmers. In its new role, the central government would improve coordination across departments which oversee the development of economic sectors as well as reduce inefficiencies in implementation. The primary role for the central government would be to invest in research and development to improve the quality of services provided and increase access to technology for use in human capital production. To encourage innovation, increase efficiency and increase the capacity to scale initiatives, greater private sector participation needs to be encouraged as well.

11.2   POLICIES FOR AGRICULTURAL DEVELOPMENT: FACILITATING GREATER NUTRIENT AVAILABILITY AND RURAL PROSPERITY THROUGH COMMERCIALIZATION AND DIVERSIFICATION

The key to success for the agricultural sector in general and farmers specifically lies in commercialization and diversification. There exists a tremendous opportunity for farmers in catering to the rising urban demand for higher value agricultural products (T. Reardon & Timmer, 2007). Diversification of production not only improves the availability and access of nutritious food for the consumers but also provides a greater capacity for the farmers to grow out of poverty and share in the benefits of economic growth (Pingali & Rosegrant, 1995). Diversification of the agricultural sector however fundamentally hinges on the ability of smallholders—which make up the majority of Indian farmers—to overcome constraints to accessing input and product markets and increase production efficiency. Smallholders often face disadvantages in accessing input markets such as credit, quality seeds, fertilizer, pesticides, farm machinery and R&D to diversify and generate a marketable surplus (Abraham & Pingali, 2017). They also lack access to output markets to sell their produce at fair prices. In the absence of commercialization in *lagging* regions, smallholders continue to practice low risk, low return production of basic staple grains. Traditionally smallholder production had the advantage of higher labor utilization and low monitoring costs through the utilization of family labor. In recent years, increasing non-farm wages have led to a rise in seasonal migration, which has led to reduced utilization of family labor. Additionally, poor economies of scale limit the scope and ability of smallholders for mechanizing or adopting new technologies and linking to urban value chains. These factors have contributed to declining farm productivity, especially in the *lagging states.*

The role of climate change in agricultural production is another major challenge for smallholder production. In the past two decades, the increasing uncertainties from changing weather patterns and resource degradation from the overuse of land and water have emerged to be additional concerns. Addressing these will be necessary for policies focused on agricultural growth in the future. In this section, we look at the interventions needed to rectify smallholder disadvantages for commercialization and improved access to technology and sustainable intensification, making agriculture climate-smart and effectively managing value chains to improve efficiency and reduce wastage.

11.2.1   *Promoting Aggregation Models and Rectifying Smallholder Disadvantages of Scale*

Institutional interventions can offset scale disadvantages faced by small farms and enable improved agricultural production. By reducing the risk associated with the adoption of new crop technologies and reducing transaction costs in market access, these interventions could help in farm diversification as well as in achieving better price realizations in the output market. Aggregation models such as FPOs and cooperatives are examples of these types of interventions. At the farm level, aggregation helps smallholders to access credit and other inputs at a more competitive cost. Access to extension services is also increased through these models at very low costs. Joint marketing of produce opens up avenues for vertical coordination (VC), access to electronic markets, trading in commodity futures and benefit from warehousing platforms.

In Table 11.2, we highlight some recommendations that differ by the type of regional development. In the *lagging states* with low agricultural productivity, FPOs have the potential to enable greater commercialization, enabling greater yields. Linkages to output markets will help incentivize the production of pulses and coarse grains, given their comparative advantage. In *agriculture-led states* and *urbanizing states*, alternative models such as contract farming are more likely to succeed since they already have higher yields. Enabling conditions for contract farming through mechanisms to enforce contracts and allowing retailers and processors to transact directly with farmers, especially in the cash crops, could be the way forward. Here, aggregation models can help reduce organization costs of engaging with a more significant number of small farms and reduce contracting costs that often exclude small farm contracts. Policy measures to financially support FPO emergence, extend financial and insurance-based services, link them to information and extension services and enable market linkages by improving connectivity will further incentivize group formation and establish linkages across the value chain.

11.2.2   *Reforming Markets to Improve Farmer Participation and Increase the Efficiency of Transactions*

Traditional markets or *mandis* are the main platforms for agricultural marketing. In *lagging states*, the primary challenge for smallholders is access to traditional markets. With small surplus produce, large distances to markets and poor rural connectivity, market participation is lower. Intermediaries benefit from the missing market and expropriate a large part of the smallholders' profit. Improving connectivity and infrastructure, therefore, is critical. Farmers also find it difficult to sell in the markets without appropriate grading and standardization of their produce. Establishing systems of grades and standards determination, checks on malpractices in weighing at the *mandis*, and information on prices further encourage market participation. These measures are vital for developing agricultural marketing systems to stimulate greater agriculture-related development in *lagging states*.

Table 11.2 Policies for enabling diversification and commercialization of farm systems

Agricultural sector	Lagging states	Agriculture-led states	Urbanizing states
Promoting aggregation models and rectifying smallholder disadvantages of scale	Promoting FPOs and cooperatives to rectify smallholder farmer disadvantages in accessing input and output markets	Linking farms to markets through contract farming. FPOs enforcing contracts and monitoring and evaluations	Creating opportunities for contract enforcement, direct procurement etc. for export-oriented production in cash crops
Reforming markets to improve participation and efficiency	Improving connectivity and marketing infrastructure	Enabling vertical coordination models	Promoting alternative platforms—E-trading, commodity futures and direct procurement for retail sectors
Increasing access to technology adoption for sustainable intensification	HYV in coarse grain and pulses, adopting other high-value crops and foods	Diversification out of staple grains towards high-value agriculture (fruits, vegetables, livestock)	Integrating ICT into agricultural systems, precision farming, to conserve natural resources
Making agriculture production systems climate-smart	Drought, heat, flood, disease-resistant technologies for crops, irrigation infrastructure and natural resource management groups	Sustainable intensification of agricultural systems, reducing land degradation through input management	Drought, heat, flood, disease-resistant technologies for crops, irrigation infrastructure and natural resource management groups
Increasing bio-availability of nutrients in the food supply chains	Increasing farm diversification and development of non-staple production systems	Increasing bio-availability of micronutrients in staple crops, creating fortification industries for processed foods, increasing demand for micronutrient-rich foods	Creating urban markets for bio-fortified crops, organic foods and foods rich in micronutrients, reducing food loss and waste through supply chain interventions

With changing demand for quality and high-value agricultural produce, alternative value chains and newer marketing platforms have emerged. Vertical coordination (VC) by which retailers form direct linkages with farms and bypass traditional markets has been growing in *agriculture-led growth states* and *urbanizing states*. Newer marketing platforms where farmers can participate in online auctions and trading such as eNAM and

Rashtriya e-Market Services Pvt. Ltd. (ReMS) in Karnataka and warehousing platforms such as the National Commodity & Derivatives Exchange (NCDEX) eMarkets Limited can be viable alternatives to existing traditional markets (Reddy, 2016). VC can be more relevant for perishable crops and farmers in regions with good linkages to market (*agriculture-led growth states*) while futures and warehousing platforms can be useful for nonperishable commodities and can emerge in low potential areas such as those in *lagging states*. Different marketing arrangements can help serve specific purposes of farms, conditioned on geographical and crop characteristics.

11.2.3   Increasing Access to Technology Adoption for Sustainable Intensification

Technology has played a critical role in enabling food security in the developing world. The Green Revolution (GR) helped in increasing yields of wheat and rice, making many countries like India self-sufficient in these grains. GR technologies were conventional plant-breeding (CPB) technologies that were limited to wheat and rice in the context of India. Additionally, implementation of GR technologies was limited to regions with access to irrigation and (or) consistent rainfall. This led to interregional disparities in agricultural development where states with comparative advantages in staple crop production benefited disproportionately in comparison to other states. Another fallout of these technologies was their impact on the environment. Because of poor management of natural resources and overuse of subsidized inputs such as fertilizers and pesticides, the Green Revolution has also resulted in depletion of water tables and the degradation of land and soil quality. The role of technology in the wake of new production challenges for diversifying food systems in the presence of climate change and environmental degradation is thus to increase yields while reducing environmental externalities through sustainable intensification.

New agricultural technologies have gone beyond conventional plant-breeding technologies of the Green Revolution to the genetically modified organisms (GMOs). The first generation of genetically modified (GM) crops have traits that give them tolerance or resistance to insects, pesticides and herbicides. In India, Bt cotton, which has an inbuilt resistance to boring pests, is the only first-generation GMO that was introduced to the agricultural sector. Second-generation GMOs are crops engineered to have increased tolerance to abiotic stress (drought, flood salinity) and increased nutrient (protein, amino acids, fatty acids, starch, vitamins, minerals and enzymes) content, enabling the creation of resilient and more nutritive crops (Buiatti, Christou, & Pastore, 2013; Flachowsky & Aulrich, 2001; C. N. Rao, Pray, & Herring, 2018). Both first- and second-generation GM technologies will prove to be critical in the wake of the food systems challenges India is facing. In *lagging states, agriculture-led states* and *urbanizing states*, GMOs can help in the reduction of climate-related risks through heat and drought resistance crops, and they can increase yield and reduce the cost of production in crops through built-in pest resistance. So far, no GMOs except Bt cotton have been allowed in the Indian agricultural sector. There has been much debate about the safety of GM crops in India and around the world. Despite no evidence being found that GMOs are detrimental to human, animal and environmental health, there has been much opposition to it, discouraging investments and innovation in agricultural R&D. India needs to have more forward-looking bio-technology policies and institutions that can allow the introduction of these new technologies into the agricultural sector. This is essential to bolster innovation and investment from the private sector and enable institutional support for the adoption of biotechnology in agriculture.

11.2.4 Making Agriculture Production Systems Climate-Smart

Given the close relationship between poverty, agriculture production and weather, developing adaptation strategies to protect smallholders from climatic risks is essential. Climate-smart agriculture (CSA) to ensure enhanced productivity, increased resilience and limited environmental externalities require a combination of technology, management practices, infrastructure and information systems that can help mitigate, reduce or withstand the effects of climate change (Lipper et al., 2014). The core elements needed for the transition to CSA are: (a) information, evidence gathering and assessment, (b) strengthening of national and local institutions, (c) evidence-based policy making and (d) financing transition (ibid). The accessibility and availability of information are crucial to making proper planting, harvesting and marketing decisions needed for agricultural growth and development. Information communication technologies (ICTs) have shown to have great potential in reducing information asymmetries and improving the efficiency of production and marketing (Aker & Fafchamps, 2015; Fischer, Byerlee, & Edmeades, 2009;

S. Mittal & Mehar, 2012). ICTs often rely on platforms on which information can be collated, analyzed and disseminated. These platforms need to be put in place to bring together context-specific information regarding weather, technical extension and markets.

Evidence-based policy making is central to the implementation of CSA, especially about biotechnology policies to enable technology adoption. Second-generation GMO crops that are heat, drought and flood resistant can play a role in reducing crop failure and improving nutrient content in plants that will be affected through climate change (C. N. Rao et al., 2018). Policy to allow the introduction of GM crops will help reduce climate-related risks and cost of production and also increase the bio-availability of nutrients that can potentially be lost due to global warming. Management of resources that goes into agricultural production needs to complement technology adoption for sustainable intensification and reduced environmental externalities. Removal of input subsidies for electricity and fertilizers is important, as these measures in the past have led to overuse of groundwater and over-application of nitrogenous fertilizers. Supplementing agricultural programs with agroforestry for carbon sequestering, soil conservation and watershed management initiatives is essential for replenishment of common-pool resources used for agricultural production. Institutional strengthening through community-based collective actions is needed to enable conservation programs. Empowering aggregation models to take up the task of common-pool resource management will reduce the cost of organization and incentivize cooperation aligned with primary economic activities. Supporting adoption of CSA and transitioning from conventional agriculture requires financing and credit support. The role of the government and policies to improve access to financial services and build infrastructure is going to be critical.

11.2.5   *Increasing Bio-availability of Quality Nutrients in the Food Supply Chain*

Modernizing supply chains is essential to reduce loss and waste and ensuring greater food and nutrient availability in the food systems. Infrastructure investments in connecting farms to markets through the construction of good quality roads, developing infrastructure in cold chains and warehouses to reduce spoilage and creating testing facilities to establish grades and standards will be important steps towards this goal. Given the experience of other developing nations and emerging economies, encouraging the participation of the private sector and sustainability-oriented businesses to increase efficiency along the supply chain is one possible channel to facilitate this transition.

Climate change poses a major threat to agricultural production and nutrient availability in the future (Myers et al., 2014). Rising temperatures during the growing season have been found to reduce nutrient availability in plants and reduce yields of crops (P. K. Aggarwal & Mall, 2002; Lobell, Schlenker, & Costa-Roberts, 2011; Schlenker & Roberts, 2009). Increasing access to good quality nutrition requires interventions that tackle this problem at multiple levels. First, improving soil quality through crop management will be important to ensure greater nutrient availability in crops. Policies that encourage diversity in production reduce dependence on rain water and research on the application of nutrients based on real time soil quality will be important. Agroforestry initiatives supported by the appropriate decentralization of common property rights have been found to be effective in enabling conservation practices such as watershed management (R. R. Banerjee, 2015; Gross-Camp, Few, & Martin, 2015; Myers et al., 2017; Sinha & Swaminathan, 1992; Steiner, Briske, Brown, & Rottler, 2018). Second, encouraging research on improving the bioavailability of nutrients in crops will also be required going forward. Currently, research and development still focus on biofortification of staple crops since staples constitute a large portion of most individuals' dietary requirements (Meenakshi et al., 2010; Qaim, Stein, & Meenakshi, 2007). Moving forward, fortification of non-staples, increasing micronutrient availability through current food safety net programs and climate technology to prevent micronutrient loss from crops due to erratic weather conditions will need to become part of the Indian agriculture and food policy innovations. Third, a more innovative approach is to create new markets for nutrition that can properly signal the value of nutrition and health in foods, especially in *urbanizing states* (Costa-Font, Gil, & Traill, 2008). This would create a demand pull for growing more nutritious crops, thus encouraging research and development into the same. For this to happen, developing food safety standards, the demand for organic products and demand for other nutritious non-staple foods through education will be important. Fourth, investments in improving nutrition content of food through fortification of processed foods will play an important role in increasing micronutrient availability in diets (Pinstrup-Andersen, 2009). Incentivizing private sector participation in developing and marketing bio-fortified foods will be important in this context.

11.3   Policies for the Nutrition Transition: Increasing Access to Good Quality Foods and Nutrients

In India, undernutrition and micronutrient deficiency simultaneously coexist with the phenomenon of rising obesity, leading to the triple burden of malnutrition. In Chap. 5, we described the multitude of pathways influencing malnutrition and the nutrition challenges different regions are faced with. In *lagging states*, the main goal for improving nutrition would be to reduce hunger and diet-related undernutrition in addition to micronutrient deficiencies among children. For *agriculture-led states* and *urbanizing states*, the main challenge would be tackling obesity and micronutrient deficiencies in both children and adults. For *urbanizing states*, in addition to reducing obesity, the policy focus needs to be on creating safety nets for reducing urban food insecurity, especially around food access because poor urban residents completely rely on purchased food (Maitra & Rao, 2015). As the nature of nutrition challenges varies across regions, a regional approach to tackle the specific problem of malnutrition should be the way forward. In Table 11.3, we provide a summary of how policies could be tailored to reduce region-specific malnutrition.

11.3.1   Intra-Household Safety Nets to Improve Nutrient Access for Women and Children

Even when healthy foods are available within the household, intra-household distribution of access to quality and quantity of nutritious foods could be different by age and gender. In countries such as Mexico and Brazil, cash transfers and conditional cash transfer (CCT) programs have been found to have positive impacts on overcoming intra-household level dynamics that reduce nutrition access. Targeting conditional cash transfers to girls in households increases their access to nutrition in addition to increasing educational outcomes (Attanasio, Gomex, Heredia, & Vera-hernández, 2005; Behrman, Parker, & Todd, 2011; Handa & Davis, 2006; Leroy, Ruel, & Verhofstadt, 2009). These CCTs are also effective in preventing the worsening of nutrition outcomes of girl children when households undergo health-related or income-related shocks (Attanasio et al., 2005; Fernald, Gertler, & Neufeld, 2008). In *agriculture-led growth states* where women's empowerment is low and incomes are relatively high, implementing labor market reforms to increase women's labor force

Table 11.3 Policies for reducing the triple burden of malnutrition

Health and nutrition	Lagging states	Agriculture-led states	Urbanizing states
Implementing intra-household safety nets to improve nutrition access for women and children	Conditional cash transfers to encourage women to purchase nutritious foods, increasing women's access to the ICDS and MDMS	Conditional cash transfers consumption to encourage women to purchase nutritious foods, increasing women's access to the ICDS and MDMS	Unconditional cash transfers and CCTs to ensure that women can access diverse foods from markets, increasing women's access to the ICDS and MDMS
Investing in health-related infrastructure such as water, sanitation	Improving water quality, building toilets, interventions for reducing new diseases that climate change may bring	Improving water quality, building and encouraging toilet use, interventions for reducing mosquitoes and pests from climate,	Increasing urban water availability, building and encouraging toilet use, interventions for reducing mosquitoes and pests from climate,
Encouraging behavior change towards more healthy nutrition consumption practices	Taxes on unhealthy foods, promoting organic foods, encouraging hand washing and proper sanitation practices, along with BCC on nutrition consumption	State focused: Behavior change (reduction in obesity), taxes on unhealthy foods, promoting organic foods, food labeling, grades and standards, with BCC on nutrition	Urban focused: Behavior change (reduction in obesity), taxes on unhealthy foods, promoting organic foods, food labeling, grades and standards
Increasing health service capacity and improving the quality of care Bolstering other safety nets to address urban food security and improve access to nutrients	CDs: Vaccines usage promotion, health insurance (reducing burden for children) Procuring and distributing non-staples, bio-fortified crops and fortified foods through the PDS, universal health insurance	NCDs: Health insurance, tertiary hospitals (reducing burden for adults) Health insurance programs to improve access to care, improving quality of the urban PDS	NCDs: Health insurance, tertiary hospitals (reducing burden for adults) Health insurance programs to improve access to care, improving quality of the urban PDS

participation and increasing women's remuneration along with CCTs could be important interventions. The effectiveness of these interventions lies in redefining the roles of women as active income-generating members within households. In *urbanizing states*, reforms in the labor markets to increase women's engagement in the labor markets and unconditional cash transfers to women will be essential interventions. Since women are relatively more empowered in these states, these changes will further increase the bargaining power of women both at home and in the workplace, thus improving child health outcomes (E. Kennedy & Peters, 1992). In *lagging states*, a combination of CCTs and in-kind transfers will remain important. In-kind food transfers through the ICDS and the MDMS programs have been found to be effective in improving nutrition outcomes within households, but they require better monitoring and effective governance in the *lagging states* (Anjana et al., 2015; Khera, 2006; P. Pingali, Mittra, & Rahman, 2016). Finally, interventions that increase the education of girl children and women, delay child marriages, provide households information on economic opportunities for women and increase safety at workplaces have been known to impact both nutrition outcomes for women and their children (R. Jensen, 2010, 2012). Improving labor conditions, investing in schools, and educating parents on investing in their girl children will thus have to remain priorities for intra-household safety net development.

11.3.2   Water and Sanitation Infrastructure for Better Health Outcomes

Poor hygiene environments increase disease burden and sickness and affect nutrient absorption. Improving water and sanitation infrastructure are essential to reduce the spread of disease, especially waterborne diseases (Mengistie, Berhane, & Worku, 2013). Infrastructure provisions for clean water and sanitation facilities also require behavior change. Unless there is a change in beliefs within households about cleanliness related to toilet use, individuals tend to avoid the use of the constructed toilet, thus defeating the purpose of improving the health environment (Spears, Ghosh, & Cumming, 2013). Behavior change programs that seek to improve the household health environment by encouraging water storage practices, encouraging hand washing before water use and after toilet use, and encouraging cleanliness in the surrounding environment have been effective in reducing malnutrition around the world (Biran et al., 2008, 2014; Lee, Rosenzweig, & Pitt, 1997; Mangyo, 2008; J. H. Rah et al., 2015). There are currently experimental trials being conducted in rural villages in India to identify the constraints and challenges for households in adopting these practices.

Looking into the future, rapid urbanization of states increases the need to invest in water and sanitation infrastructure required to improve urban food and nutrition security. This is a pressing concern in major cities where higher population density and the existence of slums—with little or no sanitation facilities—increase household vulnerability to air or waterborne communicable diseases. Climate change further threatens to worsen the potency of diseases in urban areas where water and sanitation infrastructure are inadequate. Without proper urban development strategies that incorporate both food and nutrition policies into development, the human costs of urban growth may outweigh its benefits.

11.3.3   Encouraging Behavior Change Towards More Healthy Nutrition Consumption Practices

With changing incomes and lifestyles, over-nutrition that manifests as obesity is an emerging health-related concern, especially in urban areas and among women. Greater obesity is correlated with lower productivity, health and wages of individuals and hence this phenomenon should be of increasing concern (Cawley, 2004, 2010; Cawley & Meyerhoefer, 2012; Thow et al., 2018). Greater consumption of processed food and a sedentary lifestyle can be attributed to this emerging phenomenon in urban areas. To combat the problem, behavior change communications and nutrition education could be used to nudge individuals towards healthy eating habits. Policy instruments such as taxes on unhealthy sugary foods, like in Mexico, could be useful to reduce consumption of the same (Cawley, 2015; M. A. Colchero, Salgado, Unar-Munguia, Hernandez-Avila, & Rivera-Dommarco, 2015; M. A. Colchero, Rivera-Dommarco, Popkin, & Ng, 2017). Other interventions such as nutrient labeling, the introduction of food safety standards as well as the certification of organic and healthy foods have been found to increase consumer demand for such products (Padel & Foster, 2005). Publishing scientific research on the nutrition content of foods and its effects on health has also played an essential role in increasing public awareness of consuming balanced diets. These factors can play a significant role in increasing household diet diversity as well as reducing obesity.

Tackling undernutrition within households through education interventions requires understanding the information gap and the intrahousehold dynamics that impact nutrition access. Information campaigns on the importance of breastfeeding, the importance of eating healthy and adopting healthy nutrition practices within households, the importance of consuming micronutrients in diets and so on could be the essential interventions to improve nutrition consumption within households. Research has shown that when women are empowered to make decisions with regard to these household goods, the health of the household improves (Bennett, 1988). However, it is often the case that decisions are taken either by the male members or women in positions of power. Thus involving these men and mother in laws in these behavior change campaigns while discussing women's empowerment is also crucial in ensuring greater access to nutrition within the household's threshold.

11.3.4   *Increasing Health Service Capacity and Improving the Quality of Care*

A major health threat is the rising incidence of non-communicable diseases (NCDs). NCDs such as heart disease, diabetes and some cancers, if diagnosed early, can be treated and managed. The onset of these diseases requires palliative care and lifestyle changes to manage these conditions. Thus, managing the problem of NCDs that are specific to India requires investment in research and development into preventive care, palliative care and development of diagnostic practices and treatment protocols. Sales taxes collected from unhealthy food consumption or tobacco and alcohol use can be useful in raising resources to help build such systems. These public policy tools are also known to encourage more health behaviors in individuals. Additionally, interventions that increase quality of health services provided through the public health systems, building capacity of health service providers and regulating discriminatory private health services practices will be important in ensuring the health system remains fair and equitable for those who access it.

Climate change has been associated with changing the potency of communicable diseases within locations as well as with the growth of new disease burdens in locations that were previously not susceptible to the same. In areas where water and sanitation are poor and climatic shocks threaten infrastructure services, changes to the health environment are expected to further derail progress made towards tackling communicable diseases. Thus in addition to implementing appropriate interventions that increase the quality of water and sanitation infrastructure, climate change mitigation and adaptation strategies that involve the development of vaccines and treatment protocols for treating communicable diseases are also required. Children in *lagging states* would be most vulnerable due to their lack of access to good quality healthcare services. In such situations, implementing epidemiological disease monitoring units in addition to interventions to provide timely care in the event of disease outbreak will be extremely important for reducing malnutrition. In more developed states, integrating monitoring technology with health services provisions will be essential inputs into controlling the spread of communicable diseases as well. However, cost effective interventions need greater flexibility built into the process of preventative care and treatment. For example, each state needs to be equipped with funds and technology that will best help them tackle the communicable disease with the highest disease burden.

11.3.5 *Bolstering Safety Nets to Address Urban Food Security and Improve Access to Nutrients Beyond Calories*

A robust safety net architecture has emerged in India over the last two decades (Drèze & Khera, 2017). It is a welcome change given the rising inter-personal inequality and improved fiscal capacity of the government. The policy challenge lies in the issue of the direction and design of these initiatives. The existing social protection paradigm is structured around the idea of reducing poverty and vulnerability. While this will continue to be an essential idea behind safety nets, a futuristic policy should also consider thinking about designing programs which reduce the likelihood of people falling into poverty. Social support for the poor is palliative or curative, preventive policies like insurance programs could be a new policy direction. Efficacy of such policies is also bolstered by the fact that economic shocks, like health and weather, are one of the major causes of households falling into poverty in India. Rising informal employment, where income is highly variable, has been a significant concern of late across many countries. Social protection, therefore, of various kinds, with various objectives, provide a safety net to the disadvantaged.

The design of safety net programs also needs to be linked to the changing nature of structural transformation (Croppenstedt, Knowles, & Lowder, 2017). Much of these policies currently focus on the rural areas. By 2050, India is expected to be more urban, even by the most conservative official figures. Concerns of "urbanization of poverty" have already begun to dominate scholarly debates and news headlines (Ravallion, 2002). Combined with a large share of informal urban employment structure, unhygienic living conditions, especially for the poor, make the urban food systems susceptible to malnutrition. Being net consumers of food, urban food systems are more susceptible to food price fluctuations & thus greater food insecurity during climate change events. Urbanization and NCDs have a clear association as well. In these contexts, NCDs are likely to rise faster in poorer communities—as is happening in middle- and higher-income countries (Bollyky, Templin, Cohen, & Dieleman, 2017). The role of safety nets in urban areas, therefore, will be of critical importance as India grows. The issue of labor mobility and reduced quality of life of migrants further adds to the clarion call for a robust urban safety net program (Gentilini, 2015). Debates around introducing UBI and the importance of cash transfers will therefore be a welcome addition to urban safety net discussions. In urban areas, where banking infrastructure is well-developed, cash transfers can be effective in increasing households ability to purchase diverse food. In *lagging states*, market development needs to precede a move to cash transfers. UBI, while in its inception, shall progressively become a useful social assistance program.

Health insurance schemes are definitely a welcome addition in reducing the likelihood of poverty and mortality. More developed states in south India have done well on the take-up of government health insurance programs while the underdeveloped regions have fared poorly. Greater financial literacy among the population and well-developed insurance markets should precede these interventions in order to increase its effectiveness. Also, interventions for crop or livestock insurance should be introduced as they improve the ability of smallholders to adopt new technologies and hedge risks against climate related shocks. Collectively, these risk-absorbing interventions enhance households' abilities to tide over production & consumption shocks, thus increasing household food security and reducing their risk of malnutrition.

11.4 POLICIES FOR ECONOMIC DEVELOPMENT: CREATING ECONOMIC OPPORTUNITIES FOR CATCH-UP GROWTH AND LINKING FOOD SYSTEMS TO THE JOB AGENDA

We have argued throughout the book that economic development patterns are varied across different Indian states. *Urbanizing states* have been able to leverage their comparative advantages and grow with the local and global economy. The *agriculture-led growth states* reaped the benefits of the Green Revolution and hence reduced poverty and malnutrition successfully. The *lagging states*, however, need to catch up in order to stay competitive. Aligning agricultural development to overall economic growth is essential to ensure equitable and sustainable development in these areas. In *lagging states*, the main goals will be to ensure the development of rural infrastructure, stimulate non-farm growth and reduce labor market frictions to enable better labor utilization in the economy. Dovetailed with equitable growth strategies is the importance of sustainable growth policies. Climate change has had a significant impact on all sectors of the economy and measures to mitigate its effects will require climate-smart interventions in all sectors. In *agriculture-led states* and *urbanizing states*, institutional interventions to ensure good governance (especially urban and peri-urban areas), creating the climate for sustainability-oriented investments and interventions, encouraging private sector participation and creating an environment for technological innovation will help in sustaining economic and agricultural growth. In this section (see Table 11.4 for an overview), we discuss policies that can facilitate opportunities for economic growth based on patterns of development with the intention of creating institutions to encourage climate-smart investments and boost private sector participation.

11.4.1 Improving Rural Infrastructure to Stimulate Non-farm Growth and Improve Connectivity to Urban Areas to Stimulate Rural Development

Diversification of rural livelihood sources is a critical household strategy to hedge income security risks associated with agricultural production and increase food security (Ellis, 1998). As countries structurally transform and labor transitions out of the agricultural sector, household income sources from the non-farm sector also grow (Timmer, 1988). In India, a majority of rural households have a mix of farm and non-farm income

Table 11.4   Policies for creating economic opportunities for catch-up growth

Economic growth and development	Lagging states	Agriculture-led states	Urbanizing states
Improving rural infrastructure and connectivity to urban areas	Investing in roads, power, irrigation, supply chains etc. focused on rural development	Upstream supply chain linkages to agriculture	Downstream supply chain linkages to agriculture
Reducing labor market frictions that prevent the flow of underemployed labor towards more productive economic opportunities	Women's safety, education of the labor force, creating rural employment exchanges, upskilling the labor force	Women's safety, education of the labor force, creating urban unemployment insurance, rural employment exchanges, reskilling the labor force for the non-agricultural sector	Women's safety, education of the labor force, urban unemployment insurance, urban employment exchanges, reskilling the labor force towards high-skilled jobs
Improving the capacity of urban governance bodies to facilitate urban development and climate proof major cities	Improving governance systems for small towns, investing in drinking water, infrastructure, migration, resource use etc.	Improving governance systems for small towns, investing in drinking water, infrastructure, migration, resource use etc.	Improve urban infrastructure and urban amenities, stimulating urban growth, urban export growth, drinking water, infrastructure, migration, resource use etc.
Encouraging the private sector to participate and innovate in the growth process	Developing incentives for businesses that make use of low-skilled labor force, encouraging the growth of the informal economy, businesses that innovate in value addition of agricultural products	Developing incentives for businesses that innovate in value addition of agricultural products, businesses that innovate on agriculture input development	Developing incentives for high-tech businesses that innovate on climate and environmental issues to increase global competitiveness

sources in their income portfolio (Chandrasekhar & Mehrotra, 2016). Livelihood diversification is a common strategy among the smallholders to ensure that they can make a basic living and insure themselves against unanticipated shocks. However, since the rural non-farm sector has not grown as fast as the urban non-farm sector, households that are locked into the rural non-farm sector due to credit or labor market constraints have not seen their non-farm incomes rise as quickly.

One of the simple ways to increase access to non-farm goods and labor markets is through investments in rural infrastructure (S. Aggarwal, 2018). Infrastructure investments such as roads that connect villages to towns or the development of interstate highways lower costs of transport and reduce costs related to relocation when laborers move between low productive and high productive regions. Also, investments in infrastructure such as power and irrigation help improve labor productivity on the farm, thus creating the impetus to move underemployed labor out of agriculture (Asher & Novosad, 2018). In *lagging states*, rural infrastructure along with investments in human capital are critical for enabling catch-up growth. Programs such as the MGNREGA have been vital to improving the bargaining position of agricultural laborers in these areas and increasing income security. However, without proper credit markets, individuals may not be able to save, invest or spend these incomes (R. M. Townsend, 1994, 1995). Thus programs that seek to provide UBI for individuals may not prove useful for rural development if there is no rural infrastructure development. In *agriculture-led states* and *urbanizing states*, creating upstream and downstream market linkages to enable the flow of goods and labor from agriculture to the non-agricultural sectors is essential. For the *agriculture-led growth states*, incentivizing the food processing industry, the food fortification industry and other allied food and feed industries will help redistribute agricultural surplus towards more productive uses. In *urbanizing states*, linking technology development with agricultural inputs development and innovations along the food supply chain will provide stimulus for agricultural development (McCullough, Pingali, & Stamoulis, 2008). Introducing labor-saving technologies will increase agriculture productivity and hence agriculture-related incomes. Food supply chain innovations will reduce food waste and increase price determination of agricultural produce, thus strengthening the linkages between urban growth and rural prosperity. Rural infrastructure that connects markets across states will be essential to facilitate greater flow of goods and labor in response to demand for the same.

11.4.2   Reducing Labor Market Frictions That Prevent the Flow of Underemployed Labor Towards More Productive Economic Opportunities

In many countries across the world, urban growth due to ST brought with it an increase in rural to urban migration. In India, this rural to urban transition has been low even though urban wages have continued to increase faster than rural wages. There are four reasons for this. One, low availability of skills due to low human capital investments has led to greater underemployment in the agriculture sector. Two, the absence of appropriate human capital skills, firms tend to rely on signals such as access to caste networks rather than signals of worker productivity in their hiring process. In the absence of these networks, abled bodied youth may not find it feasible to migrate towards urban jobs. Three, the inability to find sources for reskilling based on market demand also prevents those who are underemployed to move towards more productive job opportunities that require complementary skills. Lastly, women's labor force participation has been reducing due to the lack of availability of good quality jobs, lack of child care support facilities as well as low safety during their commute and at their workplaces in urban areas (Lipton, 1980; Munshi, 2011; Munshi & Rosenzweig, 2006). These factors tend to influence the ability of migrants to permanently move out of rural economy as well.

As we look ahead, reducing labor market frictions by imparting job skills to the rural population, increasing investments in human capital development through quality education and setting up employment exchanges to reduce the search costs will be required. One of the significant challenges to leverage the non-farm sector for rural prosperity is to improve the quality of jobs and to reskill the population. The rural non-farm sector mostly contains odd jobs and petty employment opportunities that hire low-skilled workers. A large portion of urban workers, especially migrants, are mostly involved in informal employment. Greater investment in improving human capital, especially vocational skills tailored to the local industry requirements, is thus essential for the complete transformation. In the *lagging states*, creating employment exchanges that channel workers towards vocational training and up-skilling their populations will be important. In *agriculture-led states*, the key would be to incentivize entrepreneurship and reskill the agriculture labor force to work in the non-agricultural sector. In *urbanizing states*, increasing capacity of the education sector to absorb more students and improve the quality of education would be significant for creating a globally competitive labor force.

Regarding improving matches between labor and firms, employment exchanges in developed countries have enabled greater employment through the use of information and communication technologies (ICT). In developed countries, the gig economy, where people transact short-term personalized labor services, has become a useful means for reducing search costs for labor services (Burtch, Carnahan, & Greenwood, 2018; Graham, Hjorth, & Lehdonvirta, 2017). In the longer term, investing in higher education institutions that contribute to national growth through R&D is essential to maintain global competitiveness. Reducing labor market frictions that prevent women from participating, such as increasing safety enforcement in transport and the workplace, changing gender norms around what constitutes women's work and increasing child care facilities to reduce their opportunity costs will be required. Bringing women into the economic growth process gives us an additional 50% chance of success.

In the food systems approach, the non-farm sector can create jobs through the development of modern agricultural value chains. Employment in logistics like aggregation, storage, processing, and so on at the agribusiness upstream and food-related services such as restaurants downstream could potentially be leveraged as the channel of employment generation. Higher demand for agricultural inputs and related technologies would generate other livelihood avenues. As NCDs and climate change create new challenges for health, having access to good quality healthcare service providers will be important. This implies that there will be a need for more service providers and research and development into treating and curing NCDs. This will increase the demand for educational institutes that provide these services. Involving the private sector to organize resources for education sector development while monitoring their quality will be a crucial step in this direction. Also, investments in developing an R&D focused labor force and creating opportunities for innovators to benefit from intellectual property rights will stimulate innovation by individuals and (or) research organizations. All these sectors will also be able to provide women with enhanced opportunities to be a part of the labor force.

11.4.3   Improving the Capacity of Urban Governance Bodies to Facilitate Urban Development and Climate Proof Major Cities

Many rural settlements in *lagging states* now exhibit urban characteristics as reflected in the quality of dwelling or changing occupational patterns (Pradhan, 2013). The government, however, continues to govern them as rural areas, which not only inhibits their overall development but also presents a slower rate of rural transformation. These middle spaces, along with the rural-urban continuum, offer enormous growth potential. Since they are the center through which much of the non-farm livelihood creation happens, these spaces are essential in facilitating the labor transition during structural transformation. These spaces—many of them far from the metropolitan cities—could themselves turn into agglomeration economies, encouraging both the migration of labor and capital from surrounding areas (Mukhopadhyay, Zérah, Samanta, & Maria, 2016). By providing services such as technological inputs to the neighboring rural areas, these peri-urban economies often bring greater economic dynamism into the local economy. India's subaltern urbanization, with the right provision of public infrastructure, could thus attract investment near the rural areas, create jobs, reduce the burden on major cities and provide a lifeline to the farmers to markets and modern technologies, thus stimulating economic growth, especially in *lagging states.*

Over the next 30 years, the key challenge for India will be to build sustainable cities. Cities, especially in *urbanizing states*, would need to host burgeoning urban populations and provide new avenues for non-farm growth while also ensuring food security for those who live in them. With regard to economic growth, supporting investments in public goods such as construction of a good quality transport sector and investments in developing climate-friendly and sustainable water and solid waste disposal systems, developing a city-wide disaster fund to reduce damages from uncertain climatic events and providing investments to develop human capital through health and education investments will be required. These types of investments will improve the quality of life in cities and thus encourage participation by businesses that drive urban growth and employment opportunities. As coastlines move inwards due to climate change, governments would also have to be prepared for urban displacements and its impact on urban food security. Relocation of those who are poor but live near the coastline should be a focus on urban development plans.

Urban food security is another major issue for the future (Tacoli, Bukhari, & Fisher, 2013). As weather changes increase uncertainty in food production, an increase in volatility of prices will also impact urban food security. Creating an investment climate that develops efficiencies along the urban food supply chains will be essential to reduce food and nutrient loss. Also, connecting local urban supply chain to the global food supply chain will be an essential strategy for maintaining urban food security. As incomes per capita in these areas increase, instituting safety net measures for the urban poor, such as UBI, employment insurance and health insurance, will be essential to ensure overall urban development and food security as we look ahead.

11.4.4 Encouraging the Private Sector and Climate-Smart Citizens to Participate and Innovate in the Growth Process

Hart (1995, 1997) shows that businesses pursuing sustainable development strategies and developing environmentally and socially responsible products have the potential to increase their long-term profitability and hence it is socially optimum for them to do so. As consumers become more conscious of sustainability as a brand and consumers demand more accountability from companies in their supply chain and labor hiring practices, developing the investment climate to encourage environmentally friendly business practices should be encouraged in India. Currently, many experts in India wrongly argue that the country should be allowed to continue along its emissions pathways since we cannot have economic development opportunities void of emissions. This type of short-term thinking can lead to significant economic losses in the future.

With regard to creating new employment opportunities for growth, creating an investment climate that encourages sustainable businesses and business practices is required. The private sector can play a role in both helping with climate change mitigation and economic development as long as they are incentivized with appropriate intellectual property rights and are guaranteed returns to their investments. Currently, regulation on the part of the government in the form of urban land ceiling rules, inflexible labor and employment policies and stringent bankruptcy laws create opportunities for rent-seeking on behalf of the government and increase the cost of doing business. Removing these hurdles while also incentivizing venture capital investments in developing sustainable businesses will be an essential step towards ensuring long-term economic development.

302 P. PINGALI ET AL.

Pingali and Aiyar (2018) suggest the integration of all individuals, firms and governments across countries into global carbon markets. The authors envision that this would help in climate mitigation in the following ways. First, individuals when financially motivated may be more likely to invest in climate-friendly technologies and purchase climate-friendly production. For example, farmers who invest in organic farms or sustainable agriculture practices can earn points from the carbon markets in addition to the revenues they make through the sales of these products. This, in turn, would incentivize firms to invest in environment-friendly technologies that lead to the development of low emissions goods and services (Lal et al., 2007; Lehmann, 2007; Lohmann et al., 2006; Montagnini & Nair, 2004; Jindal et al., 2008). However, to benefit from such a decentralized process, governments need to play a role in monitoring and measurement. Research and development into satellite technology to monitor progress, providing public research services in areas where business development is not possible and penalizing those who cheat on these markets will encourage greater compliance in & credibility of carbon trading (Fawcett, 2010; Lohmann et al., 2006). At the global level, governments can discuss progress made and set agenda on emissions reductions and clean up as we look ahead.

11.5 Conclusion

Through the various chapters in the book, we have shared the contradictions that have come to represent the India growth story. To start with, fast-growing per capita incomes have not been met with a similar pace in the reduction of either undernutrition or micronutrient deficiencies in the country. These nutritional deficiencies are outcomes of inadequate access to food (and nutrients), which are outcomes of low incomes per capita. Even as policy makers continue to fight the battle against this undernutrition, on the other end of the spectrum, the prevalence of obesity, an outcome of over-nutrition, has been on the increase. Obesity rates are keeping close pace with the growth in per capita incomes even as undernutrition reduction remains a sticky challenge. The significant fallout of increasing obesity is the risk it poses for the growth of non-communicable diseases (NCD). In combination with the growing triple burden of malnutrition, increasing incidence of NCDs poses an exponential threat for economic and health security for the future food systems in India. Second, economic growth and increasing household incomes are known to be necessary for improving nutritional outcomes. Higher purchasing power enables a better command over household resources and hence improves access to better quality food. In line with this hypothesis, in states with high economic growth, policy makers have been successful in improving food security and reducing undernutrition. However, these states now face the challenge of tackling over-nutrition and NCDs related to this malnutrition. In states with low incomes per capita, on the other hand, high undernutrition persists. Even though there have been a large number of interventions focused on reducing this nutrition burden across the country, progress towards achieving the sustainable development goal of zero hunger and malnutrition has been slow. Thus, this regional inequality in nutritional outcomes is also reflected in the regional (state-wise) disparities in economic growth.

Third, within a state, the pace of household income growth and economic development has been determined by the structural transformation strategy chosen by the state for its development. The success of these strategies in enabling state-wise economic transformation has depended upon resource endowments of the states, global and local demand as well as their political priorities. Stark differences in regional development patterns have arisen in part due to differences in comparative advantages across states that have been based on access to agro-ecological zones, natural resource endowments, differences in institutional capacity and preferences for certain types of development strategies. These differences have mediated the speed of economic transformation across states. This has caused the country to develop such that some states now resemble low-income countries from sub-Saharan Africa while other states look more similar to high-income countries from Latin America. Fourth, the primary driver of this growing regional inequality has been the continued reliance of agricultural development strategies on *staple grain production*-driven growth. By focusing on staples as the foundation for agricultural development and therefore economic growth, national economic development policy has inadvertently created and entrenched regional disparities in growth. While the national staple grain promoting policies played an important role to ensure calorie sufficiency across the country, it also inhibited diversification of the food systems, reduced local nutrient availability and led to the faster development of regions with comparative advantages in staple crop production vis-à-vis others. Widening regional income inequality has reduced access and affordability of different nutrients in household diets and contributed to the phenomenon of undernutrition in some parts of the country and rising obesity in other parts. These differences are also reflected in disparities in regional development trajectories, employment patterns, occupational patterns and incomes.

Looking ahead, we see new opportunities and challenges for the current food systems. First, higher demand for diet diversity will create new avenues for growth through diversification in the agricultural sector. Continued reliance on the staple grain policies that often lock smallholder farmers into staple grain production will prevent them from realizing net benefits from diversifying their farm production in response to the new demand. Thus, we have provided recommendations on how to facilitate the commercialization and diversification of the farm sector given these challenges. This commercialization and diversification, we believe, will be necessary for increasing on-farm nutrient availability. Technologies in agriculture can ease the land and labor constraints and increase nutrient availability in food systems provided that threats from climate change are adequately addressed. Investing in both staple and non-staple production technologies that are climate sensitive and environmentally friendly will be an important adaptation measure against the threats of climate change on the viability of the agricultural system. Improving efficiency in food supply chains is also vital for increasing nutrient availability and for linking urban growth with rural prosperity. Second, given the projections of falling fertility and an increase in aging population in the country, health technologies will be useful in reducing NCD burden only if the malnutrition pandemic is put in check. This will require additional interventions that address access to good quality food, increasing dietary diversity, improving hygiene practices and increasing access to social protection policies. Third, in order to reduce economic disparities across regions, developing region-specific growth strategies that are based on comparative advantages in states will be required. Also, investing in new comparative advantages that rely on the labor dividend and interventions that stimulate greater urban development will be required to maintain global competitiveness. For this to take place, increasing human capital through health and education interventions, reducing inequities in access to current labor markets and creating new avenues for the growth of the non-agricultural sector through entrepreneurship will be required.

References

Abraham, M., & Pingali, P. (2017). Transforming smallholder agriculture to achieve the SDGs. In L. Riesgo, S. Gomez-Y-Paloma, & K. Louhichi (Eds.), *The role of small farms in food and nutrition security*. Springer.

Aggarwal, P. K., & Mall, R. K. (2002). Climate change and rice yields in diverse agro-environments of India. II. Effect of uncertainties in scenarios and crop models on impact assessment. *Climatic Change, 52*(3), 331–343. https://doi.org/10.1023/A:1013714506779

Aggarwal, S. (2018). Do rural roads create pathways out of poverty? Evidence from India. *Journal of Development Economics, 133*, 375–395. https://doi.org/10.1016/j.jdeveco.2018.01.004

Aker, J. C., & Fafchamps, M. (2015). Mobile phone coverage and producer markets: Evidence from West Africa. *The World Bank Economic Review, 29*(2), 262–292.

Anjana, R. M., Sudha, V., Nair, D. H., Lakshmipriya, N., Deepa, M., Pradeepa, R., ... Mohan, V. (2015). Diabetes in Asian Indians—How much is preventable? Ten-year follow-up of the Chennai Urban Rural Epidemiology Study (CURES-142). *Diabetes Research and Clinical Practice, 109*(2), 253–261. https://doi.org/10.1016/j.diabres.2015.05.039

Asher, S., & Novosad, P. (2018). *Rural roads and local economic development*. Policy Research Working Paper No. WPS 8466, World Bank Group, Washington, DC.

Attanasio, O., Gomex, L. C., Heredia, P., & Vera-hernández, M. (2005). *The short-term impact of a conditional cash transfer on child health and nutrition in Colombia*. Institute of Fiscal Studies.

Banerjee, R. R. (2015). Farmers' perception of climate change, impact and adaptation strategies: A case study of four villages in the semi-arid regions of India. *Natural Hazards, 75*(3), 2829–2845.

Behrman, J. R., Parker, S. W., & Todd, P. E. (2011). Do conditional cash transfers for schooling generate lasting benefits?: A five-year followup of PROGRESA/Oportunidades. *Journal of Human Resources, 46*(1), 203–236. https://doi.org/10.1353/jhr.2011.0028

Bennett, L. (1988). The role of women in income production and intra-household allocation of resources as a determinant of child nutrition and health. *Food and Nutrition Bulletin, 10*(3), 16–26.

Biran, A., Rabie, T., Schmidt, W., Juvekar, S., Hirve, S., & Curtis, V. (2008). Comparing the performance of indicators of hand-washing practices in rural Indian households. *Tropical Medicine & International Health, 13*(2), 278–285.

Biran, A., Schmidt, W.-P., Varadharajan, K. S., Rajaraman, D., Kumar, R., Greenland, K., ... Curtis, V. (2014). Effect of a behaviour-change intervention on handwashing with soap in India (SuperAmma): A cluster-randomised trial. *The Lancet Global Health, 2*(3), e145–e154. https://doi.org/10.1016/ S2214-109X(13)70160-8

Bollyky, T. J., Templin, T., Cohen, M., & Dieleman, J. L. (2017). Lower-income countries that face the most rapid shift in noncommunicable disease burden are also the least prepared. *Health Affairs, 36*(11), 1866–1875. https://doi. org/10.1377/hlthaff.2017.0708

Buiatti, M., Christou, P., & Pastore, G. (2013). The application of GMOs in agri-culture and in food production for a better nutrition: Two different scientific points of view. *Genes & Nutrition, 8*(3), 255–270. https://doi.org/10.1007/ s12263-012-0316-4

Burtch, G., Carnahan, S., & Greenwood, B. N. (2018). Can you gig it? An empiri-cal examination of the gig economy and entrepreneurial activity. *Management Science, 64*(12), 5497–5520.

Cawley, J. (2004). The impact of obesity on wages. *The Journal of Human Resources, 39*(2), 451. https://doi.org/10.2307/3559022

Cawley, J. (2010). The economics of childhood obesity. *Health Affairs, 29*(3), 364–371. https://doi.org/10.1377/hlthaff.2009.0721

Cawley, J. (2015). An economy of scales: A selective review of obesity's economic causes, consequences, and solutions. *Journal of Health Economics, 43,* 244–268. https://doi.org/10.1016/j.jhealeco.2015.03.001

Cawley, J., & Meyerhoefer, C. (2012). The medical care costs of obesity: An instrumental variables approach. *Journal of Health Economics, 31*(1), 219–230. https://doi.org/10.1016/j.jhealeco.2011.10.003

Chandrasekhar, S., & Mehrotra, N. (2016). Doubling farmers' incomes by 2022. *Economic & Political Weekly, 51*(18), 10–13.

Colchero, M. A., Rivera-Dommarco, J., Popkin, B. M., & Ng, S. W. (2017). In Mexico, evidence of sustained consumer response two years after implementing a sugar-sweetened beverage tax. *Health Affairs, 36*(3), 564–571.

Colchero, M. A., Salgado, J. C., Unar-Munguia, M., Hernandez-Avila, M., & Rivera-Dommarco, J. A. (2015). Price elasticity of the demand for sugar sweet-ened beverages and soft drinks in Mexico. *Economics & Human Biology, 19,* 129–137.

Costa-Font, M., Gil, J. M., & Traill, W. B. (2008). Consumer acceptance, valua-tion of and attitudes towards genetically modified food: Review and implica-tions for food policy. *Food Policy, 33*(2), 99–111. https://doi.org/10.1016/j. foodpol.2007.07.002

Croppenstedt, A., Knowles, M., & Lowder, S. K. (2017). Social protection and agriculture: Introduction to the special issue. *Global Food Security, 16*(2), 0–1. https://doi.org/10.1016/j.gfs.2017.09.006

Drèze, J., & Khera, R. (2017). Recent social security initiatives in India. *World Development, 98,* 555–572. https://doi.org/10.1016/j.worlddev.2017.05.035

Ellis, F. (1998). Household strategies and rural livelihood diversification. *Journal of Development Studies, 35*(1), 1–38. https://doi.org/10.1080/00220389808422553

Fawcett, T. (2010). Personal carbon trading: A policy ahead of its time? *Energy Policy, 38*(11), 6868–6876.

Fernald, L. C. H., Gertler, P. J., & Neufeld, L. M. (2008). Role of cash in conditional cash transfer programmes for child health, growth, and development: An analysis of Mexico's Oportunidades. *Lancet, 371*(9615), 828–837. https://doi.org/10.1016/S0140-6736(08)60382-7

Fischer, R., Byerlee, D., & Edmeades, G. (2009). Can technology deliver on the yield challenge to 2050? In *How to feed the world in 2050*. Rome: FAO and Economic and Social Development Department.

Flachowsky, G., & Aulrich, K. (2001). Nutritional assessment of feeds from genetically modified organism. *Journal of Animal and Feed Sciences, 10*(Suppl. 1), 181–194. https://doi.org/10.22358/jafs/70020/2001

Gentilini, U. (2015). Revisiting the "cash versus food" debate: New evidence for an old puzzle? *The World Bank Research Observer, 31*(1), 135–167.

Graham, M., Hjorth, I., & Lehdonvirta, V. (2017). Digital labour and development: Impacts of global digital labour platforms and the gig economy on worker livelihoods. *Transfer: European Review of Labour and Research, 23*(2), 135–162.

Gross-Camp, N. D., Few, R., & Martin, A. (2015). Perceptions of and adaptation to environmental change in forest-adjacent communities in three African nations. *International Forestry Review, 17*(2), 153–164.

Handa, S., & Davis, B. (2006). The experience of conditional cash transfers in Latin America and the Caribbean. *Development Policy Review, 24*(5), 513–536. https://doi.org/10.1111/j.1467-7679.2006.00345.x

Hart, S. L. (1995). A natural-resource-based view of the firm. *Academy of Management Review, 20*(4), 986–1014.

Hart, S. L. (1997). Beyond greening: Strategies for a sustainable world. *Harvard Business Review, 75*(1), 66–77.

Jensen, R. (2010). The (perceived) returns to education and the demand for schooling. *Quarterly Journal of Economics, 125*(2), 515–548.

Jensen, R. (2012). Do labor market opportunities affect young women's work and family decisions? Experimental evidence from India. *The Quarterly Journal of Economics, 127*(2), 753–792. https://doi.org/10.1093/qje/qjs002

Jindal, R., Swallow, B., & Kerr, J. (2008, May). Forestry-based carbon sequestration projects in Africa: Potential benefits and challenges. *Natural Resources Forum, 32*(2), 116–130.

Kennedy, E., & Peters, P. (1992). Household food security and child nutrition: The interaction of income and gender of household head. *World Development, 20*(8), 1077–1085. https://doi.org/10.1016/0305-750X(92)90001-C

Khera, R. (2006). Mid-day meals in primary schools: Achievements and challenges. *Economic and Political Weekly*, *41*(46), 4742–4750. Retrieved from http://www.jstor.org/stable/4418915

Lal, R., Follett, R. F., Stewart, B. A., & Kimble, J. M. (2007). Soil carbon sequestration to mitigate climate change and advance food security. *Soil Science*, *172*(12), 943–956.

Lee, L., Rosenzweig, M. R., & Pitt, M. M. (1997). The effects of improved nutrition, sanitation, and water quality on child health in high-mortality populations. *Journal of Econometrics*, *77*(1), 209–235. https://doi.org/10.1016/S0304-4076(96)01813-1

Lehmann, J. (2007). A handful of carbon. *Nature*, *447*(7141), 143.

Leroy, J. L., Ruel, M., & Verhofstadt, E. (2009). The impact of conditional cash transfer programmes on child nutrition: A review of evidence using a programme theory framework. *Journal of Development Effectiveness*, *1*(2), 103–129. https://doi.org/10.1080/19439340902924043

Lipper, L., Thornton, P., Campbell, B. M., Baedeker, T., Braimoh, A., Bwalya, M., … Torquebiau, E. F. (2014). Climate-smart agriculture for food security. *Nature Climate Change*, *4*(12), 1068–1072. https://doi.org/10.1038/nclimate2437

Lipton, M. (1980). Migration from rural areas of poor countries: The impact on rural productivity and income distribution. *World Development*, *8*(1), 1–24. https://doi.org/10.1016/0305-750X(80)90047-9

Lobell, D. B., Schlenker, W., & Costa-Roberts, J. (2011). Climate trends and global crop production since 1980. *Science*, *333*(6042), 616–620.

Lohmann, L., Hällström, N., Österbergh, R., & Nordberg, O. (2006). *Carbon trading: A critical conversation on climate change, privatisation and power.* Uppsala: Dag Hammarskjöld Centre. Retrieved from https://www.tni.org/en/publication/carbon-trading

Maitra, C., & Rao, D. S. P. (2015). Poverty–food security nexus: Evidence from a survey of urban slum dwellers in Kolkata. *World Development*, *72*, 308–325. https://doi.org/10.1016/j.worlddev.2015.03.006

Mangyo, E. (2008). The effect of water accessibility on child health in China. *Journal of Health Economics*, *27*(5), 1343–1356.

McCullough, E. B., Pingali, P., & Stamoulis, K. G. (2008). Small farms and the transformation of food systems: An overview. In E. B. McCullough, P. L. Pingali, & K. G. Stamoulis (Eds.), *The transformation of agri-food systems: Globalisation, supply chains, and smallholder farmers* (pp. 3–46). Rome: FAO.

Meenakshi, J. V., Johnson, N. L., Manyong, V. M., DeGroote, H., Javelosa, J., Yanggen, D. R., … Meng, E. (2010). How cost-effective is biofortification in combating micronutrient malnutrition? An *ex ante* assessment. *World Development*, *38*(1), 64–75. https://doi.org/10.1016/j.worlddev.2009.03.014

Mengistie, B., Berhane, Y., & Worku, A. (2013). Household water chlorination reduces incidence of diarrhea among under-five children in rural Ethiopia: A cluster randomized controlled trial. *PLoS One, 8*(10), e77887.

Mittal, S., & Mehar, M. (2012). How mobile phones contribute to growth of small farmers? Evidence from India. *Quarterly Journal of International Agriculture, 51*(3), 227–244.

Montagnini, F., & Nair, P. K. R. (2004). Carbon sequestration: An underexploited environmental benefit of agroforestry systems. In *New vistas in agroforestry* (pp. 281–295). Dordrecht: Springer. Retrieved from http://citeseerx.ist.psu.edu/viewdoc/download?doi=10.1.1.456.8246&rep=rep1&type=pdf

Mukhopadhyay, P., Zérah, M.-H., Samanta, G., & Maria, A. (2016). *Understanding India's urban frontier: What is behind the emergence of census towns in India?* The World Bank. https://doi.org/10.1596/1813-9450-7923

Munshi, K. (2011). Strength in numbers: Networks as a solution to occupational traps. *Review of Economic Studies, 78*(3), 1069–1101. https://doi.org/10.1093/restud/rdq029

Munshi, K., & Rosenzweig, M. (2006). Traditional institutions meet the modern world: Caste, gender, and schooling choice in a globalizing economy. *American Economic Review, 96*(4), 1225–1252. https://doi.org/10.1257/aer.96.4.1225

Myers, S. S., Smith, M. R., Guth, S., Golden, C. D., Vaitla, B., Mueller, N. D., ... Huybers, P. (2017). Climate change and global food systems: Potential impacts on food security and undernutrition. *Annual Review of Public Health, 38*(1), 259–277. https://doi.org/10.1146/annurev-publhealth-031816-044356

Myers, S. S., Zanobetti, A., Kloog, I., Huybers, P., Leakey, A. D. B., Bloom, A. J., ... Usui, Y. (2014). Increasing CO_2 threatens human nutrition. *Nature, 510*(7503), 139–142.

Padel, S., & Foster, C. (2005). Exploring the gap between attitudes and behaviour: Understanding why consumers buy or do not buy organic food. *British Food Journal, 107*(8), 606–625. https://doi.org/10.1108/00070700510611002

Pingali, P., & Aiyar, A. (2018). Food, agriculture, and nutrition policy: Looking ahead to 2050. In P. P. Rachid Serraj (Ed.), *Agriculture and food systems to 2050*. World Scientific Publishing.

Pingali, P., Mittra, B., & Rahman, A. (2016, March). The bumpy road from food to nutrition security—Slow evolution of India's food policy. https://doi.org/10.1016/j.gfs.2017.05.002

Pingali, P., & Rosegrant, M. W. (1995). Agricultural commercialization and diversification: Processes and policies. *Food Policy, 20*(3), 171–185. https://doi.org/10.1016/0306-9192(95)00012-4

Pinstrup-Andersen, P. (2009). Food security: Definition and measurement. *Food Security, 1*(1), 5–7. https://doi.org/10.1007/s12571-008-0002-y

Pradhan, K. C. (2013). Unacknowledged urbanisation. *Economic and Political Weekly*. Retrieved from https://www.epw.in/journal/2013/36/special-articles/unacknowledged-urbanisation.html

Qaim, M., Stein, A. J., & Meenakshi, J. V. (2007). Economics of biofortification. *Agricultural Economics, 37*(s1), 119–133.

Rah, J. H., Cronin, A. A., Badgaiyan, B., Aguayo, V. M., Coates, S., & Ahmed, S. (2015). Household sanitation and personal hygiene practices are associated with child stunting in rural India: A cross-sectional analysis of surveys. *BMJ Open, 5*(2), e005180.

Rao, C. N., Pray, C. E., & Herring, R. J. (2018). Biotechnology for second green revolution in India: Overview of issues. In R. N. Chandrashekhar, C. E. Pray, & R. J. Herring (Eds.), *Biotechnology for a second green revolution in India* (pp. 45–74). New Delhi: Academic Foundation.

Ravallion, M. (2002). On the urbanization of poverty. *Journal of Development Economics, 68*(2), 435–442. https://doi.org/10.1016/S0304-3878(02)00021-4

Reardon, T., & Timmer, P. C. (2007). Chapter 55 Transformation of markets for agricultural output in developing countries since 1950: How has thinking changed? In *Handbook of agricultural economics* (Vol. 3, pp. 2807–2855). Elsevier. https://doi.org/10.1016/S1574-0072(06)03055-6

Reddy, A. (2016). Impact of e-markets in Karnataka, India. *Indian Journal of Agricultural Marketing, 30*(2), 31–44.

Schlenker, W., & Roberts, M. J. (2009). Nonlinear temperature effects indicate severe damages to US crop yields under climate change. *Proceedings of the National Academy of Sciences, 106*(37), 15594–15598.

Sinha, S. K., & Swaminathan, M. S. (1992). Deforestation, climate change and sustainable nutrition security: A case study of India. In N. Myers (Ed.), *Tropical forests and climate* (pp. 201–209). Dordrecht: Springer Netherlands. https://doi.org/10.1007/978-94-017-3608-4_20

Spears, D., Ghosh, A., & Cumming, O. (2013). Open defecation and childhood stunting in India: An ecological analysis of new data from 112 districts. *PLoS One, 8*(9), e73784. https://doi.org/10.1371/journal.pone.0073784

Steiner, J. L., Briske, D. D., Brown, D. P., & Rottler, C. M. (2018). Vulnerability of Southern Plains agriculture to climate change. *Climatic Change, 146*(1–2), 201–218.

Tacoli, C., Bukhari, B., & Fisher, S. (2013). *Urban poverty, food security and climate change*. Human Settlements Working Paper No. 37.

Thow, A. M., Downs, S. M., Mayes, C., Trevena, H., Waqanivalu, T., & Cawley, J. (2018). Policy and practice Fiscal policy to improve diets and prevent non-communicable diseases: From recommendations to action. *Bull World Health Organ, 96*(February), 201–210. https://doi.org/10.2471/BLT.17.195982

Timmer, P. C. (1988). Chapter 8 The agricultural transformation. *Handbook of Development Economics, 1,* 275–331. https://doi.org/10.1016/S1573-4471(88)01011-3

Townsend, R. M. (1994). Risk and insurance in village India. *Econometrica, 62*(3), 539–591.

Townsend, R. M. (1995). Consumption insurance: An evaluation of risk-bearing systems in low-income economies. *Journal of Economic Perspectives, 9*(3), 83–102. https://doi.org/10.1257/jep.9.3.83

REFERENCES

Ablett, J., Baijal, A., Beinhocker, E., Bose, A., Farrell, D., Gersch, U., ... Gupta, S. (2007). *The 'Bird of Gold': The rise of India's consumer market*. San Francisco: McKinsey Global Institute.

Abraham, M., & Pingali, P. (2017). Transforming smallholder agriculture to achieve the SDGs. In L. Riesgo, S. Gomez-Y-Paloma, & K. Louhichi (Eds.), *The role of small farms in food and nutrition security*. Springer.

Abraham, M., & Pingali, P. (2019). Shortage of pulses in India: Understanding how markets incentivize supply response. *Journal of Agribusiness in Developing and Emerging Economies*, forthcoming.

Adhikari, B. (2013). Poverty reduction through promoting alternative livelihoods: Implications for marginal drylands. *Journal of International Development, 25*(7), 947–967. https://doi.org/10.1002/jid.1820

Adhvaryu, A., & Nyshadham, A. (2016). Endowments at birth and parents' investments in children. *The Economic Journal, 126*(593), 781–820.

Aeschbach-Hertig, W., & Gleeson, T. (2012). Regional strategies for the accelerating global problem of groundwater depletion. *Nature Geoscience, 5*, 853. https://doi.org/10.1038/ngeo1617

Afridi, F. (2010). Child welfare programs and child nutrition: Evidence from a mandated school meal program in India. *Journal of Development Economics, 92*(2), 152–165. https://doi.org/10.1016/j.jdeveco.2009.02.002

Afridi, F., Mukhopadhyay, A., & Sahoo, S. (2016). Female labor force participation and child education in India: Evidence from the National Rural Employment Guarantee Scheme. *IZA Journal of Labor & Development, 5*(1), 7. https://doi.org/10.1186/s40175-016-0053-y

© The Author(s) 2019
P. Pingali et al., *Transforming Food Systems for a Rising India*,
Palgrave Studies in Agricultural Economics and Food Policy,
https://doi.org/10.1007/978-3-030-14409-8

Agarwal, B. (2010). Rethinking agricultural production collectivities. *Economic and Political Weekly, 45*(9), 64–78.

Aggarwal, P. K., & Mall, R. K. (2002). Climate change and rice yields in diverse agro-environments of India. II. Effect of uncertainties in scenarios and crop models on impact assessment. *Climatic Change, 52*(3), 331–343. https://doi.org/10.1023/A:1013714506779

Aggarwal, S. (2018). Do rural roads create pathways out of poverty? Evidence from India. *Journal of Development Economics, 133*, 375–395. https://doi.org/10.1016/j.jdeveco.2018.01.004

Aghion, P., Burgess, R., Redding, S., & Zilibotti, F. (2008). The unequal effects of liberalization: Theory and evidence from India. *American Economic Review, 98*(4), 1397–1412. https://doi.org/10.1257/aer.98.4.1397

Agüero, J. M., & Marks, M. S. (2011). Motherhood and female labor supply in the developing world: Evidence from infertility shocks. *Journal of Human Resources, 46*(4), 800–826. https://doi.org/10.1353/jhr.2011.0002

Ahmad, J. (2013). *Climate change and sustainable development in India.* New Century Publications.

Ahmad, L., Habib, R. K., Parvaze, S., & Sheraz, S. M. (2017). Agro-climatic and agro-ecological zones of India BT. In L. Ahmad, R. Habib Kanth, S. Parvaze, & S. Sheraz Mahdi (Eds.), *Experimental agrometeorology: A practical manual* (pp. 99–118). Cham: Springer International Publishing. https://doi.org/10.1007/978-3-319-69185-5_15

Ahmed, S. A., Diffenbaugh, N. S., & Hertel, T. W. (2009). Climate volatility deepens poverty vulnerability in developing countries. *Environmental Research Letters, 4*(3), 34004.

Aker, J. C. (2011). Dial "A" for agriculture: A review of information and communication technologies for agricultural extension in developing countries. *Agricultural Economics, 42*(6), 631–647. https://doi.org/10.1111/j.1574-0862.2011.00545.x

Aker, J. C., & Fafchamps, M. (2015). Mobile phone coverage and producer markets: Evidence from West Africa. *The World Bank Economic Review, 29*(2), 262–292.

Aker, J. C., Ghosh, I., & Burrell, J. (2016). The promise (and pitfalls) of ICT for agriculture initiatives. *Agricultural Economics, 47*(S1), 35–48. https://doi.org/10.1111/agec.12301

Akhtar, S., Ahmed, A., Randhawa, M. A., Atukorala, S., Arlappa, N., Ismail, T., & Ali, Z. (2013). Prevalence of vitamin A deficiency in South Asia: Causes, outcomes, and possible remedies. *Journal of Health, Population, and Nutrition, 31*(4), 413–423. Retrieved from http://www.ncbi.nlm.nih.gov/pmc/articles/PMC3905635/

Akresh, R., Verwimp, P., & Bundervoet, T. (2011). Civil war, crop failure, and child stunting in Rwanda. *Economic Development and Cultural Change, 59*(4), 777–810. https://doi.org/10.1086/660003

Akresh, R., Verwimp, P., & Bundervoet, T. (2013). Civil war, crop failure, and child stunting in Rwanda. *Economic Development and Cultural Change,* *59*(4), 777–810.

Akwabi-Ameyaw, K. (1997). Producer cooperative resettlement projects in Zimbabwe: Lessons from a failed agricultural strategy. *World Development,* *25,* 437–456.

Alaimo, K., Olson, C. M., & Frongillo, E. A., Jr. (2001). Low family income and food insufficiency in relation to overweight in US children: Is there a paradox? *Archives of Pediatrics and Adolescent Medicine, 155*(10), 1161–1167. https:// doi.org/10.1001/archpedi.155.10.1161

Alderman, H., Hoddinott, J., & Kinsey, B. (2006). Long term consequences of early childhood malnutrition. *Oxford Economic Papers, 58*(3), 450–474. https://doi.org/10.1093/oep/gpl008

Ali, M. Y., Ahmed, M. M., & Islam, M. B. (2008, April). *Homestead vegetable gardening: Meeting the need of year round vegetable requirement of farm family.* In National Workshop on Multiple Cropping held at Bangladesh Agricultural Research Council, Farmgate, Dhaka, Bangladesh, pp. 23–24.

Allen, L. H., Peerson, J. M., & Olney, D. K. (2009). Provision of multiple rather than two or fewer micronutrients more effectively improves growth and other outcomes in micronutrient-deficient children and adults. *The Journal of Nutrition, 139*(5), 1022–1030. https://doi.org/10.3945/jn.107.086199

Almond, D., & Currie, J. (2011). Killing me softly: The fetal origins hypothesis. *Journal of Economic Perspectives, 25*(3), 153–172. https://doi.org/10.1016/j. surg.2006.10.010.Use

Amirapu, A., & Subramanian, A. (2015). *Manufacturing or services? An Indian illustration of a development dilemma.* Center for Global Development Working Paper, 408.

Anjana, R. M., Sudha, V., Nair, D. H., Lakshmipriya, N., Deepa, M., Pradeepa, R., … Mohan, V. (2015). Diabetes in Asian Indians—How much is preventable? Ten-year follow-up of the Chennai Urban Rural Epidemiology Study (CURES-142). *Diabetes Research and Clinical Practice, 109*(2), 253–261. https://doi. org/10.1016/j.diabres.2015.05.039

Arimond, M., & Ruel, M. T. (2004). Dietary diversity is associated with child nutritional status: Evidence from 11 demographic and health surveys. *The Journal of Nutrition, 134*(July), 2579–2585.

Arnold, J., Javorcik, B., Lipscomb, M., & Mattoo, A. (2012). *Services reform and manufacturing performance: Evidence from India.* Retrieved from http:// www.cepr.org/pubs/new-dps/dplist.asp?dpno=8011

Arora, N. K., Pillai, R., Dasgupta, R., & Garg, P. R. (2014). Whole-of-society monitoring framework for sugar, salt, and fat consumption and noncommunicable diseases in India. *Annals of the New York Academy of Sciences, 1331*(1), 157–173. https://doi.org/10.1111/nyas.12555

Asano-Tamanoi, M. (1988). Farmers, industries, and the state: The culture of contract farming in Spain and Japan. *Comparative Studies in Society and History, 30*(3), 432–452.

Asfaw, A., & Braun, J. v. (2004). Is consumption insured against illness? Evidence on vulnerability of households to health shocks in rural Ethiopia. *Economic Development and Cultural Change, 53*(1), 115–129.

Asher, S. E., & Novosad, P. M. (2018). *Rural roads and local economic development.* Policy Research Working Paper 8466, World Bank Group, Washington, DC.

Ashok, K., Uma, K., Prahadeeswaran, M., & Jeyanthi, H. (2018). Economic and environmental performance of Bt cotton in India. In C. N. Rao, C. E. Pray, & R. J. Herring (Eds.), *Biotechnology for a second green revolution in India* (pp. 325–350). Academic Foundation.

Attanasio, O., Gomex, L. C., Heredia, P., & Vera-hernández, M. (2005). *The short-term impact of a conditional cash transfer on child health and nutrition in Colombia.* Institute of Fiscal Studies.

Attwood, D. W. (1982). *Class interests and changes in the organisation of production in the Indian sugar industry.* Paper presented at the annual meeting of the Social Science History Association (Vol. Bloomington).

Attwood, D. W. (1987). Social and political preconditions for successful cooperatives: The cooperative sugar factories of western India. In D. W. Attwood & B. S. Baviskar (Eds.), *Cooperatives and rural development.* New Delhi and Oxford: Oxford University Press.

Auffhammer, M., Ramanathan, V., & Vincent, J. R. (2006). Integrated model shows that atmospheric brown clouds and greenhouse gases have reduced rice harvests in India. *Proceedings of the National Academy of Sciences, 103*(52), 19668–19672.

Azadbakht, L., & Esmaillzadeh, A. (2011). Dietary diversity score is related to obesity and abdominal adiposity among Iranian female youth. *Public Health Nutrition, 14*(1), 62–69.

Azam, M. (2012). *The impact of Indian job guarantee scheme on labor market outcomes: Evidence from a natural experiment.* IZA Working Paper 6548, World Bank, pp. 1–34. https://doi.org/10.2139/ssrn.1941959

Babatunde, R. O., & Qaim, M. (2010). Impact of off-farm income on food security and nutrition in Nigeria. *Food Policy, 35*(4), 303–311. https://doi.org/10.1016/j.foodpol.2010.01.006

Baez, J. E., & Santos, I. V. (2007). Children's vulnerability to weather shocks: A natural disaster as a natural experiment. Syracuse University, Mimeo.

Baird, S., McIntosh, C., & Özler, B. (2011). Cash or condition? Evidence from a cash transfer experiment. *Quarterly Journal of Economics, 126*(4), 1709–1753. https://doi.org/10.1093/qje/qjr032

Bajpai, N., & Sachs, J. D. (1996). *Trends in inter-state inequalities of income in India.* Development Discussion Papers (No. 528), p. 25.

Balarajan, Y., & Reich, M. R. (2016). Political economy of child nutrition policy: A qualitative study of India's Integrated Child Development Services (ICDS) scheme. *Food Policy, 62,* 88–98. https://doi.org/10.1016/j.foodpol.2016.05.001

Balasubramanian, S. (2015). Is the PDS already a cash transfer? Rethinking India's food subsidy policies. *The Journal of Development Studies, 51*(6), 642–659. https://doi.org/10.1080/00220388.2014.997221

Ballabh, V., & Walker, T. S. (1992). Land fragmentation and consolidation in dry semi-arid tropics of India. *Artha Vijnana, 34*(4), 363–387.

Banerjee, L. (2007). Effect of flood on agricultural wages in Bangladesh: An empirical analysis. *World Development, 35*(11), 1989–2009.

Banerjee, R. R. (2015). Farmers' perception of climate change, impact and adaptation strategies: A case study of four villages in the semi-arid regions of India. *Natural Hazards, 75*(3), 2829–2845.

Bardhan, P. (1973). Size, productivity and returns to scale: An analysis of farmlevel data in Indian agriculture. *Journal of Political Economy, 81*(6), 1370–1386.

Bardhan, P. (1996). *The nature of institutional impediments to economic development* (C96-066). Berkley: Center for International & Development Research. https://ageconsearch.umn.edu/record/233429/files/cal-cider-c096-066.pdf

Barrett, C. B., Bachke, M. E., Bellemare, M. F., Michelson, H. C., Narayanan, S., & Walker, T. F. (2012). Smallholder participation in contract farming: Comparative evidence from five countries. *World Development, 40*(4), 715–730. https://doi.org/10.1016/j.worlddev.2011.09.006

Barrett, C. B., Christian, P., & Shiferaw, B. A. (2017). The structural transformation of African agriculture and rural spaces: Introduction to a special section. *Agricultural Economics, 48*(5), 1–9. https://doi.org/10.1111/agec.12382

Barrett, H. R., Browne, A. W., Hyder, A. A., Maman, S., Nyoni, J. E., Khasiani, S. A., … Sohani, S. (2005). The pervasive triad of food security, gender inequity and women's health: Exploratory research from sub-Saharan Africa. *Community Development Journal, 29*(3), 203–214.

Basu, S. (1997). Why institutional credit agencies are reluctant to lend to the rural poor: A theoretical analysis of the Indian rural credit market. *World Development, 25*(2), 267–280. https://doi.org/10.1016/S0305-750X(96)00103-9

Baviskar, B. S. (1987). Cooperatives and rural development in India. *Current Anthropology, 28*(4), 564–565.

Behrman, J. R., & Deolalikar, A. B. (1990). The intrahousehold demand for nutrients in rural South India individual estimates, fixed effects, and permanent income. *The Journal of Human Resources, 25*(4), 665–696.

Behrman, J. R., & Deolalikar, A. B. (1993). The intrahousehold distribution of market labour supply in rural South India. *Oxford Bulletin of Economics and Statistics, 55*(4), 409–421.

Behrman, J. R., Parker, S. W., & Todd, P. E. (2011). Do conditional cash transfers for schooling generate lasting benefits?: A five-year followup of PROGRESA/Oportunidades. *Journal of Human Resources, 46*(1), 203–236. https://doi.org/10.1353/jhr.2011.0028

Bell, C. (1990). Reforming property rights in land and tenancy. *World Bank Research Observer, 5*(2), 143–166.

Bellemare, M. F. (2012). As you sow, so shall you reap: The welfare impacts of contract farming. *World Development, 40*(7), 1418–1434. https://doi.org/10.1016/j.worlddev.2011.12.008

Bellemare, M. F. (2015). Rising food prices, food price volatility, and social unrest. *American Journal of Agricultural Economics, 97*(1), 1–21. https://doi.org/10.1093/ajae/aau038

Benjamin, D. (1995). Can unobserved land quality explain the inverse productivity relationship? *Journal of Development Economics, 46*, 51–84.

Benjamin, D., Reardon, T., Stamoulis, K. G., & Winters, P. (2002). *Promoting farm/non-farm linkages for rural development—Case studies from Africa & Latin America*. Rome: FAO.

Bennett, L. (1988). The role of women in income production and intra-household allocation of resources as a determinant of child nutrition and health. *Food and Nutrition Bulletin, 10*(3), 16–26.

Benziger, V. (1996). Helping small farmers make transition to high value added crops. *World Development, 24*(11), 1681–1693.

Berdegué, J. A., Balsevich, F., Flores, L., & Reardon, T. (2005). Central American supermarkets' private standards of quality and safety in procurement of fresh fruits and vegetables. *Food Policy, 30*(3), 254–269.

Bernstein, H. (2010). *Class dynamics of agrarian change*. West Hartford, CT: Kumarian Press.

Berti, P. R., Krasevec, J., & FitzGerald, S. (2004). A review of the effectiveness of agriculture interventions in improving nutrition outcomes. *Public Health Nutrition, 7*(5), 599–609. https://doi.org/10.1079/PHN2003595

Besley, T. (1995a). Property rights and investment incentives: Theory and evidence from Ghana. *Journal of Political Economy, 103*(5), 903–937.

Besley, T. (1995b). Savings, credit and insurance. In J. Behrman & T. N. Srinivasan (Eds.), *The handbook of developmental economics* (pp. 2124–2207). Amsterdam: Elsevier Science Publishers, B.V.

Besley, T., & Burgess, R. (2002). The political economy of government responsiveness: Theory and evidence from India. *The Quarterly Journal of Economics, 117*(4), 1415–1451.

Bhaduri, A. (1977). On the formation of usurious interest rates in backward agriculture. *Cambridge Journal of Economics, 1*(4), 341–352.

Bhagat, R. B. (2017). *Migration and urban transition in India: Implications for development migration and urban transition in India: Implications for development*. United Nations expert group meeting on Sustainable Cities, Human Mobility and International Migration. Retrieved from http://www.un.org/en/development/desa/population/events/pdf/expert/27/papers/V/paper-Bhagat-final.pdf

Bhalla, G. S., & Singh, G. (1997). Recent developments in Indian agriculture: A state level analysis. *Economic and Political Weekly, 32*(13), A2–A18.

Bhalla, G. S., & Singh, G. (2010). *Growth of Indian agriculture: A district level study*. Final report submitted to Planning Commission, Government of India, New Delhi.

Bhalla, G. S., & Tyagi, D. S. (1989). Spatial pattern of agricultural development in India. *Economic and Political Weekly, 24*(25), 46–56.

Bhalla, S. (1979). Real wage rates of agricultural labourers in Punjab, 1961–77: A preliminary analysis. *Economic and Political Weekly, 14*(26), A57–A68. Retrieved from http://www.jstor.org/stable/4367735

Bhalla, S. S., & Roy, P. (1988). Mis-specification in farm productivity analysis: The role of land quality. *Oxford Economic Papers, 40*(1), 55–73.

Bhanja, S. N., Mukherjee, A., Rodell, M., Wada, Y., Chattopadhyay, S., Velicogna, I., ... Famiglietti, J. S. (2017). Groundwater rejuvenation in parts of India influenced by water-policy change implementation. *Scientific Reports, 7*(1), 7453. https://doi.org/10.1038/s41598-017-07058-2

Bharadwaj, K. (1985). A view on commercialisation in Indian agriculture and the development of capitalism. *Journal of Peasant Studies, 12*(4), 7–25.

Bhattacharya, B. B., & Sakthivel, S. (2004). Regional growth disparity in India: Comparison of pre- and post-reform decades. *Economic and Political Weekly, 39*(10), 1071–1077.

Bhattacharyya, B. (1985). The role of family decision in internal migration: The case of India. *Journal of Development Economics, 18*, 51–66.

Bhattacharyya, R., Ghosh, B. N., Mishra, P. K., Mandal, B., Rao, C. S., Sarkar, D., ... Franzluebbers, A. J. (2015). Soil degradation in India: Challenges and potential solutions. *Sustainability, 7*(4), 3528–3570. https://doi.org/10.3390/su7043528

Binswanger-Mkhize, H. P. (2012). India 1960–2010: Structural change, the rural non-farm sector, and the prospects for agriculture. In *Center on Food Security and the Environment Stanford Symposium Series on Global Food Policy and Food Security in the 21st Century, Stanford University*. Citeseer.

Binswanger-Mkhize, H. P. (2013). The stunted structural transformation of the Indian economy: Agriculture, manufacturing and the rural non-farm sector. *Economic and Political Weekly, 48*, 5–13. Retrieved from https://www.epw.in/journal/2013/26-27/review-rural-affairs-review-issues/stuntedstructural-transformation-indian

Binswanger, H. P., & Khandker, S. (1992). *The impact of formal finance on the rural economy of India* (No. 949). Washington, DC.

Binswanger, H. P., & Rosenzweig, M. R. (1986). Behavioural and material determinants of production relations in agriculture. *Journal of Development Studies, 22*, 503–539.

Binswanger, H. P., & Singh, S. K. (2017). Wages, prices and agriculture: How can Indian agriculture cope with rising wages? *Journal of Agricultural Economics, 69*(2), 281–305. https://doi.org/10.1111/1477-9552.12234

Biran, A., Rabie, T., Schmidt, W., Juvekar, S., Hirve, S., & Curtis, V. (2008). Comparing the performance of indicators of hand-washing practices in rural Indian households. *Tropical Medicine & International Health, 13*(2), 278–285.

Biran, A., Schmidt, W.-P., Varadharajan, K. S., Rajaraman, D., Kumar, R., Greenland, K., ... Curtis, V. (2014). Effect of a behaviour-change intervention on handwashing with soap in India (SuperAmma): A cluster-randomised trial. *The Lancet Global Health, 2*(3), e145–e154. https://doi.org/10.1016/S2214-109X(13)70160-8

Birner, R., & Resnick, D. (2010). The political economy of policies for small-holder agriculture. *World Development, 38*(10), 1442–1452. https://doi.org/10.1016/j.worlddev.2010.06.001

Birthal, P. S., Jha, A. K., Tiongco, M. M., & Narrod, C. (2009). Farm-level impacts of vertical coordination of the food supply chain: Evidence from contract farming of milk in India. *Indian Journal of Agricultural Economics, 64*(3), 481–496.

Birthal, P. S., Joshi, P. K., & Gulati, A. (2005). *Vertical coordination in high value commodities: Implications for the smallholders.* Washington, DC: IFPRI.

Black, R. E., Victora, C. G., Walker, S. P., Bhutta, Z. A., Christian, P., de Onis, M., ... Uauy, R. (2013). Maternal and child undernutrition and overweight in low-income and middle-income countries. *The Lancet, 382*(9890), 427–451. https://doi.org/10.1016/S0140-6736(13)60937-X

Bobonis, G. J., Miguel, E., & Sharma, C. P. (2004). *Iron deficiency anemia and school participation.* Poverty Action Lab Paper (No. 7), pp. 1118–1120.

Bollyky, T. J., Templin, T., Cohen, M., & Dieleman, J. L. (2017). Lower-income countries that face the most rapid shift in noncommunicable disease burden are also the least prepared. *Health Affairs, 36*(11), 1866–1875. https://doi.org/10.1377/hlthaff.2017.0708

Bonesrønning, H. (2010). Are parental effort allocations biased by gender? *Education Economics, 18*(3), 253–268. https://doi.org/10.1080/09645290902843514

Boomiraj, K., Chakrabarti, B., Aggarwal, P. K., Choudhary, R., & Chander, S. (2010). Assessing the vulnerability of Indian mustard to climate change. *Agriculture, Ecosystems & Environment, 138*(3–4), 265–273.

Boselie, D. (2002). *Business case description: TOPS supply chain project, Thailand.* Den Bosch: Agri Supply Chain Development Program, Agrichain Competence Center, KLICT International.

Boselie, D., Henson, S., & Weatherspoon, D. (2003). Supermarket procurement practices in developing countries: Redefining the roles of the public and private sectors. *American Journal of Agricultural Economics, 85*(5), 1155–1161.

Brabin, B. J., Hakimi, M., & Pelletier, D. (2001). An analysis of anemia and pregnancy-related maternal mortality. *The Journal of Nutrition, 131*(2), 604S–615S.

Breman, J. (2016). At work in the informal economy of India: A perspective from the bottom up (OIP). *OUP Catalogue.*

Brenkert, A. L., & Malone, E. L. (2005). Modeling vulnerability and resilience to climate change: A case study of India and Indian states. *Climatic Change, 72*(1), 57–102. https://doi.org/10.1007/s10584-005-5930-3

Brinkman, H.-J., de Pee, S., Sanogo, I., Subran, L., & Bloem, M. W. (2010). High food prices and the global financial crisis have reduced access to nutritious food and worsened nutritional status and health. *The Journal of Nutrition, 140*(1), 153S–161S. https://doi.org/10.3945/jn.109.110767

Briones, R. M. (2015). Small farmers in high-value chains: Binding or relaxing constraints to inclusive growth? *World Development, 72*, 43–52. https://doi.org/10.1016/j.worlddev.2015.01.005

Buiatti, M., Christou, P., & Pastore, G. (2013). The application of GMOs in agriculture and in food production for a better nutrition: Two different scientific points of view. *Genes & Nutrition, 8*(3), 255–270. https://doi.org/10.1007/s12263-012-0316-4

Burke, M., Hsiang, S. M., & Miguel, E. (2015). Global non-linear effect of temperature on economic production. *Nature, 527*(7577), 235–239.

Burney, J. A., Davis, S. J., & Lobell, D. B. (2010). Greenhouse gas mitigation by agricultural intensification. *Proceedings of the National Academy of Sciences, 107*(26), 12052–12057.

Burney, J., & Ramanathan, V. (2014). Recent climate and air pollution impacts on Indian agriculture. *Proceedings of the National Academy of Sciences, 111*(46), 16319–16324.

Burtch, G., Carnahan, S., & Greenwood, B. N. (2018). Can you gig it? An empirical examination of the gig economy and entrepreneurial activity. *Management Science, 64*(12), 5497–5520.

Busert, L. K., Neuman, M., Rehfuess, E. A., Dulal, S., Harthan, J., Chaube, S. S., ... Manandhar, D. S. (2016). Dietary diversity is positively associated with deviation from expected height in rural Nepal—3. *The Journal of Nutrition, 146*(7), 1387–1393.

Buvik, A., & John, G. (2000). When does vertical coordination improve industrial purchasing relationships? *Journal of Marketing, 64*(4), 52–64.

Byerlee, D., de Janvry, A., & Sadoulet, E. (2009). Agriculture for development: Toward a new paradigm. *Annual Review of Resource Economics, 1*, 15–31.

Byjesh, K., Kumar, S. N., & Aggarwal, P. K. (2010). Simulating impacts, potential adaptation and vulnerability of maize to climate change in India. *Mitigation and Adaptation Strategies for Global Change, 15*(5), 413–431.

Campbell, B. M., Vermeulen, S. J., Aggarwal, P. K., Corner-Dolloff, C., Girvetz, E., Loboguerrero, A. M., ... Wollenberg, E. (2016). Reducing risks to food security from climate change. *Global Food Security, 11*, 34–43. https://doi.org/10.1016/j.gfs.2016.06.002

Carletto, C., Corral, P., & Guelfi, A. (2017). Agricultural commercialization and nutrition revisited: Empirical evidence from three African countries. *Food Policy, 67*, 106–118. https://doi.org/10.1016/j.foodpol.2016.09.020

Carrand, M., & Hartl, M. (2010). *Lightening the load: Labor-saving technologies and practices for rural women*. International Fund for Agricultural Development (IFAD)/Practical Action Publishing Ltd.

Carter, M. R., & Barrett, C. B. (2006). The economics of poverty traps and persistent poverty: An asset-based approach. *The Journal of Development Studies, 42*(2), 178–199. https://doi.org/10.1080/00220380500405261

Case, A., & Ardington, C. (2006). The impact of parental death on school outcomes: Longitudinal evidence from South Africa. *Demography, 43*(3), 401–420.

Cawley, J. (2004). The impact of obesity on wages. *The Journal of Human Resources, 39*(2), 451. https://doi.org/10.2307/3559022

Cawley, J. (2010). The economics of childhood obesity. *Health Affairs, 29*(3), 364–371. https://doi.org/10.1377/hlthaff.2009.0721

Cawley, J. (2015). An economy of scales: A selective review of obesity's economic causes, consequences, and solutions. *Journal of Health Economics, 43*, 244–268. https://doi.org/10.1016/j.jhealeco.2015.03.001

Cawley, J., & Meyerhoefer, C. (2012). The medical care costs of obesity: An instrumental variables approach. *Journal of Health Economics, 31*(1), 219–230. https://doi.org/10.1016/j.jhealeco.2011.10.003

Census. (2001). *Migration Tables. Census of India* (Vol. 1).

Chakravorty, S. (2003). Industrial location in post-reform India: Patterns of inter-regional divergence and intra-regional convergence. *Journal of Development Studies, 40*(2), 120–152. https://doi.org/10.1080/00220380412331293797

Chakravorty, S., Chandrasekhar, S., & Naraparaju, K. (2016). *Income generation and inequality in India's agricultural sector: The consequences of land fragmentation*. Indira Gandhi Institute of Development Research, Mumbai Working Papers. Indira Gandhi Institute of Development Research, Mumbai, India. Retrieved from https://econpapers.repec.org/RePEc:ind:igiwpp:2016-028

Challinor, A. J., Watson, J., Lobell, D. B., Howden, S. M., Smith, D. R., & Chhetri, N. (2014). A meta-analysis of crop yield under climate change and adaptation. *Nature Climate Change, 4*(4), 287.

Chand, R. (2012). Development policies and agricultural markets. *Economic and Political Weekly, 47*(52), 53–63.

Chand, R., Saxena, R., & Rana, S. (2015). Estimates and analysis of farm income in India, 1983–84 to 2011–12. *Economic and Political Weekly, 50*(22), 139–145.

Chand, R., Srivastava, S. K., & Singh, J. (2017). *Changing structure of rural economy of India implications for employment and growth*. New Delhi: NITI Aayog.

Chandrasekhar, S. (2011). Workers commuting between the rural and urban: Estimates from NSSO data. *Economic and Political Weekly, 46*(46), 22–25. Retrieved from http://www.jstor.org/stable/41319397

Chandrasekhar, S., & Mehrotra, N. (2016). Doubling farmers' incomes by 2022. *Economic & Political Weekly, 51*(18), 10–13.

Chandrasekhar, S., & Mukhopadhyay, A. (2017). The changing nature of rurality: Reframing the discourse on migration and commuting. In *Rural labour mobility in times of structural transformation* (pp. 183–207). Singapore: Springer Singapore. https://doi.org/10.1007/978-981-10-5628-4_9

Chappell, A., Baldock, J., & Sanderman, J. (2015). The global significance of omitting soil erosion from soil organic carbon cycling schemes. *Nature Climate Change, 6,* 187.

Chatterjee, U., Murgai, R., Narayan, A., & Rama, M. (2016). *Pathways to reducing poverty and sharing prosperity in India: Lessons from the last two decades.* World Bank.

Chatterjee, U., Murgai, R., & Rama, M. (2015). Employment outcomes along the rural-urban gradation. *Economic & Political Weekly, 50*(26 & 27), 5–10. Retrieved from http://www.epw.in/system/files/pdf/2015_50/26-27/Employment_Outcomes_along_the_RuralUrban_Gradation.pdf

Chaudhuri, A., & Maitra, P. (1997). *Determinants of land tenure contracts; Theory and evidence from rural India.* Department of Economics—Departmental Working Papers.

Chaudhuri, B., Chatterjee, B., Mazumdar, M., & Karim, S. (2017). Income ranking of Indian states and their pattern of urbanisation. In E. Denis & M.-H. Zérah (Eds.), *Subaltern urbanisation in India. Exploring urban change in South Asia* (pp. 91–118). https://doi.org/10.1007/978-81-322-3616-0_4

Chen, Y., & Zhou, L.-A. (2007). The long-term health and economic consequences of the 1959–1961 famine in China. *Journal of Health Economics, 26*(4), 659–681.

Chenery, H. B. (1960). Patterns of industrial growth. *American Economic Review, 50*(4), 624–654.

Christiaensen, L., Demery, L., & Kuhl, J. (2011). The (evolving) role of agriculture in poverty reduction—An empirical perspective. *Journal of Development Economics, 96*(2), 239–254. https://doi.org/10.1016/j.jdeveco.2010.10.006

Christiaensen, L., & Todo, Y. (2014). Poverty reduction during the rural–urban transformation—The role of the missing middle. *World Development, 63,* 43–58. https://doi.org/10.1016/j.worlddev.2013.10.002

Chu-Ping, L. (2010). Perishability as a determinant of vertical coordination. *China Agricultural Economic Review, 2*(1), 49–62. https://doi.org/10.1108/17561371011017496

Ciais, P., Reichstein, M., Viovy, N., Granier, A., Ogée, J., Allard, V., … Carrara, A. (2005). Europe-wide reduction in primary productivity caused by the heat and drought in 2003. *Nature, 437*(7058), 529–533.

Clasen, T., Boisson, S., Routray, P., Torondel, B., Bell, M., Cumming, O., … Schmidt, W. P. (2014). Effectiveness of a rural sanitation programme on diarrhoea, soil-transmitted helminth infection, and child malnutrition in Odisha, India: A cluster-randomised trial. *The Lancet Global Health, 2*(11), e645–e653. https://doi.org/10.1016/S2214-109X(14)70307-9

Colchero, M. A., Rivera-Dommarco, J., Popkin, B. M., & Ng, S. W. (2017). In Mexico, evidence of sustained consumer response two years after implementing a sugar-sweetened beverage tax. *Health Affairs, 36*(3), 564–571.

Colchero, M. A., Salgado, J. C., Unar-Munguia, M., Hernandez-Avila, M., & Rivera-Dommarco, J. A. (2015). Price elasticity of the demand for sugar sweetened beverages and soft drinks in Mexico. *Economics & Human Biology, 19*, 129–137.

Coovadia, H. M., Rollins, N. C., Bland, R. M., Little, K., Coutsoudis, A., Bennish, M. L., & Newell, M.-L. (2007). Mother-to-child transmission of HIV-1 infection during exclusive breastfeeding in the first 6 months of life: An intervention cohort study. *The Lancet, 369*(9567), 1107–1116.

Costa-Font, M., Gil, J. M., & Traill, W. B. (2008). Consumer acceptance, valuation of and attitudes towards genetically modified food: Review and implications for food policy. *Food Policy, 33*(2), 99–111. https://doi.org/10.1016/j.foodpol.2007.07.002

Croppenstedt, A., Knowles, M., & Lowder, S. K. (2017). Social protection and agriculture: Introduction to the special issue. *Global Food Security, 16*(2), 0–1. https://doi.org/10.1016/j.gfs.2017.09.006

Cruz, R. V., Harasawa, H., Lal, M., Wu, S., Anokhin, Y., Punsalmaa, B., … Ninh, N. H. (2007). Asia. In M. L. Parry, O. F. Canziani, J. P. Palutikof, P. J. van der Linden, & C. E. Hanson (Eds.), *Climate change 2007: Impacts adaptation and vulnerability. Contribution of Working Group II to the Fourth Assessment Report of the Intergovernmental Panel on Climate Change* (pp. 469–506). Cambridge: Cambridge University Press.

Currie, J., & Moretti, E. (2003). Mother's education and the intergenerational transmission of human capital: Evidence from college openings. *The Quarterly Journal of Economics, 118*(4), 1495–1532.

D'Souza, A., & Jolliffe, D. (2013). Conflict, food price shocks, and food insecurity: The experience of Afghan households. *Food Policy, 42*, 32–47. https://doi.org/10.1016/j.foodpol.2013.06.007

Daigneault, P.-M. (2014). Three paradigms of social assistance. *SAGE Open, 4*(4), 1–8. https://doi.org/10.1177/2158244014559020

De Brauw, A. (2011). Migration and child development during the food price crisis in El Salvador. *Food Policy, 36*(1), 28–40. https://doi.org/10.1016/j.foodpol.2010.11.002

de Brauw, A., & Suryanarayana, M. (2015). Linkages between poverty, food security and undernutrition: Evidence from China and India. *China Agricultural Economic Review, 7*(4), 655–667. https://doi.org/10.1108/CAER-09-2015-0117

de Janvry, A., & Subbarao, K. (1986). *Agricultural price policy and income distribution in India*. New Delhi: Oxford University Press.

de Janvry, A., Sadoulet, E., & Wolford, W. (2001). *Access to land and land policy reforms* (Vol. 3). Helsinki: UNU World Institute for Development Economics Research.

Deaton, A. (1987). Estimation of own- and cross-price elasticities from household survey data. *Journal of Econometrics, 36*(1–2), 7–30.

Deaton, A., & Drèze, J. (2009). Food and nutrition in India: Facts and interpretations. *Economic and Political Weekly, 47*(7), 42–65. https://doi.org/10.2307/40278509

Deininger, K., & Liu, Y. (2013). *Welfare and poverty impacts of India's National Rural Employment Guarantee Scheme: Evidence from Andhra Pradesh (English)*. Policy Research Working Paper No. WPS 6543, World Bank, Washington, DC.

Deininger, K., Monchuk, D., Nagarajan, H. K., & Singh, S. K. (2017). Does land fragmentation increase the cost of cultivation? Evidence from India. *The Journal of Development Studies, 53*(1), 82–98. https://doi.org/10.1080/00220388.2016.1166210

del Ninno, C., & Lundberg, M. (2005). Treading water. The long-term impact of the 1998 flood on nutrition in Bangladesh. *Economics and Human Biology, 3*(1), 67–96. https://doi.org/10.1016/j.ehb.2004.12.002

Dell, M., Jones, B. F., & Olken, B. A. (2012). Temperature shocks and economic growth: Evidence from the last half century. *American Economic Journal: Macroeconomics, 4*(3), 66–95.

Demeke, A. B., Keil, A., & Zeller, M. (2011). Using panel data to estimate the effect of rainfall shocks on smallholders food security and vulnerability in rural Ethiopia. *Climatic Change, 108*(1–2), 185–206.

Denis, E., Zerah, M.-H., & Mukhopadhyay, P. (2012). Subaltern urbanisation in India. *Economic and Political Weekly*. Retrieved from https://www.epw.in/journal/2012/30/review-urban-affairs-review-issues/subaltern-urbanisation-india.html

Deolalikar, A. B. (1988). Nutrition and labor productivity in agriculture: Estimates for rural South India. *The Review of Economics and Statistics, 70*(3), 406–413.

Desai, S., & Banerji, M. (2008). Negotiated identities: Male migration and left-behind wives in India. *Journal of Population Research, 25*(3), 337–355. https://doi.org/10.1007/BF03033894

Deshpande, R., Kailash, K. K., & Tillin, L. (2017). States as laboratories: The politics of social welfare policies in India. *India Review, 16*(1), 85–105. https://doi.org/10.1080/14736489.2017.1279928

Devaux, A., Horton, D., Velasco, C., Thiele, G., López, G., Bernet, T., … Ordinola, M. (2009). Collective action for market chain innovation in the Andes. *Collective Action for Smallholder Market Access, 34*(1), 31–38. https://doi.org/10.1016/j.foodpol.2008.10.007

Devereux, S. (2002). Can social safety nets reduce chronic poverty? *Development Policy Review*, 20(5), 657–675. https://doi.org/10.1017/S1464793106007007

Dhiman, R. C., Pahwa, S., Dhillon, G. P. S., & Dash, A. P. (2010). Climate change and threat of vector-borne diseases in India: Are we prepared? *Parasitology Research*, 106(4), 763–773. https://doi.org/10.1007/s00436-010-1767-4

Dietterich, L. H., Zanobetti, A., Kloog, I., Huybers, P., Leakey, A. D. B., Bloom, A. J., … Hasegawa, T. (2014). Increasing CO_2 threatens human nutrition. *Scientific Data*, 2, 150036.

Dileep, B. K., Grover, R. K., & Rai, K. N. (2002). Contract farming in tomato: An economic analysis. *Indian Journal of Agricultural Economics*, 52(7), 197–210.

Dinsa, G. D., Goryakin, Y., Fumagalli, E., & Suhrcke, M. (2012). Obesity and socioeconomic status in developing countries: A systematic review. *Obesity Reviews*, 13(11), 1067–1079. https://doi.org/10.1111/j.1467-789X.2012.01017.x

Dolan, C., & Humphrey, J. (2000). Governance and trade in fresh vegetables: The impact of UK supermarkets on the African horticulture industry. *Journal of Development Studies*, 37(2), 147–176.

Dorward, A., Kydd, J., Morrison, J., & Urey, I. (2004). A policy agenda for pro-poor agricultural growth. *World Development*, 32(1), 73–89.

Drewnowski, A., & Popkin, B. M. (2009). The nutrition transition: New trends in the global diet. *Nutrition Reviews*, 55(2), 31–43. https://doi.org/10.1111/j.1753-4887.1997.tb01593.x

Drèze, J., Himanshu, Khera, R., & Sen, A. (2015). Clarification on PDS leakages. *Economic and Political Weekly*, 50(39), 72–73.

Drèze, J., & Khera, R. (2017). Recent social security initiatives in India. *World Development*, 98, 555–572. https://doi.org/10.1016/j.worlddev.2017.05.035

Dubowitz, T., Levinson, D., Peterman, J. N., Verma, G., Jacob, S., & Schultink, W. (2007). Intensifying efforts to reduce child malnutrition in India: An evaluation of the Dular program in Jharkhand, India. *Food and Nutrition Bulletin*, 28(3), 266–273.

Duh, J., & Spears, D. (2016). Health and hunger: Disease, energy needs, and the Indian calorie consumption puzzle. *The Economic Journal*, 1–32. https://doi.org/10.1111/ecoj.12417

Dupont, V. (2005). *Peri-urban dynamics: Population, habitat and environment on the peripheries of large Indian metropolises: An introduction.* CSH Occasional Paper 14, Centre de Sciences Humaines, New Delhi.

Dutta, S., Ghosh, S., Gopalakrishnan, S., Bijoy, C. R., & Yasmin, H. (2013). *Climate change in India: Analysis of political economy & impact.* New Delhi: Rosa Luxemburg Stiftung-South Asia.

Dyson, T., & Maharatna, A. (1992). Bihar famine, 1966–67 and Maharashtra drought, 1970–73: The demographic consequences. *Economic and Political Weekly*, 27(26), 1325–1332.

Eastwood, R., Lipton, M., & Newell, A. (2010). Farm size. *Handbook of Agricultural Economics, 4*, 3323–3397. https://doi.org/10.1016/S1574-0072(09)04065-1

Eaton, C., & Shepherd, A. W. (2001). *Contract farming: Partnerships for growth.* Rome: FAO.

Eaton, D., Meijerink, G., & Bijman, J. (2008). *Understanding institutional arrangements—Fresh fruit and vegetable value chains in East Africa.* Markets, Chains and Sustainable Development Strategy and Policy Paper No. XX.

Ebi, K. L., & McGregor, G. (2008). Climate change, tropospheric ozone and particulate matter, and health impacts. *Environmental Health Perspectives, 116*(11), 1449.

Ellis, F. (1998). Household strategies and rural livelihood diversification. *Journal of Development Studies, 35*(1), 1–38. https://doi.org/10.1080/00220389808422553

Eswaran, M., & Kotwal, A. (1986). Access to capital and agrarian production organisation. *Economic Journal, 96*(382), 482–498.

Fafchamps, M. (2003). *Rural poverty, risk and development.* Cheltenham, UK: Edward Elgar Publishing.

Fan, S., & Chan-Kang, C. (2003). Is small beautiful? Farm size, productivity and poverty in Asian agriculture. In *Proceedings of the 25th International Conference of Agricultural Economists,* Durban, South Africa.

FAO. (2010). *The status of conservation agriculture in Southern Africa: Challenges and opportunities for expansion.* Johannesburg, South Africa.

FAO. (2015). Social protection and agriculture: Breaking the cycle of rural poverty. In *The state of food and agriculture.* Rome.

FAO. (2016). *The state of food and agriculture—Climate change, agriculture and food security.* Rome.

Fawcett, T. (2010). Personal carbon trading: A policy ahead of its time? *Energy Policy, 38*(11), 6868–6876.

Feder, G. (1985). The relation between farm size and farm productivity. *Journal of Development Economics, 18*, 297–313.

Feder, G., Just, R. E., & Zilberman, D. (1985). Adoption of agricultural innovations in developing countries: A survey. *Economic Development and Cultural Change, 33*(2), 255–298. https://doi.org/10.1086/451461

Fernald, L. C. H., Gertler, P. J., & Neufeld, L. M. (2008). Role of cash in conditional cash transfer programmes for child health, growth, and development: An analysis of Mexico's Oportunidades. *Lancet, 371*(9615), 828–837. https://doi.org/10.1016/S0140-6736(08)60382-7

Ferreira, F. H. G., & Schady, N. (2009). Aggregate economic shocks, child schooling, and child health. *The World Bank Research Observer, 24*(2), 147–181. https://doi.org/10.1093/wbro/lkp006

Ferroni, M., & Zhou, Y. (2017). The private sector and India's agricultural transformation. *Global Journal of Emerging Market Economies, 9*(1–3), 28–37. https://doi.org/10.1177/0974910117716406

Fields, G. S. (1975). Rural-urban migration, urban unemployment and underemployment, and job-search activity in LDCs. *Journal of Development Economics,* 2(2), 165–187. https://doi.org/10.1016/0304-3878(75)90014-0

Fields, G. S. (2011). Labor market analysis for developing countries. *Labour Economics,* 18(Suppl. 1), S16–S22. https://doi.org/10.1016/j. labeco.2011.09.005

Fischer, R., Byerlee, D., & Edmeades, G. (2009). Can technology deliver on the yield challenge to 2050? In *How to feed the world in 2050.* Rome: FAO and Economic and Social Development Department.

Fishman, R., Devineni, N., & Raman, S. (2015). Can improved agricultural water use efficiency save India's groundwater? *Environmental Research Letters,* 10(8), 084022.

Flachowsky, G., & Aulrich, K. (2001). Nutritional assessment of feeds from genetically modified organism. *Journal of Animal and Feed Sciences,* 10(Suppl. 1), 181–194. https://doi.org/10.22358/jafs/70020/2001

Foster, A. D., & Rosenzweig, M. R. (2007). Chapter 47, Economic development and the decline of agricultural employment (pp. 3051–3083). https://doi. org/10.1016/S1573-4471(07)04047-8

Freebairn, D. K. (1995). Did the green revolution concentrate incomes? A quantitative study of research reports. *World Development,* 23(2), 265–279. https:// doi.org/10.1016/0305-750X(94)00116-G

Gaiha, R., Jha, R., & Kulkarni, V. S. (2013). How pervasive is eating out in India? *Journal of Asian and African Studies,* 48(3), 370–386. https://doi. org/10.1177/0021909612472040

GAIN, Global Agricultural Information Report. (2017). Food and grocery product opportunities stemming from internal sector shifts. Delhi. Retrieved from https://gain.fas.usda.gov/Recent%20GAIN%20Publications/Retail%20 Foods_New%20Delhi_India_6-28-2018.pdf

Gangopadhyay, S., Lensink, R., & Yadav, B. (2015). Cash or In-kind transfers? Evidence from a randomised controlled trial in Delhi, India. *The Journal of Development Studies,* 51(6), 660–673. https://doi.org/10.1080/00220388. 2014.997219

Gentilini, U. (2015). Revisiting the "cash versus food" debate: New evidence for an old puzzle? *The World Bank Research Observer,* 31(1), 135–167.

Ghani, E., Goswami, A. G., & Kerr, W. R. (2012). *Is India's manufacturing sector moving away from cities?* Policy Research Working Papers, The World Bank. https://doi.org/10.1596/1813-9450-6271.

Ghani, E., Goswami, A. G., & Kerr, W. R. (2016). *Spatial development and agglomeration economies in services—Lessons from India.* Policy Research Working Paper No. WPS 7741, World Bank Group, Washington, DC.

Ghosh, J. (2013). Microfinance and the challenge of financial inclusion for development. *Cambridge Journal of Economics, 37*(6), 1203–1219.

Ghosh, M. (2006). Economic growth and human development in Indian states. *Economic and Political Weekly, 41*(30), 3321–3329. Retrieved from http://www.jstor.org/stable/4418499

Ghosh, P., Mookherjee, D., & Ray, D. (2001). Credit rationing in developing countries: An overview of the theory. In D. Mookherjee & D. Ray (Eds.), *Readings in the theory of economic development* (pp. 283–301). Malden, MA: Blackwell Publishing Ltd.

Gibson, J., Datt, G., Murgai, R., & Ravallion, M. (2017). For India's rural poor, growing towns matter more than growing cities. *World Development, 98*, 413–429. https://doi.org/10.1016/j.worlddev.2017.05.014

Gillespie, S., Haddad, L., Mannar, V., Menon, P., & Nisbett, N. (2013). The politics of reducing malnutrition: Building commitment and accelerating progress. *The Lancet, 382*(9891), 552–569. https://doi.org/10.1016/S0140-6736(13)60842-9

Gladwin, C. H., Thomson, A. M., Peterson, J. S., & Anderson, A. S. (2001). Addressing food security in Africa via multiple livelihood strategies of women farmers. *Food Policy, 26*(2), 177–207.

Glaeser, E. L., & Maré, D. C. (2001). Cities and skills. *Journal of Labor Economics, 19*(2), 316–342. https://doi.org/10.1086/319563

Glick, P., & Sahn, D. E. (1998). Maternal labour supply and child nutrition in West Africa. *Oxford Bulletin of Economics and Statistics, 60*(3), 325–355.

Glover, D. J. (1987). Increasing the benefits to smallholders from contract farming: Problems for farmers' organizations and policy makers. *World Development, 15*(4), 441–448.

Godfray, H. C. J., Beddington, J. R., Crute, I. R., Haddad, L., Lawrence, D., Muir, J. F., … Toulmin, C. (2010). Food security: The challenge of feeding 9 billion people. *Science, 327*(5967), 812–818. https://doi.org/10.1126/science.1185383

GOI. (2002). *Report of Inter-Ministerial Task Force on Agricultural Marketing Reforms, Department of Agriculture and Cooperation*. Retrieved from https://dmi.gov.in/Documents/ReportTaskForceAMR.pdf

GOI. (2007). *Report of the Steering Committee on Agriculture for 11th Five Year Plan*. Yojana Bhavan, New Delhi.

GOI. (2012). *Report of Task Force on Agricultural Marketing Reforms*. Directorate of Marketing and Inspection, Ministry of Agriculture and Farmers Welfare, Delhi. Retrieved from http://dmi.gov.in/Documents/ReportTaskForceAMR.pdf

GOI. (2015). *Raising agricultural productivity and making farming remunerative for farmers*. New Delhi.

GOI. (2016). *Report of the expert committee on land leasing*. New Delhi.

Gokarn, S. (2011). The price of protein. *Macroeconomics and Finance in Emerging Market Economies, 4*(2), 327–335. https://doi.org/10.1080/17520843.2011.593908

Goldman, A., & Smith, J. (1995). Agricultural transformations in India and Northern Nigeria: Exploring the nature of Green Revolutions. *World Development, 23*(2), 243–263. https://doi.org/10.1016/0305-750X(94)00115-F

Gørgens, T. (2002). Selection and stunting effects of famine: A case study of the Great Chinese Famine.

Gørgens, T., Meng, X., & Vaithianathan, R. (2012). Stunting and selection effects of famine: A case study of the Great Chinese Famine. *Journal of Development Economics, 97*(1), 99–111. https://doi.org/10.1016/j.jdeveco.2010.12.005

Government of India. (2007). *Annual report.* New Delhi.

Government of India. (2018). *Economic survey 2017–2018.*

Graham, M., Hjorth, I., & Lehdonvirta, V. (2017). Digital labour and development: Impacts of global digital labour platforms and the gig economy on worker livelihoods. *Transfer: European Review of Labour and Research, 23*(2), 135–162.

Greenstone, M., & Hanna, R. (2014). Environmental regulations, air and water pollution, and infant mortality in India. *American Economic Review, 104*(10), 3038–3072.

Griffiths, P. L., & Bentley, M. E. (2001). The nutrition transition is underway in India. *The Journal of Nutrition, 131*(10), 2692–2700. http://doi.org/0022-3166/01

Gross-Camp, N. D., Few, R., & Martin, A. (2015). Perceptions of and adaptation to environmental change in forest-adjacent communities in three African nations. *International Forestry Review, 17*(2), 153–164.

Guhathakurta, P., Sreejith, O. P., & Menon, P. A. (2011). Impact of climate change on extreme rainfall events and flood risk in India. *Journal of Earth System Science, 120*(3), 359. https://doi.org/10.1007/s12040-011-0082-5

Gulati, A., Jain, S., & Satija, N. (2014). Rising farm wages in India—The 'pull' and 'push' factors. *Journal of Land and Rural Studies, 2*(2), 261–286. https://doi.org/10.1177/2321024914534045

Gulati, S., Misra, A., Colles, S. L., Kondal, D., Gupta, N., Goel, K., ... Bhardwaj, S. (2013). Dietary intakes and familial correlates of overweight/obesity: A four-cities study in India. *Annals of Nutrition and Metabolism, 62*(4), 279–290. https://doi.org/10.1159/000346554

Gupta, R., Somanathan, E., & Dey, S. (2017). Global warming and local air pollution have reduced wheat yields in India. *Climatic Change, 140*(3–4), 593–604.

Gupta, V., Downs, S. M., Ghosh-Jerath, S., Lock, K., & Singh, A. (2016). Unhealthy fat in street and snack foods in low-socioeconomic settings in India: A case study of the food environments of rural villages and an urban slum. *Journal of Nutrition Education and Behavior, 48*(4), 269–279.e1. https://doi.org/10.1016/j.jneb.2015.11.006

Gutierrez, F. (2013, May 1). Long-term consequences of early life health shocks: Evidence from the 1980s Peruvian crisis. Available at SSRN: https://ssrn.com/abstract=2267096 or https://doi.org/10.2139/ssrn.2267096

Haggblade, S., & Hazell, P. (1989). Agricultural technology and farm-nonfarm growth linkages. *Agricultural Economics, 3*(4), 345–364.

Haggblade, S., Hazell, P., & Reardon, T. (2010). The rural non-farm economy: Prospects for growth and poverty reduction. *World Development, 38*(10), 1429–1441. https://doi.org/10.1016/j.worlddev.2009.06.008

Hallegatte, S. (2009). Strategies to adapt to an uncertain climate change. *Global Environmental Change, 19*(2), 240–247.

Hammer, J., & Spears, D. (2016). Village sanitation and child health: Effects and external validity in a randomized field experiment in rural India. *Journal of Health Economics, 48,* 135–148. https://doi.org/10.1016/j.jhealeco.2016.03.003

Handa, S., & Davis, B. (2006). The experience of conditional cash transfers in Latin America and the Caribbean. *Development Policy Review, 24*(5), 513–536. https://doi.org/10.1111/j.1467-7679.2006.00345.x

Haque, T., & Nair, J. L. (2014). *Ensuring and protecting the land leasing right of poor women in India.* Paper prepared for presentation at the "2014 World Bank Conference on Land and Poverty", The World Bank.

Harris, J. R., & Todaro, M. P. (1970). Migration, unemployment and development: A two-sector analysis. *American Economic Review, 60*(1), 126–142.

Harrison, A., & Leamer, E. (1997). Labor markets in developing countries: An agenda for research. *Journal of Labor Economics, 15*(3), S1–S19. https://doi.org/10.2307/2535423

Hart, S. L. (1995). A natural-resource-based view of the firm. *Academy of Management Review, 20*(4), 986–1014.

Hart, S. L. (1997). Beyond greening: Strategies for a sustainable world. *Harvard Business Review, 75*(1), 66–77.

Hazell, P. (2018). Urbanization, agriculture and smallholder farming. In R. Serraj & P. Pingali (Eds.), *Agriculture and food systems to 2050: Global trend, challenges and opportunities* (pp. 137–160). Singapore: World Scientific.

Hazell, P., Poulton, C., Wiggins, S., & Dorward, A. (2010). The future of small farms: Trajectories and policy priorities. *World Development, 38*(10), 1349–1361. https://doi.org/10.1016/j.worlddev.2009.06.012

Headey, D. D. (2013). Developmental drivers of nutritional change: A cross-country analysis. *World Development, 42*(1), 76–88. https://doi.org/10.1016/j.worlddev.2012.07.002

Hebbar, K. B., Venugopalan, M. V., Prakash, A. H., & Aggarwal, P. K. (2013). Simulating the impacts of climate change on cotton production in India. *Climatic Change, 118*(3–4), 701–713.

Herrendorf, B., Rogerson, R., & Valentinyi, A. (2013). Two perspectives on preferences and structural transformation. *American Economic Review, 103*(7), 2752–2789.

Herring, R. J. (2015). State science, risk and agricultural biotechnology: Bt cotton to Bt Brinjal in India. *The Journal of Peasant Studies, 42*(1), 159–186. https://doi.org/10.1080/03066150.2014.951835

Hertel, T. W., Burke, M. B., & Lobell, D. B. (2010). The poverty implications of climate-induced crop yield changes by 2030. *Global Environmental Change, 20*(4), 577–585.

Hirway, I. (2003). Identification of BPL households for poverty alleviation programmes. *Economic and Political Weekly*, 4803–4808.

Hoddinott, J. (2006). Shocks and their consequences across and within households in Rural Zimbabwe. *Journal of Development Studies, 42*(2), 201–321.

Hoddinott, J. (2008). *Social safety nets and productivity enhancing investments in agriculture*. Washington, DC: IFPRI.

Hoddinott, J., & Kinsey, B. (2001). Child growth in the time of drought. *Oxford Bulletin of Economics and Statistics, 63*(4), 409–436. https://doi.org/10.1111/1468-0084.t01-1-00227

Hoddinott, J., Maluccio, J. A., Behrman, J. R., Flores, R., & Martorell, R. (2008). Effect of a nutrition intervention during early childhood on economic productivity in Guatemalan adults. *The Lancet, 371*(9610), 411–416. https://doi.org/10.1016/S0140-6736(08)60205-6

Hoddinott, J., & Yohannes, Y. (2002). *Dietary diversity as a food security indicator*. Discussion Paper (No. 136), International Food Policy Research Institute (IFPRI), Food Consumption and Nutrition Division, Washington, DC.

Holloway, G., Nicholson, N., Delgado, C., Staal, S., & Ehui, S. (2000). Agroindustrialization through institutional innovation: Transaction costs, cooperatives and milk-market development in the east-African highlands. *Agricultural Economics, 23*, 279–288.

Horton, S., & Ross, J. (2003). The economics of iron deficiency. *Food Policy, 28*(1), 51–75.

Hossain, N., & Green, D. (2011). Living on a Spike: How is the 2011 food price crisis affecting poor people? *Oxfam Policy and Practice: Agriculture, Food and Land, 11*(5), 9–56.

Hu, D., Reardon, T., Rozelle, S., Timmer, P. C., & Wang, H. H. (2004). The emergence of supermarkets with Chinese characteristics: Challenges and opportunities for China's agricultural development. *Development Policy Review, 22*(4), 557–586.

Huang, C., Li, Z., Wang, M., & Martorell, R. (2010). Early life exposure to the 1959–1961 Chinese famine has long-term health consequences. *The Journal of Nutrition, 140*(10), 1874–1878.

Huang, J. (2006). *Taiwan in transformation, 1895–2005: The challenge of a new democracy to an old civilization*. New Brunswick, NJ: Transaction Publishers.

Ibarrola-Rivas, J. M., Kastner, T., & Nonhebel, S. (2016). How much time does a farmer spend to produce my food? An international comparison of the impact of diets and mechanization. *Resources*. https://doi.org/10.3390/resources5040047

Imai, K. S., Annim, S. K., Kulkarni, V. S., & Gaiha, R. (2014). Women's empowerment and prevalence of stunted and underweight children in rural India. *World Development, 62*, 88–105.

Imai, K. S., Gaiha, R., & Thapa, G. (2015). Does non-farm sector employment reduce rural poverty and vulnerability? Evidence from Vietnam and India. *Journal of Asian Economics, 36*, 47–61. https://doi.org/10.1016/j.asieco.2015.01.001

Imbert, C., & Papp, J. (2014). Short-term migration, rural workfare programs and urban labor markets: Evidence from India. *Center for Economic Policy Research* [Google Scholar].

IMD. (2018). *Seasonal outlook for the temperatures during March to May 2018*. Retrieved from http://www.imd.gov.in/pages/press_release_view.php?ff=20180228_pr_205

IPCC. (2014). *Mitigation of climate change. Contribution of Working Group III to the Fifth Assessment Report of the Intergovernmental Panel on Climate Change*. Cambridge, UK and New York.

Ito, J., Bao, Z., & Su, Q. (2012). Distribution effects of agricultural cooperatives in China: Exclusion of smallholders and potential gains in participation. *Food Policy, 37*(6), 700–709.

Ito, T., & Kurosaki, T. (2009). Weather risk, wages in kind, and the off-farm labor supply of agricultural households in a developing country. *American Journal of Agricultural Economics, 91*(3), 697–710. https://doi.org/10.1111/j.1467-8276.2009.01270.x

Ivanic, M., & Martin, W. (2008). Implications of higher global food prices for poverty in low-income countries. *Agricultural Economics, 39*, 405–416. https://doi.org/10.1111/j.1574-0862.2008.00347.x

Jacoby, H. G. (2017). "Well-fare" economics of groundwater in South Asia. *The World Bank Research Observer, 32*(1), 1–20.

Jacoby, H., Rabassa, M., & Skoufias, E. (2011). *Distributional implications of climate change in India (English)*. Policy Research Working Paper No. WPS 5623, World Bank Group, Washington, DC.

Jain, M. (2015). India's struggle against malnutrition—Is the ICDS program the answer? *World Development, 67*, 72–89. https://doi.org/10.1016/j.worlddev.2014.10.006

Jaruzelski, B., Staack, V., & Johnson, T. (2017). The role of private-sector R&D in agricultural innovation: Improving yields, equipment productivity, and sustainability. In S. Dutta, B. Lanvin, & S. Wunsch-Vincent (Eds.), *The global innovation index*. Ithaca, Fontainebleau, and Geneva: Cornell University, INSEAD, and WIPO.

Jayachandran, S., & Pande, R. (2017). Why are Indian children so short? The role of birth order and son preference. *American Economic Review, 107*(9), 2600–2629.

Jayal, N. G. (2013). *Citizenship and its discontents: An Indian history.* Harvard University Press.

Jayaraj, D., & Subramanian, S. (2013). On the inter-group inclusiveness of India's consumption expenditure growth. *Economic and Political Weekly, XLVIII*(10), 65–70.

Jensen, R. (2000). Agricultural volatility and investments in children. *American Economic Review, 90*(2), 399–404. https://doi.org/10.1257/aer.90.2.399

Jensen, R. (2010). The (perceived) returns to education and the demand for schooling. *Quarterly Journal of Economics, 125*(2), 515–548.

Jensen, R. (2012). Do labor market opportunities affect young women's work and family decisions? Experimental evidence from India. *The Quarterly Journal of Economics, 127*(2), 753–792. https://doi.org/10.1093/qje/qjs002

Jensen, R. T., & Miller, N. H. (2008). The impact of food price increases on caloric intake in China. *Agricultural Economics, 39*(1), 465–476. https://doi.org/10.1111/j.1574-0862.2008.00352.x

Jensen, R. T., & Miller, N. H. (2010). A revealed preference approach to measuring hunger and undernutrition (No. 16555). In Intergovernmental Panel on Climate Change (Ed.), *NBER Working Paper Series.* Cambridge, UK: Cambridge University Press.

Jha, R., Gaiha, R., & Sharma, A. (2009). Calorie and micronutrient deprivation and poverty nutrition traps in rural India. *World Development, 37*(5), 982–991. https://doi.org/10.1016/j.worlddev.2008.09.008

Jha, S., & Ramaswami, B. (2010). How can food subsidies work better? Answers from India and the Philippines. *ADB Economics Working Paper Series, 221*(221), 1–35. https://doi.org/10.2139/ssrn.1721907

Jindal, R., Swallow, B., & Kerr, J. (2008, May). Forestry-based carbon sequestration projects in Africa: Potential benefits and challenges. *Natural Resources Forum, 32*(2), 116–130.

Johnson, C., & Rogers, B. L. (1993). Children's nutritional female-headed households in the Dominican Republic. *Social Science & Medicine, 37*(11), 1293–1301.

Johnson, N. L., & Ruttan, V. W. (1994). Why are farms so small? *World Development, 22*(5), 691–706. https://doi.org/10.1016/0305-750X(94)90044-2

Johnston, B. B. F. (1970). Agriculture and structural transformation in developing countries: A survey of research. *Journal of Economic Literature, 8*(2), 369–404.

Johnston, B. B. F., & Mellor, J. W. (1961). The role of agriculture in economic development. *American Economic Review, 51*(4), 566–593.

Johnston, D., Stevano, S., Malapit, H. J., Hull, E., & Kadiyala, S. (2018). Review: Time use as an explanation for the agri-nutrition disconnect: Evidence from rural areas in low and middle-income countries. *Food Policy, 76*, 8–18. https://doi.org/10.1016/j.foodpol.2017.12.011

Jones, A. D., Hayter, A. K. M., Baker, C. P., Prabhakaran, P., Gupta, V., Kulkarni, B., ... Kumar, P. U. (2016). The co-occurrence of anemia and cardiometabolic disease risk demonstrates sex-specific sociodemographic patterning in an urbanizing rural region of southern India. *European Journal of Clinical Nutrition, 70*(3), 364–372.

Jones, A. D., Shrinivas, A., & Bezner-Kerr, R. (2014). Farm production diversity is associated with greater household dietary diversity in Malawi: Findings from nationally representative data. *Food Policy, 46*, 1–12.

Joshi, B., & Lanjouw, P. (2016). Non-farm diversification, inequality and mobility in Palanpur. *Economic and Political Weekly, 51*(26–27), 43–51.

Joshi, P., & Kumar, P. (2016). Food demand and supply projections to 2030: India. In F. Brouwer & P. K. Joshi (Eds.), *International trade and food security: The future of Indian agriculture, Part 2* (pp. 29–63). CABI Publishing.

Joy, E. J., Green, R., Agrawal, S., Aleksandrowicz, L., Bowen, L., Kinra, S., ... Dangour, A. D. (2017). Dietary patterns and non-communicable disease risk in Indian adults: Secondary analysis of Indian Migration Study data. *Public Health Nutrition, 20*, 1–10. https://doi.org/10.1017/S1368980017000416

Kaczan, D., Arslan, A., & Lipper, L. (2013). *Climate-smart agriculture? A review of current practice of agroforestry and conservation agriculture in Malawi and Zambia.* ESA Working Paper No. 13-07, Rome.

Kadiyala, S., Harris, J., Headey, D., Yosef, S., & Gillespie, S. (2014). Agriculture and nutrition in India: Mapping evidence to pathways. *Annals of the New York Academy of Sciences, 1331*(1), 43–56. https://doi.org/10.1111/nyas.12477

Kadiyala, S., Joshi, P. K., Mahendra Dev, S., Nandakumar, T., & Vyas, V. (2012). A nutrition secure India. *Economic and Political Weekly, XLVII*(8), 21–25.

Kajita, M. (1965). Land policy after land reforms in Japan. *Developing Economies, 3*(1), 88–105. https://doi.org/10.1111/j.1746-1049.1965.tb00749.x

Kalaivani, K. (2009). Prevalence & consequences of anaemia in pregnancy. *Indian Journal of Medical Research, 130*(5), 627–633.

Kapur, D., & Krishnamurthy, M. (2014). *Market towns and the dynamics of India's rural and urban transformations.* Working Paper, International Growth Center.

Kapur, D., & Nangia, P. (2015). Social protection in India: A welfare state sans public goods? *India Review, 14*(1), 73–90. https://doi.org/10.1080/147364 89.2015.1001275

Kapur, D., Sharma, S., & Agarwal, K. N. (2003). Effectiveness of nutrition education, iron supplementation or both on iron status in children. *Indian Pediatrics, 40*(12), 1131–1144.

Kattelmann, R. (2003). Glacial lake outburst floods in the Nepal Himalaya: A manageable hazard? *Natural Hazards, 28*(1), 145–154.

Kaushal, N., & Muchomba, F. M. (2015). How consumer price subsidies affect nutrition. *World Development, 74*, 25–42. https://doi.org/10.1016/j.worlddev.2015.04.006

Kebede, Y. (1992). Risk taking behaviour & new technologies: The case of producers in the Central Highlands of Ethiopia. *Quarterly Journal of International Agriculture, 31*, 269–289.

Kennedy, E., & Peters, P. (1992). Household food security and child nutrition: The interaction of income and gender of household head. *World Development, 20*(8), 1077–1085. https://doi.org/10.1016/0305-750X(92)90001-C

Kennedy, G., Ballard, T., & Dop, M. C. (2011). *Guidelines for measuring household and individual dietary diversity*. FAO.

Kennedy, G., Nantel, G., & Shetty, P. (2004). *Globalization of food systems in developing countries: Impact on food security and nutrition*. FAO.

Kennedy, L. (2017). State restructuring and emerging patterns of subnational policy-making and governance in China and India. *Environment and Planning C: Politics and Space, 35*(1), 6–24. https://doi.org/10.1177/0263774X16630551

Kes, A., & Swaminathan, H. (2006). Gender and time poverty in sub-Saharan Africa. In *Gender, time use, and poverty in Sub-Saharan Africa* (pp. 13–38). World Bank.

Khera, R. (2006). Mid-day meals in primary schools: Achievements and challenges. *Economic and Political Weekly, 41*(46), 4742–4750. Retrieved from http://www.jstor.org/stable/4418915

Khera, R. (2013). Mid-day meals: Looking ahead. *Economic & Political Weekly, 48*(32), 12–14. Retrieved from http://www.righttofoodindia.org/data/mdm/MidDay_Meals_Looking_Ahead.pdf

Khera, R. (2014). Cash vs. in-kind transfers: Indian data meets theory. *Food Policy, 46*, 116–128. https://doi.org/10.1016/j.foodpol.2014.03.009

Kherallah, M., Delgado, C., Gabre-Madhin, E., Minot, N., & Johnson, M. (2002). *Reforming agricultural markets in Africa*. Baltimore, MD: John Hopkins University.

Kidd, S. (2017). *Citizenship or charity: The two paradigms of social protection*. Pathways' Perspective on Social Policy in International Development (Issue 25).

Kingdon, G. G. (2007). The progress of school education in India. *Oxford Review of Economic Policy, 23*(2), 168–195. https://doi.org/10.1093/oxrep/grm015

Kishore, A., & Chakrabarti, S. (2015). Is more inclusive more effective? The 'New Style' public distribution system in India. *Food Policy, 55*, 117–130. https://doi.org/10.1016/j.foodpol.2015.06.006

Kjellstrom, T., Holmer, I., & Lemke, B. (2009). Workplace heat stress, health and productivity—An increasing challenge for low and middle-income countries during climate change. *Global Health Action, 2*(1), 2047.

Kochar, A. (2005). Can targeted food programs improve nutrition? An empirical analysis of India's public distribution system. *Economic Development and Cultural Change, 54*(1), 203–235. https://doi.org/10.1086/431260

Kone, Z. L., Liu, M. Y., Mattoo, A., Ozden, C., & Sharma, S. (2016). *Internal borders and migration in India*. Policy Research Working Paper No. 8244.

Koppmair, S., Kassie, M., & Qaim, M. (2017). Farm production, market access and dietary diversity in Malawi. *Public Health Nutrition, 20*(2), 325–335.

Kothawale, D. R., & Rupa Kumar, K. (2005). On the recent changes in surface temperature trends over India. *Geophysical Research Letters, 32*(18). https://doi.org/10.1029/2005GL023528

Kotwal, A., & Ramaswami, B. (2014, September). Delivering food subsidy: The state and the market. In *The Oxford handbook of food, politics, and society* (pp. 301–326). New York, NY: Oxford University Press.

Krishna, A. (2011). *One illness away: Why people become poor and how they escape poverty.* Oxford University Press.

Krishnamurthy, P., Pathania, V., & Tandon, S. (2017). Food price subsidies and nutrition: Evidence from state reforms to India's public distribution system. *Economic Development and Cultural Change, 66*(1), 55–90. https://doi.org/10.1086/694033

Krishnan, S., & Hatekar, N. (2017). Rise of the new middle class in India and its changing structure. *Economic and Political Weekly, 52*(22), 40–48. Retrieved from https://www.epw.in/journal/2017/22/special-articles/rise-new-middle-class-india-and-its-changing-structure.html

Kumar, A., Yadav, C., Jee, S., Kumar, S., & Chauhan, S. (2011). Financial innovation in Indian agricultural credit market: Progress and performance of Kisan Credit Card. *Indian Journal of Agricultural Economics, 66*(3), 418–428.

Kumar, D., Goel, N. K., Mittal, P. C., & Misra, P. (2006). Influence of infant-feeding practices on nutritional status of under-five children. *The Indian Journal of Pediatrics, 73*(5), 417–421. https://doi.org/10.1007/BF02758565

Kumar, K. R., Kumar, K. K., & Pant, G. B. (1994). Diurnal asymmetry of surface temperature trends over India. *Geophysical Research Letters, 21*(8), 677–680. https://doi.org/10.1029/94GL00007

Kumar, K. S. K., & Parikh, J. (2001). Indian agriculture and climate sensitivity. *Global Environmental Change, 11*(2), 147–154.

Kumar, P. (2006). Contract farming through agribusiness firms and state corporation: A case study in Punjab. *Economic and Political Weekly, 52*(30), A5367–A5375.

Kumar, S., & Berkman, L. F. (2015). Association of inadequately iodized salt use with underweight among young children in India. *Asia Pacific Journal of Public Health, 27*(2), 185–194.

Kumar, S. M. (2013). Does access to formal agricultural credit depend on caste? *World Development, 43,* 315–328.

Kumar, S. N., & Aggarwal, P. K. (2013). Climate change and coconut plantations in India: Impacts and potential adaptation gains. *Agricultural Systems, 117,* 45–54.

Kumar, S. N., Aggarwal, P. K., Rani, D. N. S., Saxena, R., Chauhan, N., & Jain, S. (2014). Vulnerability of wheat production to climate change in India. *Climate Research, 59*(3), 173–187.

Kumar, S. N., Aggarwal, P. K., Rani, S., Jain, S., Saxena, R., & Chauhan, N. (2011). Impact of climate change on crop productivity in Western Ghats, coastal and northeastern regions of India. *Current Science, 332*–341.

Kumar, S. N., Govindakrishnan, P. M., Swarooparani, D. N., Nitin, C., Surabhi, J., & Aggarwal, P. K. (2015). Assessment of impact of climate change on potato and potential adaptation gains in the Indo-Gangetic Plains of India. *International Journal of Plant Production, 9*(1), 151–170.

Kumar, U., & Subramanian, A. (2012). Growth in India's states in the first decade of the 21st century: Four facts. *Economic and Political Weekly, XLVIII*(3), 48–57.

Kurian, N. J. (2000). Widening regional disparities in India: Some indicators. *Economic and Political Weekly, 35*(7), 538–550. Retrieved from http://www.jstor.org/stable/4408933

Lal, R., Follett, R. F., Stewart, B. A., & Kimble, J. M. (2007). Soil carbon sequestration to mitigate climate change and advance food security. *Soil Science, 172*(12), 943–956.

Lalvani, M. (2008). Sugar co-operatives in Maharashtra: A political economy perspective. *Journal of Development Studies, 44*(10), 1474–1505. https://doi.org/10.1080/00220380802265108

Lam, W. F. (2006). Foundations of a robust social-ecological system: Irrigation institutions in Taiwan. *Journal of Institutional Economics, 2*(2), 203–226.

Lanjouw, J. O., & Lanjouw, P. (2001). The rural non-farm sector: Issues and evidence from developing countries. *Agricultural Economics, 26*(1), 1–23. https://doi.org/10.1111/j.1574-0862.2001.tb00051.x

Lanjouw, P. (2007). Does the rural nonfarm economy contribute to poverty reduction. In S. Haggblade, P. B. R. Hazell, & T. Reardon (Eds.), *Transforming the rural nonfarm economy: Opportunities and threats in the developing world* (pp. 55–82). Johns Hopkins University Press.

Lanjouw, P., & Murgai, R. (2009). Poverty decline, agricultural wages, and nonfarm employment in rural India: 1983–2004. *Agricultural Economics, 40*(2), 243–263. https://doi.org/10.1111/j.1574-0862.2009.00373.x

Lee, L., Rosenzweig, M. R., & Pitt, M. M. (1997). The effects of improved nutrition, sanitation, and water quality on child health in high-mortality populations. *Journal of Econometrics, 77*(1), 209–235. https://doi.org/10.1016/S0304-4076(96)01813-1

Lehmann, J. (2007). A handful of carbon. *Nature, 447*(7141), 143.

Lei, L., Desai, S., & Vanneman, R. (2017). *Village transportation infrastructure and women's non-agricultural employment in India: The conditioning role of community gender context.* IHDS Working Paper No. 2017-2.

Leroy, J. L., Ruel, M., & Verhofstadt, E. (2009). The impact of conditional cash transfer programmes on child nutrition: A review of evidence using a programme theory framework. *Journal of Development Effectiveness, 1*(2), 103–129. https://doi.org/10.1080/19439340902924043

Leslie, J. (1988). Women's work and child nutrition in the Third World. *World Development, 16*(11), 1341–1362.

Lewis, W. A. (1954). Economic development with unlimited supplies of labour. *The Manchester School, 22*(2), 139–191. https://doi.org/10.1111/j.1467-9957.1954.tb00021.x

Li, Y., & Rama, M. (2015). *Households or locations? Cities, catchment areas and prosperity in India.* World Bank Policy Research Working Paper No. 7473.

Lim, S. S., Fullman, N., Stokes, A., Ravishankar, N., Masiye, F., Murray, C. J. L., & Gakidou, E. (2011). Net benefits: A multicountry analysis of observational data examining associations between insecticide-treated mosquito nets and health outcomes. *PLoS Medicine, 8*(9), e1001091. https://doi.org/10.1371/journal.pmed.1001091

Lin, D. (2006). Agricultural cooperatives in Taiwan. In *2006 FFTC-NACF International Seminar on Agricultural Cooperatives in Asia: Innovations and Opportunities in the 21st Century.* Seoul, Korea.

Lindblade, K. A., Walker, E. D., Onapa, A. W., Katungu, J., & Wilson, M. L. (2000). Land use change alters malaria transmission parameters by modifying temperature in a highland area of Uganda. *Tropical Medicine & International Health, 5*(4), 263–274.

Lipper, L., Pingali, P., & Zurek, M. (2006). Less-favoured areas: Looking beyond agriculture towards ecosystem services. In R. Ruben, J. Pender, & A. Kuyvenhoven (Eds.), *Sustainable poverty reduction in less-favoured areas: Problems, options and strategies* (pp. 442–460). Wallingford, UK: CABI.

Lipper, L., Thornton, P., Campbell, B. M., Baedeker, T., Braimoh, A., Bwalya, M., ... Torquebiau, E. F. (2014). Climate-smart agriculture for food security. *Nature Climate Change, 4*(12), 1068–1072. https://doi.org/10.1038/nclimate2437

Lipton, M. (1980). Migration from rural areas of poor countries: The impact on rural productivity and income distribution. *World Development, 8*(1), 1–24. https://doi.org/10.1016/0305-750X(80)90047-9

Liu, Y., & Deininger, K. (2010). Poverty impacts of India's national rural employment guarantee scheme: Evidence from Andhra Pradesh.

Lobell, D. B., & Burke, M. B. (2010). On the use of statistical models to predict crop yield responses to climate change. *Agricultural and Forest Meteorology, 150*(11), 1443–1452. https://doi.org/10.1016/j.agrformet.2010.07.008

Lobell, D. B., Burke, M. B., Tebaldi, C., Mastrandrea, M. D., Falcon, W. P., & Naylor, R. L. (2008). Prioritizing climate change adaptation needs for food security in 2030. *Science, 319*(5863), 607–610.

Lobell, D. B., Schlenker, W., & Costa-Roberts, J. (2011). Climate trends and global crop production since 1980. *Science, 333*(6042), 616–620.

Lohmann, L., Hällström, N., Österbergh, R., & Nordberg, O. (2006). *Carbon trading: A critical conversation on climate change, privatisation and power.* Uppsala: Dag Hammarskjöld Centre. Retrieved from https://www.tni.org/en/publication/carbon-trading

Lumey, L. H., Stein, A. D., Kahn, H. S., van der Pal-de Bruin, K. M., Blauw, G. J., Zybert, P. A., & Susser, E. S. (2007). Cohort profile: The Dutch Hunger Winter families study. *International Journal of Epidemiology, 36*(6), 1196–1204. https://doi.org/10.1093/ije/dym126

Luo, Z., Mu, R., & Zhang, X. (2006). Famine and overweight in China. *Review of Agricultural Economics, 28*(3), 296–304.

Maccini, S., & Yang, D. (2009). Under the weather: Health, schooling, and economic consequences of early-life rainfall. *American Economic Review, 99*(3), 1006–1026. https://doi.org/10.1257/aer.99.3.1006

Maitra, C., & Rao, D. S. P. (2015). Poverty–food security nexus: Evidence from a survey of urban slum dwellers in Kolkata. *World Development, 72*, 308–325. https://doi.org/10.1016/j.worlddev.2015.03.006

Majra, J. P., & Gur, A. (2009). Climate change and health: Why should India be concerned? *Indian Journal of Occupational and Environmental Medicine, 13*(1), 11.

Mall, R. K., Singh, R., Gupta, A., Srinivasan, G., & Rathore, L. S. (2006). Impact of climate change on Indian agriculture: A review. *Climatic Change, 78*(2), 445–478. https://doi.org/10.1007/s10584-005-9042-x

Maluccio, J. A. (2005). Coping with the coffee crisis in Central America: The role of the Nicaraguan Red de Protección Social. *FCND Discussion Papers, 188*(Feb.), 44.

Maluccio, J. A., Hoddinott, J., Behrman, J. R., Martorell, R., Quisumbing, A. R., & Stein, A. D. (2009). The impact of improving nutrition during early childhood on education among Guatemalan adults. *The Economic Journal, 119*(537), 734–763. https://doi.org/10.1111/j.1468-0297.2009.02220.x

Mangala, K. P., & Chengappa, P. G. (2008). A novel agribusiness model for backward linkages with farmers: A case of food retail chain. *Agricultural Economics Research Review, 21*, 363–370.

Mangyo, E. (2008). The effect of water accessibility on child health in China. *Journal of Health Economics, 27*(5), 1343–1356.

Mani, G. (2016). *Study on implementation of Kisan Credit Card scheme.* Occasional Paper No. 64.

Masset, E., Leroy, J. L., & Frongillo, E. A. (2007). Can interventions to promote animal production ameliorate undernutrition? *The Journal of Nutrition, 137*(10), 2311–2316.

Matson, P. A., Parton, W. J., Power, A. G., & Swift, M. J. (1997). Agricultural intensification and ecosystem properties. *Science, 277*(5325), 504–509. https://doi.org/10.1126/science.277.5325.504

Maxwell, D. (1999). The political economy of urban food security in Sub-Saharan Africa. *World Development, 27*(11), 1939–1953. https://doi.org/10.1016/S0305-750X(99)00101-1

Mazumdar, D. (1965). Size of farm and productivity—A problem of Indian peasant agriculture. *Economica, 32*(126), 161–173.

McCullough, E. B., Pingali, P., & Stamoulis, K. G. (2008a). Small farms and the transformation of food systems: An overview. In E. B. McCullough, P. L. Pingali, & K. G. Stamoulis (Eds.), *The transformation of agri-food systems: Globalisation, supply chains, and smallholder farmers* (pp. 3–46). Rome: FAO.

McCullough, E. B., Pingali, P., & Stamoulis, K. G. (2008b). *The transformation of agri-food systems: Globalization, supply chains and smallholder farmers.* Rome: FAO.

McMichael, A. J., Woodruff, R. E., & Hales, S. (2006). Climate change and human health: Present and future risks. *The Lancet, 367*(9513), 859–869.

Meenakshi, J. V. (2016). Trends and patterns in the triple burden of malnutrition in India. *Agricultural Economics, 47*(S1), 115–134. https://doi.org/10.1111/agec.12304

Meenakshi, J. V., Johnson, N. L., Manyong, V. M., DeGroote, H., Javelosa, J., Yanggen, D. R., … Meng, E. (2010). How cost-effective is biofortification in combating micronutrient malnutrition? An ex *ante* assessment. *World Development, 38*(1), 64–75. https://doi.org/10.1016/j.worlddev.2009.03.014

Mehrotra, S. (2014). *India's skills challenge: Reforming vocational education and training to harness the demographic dividend.* Oxford University Press.

Mellor, J. W., & Johnston, B. F. (1984). The world food equation: Interrelations among development, employment, and food consumption. *Journal of Economic Literature, 22*(2), 531–574.

Melmed-Sanjak, J. (1998). *A review of the literature on land leasing arrangements in selected Asian countries.* Rome.

Mengistie, B., Berhane, Y., & Worku, A. (2013). Household water chlorination reduces incidence of diarrhea among under-five children in rural Ethiopia: A cluster randomized controlled trial. *PLoS One, 8*(10), e77887.

Menon, P., Bamezai, A., Subandoro, A., Ayoya, M. A., & Aguayo, V. (2015). Age-appropriate infant and young child feeding practices are associated with child nutrition in India: Insights from nationally representative data. *Maternal & Child Nutrition, 11*(1), 73–87.

Miguel, E., & Kremer, M. (2015). Worms: Identifying impacts on education and health in the presence of treatment externalities. *Econometrica, 72*(1), 159–217.

Minten, B., Reardon, T., & Sutradhar, R. (2010). Food prices and modern retail: The case of Delhi. *World Development, 38*(12), 1775–1787. https://doi.org/10.1016/j.worlddev.2010.04.002

Mishra, S., & Rahman, A. (2018). Does non-farm income affect food security? Evidence from India. Mimeo.

Misra, A. K. (2014). Climate change and challenges of water and food security. *International Journal of Sustainable Built Environment*, 3(1), 153–165. https://doi.org/10.1016/j.ijsbe.2014.04.006

Misra, A., Singhal, N., Sivakumar, B., Bhagat, N., Jaiswal, A., & Khurana, L. (2011). Nutrition transition in India: Secular trends in dietary intake and their relationship to diet-related non-communicable diseases. *Journal of Diabetes*, 3(4), 278–292. https://doi.org/10.1111/j.1753-0407.2011.00139.x

Mitra, A., & Marayama, M. (2009). Rural to urban migration: A district-level analysis for India. *International Journal of Migration, Health and Social Care*, 5(2), 35–53.

Mittal, N., & Meenakshi, J. V. (2015). *Utilization of ICDS services and their impact on child health outcomes—Evidence from three East Indian states.* Working Papers 247, Centre for Development Economics, Delhi School of Economics.

Mittal, S., & Mehar, M. (2012). How mobile phones contribute to growth of small farmers? Evidence from India. *Quarterly Journal of International Agriculture*, 51(3), 227–244.

MoEF. (2008). *National Action Plan for Climate Change Report.*

MoEF. (2010). *India: Greenhouse Gas Emissions 2007 executive summary.* Retrieved from http://www.moef.nic.in/downloads/public-information/Report_INCCA.pdf

Mohan, S. (2015, June 1). Junk food is feeding a malnutrition epidemic in Delhi's slums. *Scroll.* Retrieved from https://scroll.in/article/728525/junk-food-is-feeding-a-malnutrition-epidemic-in-delhis-slums

MoHFW. (2017). *India: Health of the nation's states.* MoHFW Report.

Montagnini, F., & Nair, P. K. R. (2004). Carbon sequestration: An underexploited environmental benefit of agroforestry systems. In *New vistas in agroforestry* (pp. 281–295). Dordrecht: Springer. Retrieved from http://citeseerx.ist.psu.edu/viewdoc/download?doi=10.1.1.456.8246&rep=rep1&type=pdf

Mosley, P. (2002). The African green revolution as a pro-poor policy instrument. *Journal of International Development*, 14(6), 695–724. https://doi.org/10.1002/jid.912

Motiram, S., & Naraparaju, K. (2015). Growth and deprivation in India: What does recent evidence suggest on "Inclusiveness"? *Oxford Development Studies*, 43(2), 145–164. https://doi.org/10.1080/13600818.2014.988693

Mukhopadhyay, P. (2017). Does administrative status matter for small towns in India? In E. Denis & M.-H. Zérah (Eds.), *Subaltern urbanisation in India: An introduction to the dynamics of ordinary towns* (pp. 443–469). New Delhi: Springer India. https://doi.org/10.1007/978-81-322-3616-0_17

Mukhopadhyay, P., Zérah, M.-H., Samanta, G., & Maria, A. (2016). *Understanding India's urban frontier: What is behind the emergence of census towns in India?* The World Bank. https://doi.org/10.1596/1813-9450-7923

Müller, C., Elliott, J., & Levermann, A. (2014). Food security: Fertilizing hidden hunger. *Nature Climate Change, 4*(7), 540.

Munshi, K. (2011). Strength in numbers: Networks as a solution to occupational traps. *Review of Economic Studies, 78*(3), 1069–1101. https://doi.org/10.1093/restud/rdq029

Munshi, K., & Rosenzweig, M. (2006). Traditional institutions meet the modern world: Caste, gender, and schooling choice in a globalizing economy. *American Economic Review, 96*(4), 1225–1252. https://doi.org/10.1257/aer.96.4.1225

Munshi, K., & Rosenzweig, M. (2016). Networks and misallocation: Insurance, migration, and the rural-urban wage gap. *American Economic Review, 106*(1), 46–98. https://doi.org/10.1257/aer.20131365

Murray, C. J. L., Vos, T., Lozano, R., Naghavi, M., Flaxman, A. D., Michaud, C., … Lopez, A. D. (2012). Disability-adjusted life years (DALYs) for 291 diseases and injuries in 21 regions, 1990–2010: A systematic analysis for the Global Burden of Disease Study 2010. *The Lancet, 380*(9859), 2197–2223. https://doi.org/10.1016/S0140-6736(12)61689-4

Muto, M., & Yamano, T. (2009). The impact of mobile phone coverage expansion on market participation: Panel data evidence from Uganda. *World Development, 37*(12), 1887–1896. https://doi.org/10.1016/j.worlddev.2009.05.004

Myers, S. S., Smith, M. R., Guth, S., Golden, C. D., Vaitla, B., Mueller, N. D., … Huybers, P. (2017). Climate change and global food systems: Potential impacts on food security and undernutrition. *Annual Review of Public Health, 38*(1), 259–277. https://doi.org/10.1146/annurev-publhealth-031816-044356

Myers, S. S., Zanobetti, A., Kloog, I., Huybers, P., Leakey, A. D. B., Bloom, A. J., … Usui, Y. (2014). Increasing CO_2 threatens human nutrition. *Nature, 510*(7503), 139–142.

Mythili, G., & Goedecke, J. (2016). Economics of land degradation in India. In E. Nkonya, A. Mirzabaev, & J. von Braun (Eds.), *Economics of land degradation and improvement—A global assessment for sustainable development* (pp. 431–469). Cham: Springer.

Nagaraj, R. (2009). Is services sector output overestimated? An inquiry. *Economic and Political Weekly, 44*(5), 40–45. Retrieved from http://www.jstor.org/stable/40278458

Narayanamoorthy, A., & Alli, P. (2018, January). Agriculture market reforms are a must. *The Hindu Business Line.* Retrieved from https://www.thehindubusinessline.com/opinion/agriculture-market-reforms-are-a-must/article10007561.ece

Narayanan, S. (2014a). Profits from participation in high value agriculture: Evidence of heterogeneous benefits in contract farming schemes in Southern India. *Food Policy, 44*, 142–157. https://doi.org/10.1016/j.foodpol.2013.10.010

Narayanan, S., & Gerber, N. (2017). Social safety nets for food and nutrition security in India. *Global Food Security, 15*, 65–76. https://doi.org/10.1016/j.gfs.2017.05.001

Narrod, C., Roy, D., Okello, J., Avendaño, B., Rich, K., & Thorat, A. (2007). *The role of public–private partnerships and collective action in ensuring smallholder participation in high value fruit and vegetable supply chains.* CAPRi Working Paper, Washington, DC.

National Commission for Enterprises in the Unorganised Sector (NCEUS). (2008). *Report on definitional and statistical issues relating to informal economy.*

National Sample Survey Organisation (NSSO). (2014). *Key indicators of situation of agricultural households in India.* National Sample Survey 70th Round, Ministry of Statistics and Programme Implementation, Government of India, New Delhi.

Nelson, G. C. (2001). Traits and techniques of GMOs. In A. Nelson (Ed.), *Genetically modified organisms in agriculture, economics and politics* (pp. 7–13). London: Academic Press. https://doi.org/10.1016/B978-012515422-2/50005-9

Nelson, G. C., Mensbrugghe, D., Ahammad, H., Blanc, E., Calvin, K., Hasegawa, T., ... Lotze-Campen, H. (2014). Agriculture and climate change in global scenarios: Why don't the models agree. *Agricultural Economics, 45*(1), 85–101.

Nelson, G. C., Valin, H., Sands, R. D., Havlík, P., Ahammad, H., Deryng, D., ... Willenbockel, D. (2014). Climate change effects on agriculture: Economic responses to biophysical shocks. *Proceedings of the National Academy of Sciences, 111*(9), 3274–3279. https://doi.org/10.1073/pnas.1222465110

Nguyen, A. T., Dzator, J., & Nadolny, A. (2015). Does contract farming improve productivity and income of farmers? A review of theory and evidence. *The Journal of Developing Areas, 49*(6), 531–538.

Niang, I., Ruppel, O. C., Abdrabo, M. A., Essel, A., Lennard, C., Padgham, J., & Urquhart, P. (2014). Africa. In *Regional aspects. Contribution of Working Group II to the Fifth Assessment Report of the Intergovernmental Panel on Climate Change.* Cambridge, UK: Cambridge University Press.

Nichter, M. (2008). *Global health: Why cultural perceptions, social representations, and biopolitics matter.* University of Arizona Press.

Nicklas, T. A., Baranowski, T., Cullen, K. W., & Berenson, G. (2001). Eating patterns, dietary quality and obesity. *Journal of the American College of Nutrition, 20*(6), 599–608.

Nielsen, & CII. (2012). *Emerging consumer demand: Rise of the small town Indian.*

Nirmal, R. (2017, July). Why the eNAM platform hasn't taken off despite all the fanfare. *The Hindu Business Line.* Retrieved from https://www.thehindubusinessline.com/economy/agri-business/why-the-enam-platform-hasnt-taken-off-despiteall-the-fanfare/article9776034.ece

O'Brien, K., Leichenko, R., Kelkar, U., Venema, H., Aandahl, G., Tompkins, H., ... West, J. (2004). Mapping vulnerability to multiple stressors: Climate change and globalization in India. *Global Environmental Change, 14*(4), 303–313. https://doi.org/10.1016/j.gloenvcha.2004.01.001

Office of the Registrar General & Census Commissioner. (2001). *Census of India 2001*. New Delhi: Government of India.

Ogutu, S. O., Okello, J. J., & Otieno, D. J. (2014). Impact of information and communication technology-based market information services on smallholder farm input use and productivity: The case of Kenya. *World Development, 64*, 311–321. https://doi.org/10.1016/j.worlddev.2014.06.011

Oreopoulos, P., Page, M. E., & Stevens, A. H. (2006). The intergenerational effects of compulsory schooling. *Journal of Labor Economics, 24*(4), 729–760.

Otsuka, K., Chuma, H., & Hayami, Y. (1992). Land and labor contracts in agrarian economies: Theories and facts. *Journal of Economic Literature, 30*(4), 1965–2018.

Owusu, V., Abdulai, A., & Abdul-Rahman, S. (2011). Non-farm work and food security among farm households in Northern Ghana. *Food Policy, 36*(2), 108–118. https://doi.org/10.1016/j.foodpol.2010.09.002

Paaijmans, K. P., Blanford, S., Bell, A. S., Blanford, J. I., Read, A. F., & Thomas, M. B. (2010). Influence of climate on malaria transmission depends on daily temperature variation. *Proceedings of the National Academy of Sciences, 107*(34), 15135–15139.

Padel, S., & Foster, C. (2005). Exploring the gap between attitudes and behaviour: Understanding why consumers buy or do not buy organic food. *British Food Journal, 107*(8), 606–625. https://doi.org/10.1108/00070700510611002

Paerl, H. W., & Paul, V. J. (2012). Climate change: Links to global expansion of harmful cyanobacteria. *Water Research, 46*(5), 1349–1363. https://doi.org/10.1016/j.watres.2011.08.002

Panagariya, A., Chakraborty, P., & Rao, M. G. (2014). *State level reforms, growth, and development in Indian states* (Vol. 3). Studies in Indian Economic Policies.

Panda, S. (2015). Political connections and elite capture in a poverty alleviation programme in India. *The Journal of Development Studies, 51*(1), 50–65. https://doi.org/10.1080/00220388.2014.947281

Pandey, A. K. (2014). Spatio-temporal changes in internal migration in India during post reform period. *Journal of Economic & Social Development, X*(1), 107–116.

Parker, S., & Skoufias, E. (2000). *The impact of PROGRESA on work, leisure and time allocation*. Washington, DC: International Food Policy Research Institute.

Paterson, R. R. M., & Lima, N. (2010). How will climate change affect mycotoxins in food? *Food Research International, 43*(7), 1902–1914. https://doi.org/10.1016/j.foodres.2009.07.010

Patil, S. R., Arnold, B. F., Salvatore, A. L., Briceno, B., Ganguly, S., Colford, J. M., Jr., & Gertler, P. J. (2014). The effect of India's total sanitation campaign on defecation behaviors and child health in rural Madhya Pradesh: A cluster randomized controlled trial. *PLoS Medicine, 11*(8), e1001709.

Pattnaik, I., Lahiri-Dutt, K., Lockie, S., & Pritchard, B. (2018). The feminization of agriculture or the feminization of agrarian distress? Tracking the trajectory of women in agriculture in India. *Journal of the Asia Pacific Economy, 23*(1), 138–155. https://doi.org/10.1080/13547860.2017.1394569

Patz, J. A., Campbell-Lendrum, D., Holloway, T., & Foley, J. A. (2005). Impact of regional climate change on human health. *Nature, 438*(7066), 310.

Pettengell, C. (2010). Climate change adaptation: Enabling people living in poverty to adapt. *Oxfam Policy and Practice: Climate Change and Resilience, 6*(2), 1–48.

Pindyck, R. S. (2013). Climate change policy: What do the models tell us? *Journal of Economic Literature, 51*(3), 860–872.

Pindyck, R. S., & Wang, N. (2013). The economic and policy consequences of catastrophes. *American Economic Journal: Economic Policy, 5*(4), 306–339.

Pingali, P. (2006). Westernization of Asian diets and the transformation of food systems: Implications for research and policy. *Food Policy, 32*(3), 281–298. https://doi.org/10.1016/j.foodpol.2006.08.001

Pingali, P. (2007a). Agricultural growth and economic development: A view through the globalization lens. *Agricultural Economics, 37*(Suppl. S1), 1–12. https://doi.org/10.1111/j.1574-0862.2007.00231.x

Pingali, P. (2007b). Westernization of Asian diets and the transformation of food systems: Implications for research and policy. *Food Policy, 32*(3), 281–298. https://doi.org/10.1016/j.foodpol.2006.08.001

Pingali, P. (2010). Chapter 74 Agriculture renaissance: Making 'agriculture for development' work in the 21st century. In P. Pingali & R. Evenson (Eds.), *Handbook of agricultural economics* (pp. 3867–3894). Elsevier. Retrieved from http://www.sciencedirect.com/science/article/pii/S1574007209040742

Pingali, P. (2012). Green revolution: Impacts, limits, and the path ahead. *Proceedings of the National Academy of Science, 109*(31), 12302–12308. https://doi.org/10.1073/pnas.0912953109

Pingali, P. (2015a). Agricultural policy and nutrition outcomes—Getting beyond the preoccupation with staple grains. *Food Security, 7*(3), 583–591. https://doi.org/10.1007/s12571-015-0461-x

Pingali, P. (2015b). Wringing food from the world. *Nature Geoscience, 8*(4), 252–252. https://doi.org/10.1038/ngeo2410

Pingali, P., & Aiyar, A. (2018a). Diversity in development: Inter-state differences in the India growth story. *World Food Policy, 4*(2), 57–77. Retrieved from http://www.ipsonet.org/publications/open-access/world-food-policy/wfp-volume-4-issue-2-spring-2018

Pingali, P., & Aiyar, A. (2018b). Food, agriculture, and nutrition policy: Looking ahead to 2050. In P. P. Rachid Serraj (Ed.), *Agriculture and food systems to 2050*. World Scientific Publishing.

Pingali, P., & Khwaja, Y. (2004). *Globalisation of Indian diets and the transformation of food supply systems.* Citeseer.

Pingali, P., Khwaja, Y., & Madelon, M. (2005). *Commercializing small farms: Reducing transaction cost*. ESA Working Paper (No.), 05-08.

Pingali, P., Khwaja, Y., & Madelon, M. (2007). The role of the public and private sectors in commercializing small farms and reducing transaction costs. In J. F. M. Swinnen (Ed.), *Global supply chains, standards and the poor* (pp. 260–267). Oxford, UK: CABI International.

Pingali, P., Mittra, B., & Rahman, A. (2016, March). The bumpy road from food to nutrition security—Slow evolution of India's food policy. https://doi.org/10.1016/j.gfs.2017.05.002

Pingali, P., Mittra, B., & Rahman, A. (2017). The bumpy road from food to nutrition security—Slow evolution of India's food policy. *Global Food Security, 15*, 77–84. https://doi.org/10.1016/j.gfs.2017.05.002

Pingali, P., & Rao, T. (2016). Understanding the multidimensional nature of the malnutrition problem in India. In P. Pingali & G. Feder (Eds.), *Agriculture and rural development in a globalizing world*. Routledge.

Pingali, P., Ricketts, K., & Sahn, D. E. (2015a). Agriculture for nutrition: Getting policies right. In D. E. Sahn (Ed.), *The fight against hunger and malnutrition: The role of food, agriculture and targeted policies*. Oxford, UK: Oxford University Press.

Pingali, P., Ricketts, K., & Sahn, D. E. (2015b). The fight against hunger and malnutrition: The role of food, agriculture, and targeted policies. In D. E. Sahn (Ed.), *Agriculture for nutrition*. Oxford, UK: Oxford University Press.

Pingali, P., & Rosegrant, M. W. (1995). Agricultural commercialization and diversification: Processes and policies. *Food Policy, 20*(3), 171–185. https://doi.org/10.1016/0306-9192(95)00012-4

Pingali, P., & Sunder, N. (2017). Transitioning toward nutrition-sensitive food systems in developing countries. *Annual Review of Resource Economics, 9*(1), 439–459. https://doi.org/10.1146/annurev-resource-100516-053552

Pingali, P. L., & Ricketts, K. D. (2014). Mainstreaming nutrition metrics in household surveys—Toward a multidisciplinary convergence of data systems. *Annals of the New York Academy of Sciences, 1331*(1), 249–257. https://doi.org/10.1111/nyas.12597

Pingali, P. L., Spielman, D., & Zaidi, F. (2014). Changing donor trends in assistance to agricultural research and development in Africa South of the Sahara. *The Future of African Agricultural R&D, 6*:1–6:25. https://doi.org/10.2499/9780896292123_06

Pinstrup-Andersen, P. (2009). Food security: Definition and measurement. *Food Security, 1*(1), 5–7. https://doi.org/10.1007/s12571-008-0002-y

Planning Commission. (2011). *Report of the working group on agricultural marketing infrastructure, secondary agriculture and policy required for internal and external trade for the XII five-year plan 2012–17*. New Delhi.

Plessow, R., Arora, N. K., Brunner, B., Tzogiou, C., Eichler, K., Brügger, U., & Wieser, S. (2015). Social costs of iron deficiency anemia in 6–59-month-old children in India. *PLoS One, 10*(8). https://doi.org/10.1371/journal.pone.0136581

Popkin, B. M. (1997). The nutrition transition and its health implications in lower-income countries. *Public Health Nutrition, 1*(1), 5–21.

Popkin, B. M. (1999). Urbanization, lifestyle changes and the nutrition transition. *World Development, 27*(11), 1905–1916. https://doi.org/10.1016/S0305-750X(99)00094-7

Popkin, B. M. (2003). The nutrition transition in the developing world. *Development Policy Review, 21*(5–6), 581–597. https://doi.org/10.1111/j.1467-8659.2003.00225.x

Popkin, B. M., Horton, S., Kim, S., Mahal, A., & Shuigao, J. (2001). Trends in diet, nutritional status, and diet-related noncommunicable diseases in China and India: The economic costs of the nutrition transition. *Nutrition Reviews, 59*(12), 379–390.

Poulton, C., Dorward, A., & Kydd, J. (2010). The future of small farms: New directions for services, institutions, and intermediation. *World Development, 38*(10), 1413–1428. https://doi.org/10.1016/j.worlddev.2009.06.009

Pradhan, K. C. (2013). Unacknowledged urbanisation. *Economic and Political Weekly*. Retrieved from https://www.epw.in/journal/2013/36/special-articles/unacknowledged-urbanisation.html

Prahladachar, M. (1983). Income distribution effects of the green revolution in India: A review of empirical evidence. *World Development, 11*(11), 927–944.

Prakash, P., & Kumar, P. (2016). Performance of Kisan Credit Card scheme in Tamil Nadu. *Indian Journal of Agricultural Economics, 71*(2), 191–211.

Prasad, R. (2009). Efficient fertilizer use: The key to food security and better environment. *Journal of Tropical Agriculture, 47*(1–2), 1–17.

Pray, C. E., & Nagarajan, L. (2014). The transformation of the Indian agricultural input industry: Has it increased agricultural R&D? *Agricultural Economics, 45*(S1), 145–156. https://doi.org/10.1111/agec.12138

Pretty, J., Toulmin, C., & Williams, S. (2011). Sustainable intensification in African agriculture. *International Journal of Agricultural Sustainability, 9*(1), 5–24. https://doi.org/10.3763/ijas.2010.0583

Qadir, M., Tubeileh, A., Akhtar, J., Larbi, A., Minhas, P. S., & Khan, M. A. (2008). Productivity enhancement of salt-affected environments through crop diversification. *Land Degradation & Development, 19*(4), 429–453. https://doi.org/10.1002/ldr.853

Qaim, M., Stein, A. J., & Meenakshi, J. V. (2007). Economics of biofortification. *Agricultural Economics, 37*(s1), 119–133.

Qaim, M., Subramanian, A., Naik, G., & Zilberman, D. (2006). Adoption of Bt cotton and impact variability: Insights from India. *Applied Economic Perspectives and Policy, 28*(1), 48–58.

Rah, J. H., Akhter, N., Semba, R. D., De Pee, S., Bloem, M. W., Campbell, A. A., … Kraemer, K. (2010). Low dietary diversity is a predictor of child stunting in rural Bangladesh. *European Journal of Clinical Nutrition, 64*(12), 1393.

Rah, J. H., Cronin, A. A., Badgaiyan, B., Aguayo, V. M., Coates, S., & Ahmed, S. (2015). Household sanitation and personal hygiene practices are associated with child stunting in rural India: A cross-sectional analysis of surveys. *BMJ Open, 5*(2), e005180.

Rahman, A. (2016). Universal food security program and nutritional intake: Evidence from the hunger prone KBK districts in Odisha. *Food Policy, 63,* 73–86. https://doi.org/10.1016/j.foodpol.2016.07.003

Rahman, A. (2017), Recent trends in food consumption and nutrient intake in rural India. Mimeo.

Rajib, P. (2015). Indian agricultural commodity derivatives market—In conversation with S Sivakumar, Divisional Chief Executive, Agri Business Division, ITC Ltd. *IIMB Management Review, 27*(2), 118–128. https://doi.org/10.1016/j.iimb.2015.02.002

Raman, S., Devineni, N., & Fishman, R. (2015). Can improved agricultural water use efficiency save India's groundwater? *Environmental Research Letters, 10*(8), 84022.

Ramani, S. V., & Thutupalli, A. (2015). Emergence of controversy in technology transitions: Green Revolution and Bt cotton in India. *Technological Forecasting and Social Change, 100,* 198–212. https://doi.org/10.1016/j.techfore.2015.06.018

Ramaswami, B., Birthal, P. S., & Joshi, P. K. (2009). Grower heterogeneity and the gains from contract farming: The case of Indian poultry. *Indian Growth and Development Review, 2*(1), 56–74. https://doi.org/10.1108/17538250910953462

Rao, C. H. H. (1975). *Technological change and the distribution of gains in Indian agriculture*. Macmillan Company of India.

Rao, C. H. H. (1994). *Agricultural growth, rural poverty and environmental degradation in India*. Oxford University Press.

Rao, C. N., Pray, C. E., & Herring, R. J. (2018). Biotechnology for second green revolution in India: Overview of issues. In R. N. Chandrashekhar, C. E. Pray, & R. J. Herring (Eds.), *Biotechnology for a second green revolution in India* (pp. 45–74). New Delhi: Academic Foundation.

Rao, E. J. O., Brümmer, B., & Qaim, M. (2012). Farmer participation in supermarket channels, production technology, and efficiency: The case of vegetables in Kenya. *American Journal of Agricultural Economics, 23*(3), 784–796.

Rao, M. G., Shand, R. T., & Kalirajan, K. P. (1999). Convergence of incomes across Indian states—A divergent view. *Economic and Political Weekly, 34*(13), 769–778.

Rao, N., & Kaul, V. (2018). India's integrated child development services scheme: Challenges for scaling up. *Child: Care, Health and Development, 44*(1), 31–40. https://doi.org/10.1111/cch.12531

350 REFERENCES

Rasmussen, K. M. (2001). Is there a causal relationship between iron deficiency or iron-deficiency anemia and weight at birth, length of gestation and perinatal mortality? *The Journal of Nutrition, 131*(2), 590S–603S.

Ravallion, M. (2002). On the urbanization of poverty. *Journal of Development Economics, 68*(2), 435–442. https://doi.org/10.1016/S0304-3878(02)00021-4

Ravi, S., & Engler, M. (2015). Workfare as an effective way to fight poverty: The case of India's NREGS. *World Development, 67*, 57–71. https://doi.org/10.1016/j.worlddev.2014.09.029

Ray, B. (2011). *Climate change: IPCC, water crisis, and policy riddles with reference to India and her surroundings.* Lexington Books.

Reardon, T. (1997). Using evidence of household income diversification to inform study of the rural nonfarm labor market in Africa. *World Development, 25*(5), 735–747. https://doi.org/10.1016/S0305-750X(96)00137-4

Reardon, T. (2015). The hidden middle: The quiet revolution in the midstream of agrifood value chains in developing countries. *Oxford Review of Economic Policy, 31*(1), 45–63. https://doi.org/10.1093/oxrep/grv011

Reardon, T., Barrett, C. B., Berdegué, J. A., & Swinnen, J. F. M. (2009). Agrifood industry transformation and small farmers in developing countries. *World Development, 37*(11), 1717–1727. https://doi.org/10.1016/j.worlddev.2008.08.023

Reardon, T., & Berdegué, J. A. (2002). The rapid rise of supermarkets in Latin America: Challenges and opportunities for development. *Development Policy Review, 20*(4), 371–388.

Reardon, T., Lansing, E., Minten, B., & Ababa, A. (2011). Surprised by supermarkets: Diffusion of modern food retail in India. *Journal of Agribusiness in Developing and Emerging Economies, 1*(2), 134–161. https://doi.org/10.1108/JADEE-10-2013-0040

Reardon, T., & Minten, B. (2011). Surprised by supermarkets: Diffusion of modern food retail in India. *Journal of Agribusiness in Developing and Emerging Economies, 1*(2), 134–161. https://doi.org/10.1108/20440831111167155

Reardon, T., Stamoulis, K., & Pingali, P. (2007). Rural nonfarm employment in developing countries in an era of globalization. *Agricultural Economics, 37*, 173–183. https://doi.org/10.1111/j.1574-0862.2007.00243.x

Reardon, T., & Timmer, C. P. (2014). Five inter-linked transformations in the Asian agrifood economy: Food security implications. *Global Food Security, 3*(2), 108–117. https://doi.org/10.1016/j.gfs.2014.02.001

Reardon, T., Timmer, C. P., & Minten, B. (2012). Supermarket revolution in Asia and emerging development strategies to include small farmers. *Proceedings of the National Academy of Sciences, 109*(31), 12332–12337. https://doi.org/10.1073/pnas.1003160108

Reardon, T., & Timmer, P. C. (2007). Chapter 55 Transformation of markets for agricultural output in developing countries since 1950: How has thinking changed? In *Handbook of agricultural economics* (Vol. 3, pp. 2807–2855). Elsevier. https://doi.org/10.1016/S1574-0072(06)03055-6

Reardon, T., Timmer, P. C., Barrett, C. B., & Berdegué, J. A. (2003). The rise of supermarkets in Africa, Asia, and Latin America. *American Journal of Agricultural Economics, 85*(5), 1140–1146.

Reddy, A. (2016). Impact of e-markets in Karnataka, India. *Indian Journal of Agricultural Marketing, 30*(2), 31–44.

Revi, A., Prakash, S., Mehrotra, R., Bhat, G. K., Gupta, K., & Gore, R. (2006). Goa 2100: The transition to a sustainable RUrban design. *Environment and Urbanization, 18*(1), 51–65. https://doi.org/10.1177/0956247806063941

RFST. (2005). *Impact of WTO on women in agriculture.* New Delhi.

Robert, J. (2007). The digital provide: Information (technology), market performance and welfare in the South Indian fisheries sector. *Quarterly Journal of Economics, 121*(2), 879–924.

Rodrik, D., & Subramanian, A. (2004). *From Hindu growth to productivity surge: The mystery of the Indian growth transition.* NBER Working Paper Series No. w10376.

Rojas-Downing, M. M., Nejadhashemi, A. P., Harrigan, T., & Woznicki, S. A. (2017). Climate change and livestock: Impacts, adaptation, and mitigation. *Climate Risk Management, 16*, 145–163. Retrieved from http://www.science-direct.com/science/article/pii/S221209631730027X

Roseboom, T., de Rooij, S., & Painter, R. (2006). The Dutch famine and its long-term consequences for adult health. *Early Human Development, 82*(8), 485–491.

Roseboom, T. J., Van Der Meulen, J. H. P., Ravelli, A. C. J., Osmond, C., Barker, D. J. P., & Bleker, O. P. (2001). Effects of prenatal exposure to the Dutch famine on adult disease in later life: An overview. *Molecular and Cellular Endocrinology, 185*(1–2), 93–98.

Rosegrant, M. W., Koo, J., Cenacchi, N., Ringler, C., Robertson, R., Fisher, M., … Sabbagh, P. (2014). *Food security in a world of natural resource scarcity: The role of agricultural technologies.* Washington, DC: International Food Policy Research Institute.

Roy, A. (2009). Why India cannot plan its cities: Informality, insurgence and the idiom of urbanization. *Planning Theory, 8*(1), 76–87. https://doi.org/10.1177/1473095208099299

Roy, D., & Thorat, A. (2008). Success in high value horticultural export markets for the small farmers: The case of Mahagrapes in India. *World Development, 36*, 1874–1890.

Rozelle, S., Taylor, J. E., & DeBrauw, A. (1999). Migration, remittances, and agricultural productivity in China. *American Economic Review, 89*(2), 287–291. https://doi.org/10.1257/aer.89.2.287

Ruel, M. T. (2003). Operationalizing dietary diversity: A review of measurement issues and research priorities. *The Journal of Nutrition, 133*(11), 3911S–3926S.

Sadoulet, E., Murgai, R., & de Janvry, A. (1998). *Access to land via land rental markets.*

Saha, P., & Verick, S. (2017). Casualization and shift of rural workers to non-farm activities. In *Rural labour mobility in times of structural transformation* (pp. 127–150). Singapore: Springer Singapore. https://doi.org/10.1007/978-981-10-5628-4_7

Schaffner, D. J., Schroder, W. R., & Earle, M. D. (1998). *Food marketing: An international perspective.* Boston, MA: WCB McGraw-Hill.

Schipmann, C., & Qaim, M. (2010). Spillovers from modern supply chains to traditional markets: Product innovation and adoption by smallholders. *Agricultural Economics, 41*(3–4), 361–371. https://doi.org/10.1111/j.1574-0862.2010.00438.x

Schlenker, W., & Roberts, M. J. (2009). Nonlinear temperature effects indicate severe damages to US crop yields under climate change. *Proceedings of the National Academy of Sciences, 106*(37), 15594–15598.

Schuur, E. A. G., McGuire, A. D., Schädel, C., Grosse, G., Harden, J. W., Hayes, D. J., ... Lawrence, D. M. (2015). Climate change and the permafrost carbon feedback. *Nature, 520*(7546), 171–179.

Sekhar, C. S. C., Roy, D., & Bhatt, Y. (2017). *Food inflation and food price volatility in India: Trends and determinants.* IFPRI Discussion Papers, International Food Policy Research Institute (IFPRI). Retrieved from https://econpapers.repec.org/RePEc:fpr:ifprid:1640

Semba, R. D., de Pee, S., Sun, K., Campbell, A. A., Bloem, M. W., & Raju, V. K. (2010). Low intake of vitamin A-rich foods among children, aged 12–35 months, in India: Association with malnutrition, anemia, and missed child survival interventions. *Nutrition, 26*(10), 958–962.

Sen, A. K. (1962). An aspect of Indian agriculture. *The Economic Weekly, 14*(46), 243–246.

Sen, A. K. (1966). Peasants and dualism with or without surplus labor. *Journal of Political Economy, 74*, 425–450.

Sen, A. K. (2000). *Social exclusion: Concept, application, and scrutiny.* Social Development Paper No. 1, Bangkok.

Sengupta, A., Angeli, F., Syamala, T. S., Dagnelie, P. C., & Schayck, C. P. v. (2015). Overweight and obesity prevalence among Indian women by place of residence and socio-economic status: Contrasting patterns from "underweight states" and "overweight states" of India. *Social Science and Medicine, 138*, 161–169. https://doi.org/10.1016/j.socscimed.2015.06.004

Shah, M., & Steinberg, B. (2012). *Could droughts improve human capital? Evidence from India.* Retrieved from http://www.frbsf.org/economic-research/files/Shah_Steinberg.pdf

Shankar, B., Agrawal, S., Beaudreault, A. R., Avula, L., Martorell, R., Osendarp, S., ... Mclean, M. S. (2017). Dietary and nutritional change in India: Implications for strategies, policies, and interventions. *Annals of the New York Academy of Sciences, 1395*(1), 49–59. https://doi.org/10.1111/nyas.13324

Sharma, A. (2016). Urban proximity and spatial pattern of land use and development in rural India. *The Journal of Development Studies, 52*(11), 1593–1611. https://doi.org/10.1080/00220388.2016.1166207

Sharma, A., & Pingali, P. (2016). *Does the onset of the rainy season affect crop yields in India?* Ithaca, NY: Tata-Cornell Institute for Agriculture & Nutrition.

Sharma, A., & Pingali, P. (2018). Looking beyond rice & wheat: Climate change impacts on food systems and food security in India. *World Food Policy Journal, 4*(2).

Shetty, P., Victora, C. G., Adair, L., Fall, C., Hallal, P. C., Martorell, R., ... Group, M. and C. U. S. (2012). India's diabetes time bomb. *Nature, 485*(7398), S14.

Shiao, T., Maddocks, A., Carson, C., & Loizeaux, E. (2015). 3 maps explain India's growing water risks. Washington, DC. Retrieved from https://www.wri.org/blog/2015/02/3-maps-explain-india-s-growing-water-risks

Shrestha, U. B., Gautam, S., & Bawa, K. S. (2012). Widespread climate change in the Himalayas and associated changes in local ecosystems. *PLoS One, 7*(5), e36741.

Shrinivas, A., Baylis, K., Crost, B., & Pingali, P. (2018). Do staple food subsidies improve nutrition? Retrieved from http://barrett.dyson.cornell.edu/NEUDC/paper_520.pdf

Shrivastava, U., Misra, A., Mohan, V., Unnikrishnan, R., & Bachani, D. (2017). Obesity, diabetes and cardiovascular diseases in India: Public health challenges. *Current Diabetes Reviews, 13*(1), 65–80.

Shroff, M., Griffiths, P., Adair, L., Suchindran, C., & Bentley, M. (2009). Maternal autonomy is inversely related to child stunting in Andhra Pradesh, India. *Maternal & Child Nutrition, 5*(1), 64–74.

Shroff, M. R., Griffiths, P. L., Suchindran, C., Nagalla, B., Vazir, S., & Bentley, M. E. (2011). Does maternal autonomy influence feeding practices and infant growth in rural India? *Social Science & Medicine, 73*(3), 447–455.

Sibhatu, K. T., Krishna, V. V., & Qaim, M. (2015). Production diversity and dietary diversity in smallholder farm households. *Proceedings of the National Academy of Sciences, 112*(34), 10657–10662.

Singh, A., Gupta, V., Ghosh, A., Lock, K., & Ghosh-Jerath, S. (2015). Quantitative estimates of dietary intake with special emphasis on snacking pattern and nutritional status of free living adults in urban slums of Delhi: Impact of nutrition transition. *BMC Nutrition, 1*(1), 22. https://doi.org/10.1186/s40795-015-0018-6

Singh, A., Park, A., & Dercon, S. (2013). School meals as a safety net: An evaluation of the midday meal scheme in India. *Economic Development and Cultural Change, 62*(2), 275–306.

Singh, C., & Rahman, A. (2018). Urbanising the rural: Reflections on India's National RUrban Mission. *Asia & the Pacific Policy Studies, 5*(2), 370–377. https://doi.org/10.1002/app5.234

Singh, G., & Asokan, S. R. (2005). Contract farming in India. In C. Ramesh (Ed.), *India's agricultural challenges: Reflections on policy, technology and other issues.* New Delhi: Centre for Trade and Development (CENTAD).

Singh, N., Praharaj, C., & Sandhu, J. (2016). Utilizing untapped potential of rice fallow of East and North-east India through pulse production. *Indian Journal of Genetics and Plant Breeding, 76*(4), 388–398.

Singh, P. (2015). Performance pay and information: Reducing child undernutrition in India. *Journal of Economic Behavior & Organization, 112*, 141–163.

Singh, P., Nedumaran, S., Ntare, B. R., Boote, K. J., Singh, N. P., Srinivas, K., & Bantilan, M. C. S. (2014). Potential benefits of drought and heat tolerance in groundnut for adaptation to climate change in India and West Africa. *Mitigation and Adaptation Strategies for Global Change, 19*(5), 509–529.

Singh, S. (2002). Contracting out solutions: Political economy of contract farming in the Indian Punjab. *World Development, 30*(9), 1621–1638.

Singh, S. (2011). FDI in retail: Misplaced expectations and half-truths. *Economic and Political Weekly, 47*(51), 13–16.

Singh, V. K., Kumar, A., Singh, R. D., & Yadava, K. N. S. (2011). Changing pattern of internal migration in India: Some evidences from census data. *International Journal of Current Research, 3*, 289–295.

Sinha, S. K., & Swaminathan, M. S. (1992). Deforestation, climate change and sustainable nutrition security: A case study of India. In N. Myers (Ed.), *Tropical forests and climate* (pp. 201–209). Dordrecht: Springer Netherlands. https://doi.org/10.1007/978-94-017-3608-4_20

Skoufias, E., Rabassa, M., & Olivieri, S. (2011, April 1). *The poverty impacts of climate change: A review of the evidence.* World Bank Policy Research Working Paper No. 5622. Available at SSRN: https://ssrn.com/abstract=1803002

Smit, B., Burton, I., Klein, R. J. T., & Wandel, J. (2000). An anatomy of adaptation to climate change and variability. In *Climatic change* (Vol. 45, pp. 223–251). Springer. https://doi.org/10.1023/A:1005661622966

Smit, B., & Wandel, J. (2006). Adaptation, adaptive capacity and vulnerability. *Global Environmental Change, 16*(3), 282–292.

Smith, L. C. (2015). The great Indian calorie debate: Explaining rising undernourishment during India's rapid economic growth. *Food Policy, 50*, 53–67. https://doi.org/10.1016/j.foodpol.2014.10.011

Soby, S. D. (2013). The end of the Green Revolution. *Journal of Agricultural and Environmental Ethics, 26*(3), 537–546. https://doi.org/10.1007/s10806-012-9393-z

Somanathan, E., Prabhakar, R., & Mehta, B. S. (2009). Decentralization for cost-effective conservation. *Proceedings of the National Academy of Sciences, 106*(11), 4143–4147.

Somanathan, E., & Somanathan, R. (2009). Climate change: Challenges facing India's poor. *Economic and Political Weekly, 44*(31), 51–58.

Somanathan, E., Somanathan, R., Sudarshan, A., & Tewari, M. (2015). *The impact of temperature on productivity and labor supply: Evidence from Indian manufacturing.* Working Paper.

Soora, N. K., Aggarwal, P. K., Saxena, R., Rani, S., Jain, S., & Chauhan, N. (2013). An assessment of regional vulnerability of rice to climate change in India. *Climatic Change, 118*(3–4), 683–699.

Spears, D., Ghosh, A., & Cumming, O. (2013). Open defecation and childhood stunting in India: An ecological analysis of new data from 112 districts. *PLoS One, 8*(9), e73784. https://doi.org/10.1371/journal.pone.0073784

Speers, A. E., Besedin, E. Y., Palardy, J. E., & Moore, C. (2016). Impacts of climate change and ocean acidification on coral reef fisheries: An integrated ecological–economic model. *Ecological Economics, 128*, 33–43. https://doi.org/10.1016/j.ecolecon.2016.04.012

Srivastava, A., Kumar, S. N., & Aggarwal, P. K. (2010). Assessment on vulnerability of sorghum to climate change in India. *Agriculture, Ecosystems & Environment, 138*(3–4), 160–169.

Srivastava, R. (1989). Interlinked modes of exploitation in Indian agriculture during transition: A case study. *The Journal of Peasant Studies, 16*(4), 493–522. https://doi.org/10.1080/03066158908438404

Stein, A. D., Wang, M., Digirolamo, A., Grajeda, R., Ramakrishnan, U., Ramirez-zea, M., … Inter-, S. (2008). Nutritional supplementation in early childhood, schooling, and intellectual functioning in adulthood. *Archives of Pediatrics & Adolescent Medicine, 162*(7), 612–618.

Steiner, J. L., Briske, D. D., Brown, D. P., & Rottler, C. M. (2018). Vulnerability of Southern Plains agriculture to climate change. *Climatic Change, 146*(1–2), 201–218.

Steyn, N. P., Nel, J. H., Nantel, G., Kennedy, G., & Labadarios, D. (2006). Food variety and dietary diversity scores in children: Are they good indicators of dietary adequacy? *Public Health Nutrition, 9*(5), 644–650.

Stockbridge, M., Dorward, A., & Kydd, J. (2003). *Farmer organizations for market access: Learning from success.* Volume Briefing Paper. London, UK: Wye College, University of London.

Strauss, J., & Thomas, D. (1998). Health, nutrition, and economic development. *Journal of Economic Literature, 36*(2), 766–817.

Sturm, R., Ringel, J. S., & Andreyeva, T. (2004). Increasing obesity rates and disability trends. *Health Affairs, 23*(2), 199–205.

Subbarao, G. V., Arango, J., Masahiro, K., Hooper, A. M., Yoshihashi, T., Ando, Y., … Iwanaga, M. (2017). Genetic mitigation strategies to tackle agricultural GHG emissions: The case for biological nitrification inhibition technology. *Plant Science, 262,* 165–168. https://doi.org/10.1016/j.plantsci.2017.05.004

Subramanian, A., & Qaim, M. (2011). Interlocked village markets and trader idiosyncrasy in rural India. *Journal of Agricultural Economics, 62*(3), 690–709. https://doi.org/10.1111/j.1477-9552.2011.00309.x

Subramanian, S., & Deaton, A. (1996). The demand of food and calories. *Journal of Political Economy, 104*(1), 133–162.

Sutherst, R. W. (2004). Global change and human vulnerability to vector-borne diseases. *Clinical Microbiology Reviews, 17*(1), 136–173.

Swain, B. B. (2011). Contract farming in Andhra Pradesh: A case of rice seed and gherkin. *Economic and Political Weekly, 46*(42), 60–68.

Swinburn, B. A., Sacks, G., Hall, K. D., McPherson, K., Finegood, D. T., Moodie, M. L., & Gortmaker, S. L. (2011). The global obesity pandemic: Shaped by global drivers and local environments. *The Lancet, 378*(9793), 804–814. https://doi.org/10.1016/S0140-6736(11)60813-1

Swinnen, J. F. M., & Maertens, M. (2007). Globalization, privatization, and vertical coordination in food value chains in developing and transition countries. *Agricultural Economics, 37*, 89–102. https://doi.org/10.1111/j.1574-0862.2007.00237.x

Swinnen, J., & Squicciarini, P. (2012). Mixed messages on prices and food security. *Science, 335*(6067), 405–406. https://doi.org/10.1126/science.1210806

Tacoli, C., Bukhari, B., & Fisher, S. (2013). *Urban poverty, food security and climate change.* Human Settlements Working Paper No. 37.

Tanser, F. C., Sharp, B., & le Sueur, D. (2003). Potential effect of climate change on malaria transmission in Africa. *The Lancet, 362*(9398), 1792–1798. https://doi.org/10.1016/S0140-6736(03)14898-2

Tarozzi, A. (2005). The Indian public distribution system as provider of food security: Evidence from child nutrition in Andhra Pradesh. *European Economic Review, 49*(5), 1305–1330. https://doi.org/10.1016/j.euroecorev.2003.08.015

Taylor, J. E., & Wyatt, T. J. (1996). The shadow value of migrant remittances, income and inequality in a household—Farm economy. *Journal of Development Studies, 32*(6), 899–911.

Taylor, R. G., Scanlon, B., Döll, P., Rodell, M., Van Beek, R., Wada, Y., ... Edmunds, M. (2013). Ground water and climate change. *Nature Climate Change, 3*(4), 322.

Thakur, N., Chandra, J., Pemde, H., & Singh, V. (2014). Anemia in severe acute malnutrition. *Nutrition, 30*(4), 440–442.

Thior, I., Lockman, S., Smeaton, L. M., Shapiro, R. L., Wester, C., Heymann, S. J., ... Kim, S. (2006). Breastfeeding plus infant zidovudine prophylaxis for 6 months vs formula feeding plus infant zidovudine for 1 month to reduce mother-to-child HIV transmission in Botswana: A randomized trial: The Mashi Study. *JAMA, 296*(7), 794–805.

Thomas, D., Strauss, J., & Henriques, M. (1991). How does mother's education affect child height? *The Journal of Human Resources, 26*(2), 183–211.

Thorat, S. (2009). Economic exclusion and poverty linkages: A reflection on concept, consequences, and remedies in an Asian context. In J. von Braun, R. V. Hill, & R. Pandya-Lorch (Eds.), *The poorest and hungry assessments, analyses, and actions.* Washington, DC: International Food Policy Research Institute.

Thornton, P. K., van de Steeg, J., Notenbaert, A., & Herrero, M. (2009). The impacts of climate change on livestock and livestock systems in developing countries: A review of what we know and what we need to know. *Agricultural Systems, 101*(3), 113–127. https://doi.org/10.1016/j.agsy.2009.05.002

Thow, A. M., Downs, S. M., Mayes, C., Trevena, H., Waqanivalu, T., & Cawley, J. (2018). Policy and practice Fiscal policy to improve diets and prevent noncommunicable diseases: From recommendations to action. *Bull World Health Organ, 96*(February), 201–210. https://doi.org/10.2471/BLT.17.195982

Timmer, C. P. (1989). Food price policy. *Food Policy, 14*(1), 17–27. https://doi.org/10.1016/0306-9192(89)90023-7

Timmer, C. P. (2017). Food security, structural transformation, markets and government policy. *Asia and the Pacific Policy Studies, 4*(1), 4–19. https://doi.org/10.1002/app5.161

Timmer, P. C. (1988). Chapter 8 The agricultural transformation. *Handbook of Development Economics, 1,* 275–331. https://doi.org/10.1016/S1573-4471(88)01011-3

Timmer, P. C., & Akkus, S. (2008). *The structural transformation as a pathway out of poverty: Analytics, empirics and politics.* Working Paper No. 150, Washington, DC.

Tirivayi, N., Knowles, M., & Davis, B. (2016). The interaction between social protection and agriculture: A review of evidence. *Global Food Security, 10,* 52–62. https://doi.org/10.1016/j.gfs.2016.08.004

Todaro, M. P. (1969). A model of labor migration and urban unemployment in less developed countries. *The American Economic Review, 59*(1), 138–148. https://doi.org/10.2307/1811100

Tomich, T. P., Kilby, P., & Johnston, B. F. (1995). *Transforming agrarian economies: Opportunities seized, opportunities missed.* Cornell University Press.

Townsend, R., Benfica, R. M., Prasann, A., & Lee, M. (2017). *Future of food: Shaping the food system to deliver jobs.* Washington, DC: World Bank.

Townsend, R. M. (1994). Risk and insurance in village India. *Econometrica, 62*(3), 539–591.

Townsend, R. M. (1995). Consumption insurance: An evaluation of risk-bearing systems in low-income economies. *Journal of Economic Perspectives, 9*(3), 83–102. https://doi.org/10.1257/jep.9.3.83

Trebbin, A. (2014). Linking small farmers to modern retail through producer organizations—Experiences with producer companies in India. *Food Policy, 45,* 35–44. https://doi.org/10.1016/j.foodpol.2013.12.007

Trebbin, A., & Franz, M. (2010). Exclusivity of private governance structures in agrofood networks: Bayer and the food retailing and processing sector in India. *Environment and Planning, 42,* 2043–2057.

Tumbe, C. (2014). The Great Indian Migration Wave, 1870–2010, Persistence & Consequences. Mimeo, The Economic Growth Center, Yale University.

USDA. (2018). GAIN Report No. IN8081. Retrieved from https://gain.fas. usda.gov/Recent%20GAIN%20Publications/Retail%20Foods_New%20 Delhi_India_6-28-2018.pdf

Vaidyanathan, A. (1994). Agrarian relations in the context of new agricultural technology: An issues paper. *Indian Journal of Agricultural Economics, 49*(3), 317–329.

Varshney, A. (1998). *Democracy, development, and the countryside: Urban-rural struggles in India.* https://doi.org/10.1017/CBO9780511609367

Vedwan, N., & Rhoades, R. E. (2001). Climate change in the Western Himalayas of India. *Climate Research, 19*(2), 109–117. Retrieved from http://www.jstor. org/stable/24866773

Vellakkal, S., Fledderjohann, J., Basu, S., Agrawal, S., Ebrahim, S., Campbell, O., ... Stuckler, D. (2015). Food price spikes are associated with increased malnutrition among children in Andhra Pradesh, India. *The Journal of Nutrition, 145*(8), 1942–1949. https://doi.org/10.3945/jn.115.211250

Vermeulen, S. J., Aggarwal, P. K., Ainslie, A., Angelone, C., Campbell, B. M., Challinor, A. J., ... Kristjanson, P. (2012). Options for support to agriculture and food security under climate change. *Environmental Science & Policy, 15*(1), 136–144.

Verwimp, P. (2012). Undernutrition, subsequent risk of mortality and civil war in Burundi. *Economics and Human Biology, 10*(3), 221–231. https://doi. org/10.1016/j.ehb.2011.09.007

Vetter, S. H., Sapkota, T. B., Hillier, J., Stirling, C. M., Macdiarmid, J. I., Aleksandrowicz, L., ... Smith, P. (2017). Greenhouse gas emissions from agricultural food production to supply Indian diets: Implications for climate change mitigation. *Agriculture, Ecosystems & Environment, 237*(Suppl. C), 234–241. https://doi.org/10.1016/j.agee.2016.12.024

Victora, C. G., Adair, L., Fall, C., Hallal, P. C., Martorell, R., Richter, L., ... Group, M. and C. U. S. (2008). Maternal and child undernutrition: Consequences for adult health and human capital. *The Lancet, 371*(9609), 340–357.

von Braun, J. (1995). Agricultural commercialization: Impacts on income and nutrition and implications for policy. *Food Policy, 20*(3), 187–202. https://doi. org/10.1016/0306-9192(95)00013-5

Wang, H., Moustier, P., & Loc, N. T. T. (2014). Economic impact of direct marketing and contracts: The case of safe vegetable chains in northern Vietnam. *Food Policy, 47*, 13–23.

Wang, H. H., Wang, Y., & Delgado, M. S. (2014). The transition to modern agriculture: Contract farming in developing economies. *American Journal of Agricultural Economics, 96*(5), 1257–1271.

Wang, Y. C., McPherson, K., Marsh, T., Gortmaker, S. L., & Brown, M. (2011). Health and economic burden of the projected obesity trends in the USA and the UK. *The Lancet, 378*(9793), 815–825. https://doi.org/10.1016/S0140-6736(11)60814-3

Watanabe, T., Ives, J. D., & Hammond, J. E. (1994). Rapid growth of a glacial lake in Khumbu Himal, Himalaya: Prospects for a catastrophic flood. *Mountain Research and Development, 14*(4), 329–340.

Watts, N., Adger, W. N., Agnolucci, P., Blackstock, J., Byass, P., Cai, W., ... Cooper, A. (2015). Health and climate change: Policy responses to protect public health. *The Lancet, 386*(10006), 1861–1914.

Webb, P., & Block, S. (2012). Support for agriculture during economic transformation: Impacts on poverty and undernutrition. *Proceedings of the National Academy of Sciences, 109*(31), 12309–12314. https://doi.org/10.1073/pnas.0913334108

Webb, P., & Block, S. (2013). Nutrition information and formal schooling as inputs to child nutrition. *Economic Development and Cultural Change, 52*(4), 801–820.

Weitzman, M. L. (2014). Fat tails and the social cost of carbon. *American Economic Review, 104*(5), 544–546.

Wigand, C., Ardito, T., Chaffee, C., Ferguson, W., Paton, S., Raposa, K., ... Watson, E. (2017). A climate change adaptation strategy for management of coastal marsh systems. *Estuaries and Coasts, 40*(3), 682–693.

Wodon, Q., & Zaman, H. (2010). Higher food prices in Sub-Saharan Africa: Poverty impact and policy responses. *The World Bank Research Observer, 25*(1), 157–176. https://doi.org/10.1093/wbro/lkp018

Wollenberg, E., Richards, M., Smith, P., Havlík, P., Obersteiner, M., Tubiello, F. N., ... Campbell, B. M. (2016). Reducing emissions from agriculture to meet the 2 °C target. *Global Change Biology, 22*(12), 3859–3864. https://doi.org/10.1111/gcb.13340

World Bank. (2015). *Ending poverty and hunger by 2030: An agenda for the global food system.* Retrieved from http://documents.worldbank.org/curated/en/700061468334490682/pdf/95768-REVISED-WP-PUBLIC-Box391467B-Ending-Poverty-and-Hunger-by-2030-FINAL.pdf

Xiang, J., Bi, P., Pisaniello, D., & Hansen, A. (2014). Health impacts of workplace heat exposure: An epidemiological review. *Industrial Health, 52*(2), 91–101.

Yip, R. (2000). Significance of an abnormally low or high hemoglobin concentration during pregnancy: Special consideration of iron nutrition. *The American Journal of Clinical Nutrition, 72*(1), 272S–279S.

Zhang, K. H., & Song, S. (2003). Rural-urban migration and urbanization in China: Evidence from time-series and cross-section analyses. *China Economic Review, 14*(4), 386–400. https://doi.org/10.1016/j.chieco.2003.09.018

Ziska, L. H., Gebhard, D. E., Frenz, D. A., Faulkner, S., Singer, B. D., & Straka, J. G. (2003). Cities as harbingers of climate change: Common ragweed, urbanization, and public health. *Journal of Allergy and Clinical Immunology, 111*(2), 290–295.

INDEX[1]

---

[1] Note: Page numbers followed by 'n' refer to notes.

© The Author(s) 2019
P. Pingali et al., *Transforming Food Systems for a Rising India*,
Palgrave Studies in Agricultural Economics and Food Policy,
https://doi.org/10.1007/978-3-030-14409-8

CPSIA information can be obtained
at www.ICGtesting.com
Printed in the USA
LVHW101710220519
618494LV00008BA/222/P